Avizandum Legislation on

International Private Law in Scotland

Editors

Professor Elizabeth B Crawford

LLB (Hons), PhD, Solicitor
Professor of International Private Law,
University of Glasgow

and

Dr Janeen M Carruthers

LLB (Hons), Dip LP, PhD, Solicitor
Reader in Conflict of Laws,
University of Glasgow

Avizandum Publishing Ltd
Edinburgh
2007

Published by
Avizandum Publishing Ltd
58 Candlemaker Row
Edinburgh EH1 2QE

First published 2007

ISBN 978-1-904968-23-8

British Library Cataloguing in Publication Data
A catalogue record for this book is available from the British Library

Typeset by AFS Image Setters Ltd, Glasgow
Printed and bound by Bell & Bain Ltd, Glasgow

EDITORS' PREFACE

This is an entirely new publication in an area of Scots law which, increasingly, has become legislation based and subject to European and global regulation. The legislative profile of the subject today is in striking contrast with its largely common law character as late as 1970. It is essential for lawyers to have ready access to relevant materials, the more so in view of the varied sources from which the legislative materials derive: the Scottish Parliament, the UK Parliament, the EU Institutions, and the Hague Conference on Private International Law. This collection of materials is wide-ranging in subject matter, as dictated by the nature of Scots international private law, which is co-extensive with the entirety of Scots private law.

This book is intended to be a resource for students and for practitioners, and to stand as a companion to Crawford and Carruthers, *International Private Law in Scotland* (2nd edn, 2006, W Green & Sons).

The materials are arranged in six Parts, namely: Part I (Statutes – UK and ASP); Part II (Statutory Instruments); Part III (Scottish Statutory Instruments); Part IV (EC Materials); Part V (International Conventions); and Part VI (Draft Material).

The unremitting nature of the European harmonisation programme means that legislative revision and refinement exercises must be logged, and projected changes, where near completion, must be intimated. We are pleased that it has been possible to include the final version of Rome II (choice of law rules for non-contractual obligations). We have included the most up-to-date version of the draft Lugano Convention. We have taken the decision not to include the proposed Rome I Regulation (choice of law rules for contractual obligations), negotiations at a European level being ongoing, and the attitude of the UK towards the instrument being unsettled.

In general, where a UK statute has been amended by a later instrument (examples being the Prescription and Limitation (Scotland) Act 1973, and the Divorce (Scotland) Act 1976), our practice is to present the Act in its amended form, incorporating later changes. An important exception to this practice concerns section 2 of the Family Law (Scotland) Act 2006, which inserts a new provision (section 20A) into the Marriage (Scotland) Act 1977; in this instance, the new provision is narrated in both places.

Changes to the wording of an original enactment are indicated by the use of square brackets round the affected text. The use of '[...]' indicates a repealed provision. The use of '...' indicates provisions which, in our discretion, have been omitted for reasons of relevance or brevity.

EBC
JMC
University of Glasgow
August 2007

CONTENTS

PART I

STATUTES (UK AND ASP)

FOREIGN MARRIAGE ACT 1892
(1892 c 23)

1   Validity of marriages solemnized abroad in manner provided by Act

(1)   All marriages between parties of whom at least one is a United Kingdom national solemnized in the manner in this Act provided in any foreign country or place by or before a marriage officer within the meaning of this Act shall be as valid in law as if the same had been solemnized in the United Kingdom with a due observance of all forms required by law.

(2)   In this Act 'United Kingdom national' means a person who is—

(a)   a British citizen, a [British overseas territories citizen] a British Overseas citizen or a British National (Overseas); or

(b)   a British subject under the British Nationality Act 1981; or

(c)   a British protected person, within the meaning of that Act.

4   Consent to marriage and power to forbid marriage

...

[(3)   No consent shall be required to a marriage under this Act in respect of a party domiciled in Scotland.]

7   Oath before marriage

Before a marriage is solemnized under this Act, each of the parties intending marriage shall appear before the marriage officer, and make, and subscribe in a book kept by the officer for the purpose, an oath—

(a)   that he or she believes that there is not any impediment to the marriage by reason of kindred or alliance, or otherwise; and

(b)   that both of the parties have for three weeks immediately preceding had their usual residence within the district of the marriage officer; and

[(c)   where either party is under the age of eighteen years and domiciled in a country other than Scotland—

(i)   that any consent to the marriage which is required in respect of that party has been obtained,

(ii)   that the necessity of obtaining any such consent in respect of that party has been dispensed with, or

(iii)   if that party is domiciled in England and Wales or in a country outside the United Kingdom, either that he or she is a widow or widower or that there is no person having authority to give any such consent.]

8   Solemnization of marriage at office in presence of marriage officer and two witnesses

(1)   After the expiration of fourteen days after the notice of an intended marriage has been entered under this Act, then, if no lawful impediment to the marriage is shown to the satisfaction of the marriage officer, and the marriage has not been forbidden in manner provided by this Act, the marriage may be solemnized under this Act.

[(2)   Every such marriage shall be solemnised—

(a)   at the official house of the marriage officer, with open doors, between 8 am and 6 pm, in the presence of two or more witnesses;

(b)   by the marriage officer or, if the parties so desire, by another person in his presence; and
(c)   according to such form and ceremony as the parties see fit to adopt.
(3)   Where (apart from this subsection) it would not be stated or otherwise indicated in the course of the ceremony adopted by the parties that neither of them knows of any lawful impediment to their marriage, then, in some part of the ceremony and in the presence of the marriage officer and witnesses, they shall each declare—

'I solemnly declare that I know not of any lawful impediment why A.B. [or C.D.] may not be joined in matrimony to C.D. [or A.B.].'

(4)   Where (apart from this subsection) it would not be stated by each of the parties in the course of the ceremony adopted by them that he or she takes the other as wife or husband, then, in some part of the ceremony and in the presence of the marriage officer and witnesses, each of the parties shall say to the other—

'I call upon these persons here present to witness that I A.B. [or C.D.] take thee C.D. [or A.B.] to be my lawful wedded wife or husband'.]

13   Avoidance of objections to marriages on account of want of formalities or authority of officer

(1)   After a marriage has been solemnized under this Act it shall not be necessary, in support of the marriage, to give any proof of the residence for the time required by or in pursuance of this Act of either of the parties previous to the marriage, or of the consent of any person whose consent thereto is required by law, nor shall any evidence to prove the contrary be given in any legal proceeding touching the validity of the marriage.
(2)   Where a marriage purports to have been solemnized and registered under this Act in the official house of a British ambassador or counsel, [...] it shall not be necessary in support of the marriage, to give any proof of the authority of the marriage officer by or before whom the marriage was solemnized and registered, nor shall any evidence to prove his want of authority, whether by reason of his not being a duly authorized marriage officer or of any prohibitions or restrictions under the marriage regulations or otherwise, be given in any legal proceeding touching the validity of the marriage.

18   Registration of marriages solemnized under local law

(1)   Subject to the marriage regulations, a British consul, or person authorised to act as British consul, on being satisfied by personal attendance that a marriage between parties, of whom one at least is a [United Kingdom national], has been duly solemnized in a foreign country, in accordance with the local law of the country, and on payment of the proper fee, may register the marriage in accordance with the marriage regulations as having been so solemnized, and thereupon this Act shall apply as if the marriage had been registered in pursuance of this Act, except that nothing in this Act shall affect the validity of the marriage so solemnized.
[(2)   In the case of such marriages solemnized as aforesaid at which a British consul, or person authorised to act as British consul, has not attended, His Majesty may by Order in Council provide in such classes of cases, and subject to such conditions, as may be prescribed by the Order—
(a)   for the transmission to and receipt by the Registrars General of Births, Deaths and Marriages in England, Scotland and Northern Ireland, respectively, of certificates of such marriages issued in accordance with the local law; and
(b)   for the issue by those Registrars-General, on payment of such fees as may be prescribed by the Order, of certified copies of such certificates received by them, and for enabling such certified copies to be received in evidence.
(3)   Any Order in Council made under the foregoing provisions of this section may be varied or revoked by a subsequent Order in Council, and any Order in

Council made under this section shall be laid forthwith before each House of Parliament.]

19 Power to refuse solemnization of marriage where marriage inconsistent with international law

A marriage officer shall not be required to solemnize a marriage, or to allow a marriage to be solemnized in his presence, if in his opinion the solemnization thereof would be inconsistent with international law or the comity of nations;

Provided that any person requiring his marriage to be solemnized shall, if the officer refuses to solemnize it or allow it to be solemnized in his presence, have the right to appeal to the Secretary of State given by this Act.

22 Validity of marriages solemnized by chaplains of HM forces serving abroad and other persons

(1) A marriage solemnized in any foreign territory by a chaplain serving with any part of the naval, military or air forces of His Majesty serving in that territory or by a person authorised, either generally or in respect of the particular marriage, by the commanding officer of any part of those forces serving in that territory shall, subject as hereinafter provided, be as valid in law as if the marriage had been solemnized in the United Kingdom with a due observance of all forms required by law:

[(1A) Subsection (1) above shall not apply to a marriage unless—
    (a) at least one of the parties to the marriage is a person who—
        (i) is a member of the said forces serving in the foreign territory concerned or is employed in that territory in such other capacity as may be prescribed by Order in Council; or
        (ii) is a child of a person falling within sub-paragraph (i) above and has his home with that person in that territory; and
    (b) such other conditions as may be so prescribed are complied with.

(1B) In determining for the purposes of subsection (1A) above whether one person is the child of another, a person who is or was treated by another as a child of the family in relation to—
    (a) a marriage to which the other is or was a party, or
    (b) a civil partnership in which the other is or was a civil partner,
shall be regarded as the other's child.]

(2) In this section the expression 'foreign territory' means territory other than—
    (a) any part of His Majesty's dominions;
    (b) any British protectorate; or
    (c) any other country or territory under His Majesty's protection or suzerainty or in which His Majesty has for the time being jurisdiction:
Provided that His Majesty may by Order in Council direct that—
        (i) any British protectorate or any such other country or territory as is referred to in paragraph (c) hereof; or
        (ii) any part of His Majesty's dominions which has been occupied by a State at war with His Majesty and in which the facilities for marriage in accordance with the local law have not in the opinion of His Majesty been adequately restored;
shall, while the Order remains in force, be treated as foreign territory for the purposes of this section.

(3) Any reference in this section to foreign territory, to forces serving in foreign territory and to persons employed in foreign territory shall include references to ships which are for the time being in the waters of any foreign territory, to forces serving in any such ship and to persons employed in any such ship, respectively.

(4) His Majesty may by Order in Council provide for the registration of marriages solemnized under this section.

(5)   Where a marriage purports to have been solemnized under this section, it shall not be necessary in any legal proceeding touching the validity of the marriage to prove the authority of the person by or before whom it was solemnized, nor shall any evidence to prove his want of authority be given in any such proceeding.

(6)   Any Order in Council made under the foregoing provisions of this section may be varied or revoked by a subsequent Order in Council, and any Order in Council made under this section shall be laid forthwith before each House of Parliament.

23   Savings
Nothing in this Act shall confirm or impair or in anywise affect the validity in law of any marriage solemnized beyond the seas, otherwise than as herein provided, and this Act shall not extend to the marriage of any of the Royal family.

ADMINISTRATION OF JUSTICE ACT 1920
(1920 c 81)

PART II
RECIPROCAL ENFORCEMENT OF JUDGMENTS IN THE UNITED KINGDOM AND IN OTHER PARTS OF HIS MAJESTY'S DOMINIONS

9   Enforcement in the United Kingdom of judgments obtained in superior courts in other British dominions

(1)   Where a judgment has been obtained in a superior court in any part of His Majesty's dominions outside the United Kingdom to which this Part of this Act extends, the judgment creditor may apply to the High Court in England or [Northern Ireland] or to the Court of Session in Scotland, at any time within twelve months after the date of the judgment, or such longer period as may be allowed by the court, to have the judgment registered in the court, and on any such application the court may, if in all the circumstances of the case they think it just and convenient that the judgment should be enforced in the United Kingdom, and subject to the provisions of this section, order the judgment to be registered accordingly.

(2)   No judgment shall be ordered to be registered under this section if—
(a)   the original court acted without jurisdiction; or
(b)   the judgment debtor, being a person who was neither carrying on business nor ordinarily resident within the jurisdiction of the original court, did not voluntarily appear or otherwise submit or agree to submit to the jurisdiction of that court; or
(c)   the judgment debtor, being the defendant in the proceedings, was not duly served with the process of the original court and did not appear, notwithstanding that he was ordinarily resident or was carrying on business within the jurisdiction of that court or agreed to submit to the jurisdiction of that court; or
(d)   the judgment was obtained by fraud; or
(e)   the judgment debtor satisfies the registering court either that an appeal is pending, or that he is entitled and intends to appeal, against the judgment; or
(f)   the judgment was in respect of a cause of action which for reasons of public policy or for some other similar reason could not have been entertained by the registering court.

(3)   Where a judgment is registered under this section—
(a)   the judgment shall, as from the date of registration, be of the same force and effect, and proceedings may be taken thereon, as if it had been a judgment

originally obtained or entered up on the date of registration in the registering court;

(b)   the registering court shall have the same control and jurisdiction over the judgment as it has over similar judgments given by itself, but in so far only as relates to execution under this section;

(c)   the reasonable costs of and incidental to the registration of the judgment (including the costs of obtaining a certified copy thereof from the original court and of the application for registration) shall be recoverable in like manner as if they were sums payable under the judgment.

(4)   Rules of court shall provide—

(a)   for service on the judgment debtor of notice of the registration of a judgment under this section; and

(b)   for enabling the registering court on an application by the judgment debtor to set aside the registration of a judgment under this section on such terms as the court thinks fit; and

(c)   for suspending the execution of a judgment registered under this section until the expiration of the period during which the judgment debtor may apply to have the registration set aside.

(5)   In any action brought in any court in the United Kingdom on any judgment which might be ordered to be registered under this section, the plaintiff shall not be entitled to recover any costs of the action unless an application to register the judgment under this section has previously been refused or unless the court otherwise orders.

12   Interpretation

(1)   In this Part of this Act, unless the context otherwise requires—

The expression 'judgment' means any judgment or order given or made by a court in any civil proceedings, whether before or after the passing of this Act, whereby any sum of money is made payable, and includes an award in proceedings on an arbitration if the award has, in pursuance of the law in force in the place where it was made, become enforceable in the same manner as a judgment given by a court in that place:

The expression 'original court' in relation to any judgment means the court by which the judgment was given:

The expression 'registering court' in relation to any judgment means the court by which the judgment was registered:

The expression 'judgment creditor' means the person by whom the judgment was obtained, and includes the successors and assigns of that person:

The expression 'judgment debtor' means the person against whom the judgment was given, and includes any person against whom the judgment is enforceable in the place where it was given.

(2)   Subject to rules of court, any of the powers conferred by this Part of this Act on any court may be exercised by a judge of the court.

14   Extent of Part II of Act

(1)   Where His Majesty is satisfied that reciprocal provisions have been made by the legislature of any part of His Majesty's dominions outside the United Kingdom for the enforcement within that part of His dominions of judgments obtained in the High Court in England, the Court of Session in Scotland, and the [High Court in Northern Ireland], His Majesty may by Order in Council declare that this Part of this Act shall extend to that part of His dominions, and on any such Order being made this Part of this Act shall extend accordingly.

(2)   An Order in Council under this section may be varied or revoked by a subsequent Order.

[(3)   Her Majesty may by Order in Council under this section consolidate any Orders in Council under this section which are in force when the consolidating Order is made.]

FOREIGN JUDGMENTS (RECIPROCAL ENFORCEMENT) ACT 1933
(1933 c 13)

PART I
REGISTRATION OF FOREIGN JUDGMENTS

1 Power to extend Part I of Act to foreign countries giving reciprocal treatment

(1) [If, in the case of any foreign country, Her Majesty is satisfied that, in the event of the benefits conferred by this Part of this Act being extended to, or to any particular class of, judgments given in the courts of that country or in any particular class of those courts, substantial reciprocity of treatment will be assured as regards the enforcement in that country of similar judgments given in similar courts of the United Kingdom, She may by order in Council direct—

(a) that this Part of this Act shall extend to that country;

(b) that such courts of that country as are specified in the Order shall be recognised courts of that country for the purposes of this Part of this Act; and

(c) that judgments of any such recognised court, or such judgments of any class so specified, shall, if within subsection (2) of this section, be judgments to which this Part of this Act applies.

(2) Subject to subsection (2A) of this section, a judgment of a recognised court is within this subsection if it satisfies the following conditions, namely—

(a) it is either final and conclusive as between the judgment debtor and the judgment creditor or requires the former to make an interim payment to the latter; and

(b) there is payable under it a sum of money, not being a sum payable in respect of taxes or other charges of a like nature or in respect of a fine or other penalty; and

(c) it is given after the coming into force of the Order in Council which made that court a recognised court.

(2A) The following judgments of a recognised court are not within subsection (2) of this section—

(a) a judgment given by that court on appeal from a court which is not a recognised court;

(b) a judgment or other instrument which is regarded for the purposes of its enforcement as a judgment of that court but which was given or made in another country;

(c) a judgment given by that court in proceedings founded on a judgment of a court in another country and having as their object the enforcement of that judgment.]

(3) For the purposes of this section, a judgment shall be deemed to be final and conclusive notwithstanding that an appeal may be pending against it, or that it may still be subject to appeal, in the courts of the country of the original court.

(4) His Majesty may by a subsequent Order in Council vary or revoke any Order previously made under this section.

[(5) Any Order in council made under this section before its amendment by the Civil Jurisdiction and Judgments Act 1982 which deems any court of a foreign country to be a superior court of that country for the purposes of this Part of this Act shall (without prejudice to subsection (4) of this section) have effect from the time of that amendment as if it provided for that court to be a recognised court of that country for those purposes, and for any final and conclusive judgment of that court, if within subsection (2) of this section, to be a judgment to which this Part of this Act applies.]

2 Application for, and effect of, registration of foreign judgment

(1) A person, being a judgment creditor under a judgment to which this Part of this Act applies, may apply to the High Court at any time within six years after

the date of the judgment, or, where there have been proceedings by way of appeal against the judgment, after the date of the last judgment given in those proceedings, to have the judgment registered in the High Court, and on any such application the court shall, subject to proof of the prescribed matters and to the other provisions of this Act, order the judgment to be registered:

Provided that a judgment shall not be registered if at the date of the application—

(a)   it has been wholly satisfied; or

(b)   it could not be enforced by execution in the country of the original court.

(2)   Subject to the provisions of this Act with respect to the setting aside of registration—

(a)   a registered judgment shall, for the purposes of execution, be of the same force and effect; and

(b)   proceedings may be taken on a registered judgment; and

(c)   the sum for which a judgment is registered shall carry interest; and

(d)   the registering court shall have the same control over the execution of a registered judgment;

as if the judgment had been a judgment originally given in the registering court and entered on the date of registration:

Provided that execution shall not issue on the judgment so long as, under this Part of this Act and the Rules of Court made thereunder, it is competent for any party to make an application to have the registration of the judgment set aside, or, where such an application is made, until after the application has been finally determined.

(4)   If at the date of the application for registration the judgment of the original court has been partly satisfied, the judgment shall not be registered in respect of the whole sum payable under the judgment of the original court, but only in respect of the balance remaining payable at that date.

(5)   If, on an application for the registration of a judgment, it appears to the registering court that the judgment is in respect of different matters and that some, but not all, of the provisions of the judgment are such that if those provisions had been contained in separate judgments those judgments could properly have been registered, the judgment may be registered in respect of the provisions aforesaid but not in respect of any other provisions contained therein.

(6)   In addition to the sum of money payable under the judgment of the original court, including any interest which by the law of the country of the original court becomes due under the judgment up to the time of registration, the judgment shall be registered for the reasonable costs of and incidental to registration, including the costs of obtaining a certified copy of the judgment from the original court.

4   Cases in which registered judgments must, or may, be set aside

(1)   On an application in that behalf duly made by any party against whom a registered judgment may be enforced, the registration of the judgment—

(a)   shall be set aside if the registering court is satisfied—

(i)   that the judgment is not a judgment to which this Part of this Act applies or was registered in contravention of the foregoing provisions of this Act; or

(ii)   that the courts of the country of the original court had no jurisdiction in the circumstances of the case; or

(iii)   that the judgment debtor, being the defendant in the proceedings in the original court, did not (notwithstanding that process may have been duly served on him in accordance with the law of the country of the original court) receive notice of those proceedings in sufficient time to enable him to defend the proceedings and did not appear; or

(iv)   that the judgment was obtained by fraud; or

(v) that the enforcement of the judgment would be contrary to public policy in the country of the registering court; or

(vi) that the rights under the judgment are not vested in the person by whom the application for registration was made;

(b) may be set aside if the registering court is satisfied that the matter in dispute in the proceedings in the original court had previously to the date of the judgment in the original court been the subject of a final and conclusive judgment by a court having jurisdiction in the matter.

(2) For the purposes of this section the courts of the country of the original court shall, subject to the provisions of subsection (3) of this section, be deemed to have had jurisdiction—

(a) in the case of a judgment given in an action in personam—

(i) if the judgment debtor, being a defendant in the original court, submitted to the jurisdiction of that court by voluntarily appearing in the proceedings [...]; or

(ii) if the judgment debtor was plaintiff in, or counter-claimed in, the proceedings in the original court; or

(iii) if the judgment debtor, being a defendant in the original court, had before the commencement of the proceedings agreed, in respect of the subject matter of the proceedings, to submit to the jurisdiction of that court or of the courts of the country of that court; or

(iv) if the judgment debtor, being a defendant in the original court, was at the time when the proceedings were instituted resident in, or being a body corporate had its principal place of business in, the country of that court; or

(v) if the judgment debtor, being a defendant in the original court, had an office or place of business in the country of that court and the proceedings in that court were in respect of a transaction effected through or at that office or place;

(b) in the case of a judgment given in an action of which the subject matter was immovable property or in an action in rem of which the subject matter was movable property, if the property in question was at the time of the proceedings in the original court situate in the country of that court;

(c) in the case of a judgment given in an action other than any such action as is mentioned in paragraph (a) or paragraph (b) of this subsection, if the jurisdiction of the original court is recognised by the law of the registering court.

(3) Notwithstanding anything in subsection (2) of this section, the courts of the country of the original court shall not be deemed to have had jurisdiction—

(a) if the subject matter of the proceedings was immovable property outside the country of the original court; or

[...]

(c) if the judgment debtor, being a defendant in the original proceedings, was a person who under the rules of public international law was entitled to immunity from the jurisdiction of the courts of the country of the original court and did not submit to the jurisdiction of that court.

5 Powers of registering court on application to set aside registration

(1) If, on an application to set aside the registration of a judgment, the applicant satisfies the registering court either that an appeal is pending, or that he is entitled and intends to appeal, against the judgment, the court, if it thinks fit, may, on such terms as it may think just, either set aside the registration or adjourn the application to set aside the registration until after the expiration of such period as appears to the court to be reasonably sufficient to enable the applicant to take the necessary steps to have the appeal disposed of by the competent tribunal.

(2) Where the registration of a judgment is set aside under the last foregoing subsection, or solely for the reason that the judgment was not at the date of the application for registration enforceable by execution in the country of the original

court, the setting aside of the registration shall not prejudice a further application to register the judgment when the appeal has been disposed of or if and when the judgment becomes enforceable by execution in that country, as the case may be.

(3)   Where the registration of a judgment is set aside solely for the reason that the judgment, notwithstanding that it had at the date of the application for registration been partly satisfied, was registered for the whole sum payable thereunder, the registering court shall, on the application of the judgment creditor, order judgment to be registered for the balance remaining payable at that date.

6   Foreign judgments which can be registered not to be enforceable otherwise

No proceedings for the recovery of a sum payable under a foreign judgment, being a judgment to which this Part of this Act applies, other than proceedings by way of registration of the judgment, shall be entertained by any court in the United Kingdom.

7   Power to apply Part I of Act to British dominions, protectorates and mandated territories

(1)   His Majesty may by Order in Council direct that this Part of this Act shall apply to His Majesty's dominions outside the United Kingdom and to judgments obtained in the courts of the said dominions as it applies to foreign countries and judgments obtained in the courts of foreign countries, and, in the event of His Majesty so directing, this Act shall have effect accordingly and Part II of the Administration of Justice Act 1920, shall cease to have effect except in relation to those parts of the said dominions to which it extends at the date of the Order.

(2)   If at any time after His Majesty has directed as aforesaid an Order in Council is made under section one of this Act extending Part I of this Act to any part of His Majesty's dominions to which the said Part II extends as aforesaid, the said Part II shall cease to have effect in relation to that part of His Majesty's dominions.

(3)   References in this section to His Majesty's dominions outside the United Kingdom shall be construed as including references to any territories which are under His Majesty's protection and to any territories in respect of which a mandate under the League of Nations has been accepted by His Majesty.

PART II
MISCELLANEOUS AND GENERAL

8   General effect of certain foreign judgments

(1)   Subject to the provisions of this section, a judgment to which Part I of this Act applies or would have applied if a sum of money had been payable thereunder, whether it can be registered or not, and whether, if it can be registered, it is registered or not, shall be recognised in any court in the United Kingdom as conclusive between the parties thereto in all proceedings founded on the same cause of action and may be relied on by way of defence or counter-claim in any such proceedings.

(2)   This section shall not apply in the case of any judgment—

(a)   where the judgment has been registered and the registration thereof has been set aside on some ground other than—

(i)   that a sum of money was not payable under the judgment; or

(ii)   that the judgment had been wholly or partly satisfied; or

(iii)   that at the date of the application the judgment could not be enforced by execution in the country of the original court; or

(b)   where the judgment has not been registered, it is shown (whether it could have been registered or not) that if it had been registered the registration thereof would have been set aside on an application for that purpose on some ground other than one of the grounds specified in paragraph (a) of this subsection.

(3) Nothing in this section shall be taken to prevent any court in the United Kingdom recognising any judgment as conclusive of any matter of law or fact decided therein if that judgment would have been so recognised before the passing of this Act.

9 Power to make foreign judgments unenforceable in United Kingdom if no reciprocity
(1) If it appears to His Majesty that the treatment in respect of recognition and enforcement accorded by the courts of any foreign country to judgments given in the [...] courts of the United Kingdom is substantially less favourable than that accorded by the courts of the United Kingdom to judgments of the [...] courts of that country, His Majesty may by Order in Council apply this section to that country.
(2) Except in so far as His Majesty may by Order in Council under this section otherwise direct, no proceedings shall be entertained in any court in the United Kingdom for the recovery of any sum alleged to be payable under a judgment given in a court of a country to which this section applies.
(3) His Majesty may by a subsequent Order in Council vary or revoke any Order previously made under this section.

[10A Arbitration awards
The provisions of this Act, except sections 1(5) and 6, shall apply, as they apply to a judgment, in relation to an award in proceedings on an arbitration which has, in pursuance of the law in force in the place where it was made, become enforceable in the same manner as a judgment given by a court in that place.]

11 Interpretation
(1) In this Act, unless the context otherwise requires, the following expressions have the meanings hereby assigned to them respectively, that is to say—
'Appeal' includes any proceeding by way of discharging or setting aside a judgment or an application for a new trial or a stay of execution;
'Country of the original court' means the country in which the original court is situated;
['Court', except in section 10 of this Act, includes a tribunal;]
'Judgment' means a judgment or order given or made by a court in any civil proceedings, or a judgment or order given or made by a court in any criminal proceedings for the payment of a sum of money in respect of compensation or damages to an injured party;
'Judgment creditor' means the person in whose favour the judgment was given and includes any person in whom the rights under the judgment have become vested by succession or assignment or otherwise;
'Judgment debtor' means the person against whom the judgment was given, and includes any person against whom the judgment is enforceable under the law of the original court;
[...]
'Original court' in relation to any judgment means the court by which the judgment was given;
'Prescribed' means prescribed by rules of court;
'Registration' means registration under Part I of this Act, and the expressions 'register' and 'registered' shall be construed accordingly;
'Registering court' in relation to any judgment means the court to which an application to register the judgment is made.
(2) For the purposes of this Act, the expression 'action in personam' shall not be deemed to include any matrimonial cause or any proceedings in connection with any of the following matters, that is to say, matrimonial matters, administration of the estates of deceased persons, bankruptcy, winding up of companies, lunacy, or guardianship of infants.

12   Application to Scotland
This Act in its application to Scotland shall have effect subject to the following modifications:—
(a)   For any reference to the High Court [...] there shall be substituted a reference to the Court of Session:
(b)   The Court of Session shall, subject to the provisions of subsection (2) of section three of this Act, have power by Act of Sederunt to make rules for the purposes specified in subsection (1) of the said section:
(c)   Registration under Part I of this Act shall be effected by registering in the Books of Council and Session or in such manner as the Court of Session may by Act of Sederunt prescribe:
(d)   [...]
(e)   For any reference to the entering of a judgment there shall be substituted a reference to the signing of the interlocutor embodying the judgment.

MAINTENANCE ORDERS ACT 1950
(1950 c 37)

PART II
ENFORCEMENT

16   Application of Part II
(1)   Any order to which this section applies (in this Part of this Act referred to as a maintenance order) made by a court in any part of the United Kingdom may, if registered in accordance with the provisions of this Part of this Act in a court in another part of the United Kingdom, be enforced in accordance with those provisions in that other part of the United Kingdom.
(2)   This section applies to the following orders, that is to say—
(a)   an order for alimony, maintenance or other payments made or deemed to be made by a court in England under any of the following enactments:—
   (i)   [sections 15 to 17, 19 to 22, 30, 34 and 35 of the Matrimonial Causes Act 1965 and sections 22, 23(1), (2) and (4) and 27 of the Matrimonial Causes Act 1973 and section 14 or 17 of the Matrimonial and Family Proceedings Act 1984];
   (ii)   [Part I of the Domestic Proceedings and Magistrates' Courts Act 1978];
   (iii)   [Schedule 1 to the Children Act 1989];
   [...]
   (v)   [paragraph 23 of Schedule 2 to the Children Act 1989], or section forty-three of the National Assistance Act 1948;
   [(vi)   section 18 of the Supplementary Benefits Act 1976;]
   [...]
   [(viii)   section 106 of the Social Security Administration Act 1992;
   (ix)   Part 1, 8 or 9 of Schedule 5 to the Civil Partnership Act 2004, Schedule 6 to that Act or paragraph 5 or 9 of Schedule 7 to that Act];
(b)   a decree for payment of aliment granted by a court in Scotland, including—
   (i)   an order for the payment of an annual or periodical allowance under section two of the Divorce (Scotland) Act 1938, [an order for the payment of a periodic allowance or a capital sum under section 26 of the Succession (Scotland) Act 1964 or section 5 of the Divorce (Scotland) Act 1976; or section 29 of the Matrimonial and Family Proceedings Act 1984; or an order for financial provision in the form of a monetary payment under section 8 of the Family Law (Scotland) Act 1985];
   (ii)   an order for the payment of weekly or periodical sums under subsection (2) of section three or subsection (4) of section five of the Guardianship of Infants Act 1925;

(iii) an order for the payment of sums in respect of aliment under sub-section (3) of section one of the Illegitimate Children (Scotland) Act 1930;

(iv) a decree for payment of aliment under section forty-four of the National Assistance Act 1948, or under section twenty-six of the Children Act 1948; and

(v) [an order under section forty-three of the National Assistance Act 1948];

[(vi) a contribution order under section 80 of, or a decree or an order made under section 81 of, the Social Work (Scotland) Act 1968;

(vii) an order for the payment of weekly or other periodical sums under subsection (3) of section 11 of the Guardianship Act 1973;

(viii) an order made on an application under section 18 or 19(8) of the Supplementary Benefits Act 1976;

(ix) an order made on an application under section 106 of the Social Security Administration Act 1992;

(x) an order made on an application under Schedule 11 to the Civil Partnership Act 2004];

(c) an order for alimony, maintenance or other payments made by a court in Northern Ireland under or by virtue of any of the following enactments:—

(i) subsection (2) of section seventeen, subsections (2) to (7) of section nineteen, subsection (2) of section twenty, section twenty-two or subsection (1) of section twenty-eight of the Matrimonial Causes Act (Northern Ireland) 1939;

(ii) [Schedule 1 to the Children (Northern Ireland) Order 1995;]

[...]

[(iv) Article 41 of the Children (Northern Ireland) Order 1995 or Article 101 of the Health and Personal Social Services (Northern Ireland) Order 1972;

(v) any enactment of the Parliament of Northern Ireland containing provisions corresponding with section 22(1), 34 or 35 of the Matrimonial Causes Act 1965, with section 22, 23(1), (2) or (4) or 27 of the Matrimonial Causes Act 1973;

(vi) Article 23 or 24 of the Supplementary Benefits (Northern Ireland) Order 1977;

(vii) the Domestic Proceedings (Northern Ireland) Order 1980;

(viii) any enactment applying in Northern Ireland and corresponding to section 106 of the Social Security Administration Act 1992;

(ix) Article 18 or 21 of the Matrimonial and Family Proceedings (Northern Ireland) Order 1989;

[(x) Part 1, 7 or 8 of Schedule 15 to the Civil Partnership Act 2004, Schedule 16 to that Act or paragraph 5 or 9 of Schedule 17 to that Act.]

(3) For the purposes of this section, any order made before the commencement of the Matrimonial Causes Act (Northern Ireland) 1939, being an order which, if that Act had been in force, could have been made under or by virtue of any provision of that Act, shall be deemed to be an order made by virtue of that provision.

17 Procedure for registration of maintenance orders

(1) An application for the registration of a maintenance order under this Part of this Act shall be made in the prescribed manner to the appropriate authority, that is to say—

(a) where the maintenance order was made by a court of summary jurisdiction in England, a justice or justices acting [in the same local justice area] as the court which made the order;

(b) where the maintenance order was made by a court of summary jurisdiction in Northern Ireland, a resident magistrate acting for the same petty sessions district as the court which made the order;

(c)   in every other case, the prescribed officer of the court which made the order.

(2)   If upon application made as aforesaid by or on behalf of the person entitled to payments under a maintenance order it appears that the person liable to make those payments resides in another part of the United Kingdom, and that it is convenient that the order should be enforceable there, the appropriate authority shall cause a certified copy of the order to be sent to the prescribed officer of a court in that part of the United Kingdom in accordance with the provisions of the next following subsection.

(3)   The Court to whose officer the certified copy of a maintenance order is sent under this section shall be—

(a)   where the maintenance order was made by a superior court, the Supreme Court of Judicature in England, the Court of Session or the Supreme Court of Judicature of Northern Ireland, as the case may be;

(b)   in any other case, a court of summary jurisdiction acting for the place in England or Northern Ireland in which the defendant appears to be, or as the case may be, the sheriff court in Scotland within the jurisdiction of which he appears to be.

(4)   Where the prescribed officer of any court receives a certified copy of a maintenance order sent to him under this section, he shall cause the order to be registered in that court in the prescribed manner, and shall give notice of the registration in the prescribed manner to the prescribed officer of the court which made the order.

(5)   The officer to whom any notice is given under the last foregoing subsection shall cause particulars of the notice to be registered in his court in the prescribed manner.

(6)   Where the sums payable under a maintenance order, being an order made by a court of summary jurisdiction in England or Northern Ireland, are payable to or through an officer of any court, that officer shall, if the person entitled to the payments so requests, make an application on behalf of that person for the registration of the order under this Part of this Act; but the person at whose request the application is made shall have the same liability for costs properly incurred in or about the application as if the application had been made by him.

(7)   An order which is for the time being registered under this Part of this Act in any court shall not be registered thereunder in any other court.

18   Enforcement of registered orders

(1)   Subject to the provisions of this section, a maintenance order registered under this Part of this Act in a court in any part of the United Kingdom may be enforced in that part of the United Kingdom in all respects as if it had been made by that court and as if that court had had jurisdiction to make it; and proceedings for or with respect to the enforcement of any such order may be taken accordingly.

[(1A)   Does not apply to Scotland.]

(1B)   A maintenance order made in Scotland which is registered under this Part of this Act in the Supreme Court in England or Northern Ireland shall, if interest is by the law of Scotland recoverable under the order, carry the like interest in accordance with subsection (1) of this section.

...

21   Discharge and variation of maintenance orders registered in superior courts

(1)   The registration of a maintenance order in a superior court under this Part of this Act shall not confer on that court any power to vary or discharge the order, or affect any jurisdiction of the court in which the order was made to vary or discharge the order.

(2)   Where a maintenance order made in Scotland is for the time being—

[(a)   registered under this Part of this Act in a superior court and not regis-

tered under Part I of the Maintenance Orders Act 1958 [or under section 36 of
the Civil Jurisdiction and Judgments Act 1982], or

    (b)   registered in a court in England under that Part of that Act [of 1958] by
virtue of section 1(2) of that Act [of 1958],

    [(c)   registered in a court in Northern Ireland under section 36 of the Civil
Jurisdiction and Judgments Act 1982,]

the person liable to make payments under the order may, upon application made
to that court in the prescribed manner, adduce before that court any evidence
upon which he would be entitled to rely in any proceedings brought before the
court by which the order was made for the variation or discharge of the order.

   ...

22 Discharge and variation of maintenance orders registered in summary or sheriff courts

(1)   Where a maintenance order is for the time being registered under this Part
of this Act in a court of summary jurisdiction or sheriff court, that court may, upon
application made in the prescribed manner by or on behalf of the person liable to
make periodical payments under the order or the person entitled to those payments,
by order make such variation as the court thinks fit in the rate of the payments
under the maintenance order; but no such variation shall impose on the person
liable to make payments under the maintenance order a liability to make payments
in excess of the maximum rate (if any) authorised by the law for the time being in
force in the part of the United Kingdom in which the maintenance order was made.

   ...

(2)   For the purposes of subsection (1) of this section, a court in any part of the
United Kingdom may take notice of the law in force in any other part of the
United Kingdom.

   ...

(4)   Except as provided by subsection (1) of this section, no variation shall be
made in the rate of the payments under a maintenance order which is for the time
being registered under this Part of this Act in a court of summary jurisdiction or
sheriff court, but without prejudice to any power of the court which made the
order to discharge it or vary it otherwise than in respect of the rate of the payments thereunder.

(5)   Where a maintenance order is for the time being registered under this Part
of this Act in a court of summary jurisdiction or sheriff court—

    (a)   the person entitled to payments under the order or the person liable to
make payments under the order may, upon application made in the prescribed
manner to the court by which the order was made, or in which the order is
registered, as the case may be, adduce in the prescribed manner before the court
in which the applications is made any evidence on which he would be entitled
to rely in proceedings for the variation or discharge of the order;

    (b)   the court in which the application is made shall cause a transcript or
summary of that evidence, signed by the deponent, to be sent to the prescribed
officer of the court in which the order is registered or of the court by which the
order was made, as the case may be; and in any proceedings for the variation or
discharge of the order the transcript or summary shall be evidence of the facts
stated therein.

PART III

GENERAL

...

27 General provisions as to jurisdiction

(1)   Nothing in this Act shall be construed as derogating from any jurisdiction
exercisable, apart from the provisions of this Act, by any court in any part of the
United Kingdom.

(2) It is hereby declared that any jurisdiction conferred by Part I of this Act, or any enactment therein referred to, upon a court in any part of the United Kingdom is exercisable notwithstanding that any party to the proceedings is not domiciled in that part of the United Kingdom; and any jurisdiction so conferred in affiliation proceedings shall be exercisable notwithstanding that the child to whom the proceedings relate was not born in that part of the United Kingdom.

(3) For the avoidance of doubt it is hereby declared that in relation to proceedings in which the sheriff has jurisdiction by virtue of the provisions of this Act there are the same rights of appeal and of remit to the Court of Session as there are in relation to the like proceedings in which the sheriff has jurisdiction otherwise than by virtue of the said provisions.

WILLS ACT 1963
(1963 c 44)

1 General rule as to formal validity

A will shall be treated as properly executed if its execution conformed to the internal law in force in the territory where it was executed, or in the territory where, at the time of its execution or of the testator's death, he was domiciled or had his habitual residence, or in a state of which, at either of those times, he was a national.

2 Additional rules

(1) Without prejudice to the preceding section, the following shall be treated as properly executed—

(a) a will executed on board a vessel or aircraft of any description, if the execution of the will conformed to the internal law in force in the territory with which, having regard to its registration (if any) and other relevant circumstances, the vessel or aircraft may be taken to have been most closely connected;

(b) a will so far as it disposes of immovable property, if its execution conformed to the internal law in force in the territory where the property was situated;

(c) a will so far as it revokes a will which under this Act would be treated as properly executed or revokes a provision which under this Act would be treated as comprised in a properly executed will, if the execution of the later will conformed to any law by reference to which the revoked will or provision would be so treated;

(d) a will so far as it exercises a power of appointment, if the execution of the will conformed to the law governing the essential validity of the power.

(2) A will so far as it exercises a power of appointment shall not be treated as improperly executed by reason only that its execution was not in accordance with any formal requirements contained in the instrument creating the power.

3 Certain requirements to be treated as formal

Where (whether in pursuance of this Act or not) a law in force outside the United Kingdom falls to be applied in relation to a will, any requirement of that law whereby special formalities are to be observed by testators answering a particular description, or witnesses to the execution of a will are to possess certain qualifications, shall be treated, notwithstanding any rule of that law to the contrary, as a formal requirement only.

4 Construction of wills

The construction of a will shall not be altered by reason of any change in the testator's domicile after the execution of the will.

6 Interpretation

(1) In this Act—

'internal law' in relation to any territory or state means the law which would apply in a case where no question of the law in force in any other territory or state arose;

'state' means a territory or group of territories having its own law of nationality;

'will' includes any testamentary instrument or act, and 'testator' shall be construed accordingly.

(2)   Where under this Act the internal law in force in any territory or state is to be applied in the case of a will, but there are in force in that territory or state two or more systems of internal law relating to the formal validity of wills, the system to be applied shall be ascertained as follows—

(a)   if there is in force throughout the territory or state a rule indicating which of those systems can properly be applied in the case in question, that rule shall be followed; or

(b)   if there is no such rule, the system shall be that with which the testator was most closely connected at the relevant time, and for this purpose the relevant time is the time of the testator's death where the matter is to be determined by reference to circumstances prevailing at his death, and the time of execution of the will in any other case.

(3)   In determining for the purposes of this Act whether or not the execution of a will conformed to a particular law, regard shall be had to the formal requirements of that law at the time of execution, but this shall not prevent account being taken of an alteration of law affecting wills executed at that time if the alteration enables the will to be treated as properly executed.

7   Short title, commencement, repeal and extent
(1)   This Act may be cited as the Wills Act 1963.
(2)   This Act shall come into operation on 1st January 1964.
(3)   The Wills Act 1861 is hereby repealed.
(4)   This Act shall not apply to a will of a testator who died before the time of the commencement of this Act and shall apply to a will of a testator who dies after that time whether the will was executed before or after that time, but so that the repeal of the Wills Act 1861 shall not invalidate a will executed before that time.

SUCCESSION (SCOTLAND) ACT 1964
(1964 c 41)

PART II
LEGAL AND OTHER PRIOR RIGHTS IN ESTATES OF DECEASED PERSONS

8   Prior rights of surviving spouse, on intestacy, in dwelling house and furniture
(1)   Where a person dies intestate leaving a spouse [or civil partner], and the intestate estate includes a relevant interest in a dwelling house to which this section applies, the surviving spouse [or civil partner] shall be entitled to receive out of the intestate estate—

(a)   where the value of the relevant interest does not exceed [£300,000 or such larger amount as may from time to time be fixed by order of the Secretary of State]—

(i)   if subsection (2) of this section does not apply, the relevant interest;

(ii)   if the said subsection (2) applies, a sum equal to the value of the relevant interest;

(b)   in any other case, the sum of [£300,000 or such larger amount as may from time to time be fixed by order of the Secretary of State]:

Provided that, if the intestate estate comprises a relevant interest in two or more dwelling houses to which this section applies, this subsection shall have effect only in relation to such one of them as the surviving spouse [or civil partner] may elect for the purposes of this subsection within six months of the date of death of the intestate.

(2) This subsection shall apply for the purposes of paragraph (a) of the foregoing subsection if—

(a) the dwelling house forms part only of the subjects comprised in one tenancy or lease under which the intestate was the tenant; or

(b) the dwelling house forms the whole or part of subjects an interest in which is comprised in the intestate estate and which were used by the intestate for carrying on a trade, profession or occupation, and the value of the estate as a whole would be likely to be substantially diminished if the dwelling house were disposed of otherwise than with the assets of the trade, profession or occupation.

(3) Where a person dies intestate leaving a spouse [or civil partner], and the intestate estate includes the furniture and plenishings of a dwelling house to which this section applies (whether or not the dwelling house is comprised in the intestate estate), the surviving spouse [or civil partner] shall be entitled to receive out of the intestate estate—

(a) where the value of the furniture and plenishings does not exceed [£24,000 or such larger amount as may from time to time be fixed by order of the Secretary of State], the whole thereof;

(b) in any other case, such part of the furniture and plenishings, to a value not exceeding [£24,000 or such larger amount as may from time to time be fixed by order of the Secretary of State], as may be chosen by the surviving spouse [or civil partner]:

Provided that, if the intestate estate comprises the furniture and plenishings of two or more such dwelling houses, this subsection shall have effect only in relation to the furniture and plenishings of such one of them as the surviving spouse [or civil partner] may elect for the purposes of this subsection within six months of the date of death of the intestate.

(4) This section applies, in the case of any intestate, to any dwelling house in which the surviving spouse [or civil partner] of the intestate was ordinarily resident at the date of death of the intestate.

(5) Where any question arises as to the value of any furniture or plenishings, or of any interest in a dwelling house, for the purposes of any provision of this section the question shall be determined by arbitration by a single arbiter appointed, in default of agreement, by the sheriff of the county in which the intestate was domiciled at the date of his death or, if that county is uncertain or the intestate was domiciled furth of Scotland, the sheriff of the Lothians and Peebles at Edinburgh.

(6) In this section—

(a) 'dwelling house' includes a part of a building occupied (at the date of death of the intestate) as a separate dwelling; and any reference to a dwelling house shall be construed as including any garden or portion of ground attached to, and usually occupied with, the dwelling house or otherwise required for the amenity or convenience of the dwelling house;

(b) 'furniture and plenishings' includes garden effects, domestic animals, plate, plated articles, linen, china, glass, books, pictures, prints, articles of household use and consumable stores; but does not include any article or animal used at the date of death of the intestate for business purposes, or money or securities for money, or any heirloom;

(c) 'heirloom', in relation to an intestate estate, means any article which has associations with the intestate's family of such nature and extent that it ought to pass to some member of that family other than the surviving spouse of the intestate;

(d) 'relevant interest', in relation to a dwelling house, means the interest therein of an owner, or the interest therein of a tenant, subject in either case to any heritable debt secured over the interest; and for the purposes of this definition 'tenant' means a tenant under a tenancy or lease (whether of the dwelling house alone or of the dwelling house together with other subjects) which is not a tenancy to which the Rent and Mortgage Interest Restrictions Acts 1920 to 1939 apply

9 Prior right of surviving spouse to financial provision on intestacy

(1)   Where a person dies intestate and is survived by a husband, [wife or civil partner the survivor] shall be entitled to receive out of the intestate estate—

(a)   if the intestate is survived by issue the sum of [£42,000 or such larger amount as may from time to time be fixed by order of the Secretary of State], or

(b)   if the intestate is not survived by issue the sum of [£75,000 or such larger amount as may from time to time be fixed by order of the Secretary of State], together with, in either case, interest at the rate of 4 per cent. per annum [or, at such rate as may from time to time be fixed by order of the Secretary of State], on such sum from the date of the intestate's death until payment:

Provided that where the surviving spouse [or civil partner] is entitled to receive a legacy out of the estate of the intestate (other than a legacy of any dwelling house to which the last foregoing section applies or of any furniture and plenishings of any such dwelling house), he or she shall, unless he or she renounces the legacy, be entitled under this subsection to receive only such sum, if any, as remains after deducting from the sum fixed by virtue of paragraph (a) of this subsection or the sum fixed by virtue of paragraph (b) of this subsection, as the case may be, the amount or value of the legacy.

(2)   Where the intestate estate is less than the amount which the surviving spouse or civil partner is entitled to receive by virtue of subsection (1) of this section the right conferred by the said subsection on the surviving spouse [or civil partner] shall be satisfied by the transfer to him or her of the whole of the intestate estate.

(3)   The amount which the surviving spouse [or civil partner] is entitled to receive by virtue of subsection (1) of this section shall be borne by, and paid out of, the parts of the intestate estate consisting of heritable and moveable property respectively in proportion to the respective amounts of those parts.

(4)   Where by virtue of subsection (2) of this section a surviving spouse [or civil partner] has right to the whole of the intestate estate, he or she shall have the right to be appointed executor.

(5)   The rights conferred by the Intestate Husband's Estate (Scotland) Acts 1911 to 1959 on a surviving spouse in his or her deceased spouse's estate shall not be exigible out of the estate of any person dying after the commencement of this Act.

(6)   For the purposes of this section—

(a)   the expression 'intestate estate' means so much of the net intestate estate as remains after the satisfaction of any claims under the last foregoing section; and

(b)   the expression 'legacy' includes any payment or benefit to which a surviving spouse [or civil partner] becomes entitled by virtue of any testamentary disposition; and the amount or value of any legacy shall be ascertained as at the date of the intestate's death.

ADMINISTRATION OF ESTATES ACT 1971
(1971 c 25)

RECIPROCAL RECOGNITION OF GRANTS

1 Recognition in England and Wales of Scottish confirmations and Northern Irish grants of representation

(1)   Where a person dies domiciled in Scotland—

(a)   a confirmation granted in respect of all or part of his estate and noting his Scottish domicile, and

(b)   a certificate of confirmation, noting his Scottish domicile and relating to one or more items of his estate,

shall, without being resealed, be treated for the purposes of the law of England and Wales as a grant of representation (in accordance with subsection (2) below) to the executors named in the confirmation or certificate in respect of the property of the deceased of which according to the terms of the confirmation they are executors or, as the case may be, in respect of the item or items of property specified in the certificate of confirmation.

(2)   Where by virtue of subsection (1) above a confirmation or certificate of confirmation is treated for the purposes of the law of England and Wales as a grant of representation to the executors named therein then, subject to subsections (3) and (5) below, the grant shall be treated—

(a)   as a grant of probate where it appears from the confirmation or certificate that the executors so named are executors nominate; and

(b)   in any other case, as a grant of letters of administration.

(3)   Section 7 of the Administration of Estates Act 1925 (executor of executor represents original testator) shall not, by virtue of subsection (2)(a) above, apply on the death of an executor named in a confirmation or certificate of confirmation.

(4)   Subject to subsection (5) below, where a person dies domiciled in Northern Ireland a grant of probate of his will or letters of administration in respect of his estate (or any part of it) made by the High Court in Northern Ireland and noting his domicile there shall, without being resealed, be treated for the purposes of the law of England and Wales as if it had been originally made by the High Court in England and Wales.

(5)   Notwithstanding anything in the preceding provisions of this section, a person who is a personal representative according to the law of England and Wales by virtue only of those provisions may not be required, under section 25 of the Administration of Estates Act 1925, to deliver up his grant to the High Court.

(6)   This section applies in relation to confirmations, probates and letters of administration granted before as well as after the commencement of this Act, and in relation to a confirmation, probate or letters of administration granted before the commencement of this Act, this section shall have effect as if it had come into force immediately before the grant was made.

(7)   In this section 'confirmation' includes an additional confirmation, and the term 'executors', where used in relation to a confirmation or certificate of confirmation, shall be construed according to the law of Scotland.

2   Recognition in Northern Ireland of English grants of representation and Scottish confirmations

(1)   Where a person dies domiciled in England and Wales a grant of probate of his will or letters of administration in respect of his estate (or any part of it) made by the High Court in England and Wales and noting his domicile there shall, without being resealed, be treated for the purposes of the law of Northern Ireland as if it had been originally made by the High Court in Northern Ireland.

(2)   Where a person dies domiciled in Scotland—

(a)   a confirmation granted in respect of all or part of his estate and noting his Scottish domicile, and

(b)   a certificate of confirmation noting his Scottish domicile and relating to one or more items of his estate,

shall, without being resealed, be treated for the purposes of the law of Northern Ireland as a grant of representation (in accordance with subsection (3) below) to the executors named in the confirmation or certificate in respect of the property of the deceased of which according to the terms of the confirmation they are executors or, as the case may be, in respect of the item or items of property specified in the certificate of confirmation.

(3)   Where by virtue of subsection (2) above a confirmation or certificate of confirmation is treated for the purposes of the law of Northern Ireland as a grant of representation to the executors named therein then, subject to subsection (4) below, the grant shall be treated—

(a)   as a grant of probate where it appears from the confirmation or certificate that the executors so named are executors nominate; and

(b)   in any other case, as a grant of letters of administration.

(4)   Notwithstanding anything in any enactment or rule of law, subsection (3)(a) above shall not operate to entitle an executor of a sole or last surviving executor of a testator, whose will has been proved in Scotland only, to act as the executor of that testator.

(5)   This section applies in relation to probates, letters of administration and confirmations granted before as well as after the commencement of this Act, and—

(a)   in relation to a probate, letters of administration or confirmation granted, and resealed in Northern Ireland, before the commencement of this Act, this section shall have effect as if it had come into force immediately before the grant was so resealed; and

(b)   a probate, letters of administration or confirmation granted but not resealed in Northern Ireland before the commencement of this Act shall, for the purposes of this section, be treated as having been granted at the commencement of this Act.

(6)   In this section 'confirmation' includes an additional confirmation, and the term 'executors', where used in relation to a confirmation or certificate of confirmation shall be construed according to the law of Scotland.

3   Recognition in Scotland of English and Northern Irish grants of representation

(1)   Where a person dies domiciled in England and Wales or in Northern Ireland a grant of probate or letters of administration—

(a)   from the High Court in England and Wales and noting his domicile there, or

(b)   from the High Court in Northern Ireland and noting his domicile there,

shall, without being resealed, be of the like force and effect and have the same operation in relation to property in Scotland as a confirmation given under the seal of office of the Commissariot of Edinburgh to the executor or administrator named in the probate or letters of administration.

(2)   This section applies in relation to probates and letters of administration granted before as well as after the commencement of this Act, and in relation to a probate or letters of administration granted before the commencement of this Act, this section shall have effect as if it had come into force immediately before the grant was made.

4   Evidence of grants

(1)   In England and Wales and in Northern Ireland—

(a)   a document purporting to be a confirmation, additional confirmation or certificate of confirmation given under the seal of office of any commissariot in Scotland shall, except where the contrary is proved, be taken to be such a confirmation, additional confirmation or certificate of confirmation without further proof; and

(b)   a document purporting to be a duplicate of such a confirmation or additional confirmation and to be given under such a seal shall be receivable in evidence in like manner and for the like purposes as the confirmation or additional confirmation of which it purports to be a duplicate.

(2)   In England and Wales and in Scotland—

(a)   a document purporting to be a grant of probate or of letters of administration issued under the seal of the High Court in Northern Ireland or of the principal or district probate registry there shall, except where the contrary is proved, be taken to be such a grant without further proof; and

(b)   a document purporting to be a copy of such a grant and to be sealed with such a seal shall be receivable in evidence in like manner and for the like purposes as the grant of which it purports to be a copy.

(3)   In Scotland and in Northern Ireland—

(a)   a document purporting to be a grant of probate or of letters of adminis- tration issued under the seal of the High Court in England and Wales or of the principal or a district probate registry there shall, except where the contrary is proved, be taken to be such a grant without further proof; and

(b)   a document purporting to be a copy of such a grant and to be sealed with such a seal shall be receivable in evidence in like manner and for the like purposes as the grant of which it purports to be a copy.

5   Property outside Scotland of which deceased was trustee

(1)   A confirmation or additional confirmation granted in respect of property situated in Scotland of a person who died domiciled there, which notes that domi- cile, may contain or have appended thereto and signed by the sheriff clerk a note or statement of property in England and Wales or in Northern Ireland held by the deceased in trust, being a note or statement which has been set forth in any inven- tory recorded in the books of the court of which the sheriff clerk is clerk.

(2)   Section 1 or, as the case may be, section 2 of this Act shall apply in relation to property specified in such a note or statement as is mentioned in subsection (1) above as it applies in relation to property specified in the confirmation or addi- tional confirmation concerned.

6   Inventory of Scottish estate may include real estate in any part of the United Kingdom

(1)   It shall be competent to include in the inventory of the estate of any person who dies domiciled in Scotland any real estate of the deceased situated in England and Wales or Northern Ireland, and accordingly in section 9 of the Confirmation of Executors (Scotland) Act 1858 the word 'personal' wherever it occurs is hereby repealed.

(2)   Section 14(2) of the Succession (Scotland) Act 1964 (act of sederunt to pro- vide for description of heritable property) shall apply in relation to such real estate as aforesaid as it applies in relation to heritable property in Scotland.

MAINTENANCE ORDERS (RECIPROCAL ENFORCEMENT) ACT 1972
(1972 c 18)

PART I
RECIPROCAL ENFORCEMENT OF MAINTENANCE ORDERS MADE IN UNITED KINGDOM OR RECIPROCATING COUNTRY

Designation of reciprocating countries

1   Orders in Council designating reciprocating countries*

(1)   Her Majesty, if satisfied that, in the event of the benefits conferred by this Part of this Act being applied to, or to particular classes of, maintenance orders made by the courts of any country or territory outside the United Kingdom, similar benefits will in that country or territory be applied to, or to those classes of, maintenance orders made by the courts of the United Kingdom, may by Order in

*In relation to maintenance orders made by courts in the United Kingdom or by courts in a State specified in Sch 1 to SI 1995/2709 section 1 does not apply.

Council designate that country or territory as a reciprocating country for the purposes of this Part of this Act; and, subject to subsection (2) below, in this Part of this Act 'reciprocating country' means a country or territory that is for the time being so designated.

(2)   A country or territory may be designated under subsection (1) above as a reciprocating country either as regards maintenance orders generally, or as regards maintenance orders other than those of any specified class, or as regards maintenance orders of one or more specified classes only; and a country or territory which is for the time being so designated otherwise than as regards maintenance orders generally shall for the purposes of this Part of this Act be taken to be a reciprocating country only as regards maintenance orders of the class to which the designation extends.

Orders made by courts in the United Kingdom

2   Transmission of maintenance order made in United Kingdom for enforcement in reciprocating country

(1)   Subject to subsection (2) below, where the payer under a maintenance order made, whether before or after the commencement of this Part of this Act, by a court in the United Kingdom is residing [or has assets] in a reciprocating country, the payee under the order may apply for the order to be sent to that country for enforcement.

(2)   Subsection (1) above shall not have effect in relation to a provisional order or to an order made by virtue of a provision of Part II of this Act.

(3)   Every application under this section shall be made in the prescribed manner to the prescribed officer of the court which made the maintenance order to which the application relates.

(4)   If, on an application duly made under this section to the prescribed officer of a court in the United Kingdom, that officer is satisfied that the payer under the maintenance order to which the application relates is residing [or has assets] in a reciprocating country, the following documents, that is to say—

(a)   a certified copy of the maintenance order;

(b)   a certificate signed by that officer certifying that the order is enforceable in the United Kingdom;

(c)   a certificate of arrears so signed;

(d)   a statement giving such information as the officer possesses as to the whereabouts of the payer [and the nature and location of his assets in that country];

(e)   a statement giving such information as the officer possesses for facilitating the identification of the payer; and

(f)   where available, a photograph of the payer;

shall be sent by that officer to the Secretary of State with a view to their being transmitted by the Secretary of State to the responsible authority in the reciprocating country if he is satisfied that the statement relating to the whereabouts of the payer and the nature and location of his assets in that country gives sufficient information to justify that being done.

(5)   Nothing in this section shall be taken as affecting any jurisdiction of a court in the United Kingdom with respect to a maintenance order to which this section applies, and any such order may be enforced, varied or revoked accordingly.

5   Variation and revocation of maintenance order made in United Kingdom

(1)   This section applies to a maintenance order a certified copy of which has been sent to a reciprocating country in pursuance of section 2 of this Act and to a maintenance order made by virtue of section 3 or 4 thereof which has been confirmed by a competent court in such a country.

(2)   A court in the United Kingdom having power to vary a maintenance order

to which this section applies shall have power to vary that order by a provisional order.

(3)   Where the payer under a maintenance order to which this section applies is for the time being residing in a reciprocating country, the court shall not, on an application made by the payee under the order for the variation of the order, vary the order by increasing the rate of the payments thereunder otherwise than by a provisional order.

[(3A)   It shall not be necessary for the payee under a maintenance order to which this section applies to intimate to any person the making by him of an application for a provisional order varying the said maintenance order by increasing the rate of the payments thereunder.]

(4)   Where a court in the United Kingdom makes a provisional order varying a maintenance order to which this section applies, the prescribed officer of the court shall send in the prescribed manner to the court in a reciprocating country having power to confirm the provisional order a certified copy of the provisional order together with a document, authenticated in the prescribed manner, setting out or summarising the evidence given in the proceedings.

(5)   Where a certified copy of a provisional order made by a court in a reciprocating country, being an order varying or revoking a maintenance order to which this section applies, together with a document, duly authenticated, setting out or summarising the evidence given in the proceedings in which the provisional order was made, is received by the court in the United Kingdom which made the maintenance order, that court may confirm or refuse to confirm the provisional order and, if that order is an order varying the maintenance order, confirm it either without alteration or with such alterations as it thinks reasonable.

(6)   Where a certified copy of a provisional order varying or revoking a maintenance order to which this section applies is received by a court as mentioned in subsection (5) above, the prescribed officer of that court shall intimate to the payee under the maintenance order, in the prescribed manner, that the provisional order has been received as aforesaid and that, unless the payee enters appearance within the prescribed period, the court will confirm the provisional order under this section.

(7)   Where a maintenance order to which this section applies has been varied by an order (including a provisional order which has been confirmed) made by a court in the United Kingdom or by a competent court in a reciprocating country, the maintenance order shall, as from [the date on which under the provisions of the order the variation is to take effect], have effect as varied by that order and, where that order was a provisional order, as if that order had been made in the form in which it was confirmed and as if it had never been a provisional order.

(8)   Where a maintenance order to which this section applies has been revoked by an order made by a court in the United Kingdom or by a competent court in a reciprocating country, including a provisional order made by the last-mentioned court which has been confirmed by a court in the United Kingdom, the maintenance order shall, as from [the date on which under the provisions of the order the revocation is to take effect], be deemed to have ceased to have effect except as respects any arrears due under the maintenance order at that date.

(9)   Where before a maintenance order made by virtue of section 3 or 4 of this Act is confirmed a document, duly authenticated, setting out or summarising evidence taken in a reciprocating country for the purpose of proceedings relating to the confirmation of the order is received by the court in the United Kingdom which made the order, or that court, in compliance with a request made to it by a court in such a country, takes the evidence of a person residing in the United Kingdom for the purpose of such proceedings, the court in the United Kingdom which made the order shall consider that evidence and if, having done so, it appears to it that the order ought not to have been made—

(a)   it shall, in such manner as may be prescribed, give to the person on whose application the maintenance order was made an opportunity to consider that evidence, to make representations with respect to it and to adduce further evidence; and

(b)   after considering all the evidence and any representations made by that person, it may revoke the maintenance order.

(10)   *[Substitutes subsections (3), (3A) and (6) above for Scotland.]*

Orders made by courts in reciprocating countries

6   Registration in United Kingdom court of maintenance order made in reciprocating country

(1)   This section applies to a maintenance order made, whether before or after the commencement of this Part of this Act, by a court in a reciprocating country, including such an order made by such a court which has been confirmed by a court in another reciprocating country but excluding a provisional order which has not been confirmed.

(2)   Where a certified copy of an order to which this section applies is received by the Secretary of State from the responsible authority in a reciprocating country, and it appears to the Secretary of State that the payer under the order is residing [or has assets] in the United Kingdom, he shall send the copy of the order to the prescribed officer of the appropriate court.

(3)   Where the prescribed officer of the appropriate court receives from the Secretary of State a certified copy of an order to which this section applies, he shall, subject to subsection (4) below, register the order in the prescribed manner in that court.

(4)   Before registering an order under this section an officer of a court shall take such steps as he thinks fit for the purpose of ascertaining whether the payer under the order is residing [or has assets] within the jurisdiction of the court, and if after taking those steps he is satisfied that the payer is not [residing and has no assets within the jurisdiction of the court] he shall return the certified copy of the order to the Secretary of State with a statement giving such information as he possesses as to the whereabouts of the payer [and the nature and location of his assets].

7   Confirmation by United Kingdom court of provisional maintenance order made in reciprocating country*

(1)   This section applies to a maintenance order made, whether before or after the commencement of this Part of this Act, by a court in a reciprocating country being a provisional order.

(2)   Where a certified copy of an order to which this section applies together with—

(a)   a document, duly authenticated, setting out or summarising the evidence given in the proceedings in which the order was made; and

(b)   a statement of the grounds on which the making of the order might have been opposed by the payer under the order,

is received by the Secretary of State from the responsible authority in a reciprocating country, and it appears to the Secretary of State that the payer under the order is residing in the United Kingdom, he shall send the copy of the order and documents which accompanied it to the prescribed officer of the appropriate court, and that court shall—

(i)   if the payer under the order establishes any grounds on which he might have opposed the making of the order in the proceedings in which the order was made, refuse to confirm the order; and

---

*Section 7 is repealed in relation to maintenance orders made by courts in the United Kingdom, the Republic of Ireland or a Hague Convention country.

(ii)   in any other case, confirm the order either without alteration or with such alterations as it thinks reasonable.

(3)   In any proceedings for the confirmation under this section of a provisional order, the statement received from the court which made the order of the grounds on which the making of the order might have been opposed by the payer under the order shall be conclusive evidence that the payer might have opposed the making of the order on any of those grounds.

(4)   [On receiving a certified copy of a provisional order sent to him in pursuance of subsection (2) above the prescribed officer of the appropriate court shall intimate to the payer under the order, in the prescribed manner, that the order has been received as aforesaid and that, unless the payer enters appearance within the prescribed period, the court will confirm the order under this section.]

(5)   The prescribed officer of a court having power under this section to confirm a provisional order shall, if the court confirms the order, register the order in the prescribed manner in that court, and shall, if the court refuses to confirm the order, return the certified copy of the order and the documents which accompanied it to the Secretary of State.

...

(6)   [If such intimation as is mentioned in subsection (4) above cannot be given to the payer under a provisional order in pursuance of that subsection] the officer by whom the certified copy of the order was received shall return that copy and the documents which accompanied it to the Secretary of State with a statement giving such information as he possesses as to the whereabouts of the payer.

(7)   This section shall apply to Scotland subject to the following modifications:—

(a), (b)   [modify subsections (4) and (6) above]

(c)   in any proceedings for the confirmation under this section of a provisional order made by a court in a reciprocating country, the sheriff shall apply the law in force in that country with respect to the sufficiency of evidence.

(8)   [Applies to Northern Ireland.]

8   Enforcement of maintenance order registered in United Kingdom court

(1)   Subject to subsection (2) below, a registered order may be enforced in the United Kingdom as if it had been made by the registering court and as if that court had had jurisdiction to make it; and proceedings for or with respect to the enforcement of any such order may be taken accordingly.

(2)–(5)   [Do not apply to Scotland.]

(6)   In any proceedings for or with respect to the enforcement of an order which is for the time being registered in any court under this Part of this Act a certificate of arrears sent to the prescribed officer of the court shall be [sufficient evidence] of the facts stated therein.

(7)   Subject to subsection (8) below, sums of money payable under a registered order shall be payable in accordance with the order as from the date on which they are required to be paid under the provisions of the order.

(8)   The court having power under section 7 of this Act to confirm a provisional order may, if it decides to confirm the order, direct that the sums of money payable under it shall be deemed to have been payable in accordance with the order as from the date on which they are required to be paid under the provisions of the order or such later date, as it may specify; and subject to any such direction, a maintenance order registered under the said section 7 shall be treated as if it had been made in the form in which it was confirmed and as if it had never been a provisional order.

(9)   In the application of this section to Scotland—

(a)   subsections (2) to (5) shall be omitted; and

(b)   in subsection (6), for the word 'evidence' there shall be substituted the words 'sufficient evidence'.

[...]

9   Variation and revocation of maintenance order registered in United Kingdom court

(1)   Subject to the provisions of this section, the registering court—

(a)   shall have the like power, on an application made by the payer or payee under a registered order, to vary or revoke the order as if it had been made by the registering court and as if that court had had jurisdiction to make it; and

(b)   shall have power to vary or revoke a registered order by a provisional order.

[(1A)   The powers conferred by subsection (1) above are not exercisable in relation to so much of a registered order as provides for the payment of a lump sum.

(1B)   The registering court shall not vary or revoke a registered order if neither the payer nor the payee under the order is resident in the United Kingdom.]

...

Supplemental

...

21   Interpretation of Part I

(1)   In this Part of this Act—

'affiliation order' means an order (however described) adjudging, finding or declaring a person to be the father of a child, whether or not it also provides for the maintenance of the child;

'the appropriate court' in relation to a person residing [or having assets] in England and Wales or in Northern Ireland means a magistrates' court, and in relation to a person residing [or having assets] in Scotland means [a sheriff court], within the jurisdiction of which that person is residing [or has assets];

'certificate of arrears', in relation to a maintenance order, means a certificate certifying that the sum specified in the certificate is to the best of the information or belief of the officer giving the certificate the amount of the arrears due under the order at the date of the certificate or, as the case may be, that to the best of his information or belief there are no arrears due thereunder at that date;

'certified copy', in relation to an order of a court, means a copy of the order certified by the proper officer of the court to be a true copy;

'court' includes any tribunal or person having power to make, confirm, enforce, vary or revoke a maintenance order;

[...]

'maintenance order' means an order (however described) of any of the following descriptions, that is to say—

(a)   an order (including an affiliation order or order consequent upon an affiliation order) which provides for the [payment of a lump sum or the making of periodical payments] towards the maintenance of any person, being a person whom the person liable to make payments under the order is, according to the law applied in the place where the order was made, liable to maintain;

[(aa)   an order which has been made in Scotland, on or after the granting of a decree of divorce, for the payment of a periodical allowance by one party to the marriage to the other party;] and

(b)   an affiliation order or order consequent upon an affiliation order, being an order which provides for the payment by a person adjudged, found or declared to be a child's father of expenses incidental to the child's birth or, where the child has died, of his funeral expenses,

and, in the case of a maintenance order which has been varied, means that order as varied;

'order', as respects Scotland, includes any interlocutor, and any decree or provision contained in an interlocutor;

'payee', in relation to a maintenance order, means the person entitled to the payments for which the order provides;

'payer', in relation to a maintenance order, means the person liable to make payments under the order;

...

'provisional order' means (according to the context)—

(a)   an order made by a court in the United Kingdom which is provisional only and has no effect unless and until confirmed, with or without alteration, by a competent court in a reciprocating country; or

(b)   an order made by a court in a reciprocating country which is provisional only and has no effect unless and until confirmed, with or without alteration, by a court in the United Kingdom having power under this Part of this Act to confirm it;

'reciprocating country' has the meaning assigned to it by section 1 of this Act;

'registered order' means a maintenance order which is for the time being registered in a court in the United Kingdom under this Part of this Act;

'registering court', in relation to a registered order, means the court in which that order is for the time being registered under this Part of this Act;

'the responsible authority', in relation to a reciprocating country, means any person who in that country has functions similar to those of the Secretary of State under this Part of this Act;

['revoke' and 'revocation' include discharge].

(2)   For the purposes of this Part of this Act an order shall be taken to be a maintenance order so far (but only so far) as it relates to the[payment of a lump sum or the making of periodical payments] as mentioned in paragraph (a) of the definition of 'maintenance order' in subsection (1) above, [to the payment of a periodical allowance as mentioned in paragraph (aa) of that definition] or to the payment by a person adjudged, found or declared to be a child's father of any such expenses as are mentioned in paragraph (b) of that definition.

(3)   Any reference in this Part of this Act to the payment of money for the maintenance of a child shall be construed as including a reference to the payment of money for the child's education.

PART II
RECIPROCAL ENFORCEMENT OF CLAIMS FOR THE RECOVERY OF MAINTENANCE

25 Convention countries

(1)   Her Majesty may by Order in Council declare that any country or territory specified in the Order, being a country or territory outside the United Kingdom to which the Maintenance Convention extends, is a convention country for the purposes of this Part of this Act.

(2)   In this section 'the Maintenance Convention' means the United Nations Convention on the Recovery Abroad of Maintenance done at New York on 20th June 1956.

26 Application by person in United Kingdom for recovery, etc of maintenance in convention country

(1)   Where a person in the United Kingdom ('the applicant') claims to be entitled to recover in a convention country maintenance from another person, and that other person is for the time being subject to the jurisdiction of that country, the applicant may apply to the Secretary of State, in accordance with the provisions of this section, to have his claim for the recovery of maintenance from that other person transmitted to that country.

(2)   Where the applicant seeks to vary any provision made in a convention country for the payment by any other person of maintenance to the applicant, and

that other person is for the time being subject to the jurisdiction of that country, the applicant may apply to the Secretary of State, in accordance with the provisions of this section, to have his application for the variation of that provision transmitted to that country.

(3)   An application to the Secretary of State under subsection (1) or (2) above shall be made through the appropriate officer, and that officer shall assist the applicant in completing an application which will comply with the requirements of the law applied by the convention country and shall send the application to the Secretary of State, together with such other documents, if any, as are required by that law.

[(3A)   An application under subsection (1) or (2) above, for the purpose of recovering maintenance from a person in a specified State within the meaning of the Recovery of Maintenance (United States of America) Order 1993, and a certificate signed by a justice of the peace or, where the applicant is residing in Scotland, the sheriff, to the effect that the application sets forth facts from which it may be determined that the respondent owes a duty to maintain the applicant and any other person named in the application and that a court in the specified State may obtain jurisdiction of the respondent or his property, shall be registered in the court in the prescribed manner by the appropriate officer or, in Scotland, by the sheriff clerk in the Maintenance Orders (Reciprocal Enforcement) Act 1972 register.]

(4)   On receiving an application from the appropriate officer the Secretary of State shall transmit it, together with any accompanying documents, to the appropriate authority in the convention country, unless he is satisfied that the application is not made in good faith or that it does not comply with the requirements of the law applied by that country.

(5)   The Secretary of State may request the appropriate officer to obtain from the court of which he is an officer such information relating to the application as may be specified in the request, and it shall be the duty of the court to furnish the Secretary of State with the information he requires.

[(6)   The appropriate officer for the purposes of this section is—

...

(c)   where the applicant is residing in Scotland, the sheriff clerk or sheriff clerk depute of the sheriff court within the jurisdiction of which the applicant is residing.]

31   Application by person in convention country for recovery of maintenance in Scotland

(1)   Where the [Secretary of the Law Society of Scotland who shall send the application and any accompanying documents to a solicitor practising in the sheriff court within the jurisdiction of which that other person resides or to such other solicitor practising in Scotland as appears to the Secretary to be appropriate, for the purposes of enabling the solicitor to take] on behalf of the applicant such steps as appear to the solicitor appropriate in respect of the application.

[(1A)   Proceedings arising out of an application under subsection (1) above shall be treated as an action for aliment within the meaning of the Family Law (Scotland) Act 1985 and, subject to subsections (1B) to (1D) below, the provisions of that Act relating to aliment shall apply in relation to claims for maintenance in such proceedings and decrees therein.

(1B)   Without prejudice to subsection (2) below, any proceedings mentioned in subsection (1A) above shall be brought in the sheriff court.

(1C)   In its application to proceedings mentioned in subsection (1A) above, section 5 of the said Act of 1985 (power to vary or recall decree of aliment) shall be subject to section 34(1) of this Act.

(1D)   Where an application under subsection (1) above is for the recovery of maintenance from a person who is a former spouse of the applicant—

(a)   then, for the purposes of the said Act of 1985, there shall be assumed to be an obligation of aliment within the meaning of that Act owed by the former spouse to the applicant;

(b)   section 2(7) and (8) of that Act shall not apply; and

(c)   an order for payment of maintenance in proceedings arising out of the application—

(i)   shall, if subsisting at the death of the party making the payment, continue to operate against that party's estate, but without prejudice to the power of the court to vary or recall the order; and

(ii)   shall cease to have effect on the remarriage or death of the party receiving payment, except in relation to any arrears due under it.]

(2)   Where in any proceedings arising out of such an application as aforesaid the sheriff [, or (on appeal or remit) the Court of Session,] makes an order containing a provision requiring the payment of maintenance, [the order shall be registered forthwith in the prescribed manner in the appropriate sheriff court by the sheriff clerk or sheriff clerk depute of that sheriff court; and where an order of the Court of Session varies or revokes a registered order of the sheriff, the said sheriff clerk or sheriff clerk depute shall amend the register accordingly.]

[(2A)   In subsection (2) above 'the appropriate sheriff court' means the sheriff court making the order or (where the order is an order of the Court of Session) from which the remit or appeal has come.]

(3)   Without prejudice to the generality of the powers conferred on the Court of Session by section 32 of the Sheriff Courts (Scotland) Act 1971 to regulate by act of sederunt the procedure of the sheriff court, the said powers shall include power to prescribe the decrees granted, or other things done, by the sheriff, or an officer of the sheriff court, under this Part of this Act, notice of which is to be given to such persons as the act of sederunt may provide and the manner in which such notice shall be given.

[(4)   Where an application under subsection (1) above is for the recovery of maintenance from a person who is a former spouse of the applicant an order containing a provision requiring the payment of such maintenance for the benefit of the applicant shall not be made in respect of that application unless—

[(i)   the marriage between the applicant and the said former spouse has been dissolved by a divorce which has been obtained in a country or territory outside the United Kingdom and which is recognised as valid by the law of Scotland;

(ii)   an order for the payment of maintenance for the benefit of the applicant as a divorced person has, in or by reason of, or subsequent to, the divorce proceedings, been made by a court in a convention country;

(iia)   in a case where the order mentioned in paragraph (ii) above was made by a court of a different country from that in which the divorce was obtained, either the applicant or the said former spouse was resident in that different country at the time the application for the order so mentioned was made; and]

(iii)   the court making the order under this section is satisfied that the former spouse of the applicant has failed to comply with the order mentioned in paragraph (ii) above.

[(4A)   In subsection (4)(i) above the reference to the dissolution of a marriage by divorce shall be construed as including a reference to the annulment of a purported marriage and any reference to a marriage, a divorce, a divorced person, a former spouse or divorce proceedings shall be construed accordingly.]

(5)   [...]

(6)   Section 8 of the Law Reform (Miscellaneous Provisions) (Scotland) Act 1966 (which relates to the variation and recall by the sheriff of certain orders made by the Court of Session) shall not apply to an order of the Court of Session registered under subsection (2) above.]

MATRIMONIAL PROCEEDINGS (POLYGAMOUS MARRIAGES) ACT 1972
(1972 c 38)

2　Matrimonial relief and declarations as to validity in respect of polygamous marriages: Scotland

(1)　A court in Scotland shall not be precluded from entertaining proceedings for, or granting, any such decree as is mentioned in subsection (2) below by reason only that [either party to the marriage is, or has during the subsistence of the marriage been, married to more than one person].

(2)　The decrees referred to in subsection (1) above are—

　(a)　a decree of divorce;

　(b)　a decree of nullity of marriage;

　(c)　[...]

　[(d)　a decree of separation;

　(e)　a decree of aliment;]

　(f)　a decree of declarator that a marriage is valid or invalid;

　(g)　any other decree involving a determination as to the validity of a marriage;

and the reference in subsection (1) above to granting such a decree as aforesaid includes a reference to making any ancillary [or incidental] order which the court has power to make in proceedings for such a decree.

[(3)　Provision may be made by rules of court—

　(a)　for requiring notice of proceedings brought by virtue of this section to be served on any additional spouse of a party to the marriage in question; and

　(b)　for conferring on any such additional spouse the right to be heard in the proceedings,

in such cases as may be specified in the rules.]

DOMICILE AND MATRIMONIAL PROCEEDINGS ACT 1973
(1973 c 45)

1　Abolition of wife's dependent domicile

(1)　Subject to subsection (2) below, the domicile of a married woman as at any time after the coming into force of this section shall, instead of being the same as her husband's by virtue only of marriage, be ascertained by reference to the same factors as in the case of any other individual capable of having an independent domicile.

(2)　Where immediately before this section came into force a woman was married and then had her husband's domicile by dependence, she is to be treated as retaining that domicile (as a domicile of choice, if it is not also her domicile of origin) unless and until it is changed by acquisition or revival of another domicile either on or after the coming into force of this section.

(3)　This section extends to England and Wales, Scotland and Northern Ireland.

4　Dependent domicile of child not living with his father*

(1)　Subsection (2) of this section shall have effect with respect to the dependent domicile of a child as at any time after the coming into force of this section when his father and mother are alive but living apart.

(2)　The child's domicile as at that time shall be that of his mother if—

　(a)　he then has his home with her and has no home with his father; or

　(b)　he has at any time had her domicile by virtue of paragraph (a) above and has not since had a home with his father.

(3)　As at any time after the coming into force of this section, the domicile of a child whose mother is dead shall be that which she last had before she died if at

---

* In relation to Scotland s 4 is repealed: Family Law (Scotland) Act 2006, Sch 3, para 1.

her death he had her domicile by virtue of subsection (2) above and he has not since had a home with his father.

(4)   Nothing in this section prejudices any existing rule of law as to the cases in which a child's domicile is regarded as being, by dependence, that of his mother.

(5)   In this section, 'child' means a person incapable of having an independent domicile.

(6)   This section extends to England and Wales [...] and Northern Ireland.

7 Jurisdiction of Court of Session

(1)   Subsections [(2A) to (10)] below shall have effect, subject to section 12(6) of this Act, with respect to the jurisdiction of the Court of Session to entertain—

(a)   an action for divorce, separation, declarator of nullity of marriage, or declarator of marriage; and

[(aa)   an action for declarator of recognition, or non-recognition, of a relevant foreign decree.]

[...]

[(2A)   The Court shall have jurisdiction to entertain an action for divorce or separation if (and only if)—

(a)   the Scottish courts have jurisdiction under the Council Regulation; or

(b)   the action is an excluded action and either of the parties to the marriage in question is domiciled in Scotland on the date when the action is begun.]

(3)   The Court shall have jurisdiction to entertain an action for declarator of marriage if (and only if) either of the parties to the marriage—

(a)   is domiciled in Scotland on the date when the action is begun; or

(b)   was habitually resident in Scotland throughout the period of one year ending with that date; or

(c)   died before that date and either—

(i)   was at death domiciled in Scotland, or

(ii)   had been habitually resident in Scotland throughout the period of one year ending with the date of death.

[(3A)   The Court shall have jurisdiction to entertain an action for declarator of nullity of marriage [or for declarator of recognition, or non-recognition, of a relevant foreign decree] if (and only if)—

(a)   the Scottish courts have jurisdiction under the Council Regulation; or

(b)   the action is one to which subsection (3B) below applies and either of the parties to the marriage—

(a)   is domiciled in Scotland on the date when the action is begun; or

(b)   died before that date and either—

(i)   was at death domiciled in Scotland; or

(ii)   had been habitually resident in Scotland throughout the period of one year ending with the date of death.

(3B)   This subsection applies to an action—

(a)   which is an excluded action; or

(b)   where one of the parties to the marriage died before the date when the action is begun.]

[...]

(5)   The Court shall, at any time when proceedings are pending in respect of which it has jurisdiction by virtue of subsection (2), (2A), (3) or (3A) above (or of this subsection), also have jurisdiction to entertain other proceedings, in respect of the same marriage, for divorce, separation or declarator of marriage, or declarator of nullity of marriage, notwithstanding that jurisdiction would not be exercisable under any of those subsections.

[(5A)   Subsection (5) does not give the Court jurisdiction to entertain proceedings in contravention of Article 6 of the Council Regulation.]

(6)   Nothing in this section affects the rules governing the jurisdiction of the

Court of Session to entertain, in an action for divorce, an application for payment by a co-defender of damages or expenses.

(7)   The foregoing provisions of this section are without prejudice to any rule of law whereby the Court of Session has jurisdiction in certain circumstances to entertain actions for separation as a matter of necessity and urgency.

(8)   No action for divorce in respect of a marriage shall be entertained by the Court of Session by virtue of this section while proceedings for divorce or nullity of marriage, begun before the commencement of this Act, are pending (in respect of the same marriage) in England and Wales, Northern Ireland, the Channel Islands or the Isle of Man; and provision may be made by rules of court as to when, for the purposes of this subsection, proceedings are to be treated as begun or pending in any of those places.

[(9)   In this section, 'relevant foreign decree' means a decree of divorce, nullity or separation granted outwith a member state of the European Union.

(10)   References in subsection (3A) to a marriage shall, in the case of an action for declarator of recognition, or non-recognition, of a relevant foreign decree, be construed as references to the marriage to which the relevant foreign decree relates.]

8   Jurisdiction of sheriff court in respect of actions for separation

(1)   Subsections (2) to [(6)] below shall have effect, subject to section 12(6) of this Act, with respect to the jurisdiction of the sheriff court to entertain—

[(a)   an action for separation or divorce; and

(b)   an action for declarator of recognition, or non-recognition, of a relevant foreign decree.]

(2)   The court shall have jurisdiction to entertain an action for separation or divorce [or for declarator of recognition, or non-recognition, of a relevant foreign decree] if (and only if)—

(a)   either—

(i)   the Scottish courts have jurisdiction under the Council Regulation; or

(ii)   the action is an excluded action and either party to the marriage in question is domiciled in Scotland at the date when the action is begun; and

(b)   either party to the marriage—

(i)   was resident in the sheriffdom for a period of forty days ending with that date, or

(ii)   had been resident in the sheriffdom for a period of not less than forty days ending not more than forty days before the said date, and has no known residence in Scotland at that date.

(3)   In respect of any marriage, the court shall have jurisdiction to entertain an action for separation or divorce (notwithstanding that jurisdiction would not be exercisable under subsection (2) above) if it is begun at a time when an original action is pending in respect of the marriage; and for this purpose 'original action' means an action in respect of which the court has jurisdiction by virtue of subsection (2), or of this subsection.

[(3A)   Subsection (3) does not give the court jurisdiction to entertain an action in contravention of Article 6 of the Council Regulation.]

(4)   The foregoing provisions of this section are without prejudice to any jurisdiction of a sheriff court to entertain an action of separation or divorce remitted to it in pursuance of any enactment or rule of court, provided that entertaining the action would not contravene Article 6 of the Council Regulation.

[(5)   In this section, 'relevant foreign decree' has the meaning given by section 7(9).

(6)   References in subsection (2) to a marriage shall, in the case of an action for declarator of recognition, or non-recognition, of a relevant foreign decree, be construed as references to the marriage to which the relevant foreign decree relates.]

10   Ancillary and collateral orders

(1)   Where after the commencement of this Act an application is competently made to the Court of Session or to a sheriff court for the making, or the variation or recall, of an order which is ancillary or collateral to an action for any of the following remedies, namely, divorce, separation, declarator of marriage and declarator of nullity of marriage (whether the application is made in the same proceedings or in other proceedings and whether it is made before or after the pronouncement of a final decree in the action), then, if the court has or, as the case may be, had by virtue of this Act or of any enactment or rule of law in force before the commencement of this Act jurisdiction to entertain the action, it shall have jurisdiction to entertain the application whether or not it would have jurisdiction to do so apart from this subsection.

[(1A)   For the purposes of subsection (1) above, references to an application for the making, or the variation or recall, of an order are references to the making, or the variation or recall, of an order relating to children, aliment, financial provision on divorce, judicial separation, nullity of marriage or expenses.

(1B)   Subsection (1) above does not give the Court of Session or a sheriff court jurisdiction to entertain an application in proceedings where—

(a)   the court is exercising jurisdiction in the proceedings by virtue of Article 3 of the Council Regulation; and

(b)   the making or variation of an order in consequence of the application would contravene [Article 6] of the Council Regulation.]

(2)   It is hereby declared that where—

(a)   the Court of Session has jurisdiction by virtue of this section to entertain an application for the variation or recall as respects any person of an order made by it, and

(b)   the order is one to which section 8 (variation and recall by the sheriff of certain orders made by the Court of Session) of the Law Reform (Miscellaneous Provisions) (Scotland) Act 1966 applies,

then, for the purposes of any application under the said section 8 for the variation or recall of the order in so far as it relates to that person, the sheriff, as defined in that section, has jurisdiction as respects that person to exercise the power conferred on him by that section.

11   Sisting of certain actions

[(1)]   The provisions of Schedule 3 to this Act shall have effect with respect to the sisting of actions for any of the following remedies, namely, divorce, separation, declarator of marriage or declarator of nullity of marriage, and with respect to the other matters mentioned in that Schedule; but nothing in that Schedule—

(a)   requires or authorises a sist of an action which is pending when this Act comes into force; or

(b)   prejudices any power to sist an action which is exercisable by any court apart from the Schedule.

[(2)   Subsection (1) above and Schedule 3 to this Act and any power mentioned in subsection (1)(b) are subject to Article 19 of the Council Regulation.]

SCHEDULE 3
SISTING OF CONSISTORIAL ACTIONS (SCOTLAND)

Mandatory sists

8.   Where before the beginning of the proof in any action for divorce which is continuing in the Court of Session [or in the Sheriff Court] it appears to the Court [concerned] on the application of a party to the marriage—

(a)   that in respect of the same marriage proceedings for divorce or nullity of marriage are continuing in a related jurisdiction; and

(b)   that the parties to the marriage have resided together after the marriage was contracted; and

(c)   that the place where they resided together when the action in the Court was begun or, if they did not then reside together, where they last resided together before the date on which that action was begun is in that jurisdiction; and

(d)   that either of the said parties was habitually resident in that jurisdiction throughout the year ending with the date on which they last resided together before the date on which that action was begun;

it shall be the duty of the Court, subject to paragraph 10(2) below, to sist the action before it.

9.—(1)   Where before the beginning of the proof in any consistorial action which is continuing in the Court of Session or in a sheriff court, it appears to the court concerned—

(a)   that any other proceedings in respect of the marriage in question or capable of affecting its validity are continuing in another jurisdiction, and

(b)   that the balance of fairness (including convenience) as between the parties to the marriage is such that it is appropriate for those other proceedings to be disposed of before further steps are taken in the action in the said court,

the court may then if it thinks fit sist that action.

(2)   In considering the balance of fairness and convenience for the purposes of sub-paragraph (1)(b) above, the court shall have regard to all factors appearing to be relevant, including the convenience of witnesses and any delay or expense which may result from the proceedings being sisted, or not being sisted.

(3)   Sub-paragraph (1) above is without prejudice to the duty imposed [...] by paragraph 8 above.

(4)   If, at any time after the beginning of the proof in any consistorial action which is pending in the Court of Session or a sheriff court, the court concerned is satisfied that a person has failed to perform the duty imposed on him in respect of the action and any such other proceedings as aforesaid by paragraph 7 above, sub-paragraph (1) of this paragraph shall have effect in relation to that action and to the other proceedings as if the words 'before the beginning of the proof' were omitted; but no action in respect of the failure of a person to perform such a duty shall be competent.

PRESCRIPTION AND LIMITATION (SCOTLAND) ACT 1973
(1973 c 52)

[23A   Private international law application

(1)   Where the substantive law of a country other than Scotland falls to be applied by a Scottish court as the law governing an obligation, the court shall apply any relevant rules of law of that country relating to the extinction of the obligation or the limitation of time within which proceedings may be brought to enforce the obligation to the exclusion of any corresponding rule of Scots law.

(2)   This section shall not apply where it appears to the court that the application of the relevant foreign rule of law would be incompatible with the principles of public policy applied by the court.

(3)   This section shall not apply in any case where the application of the corresponding rule of Scots law has extinguished the obligation, or barred the bringing of proceedings prior to the coming into force of the Prescription and Limitation (Scotland) Act 1984.]

EVIDENCE (PROCEEDINGS IN OTHER JURISDICTIONS) ACT 1975
(1975 c 34)

1   Application to United Kingdom court for assistance in obtaining evidence for civil proceedings in other court

Where an application is made to the High Court, the Court of Session or the High Court of Justice in Northern Ireland for an order for evidence to be obtained in the part of the United Kingdom in which it exercises jurisdiction, and the court is satisfied—

(a)   that the application is made in pursuance of a request issued by or on behalf of a court or tribunal ('the requesting court') exercising jurisdiction in any other part of the United Kingdom or in a country or territory outside the United Kingdom; and

(b)   that the evidence to which the application relates is to be obtained for the purposes of civil proceedings which either have been instituted before the requesting court or whose institution before that court is contemplated,

the High Court, Court of Session or High Court of Justice in Northern Ireland, as the case may be, shall have the powers conferred on it by the following provisions of this Act.

DIVORCE (SCOTLAND) ACT 1976
(1976 c 39)

[3A   Postponement of decree of divorce where religious impediment to remarry exists

(1)   Notwithstanding that irretrievable breakdown of a marriage has been established in an action for divorce, the court may—

(a)   on the application of a party ('the applicant'); and

(b)   if satisfied—

(i)   that subsection (2) applies; and

(ii)   that it is just and reasonable to do so,

postpone the grant of decree in the action until it is satisfied that the other party has complied with subsection (3).

(2)   This subsection applies where—

(a)   the applicant is prevented from entering into a religious marriage by virtue of a requirement of the religion of that marriage; and

(b)   the other party can act so as to remove, or enable or contribute to the removal of, the impediment which prevents that marriage.

(3)   A party complies with this subsection by acting in the way described in subsection (2)(b).

(4)   The court may, whether or not on the application of a party and notwithstanding that subsection (2) applies, recall a postponement under subsection (1).

(5)   The court may, before recalling a postponement under subsection (1), order the other party to produce a certificate from a relevant religious body confirming that the other party has acted in the way described in subsection 2(b).

(6)   For the purposes of subsection (5), a religious body is 'relevant' if the applicant considers the body competent to provide the confirmation referred to in that subsection.

(7)   In this section—

'religious marriage' means a marriage solemnised by a marriage celebrant of a prescribed religious body, and 'religion of that marriage' shall be construed accordingly;

'prescribed' means prescribed by regulations made by the Scottish Ministers.

(8)   Any reference in this section to a marriage celebrant of a prescribed religious body is a reference to—

(a)   a minister, clergyman, pastor or priest of such a body;

(b)   a person who has, on the nomination of such a body, been registered under section 9 of the Marriage (Scotland) Act 1977 (c 15) as empowered to solemnise marriages; or

(c)   any person who is recognised by such a body as entitled to solemnise marriages on its behalf.

(9)   Regulations under subsection (7) shall be made by statutory instrument; and any such instrument shall be subject to annulment in pursuance of a resolution of the Scottish Parliament.]

MARRIAGE (SCOTLAND) ACT 1977
(1977 c 15)

1   Minimum age for marriage

(1)   No person domiciled in Scotland may marry before he attains the age of 16.

(2)   A marriage solemnised in Scotland between persons either of whom is under the age of 16 shall be void.

3   Notice of intention to marry

...

(5)   A party to a marriage intended to be solemnised in Scotland who is not domiciled in any part of the United Kingdom is required, if practicable, to submit under subsection (1)(c) above a certificate, issued by a competent authority in the state in which the party is domiciled, to the effect that he is not known to be subject to any legal incapacity (in terms of the law of that state) which would prevent his marrying:

Provided that such a party—

(i)   may, where under the law of the state in which he is domiciled his personal law is that of another foreign state, submit in lieu of the said certificate a like certificate issued by a competent authority in that other state;

(ii)   need not submit a certificate under paragraph (c) of subsection (1) above,

(a)   if he has been resident in the United Kingdom for a period of 2 or more years immediately before the date on which he submits a marriage notice under that subsection in respect of the said marriage; or

(b)   [if no such certificate has been issued only by reason of the fact that the validity of a divorce or annulment granted by a court of civil jurisdiction in Scotland or entitled to recognition in Scotland under section 44 or 45 of the Family Law Act 1986 is not recognised in the state in which the certificate would otherwise have been issued.]

5   Objections to marriage

...

(4)   For the purposes of [this section] and section 6 of this Act, there is a legal impediment to a marriage where—

(a)   that marriage would be void by virtue of section 2(1) of this Act;

(b)   one of the parties is, or both are, already married [or in civil partnership];

(c)   one or both of the parties will be under the age of 16 on the date of solemnisation of the intended marriage;

(d)   one or both of the parties is or are incapable of understanding the nature of a marriage ceremony or of consenting to marriage;

(e)   both parties are of the same sex; or

(f)   one or both of the parties is, or are, not domiciled in Scotland and, on a ground other than one mentioned in paragraphs (a) to (e) above, a marriage in Scotland between the parties would be void ab initio according to the law of the domicile of the party or parties as the case may be.

...

7   Marriage outside Scotland where a party resides in Scotland

(1)   Where a person residing in Scotland is a party to a marriage intended to be solemnised in—

(a)   England or Wales with a party residing in England or Wales and desires; or

(b)   any country, territory or place outside Great Britain, and, for the purpose of complying with the law in force in that country, territory or place, is required to obtain from a competent authority in Scotland,

a certificate in respect of his legal capacity to marry, he may submit, in the form and with the fee and documents specified in section 3(1)(a), (b) [and (d)] of this Act, notice of intention to marry to the district registrar for the district in which he resides (the said registrar being in this section referred to as the 'appropriate registrar') as if it were intended that the marriage should be solemnised in that district, and sections 3(2) and (3) and 4 of this Act shall apply accordingly.

(2)   The appropriate registrar shall, if satisfied (after consultation, if the appropriate registrar considers it necessary, with the Registrar General) that a person who has by virtue of subsection (1) above submitted a marriage notice to him is not subject to any legal incapacity (in terms of Scots law) which would prevent his marrying, issue to that person a certificate in the prescribed form that he is not known to be subject to any such incapacity:

Provided that the certificate shall not be issued earlier than 14 days after the date of receipt (as entered by the appropriate registrar in the marriage notice book) of the marriage notice.

(3)   Any person may, at any time before a certificate is issued under subsection (2) above, submit to the appropriate registrar an objection in writing to such issue; and the objection shall be taken into account by the appropriate registrar in deciding whether, in respect of the person to whom the certificate would be issued, he is satisfied as mentioned in the said subsection (2).

[(4)   For the purpose of subsection (3) above, an objection which is submitted by electronic means is to be treated as in writing if it is received in a form which is legible and capable of being used for subsequent reference.]

20   Second marriage ceremony

(1)   Where two persons have gone through a marriage ceremony with each other outside the United Kingdom, whether before or after the commencement of this Act, but they are not, or are unable to prove that they are, validly married to each other in Scots law, an authorised registrar, on an application made to him by those persons, may, subject to the approval of the Registrar General and to subsection (2) below, solemnise their marriage as if they had not already gone through a marriage ceremony with each other.

(2)   Sections 3 to 6 and 18 and 19 of this Act shall apply for the purpose of solemnising a marriage under this section except that—

(a)   there shall be submitted to the authorised registrar a statutory declaration by both parties—

(i)   stating that they have previously gone through a marriage ceremony with each other; and

(ii)   specifying the date and place at which, and the circumstances in which, they went through that ceremony;

(b)   section 5(4)(b) of this Act shall not apply in respect of the parties already being married to each other;

(c)   the Marriage Schedule shall contain such modifications as the Registrar General may direct to indicate that the parties have previously gone through a marriage ceremony with each other; and

...

[20A Grounds on which marriage void

(1) Where subsection (2) or (3) applies in relation to a marriage solemnised in Scotland, the marriage shall be void.

(2) This subsection applies if at the time of the marriage ceremony a party to the marriage who was capable of consenting to the marriage purported to give consent but did so by reason only of duress or error.

(3) This subsection applies if at the time of the marriage ceremony a party to the marriage was incapable of—

(a) understanding the nature of marriage; and

(b) consenting to the marriage.

(4) If a party to a marriage purported to give consent to the marriage other than by reason only of duress or error, the marriage shall not be void by reason only of that party's having tacitly withheld consent to the marriage at the time when it was solemnised.

(5) In this section 'error' means—

(a) error as to the nature of the ceremony; or

(b) a mistaken belief held by a person ('A') that the other party at the ceremony with whom A purported to enter into a marriage was the person whom A had agreed to marry.]

22 Interpreters at marriage ceremony

(1) Where the person by whom a marriage is to be solemnised under this Act considers that it is necessary or desirable, he may use the services of an interpreter (not being a party or a witness to the marriage) at the marriage ceremony.

(2) The interpreter shall—

(a) before the marriage ceremony, sign a written statement that he understands, and is able to converse in, any language in respect of which he is to act as interpreter at that ceremony; and

(b) immediately after the marriage ceremony, furnish the person solemnising the marriage with a certificate written in English and signed by the interpreter that he has faithfully acted as interpreter at that ceremony.

(3) Any fee for the services of the interpreter shall be paid by the parties to the marriage.

UNFAIR CONTRACT TERMS ACT 1977
(1977 c 50)

27 Choice of law clauses

(1) Where the [law applicable to] a contract is the law of any part of the United Kingdom only by choice of the parties (and apart from that choice would be the law of some country outside the United Kingdom) sections 2 to 7 and 16 to 21 of this Act do not operate as part [of the law applicable to the contract].

(2) This Act has effect notwithstanding any contract term which applies or purports to apply the law of some country outside the United Kingdom, where (either or both)—

(a) the term appears to the court, or arbitrator or arbiter to have been imposed wholly or mainly for the purpose of enabling the party imposing it to evade the operation of this Act; or

[(b) the contract is a consumer contract as defined in Part II of this Act, and the consumer at the date when the contract was made was habitually resident in the United Kingdom, and the essential steps necessary for the making of the contract were taken there, whether by him or by others on his behalf.]

(3) [Substitutes (2)(b) above for Scotland.]

ADOPTION (SCOTLAND) ACT 1978
(1978 c 28)

PART IV
STATUS OF ADOPTED CHILDREN

38 Meaning of 'adoption order' in Part IV

(1)   In this Part 'adoption order' means—

(a)   an adoption order within the meaning of section 65(1);

(b)   an adoption order under the Children Act 1975, the Adoption Act 1958, the Adoption Act 1950 or any enactment repealed by the Adoption Act 1950;

(c)   an order effecting an adoption made in England, Wales, Northern Ireland, the Isle of Man or any of the Channel Islands;

[(cc) a Convention adoption;]

(d)   an 'overseas adoption' within the meaning of section 65(2); or

(e)   any other adoption recognised by the law of Scotland; and cognate expressions shall be construed accordingly.

(2)   The definition of adoption order includes, where the context admits, an adoption order which took effect before the commencement of the Children Act 1975.

39 Status conferred by adoption

(1)   [A child who is the subject of an adoption order shall be treated in law—

(a)   where the adopters are a married couple, as if—

(i)   he had been born as a [...] child of the marriage (whether or not he was in fact born after the marriage was constituted); and

(ii)   [subject to subsection (2A)] he were not the child of any person other than the adopters;

(b)   where the adoption order is made by virtue of section 15(1)(aa) as if—

(i)   he had been born as a [...] child of the marriage between the adopter and the natural parent to whom the adopter is married (whether or not he was in fact born after the marriage was constituted); and

(ii)   [subject to subsection (2A)] he were not the child of any person other than the adopter and that natural parent; and

(c)   in any other case, as if—

(i)   he had been born as a [...] child of the adopter; and

(ii)   [subject to subsection (2A)] he were not the child of any person other than the adopter.]

(2)   Where [a] child has been adopted by one of his natural parents as sole adoptive parent and the adopter thereafter marries the other natural parent, subsection (1) shall not affect any enactment or rule of law whereby, by virtue of the marriage, the child is rendered the [...] child of both natural parents.

[(2A)   Where, in the case of a child adopted under a Convention adoption, the Court of Session is satisfied, on an application under this subsection—

(a)   that under the law of the country in which the adoption was effected the adoption is not a full adoption;

(b)   that the consents referred to in Article 4(c) and (d) of the Convention have not been given for a full adoption, or that the United Kingdom is not the receiving State (within the meaning of Article 2 of the Convention); and

(c)   that it would be more favourable to the child for a direction to be given under this subsection,

the Court may direct that sub-paragraph (ii) of, as the case may be, paragraph (a), (b) or (c) of subsection (1) shall not apply, or shall not apply to such extent as may be specified in the direction: and in this subsection 'full adoption' means an adoption by virtue of which the child falls to be treated in law as if he were not the child of any person other than the adopters or adopter.]

(3)   This section has effect—

(a)   in the case of an adoption before 1st January 1976, from that date, and
(b)   in the case of any other adoption, from the date of the adoption.
(4)   Subject to the provisions of this Part, this section—
      (a) applies for the construction of enactments or instruments passed or made
before or after the commencement of this Act so far as the context admits; and
      (b) does not affect things done or events occurring before the adoption or,
where the adoption took place before 1st January 1976, before that date.
(5)   This section has effect subject to the provisions of section 44.

[...]

41   Miscellaneous enactments
(1)   Section 39 does not apply in determining the forbidden degrees of con-
sanguinity and affinity in respect of the law relating to marriage [, to the eligibility
of persons to register as civil partners of each other] or in respect of the crime of
incest, except that, on the making of an adoption order, the adopter and the child
shall be deemed, for all time coming, to be within the said forbidden degrees in
respect of the law relating to marriage and incest [, to such eligibility and to
incest].
(2)   [S]ection 39 does not apply for the purposes of any provision of—
      (a)   [the British Nationality Act 1981],
      (b)   the Immigration Act 1971,
      (c)   any instrument having effect under an enactment within paragraph (a)
or (b), or
      (d)   any other law for the time being in force which determines [British citizen-
ship, British Overseas Territories citizenship, the status of a British National
(Overseas) or British Overseas citizenship].

42   Pensions
Section 39(1) does not affect entitlement to a pension which is payable to or for the
benefit of a child and is in payment at the time of his adoption.

43   Insurance
Where a child is adopted whose natural parent has effected an insurance with a
friendly society or a collecting society or an industrial insurance company for the
payment on the death of the child of money for funeral expenses, the rights and
liabilities under the policy shall by virtue of the adoption be transferred to the
adoptive parents who shall for the purposes of the enactments relating to such
societies and companies be treated as the person who took out the policy.

44   Effect of s 39 on succession and *inter vivos* deed
Section 39 (status conferred by adoption) does not affect the existing law relating
to adopted persons in respect of—
      (a)   the succession to a deceased person (whether testate or intestate), and
      (b)   the disposal of property by virtue of any *inter vivos* deed.

STATE IMMUNITY ACT 1978
(1978 c 33)

1   General immunity from jurisdiction
(1)   A State is immune from the jurisdiction of the courts of the United Kingdom except as provided in the following provisions of this Part of this Act.
(2)   A court shall give effect to the immunity conferred by this section even
though the State does not appear in the proceedings in question.

2   Submission to jurisdiction
(1)   A State is not immune as respects proceedings in respect of which it has
submitted to the jurisdiction of the courts of the United Kingdom.
(2)   A State may submit after the dispute giving rise to the proceedings has

arisen or by a prior written agreement; but a provision in any agreement that it is to be governed by the law of the United Kingdom is not to be regarded as a submission.

(3)   A State is deemed to have submitted—

(a)   if it has instituted the proceedings; or

(b)   subject to subsections (4) and (5) below, if it has intervened or taken any step in the proceedings.

(4)   Subsection (3)(b) above does not apply to intervention or any step taken for the purpose only of—

(a)   claiming immunity; or

(b)   asserting an interest in property in circumstances such that the State would have been entitled to immunity if the proceedings had been brought against it.

(5)   Subsection (3)(b) above does not apply to any step taken by the State in ignorance of facts entitling it to immunity if those facts could not reasonably have been ascertained and immunity is claimed as soon as reasonably practicable.

(6)   A submission in respect of any proceedings extends to any appeal but not to any counter-claim unless it arises out of the same legal relationship or facts as the claim.

(7)   The head of a State's diplomatic mission in the United Kingdom, or the person for the time being performing his functions, shall be deemed to have authority to submit on behalf of the State in respect of any proceedings; and any person who has entered into a contract on behalf of and with the authority of a State shall be deemed to have authority to submit on its behalf in respect of proceedings arising out of the contract.

3   Commercial transactions and contracts to be performed in United Kingdom

(1)   A State is not immune as respects proceedings relating to—

(a)   a commercial transaction entered into by the State; or

(b)   an obligation of the State which by virtue of a contract (whether a commercial transaction or not) falls to be performed wholly or partly in the United Kingdom.

(2)   This section does not apply if the parties to the dispute are States or have otherwise agreed in writing; and subsection (1)(b) above does not apply if the contract (not being a commercial transaction) was made in the territory of the State concerned and the obligation in question is governed by its administrative law.

(3)   In this section 'commercial transaction' means—

(a)   any contract for the supply of goods or services;

(b)   any loan or other transaction for the provision of finance and any guarantee or indemnity in respect of any such transaction or of any other financial obligation; and

(c)   any other transaction or activity (whether of a commercial, industrial, financial, professional or other similar character) into which a State enters or in which it engages otherwise than in the exercise of sovereign authority;

but neither paragraph of subsection (1) above applies to a contract of employment between a State and an individual.

4   Contracts of employment

(1)   A State is not immune as respects proceedings relating to a contract of employment between the State and an individual where the contract was made in the United Kingdom or the work is to be wholly or partly performed there.

(2)   Subject to subsection (3) and (4) below, this section does not apply if—

(a)   at the time when the proceedings are brought the individual is a national of the State concerned; or

(b)   at the time when the contract was made the individual was neither a national of the United Kingdom nor habitually resident there; or

(c)   the parties to the contract have otherwise agreed in writing.

(3)   Where the work is for an office, agency or establishment maintained by the State in the United Kingdom for commercial purposes, subsection (2)(a) and (b) above do not exclude the application of this section unless the individual was, at the time when the contract was made, habitually resident in that State.

(4)   Subsection (2)(c) above does not exclude the application of this section where the law of the United Kingdom requires the proceedings to be brought before a court of the United Kingdom.

(5)   In subsection (2)(b) above 'national of the United Kingdom' [means—

(a)   a British citizen, a British overseas territories citizen, a British National (Overseas) or a British Overseas citizen; or

(b)   a person who under the British Nationality Act 1981 is a British subject; or

(c)   a British protected person (within the meaning of that Act)].

(6)   In this section 'proceedings relating to a contract of employment' includes proceedings between the parties to such a contract in respect of any statutory rights or duties to which they are entitled or subject as employer or employee.

5   Personal injuries and damage to property

A State is not immune as respects proceedings in respect of—

(a)   death or personal injury; or

(b)   damage to or loss of tangible property,

caused by an act or omission in the United Kingdom.

6   Ownership, possession and use of property

(1)   A State is not immune as respects proceedings relating to—

(a)   any interest of the State in, or its possession or use of, immovable property in the United Kingdom; or

(b)   any obligation of the State arising out of its interest in, or its possession or use of, any such property.

(2)   A State is not immune as respects proceedings relating to any interest of the State in movable or immovable property, being an interest arising by way of succession, gift or bona vacantia.

(3)   The fact that a State has or claims an interest in any property shall not preclude any court from exercising in respect of it any jurisdiction relating to the estates of deceased persons or persons of unsound mind or to insolvency, the winding up of companies or the administration of trusts.

(4)   A court may entertain proceedings against a person other than a State notwithstanding that the proceedings relate to property—

(a)   which is in the possession or control of a State; or

(b)   in which a State claims an interest,

if the State would not have been immune had the proceedings been brought against it or, in a case within paragraph (b) above, if the claim is neither admitted nor supported by prima facie evidence.

9   Arbitrations

(1)   Where a State has agreed in writing to submit a dispute which has arisen, or may arise, to arbitration, the State is not immune as respects proceedings in the courts of the United Kingdom which relate to the arbitration.

(2)   This section has effect subject to any contrary provision in the arbitration agreement and does not apply to any arbitration agreement between States.

14   States entitled to immunities and privileges

(1)   The immunities and privileges conferred by this Part of this Act apply to any foreign or commonwealth State other than the United Kingdom; and references to a State include references to—

(a)   the sovereign or other head of that State in his public capacity;

(b)   the government of that State; and

(c)   any department of that government,

but not to any entity (hereafter referred to as a 'separate entity') which is distinct from the executive organs of the government of the State and capable of suing or being sued.

(2)   A separate entity is immune from the jurisdiction of the courts of the United Kingdom if, and only if—

(a)   the proceedings relate to anything done by it in the exercise of sovereign authority; and

(b)   the circumstances are such that a State (or, in the case of proceedings to which section 10 above applies, a State which is not a party to the Brussels Convention) would have been so immune.

(3)   If a separate entity (not being a State's central bank or other monetary authority) submits to the jurisdiction in respect of proceedings in the case of which it is entitled to immunity by virtue of subsection (2) above, subsections (1) to (4) of section 13 above shall apply to it in respect of those proceedings as if references to a State were references to that entity.

(4)   Property of a State's central bank or other monetary authority shall not be regarded for the purposes of subsection (4) of section 13 above as in use or intended for use for commercial purposes; and where any such bank or authority is a separate entity subsections (1) to (3) of that section shall apply to it as if references to a State were references to the bank or authority.

(5)   Section 12 above applies to proceedings against the constituent territories of a federal State; and Her Majesty may by Order in Council provide for the other provisions of this Part of this Act to apply to any such constituent territory specified in the Order as they apply to a State.

(6)   Where the provisions of this Part of this Act do not apply to a constituent territory by virtue of any such Order subsections (2) and (3) above shall apply to it as if it were a separate entity.

CIVIL JURISDICTION AND JUDGMENTS ACT 1982
(1982 c 27)

PART I
IMPLEMENTATION OF THE CONVENTIONS

Main implementing provisions

1   Interpretation of references to the Conventions and Contracting States

(1)   In this Act—

'the 1968 Convention' means the Convention on jurisdiction and the enforcement of judgments in civil and commercial matters (including the Protocol annexed to that Convention), signed at Brussels on 27th September 1968;

'the 1971 Protocol' means the Protocol on the interpretation of the 1968 Convention by the European Court, signed at Luxembourg on 3rd June 1971;

'the Accession Convention' means the Convention on the accession to the 1968 Convention and the 1971 Protocol of Denmark, the Republic of Ireland and the United Kingdom, signed at Luxembourg on 9th October 1978;

['the 1982 Accession Convention' means the Convention on the accession of the Hellenic Republic to the 1968 Convention and the 1971 Protocol, with the adjustments made to them by the Accession Convention, signed at Luxembourg on 25th October 1982;]

['the 1989 Accession Convention' means the Convention on the accession of the Kingdom of Spain and the Portuguese Republic to the 1968 Convention and the 1971 Protocol, with the adjustments made to them by the Accession Convention and the 1982 Accession Convention, signed at Donostia – San Sebastián on 26th May 1989;]

['the 1996 Accession Convention' means the Convention on the accession of the

Republic of Austria, the Republic of Finland and the Kingdom of Sweden to the 1968 Convention and the 1971 Protocol, with the adjustments made to them by the Accession Convention, the 1982 Accession Convention and the 1989 Accession Convention, signed at Brussels on 29th November 1996;]

['the [Brusssels Conventions'] means the 1968 Convention, the 1971 Protocol, the Accession Convention, the 1982 Accession Convention and the 1989 Accession Convention;]

['the Lugano Convention' means the Convention on jurisdiction and the enforcement of judgments in civil and commercial matters (including the Protocols annexed to that Convention) opened for signature at Lugano on 16th September 1988 and signed by the United Kingdom on 18th September 1989;]

['the Regulation' means Council Regulation (EC) No 44/2001 of 22nd December 2000 on jurisdiction and the recognition and enforcement of judgments in civil and commercial matters, as amended from time to time and as applied by the Agreement made on 19th October 2005 between the European Community and the Kingdom of Denmark on jurisdiction and the recognition and enforcement of judgments in civil and commercial matters].

(2)   In this Act, unless the context otherwise requires—

(a)   references to, or to any provision of, the 1968 Convention or the 1971 Protocol are references to that Convention, Protocol or provision as amended by the Accession Convention [, the 1982 Accession Convention, the 1989 Accession Convention and the 1996 Accession Convention]; and

[(aa)   references to, or to any provision of, the Lugano Convention are references to that Convention as amended on the accession to it of Poland; and]

(b)   [any reference in any provision to a numbered Article without more is a reference—

(i)   to the Article so numbered of the 1968 Convention, in so far as the provision applies in relation to that Convention, and

(ii)   to the Article so numbered of the Lugano Convention, in so far as the provision applies in relation to that Convention,]

and any reference to a sub-division of a numbered Article shall be construed accordingly.

(3)   [In this Act—

'Contracting State', without more, in any provision means—

(a)   in the application of the provision in relation to the Brussels Conventions, a Brussels Contracting State; and

(b)   in the application of the provision in relation to the Lugano Convention, a Lugano Contracting State;]

['Brussels Contracting State' means a state which is one of the original parties to the 1968 Convention or one of the parties acceding to that Convention under the Accession Convention, or under the 1982 Accession Convention, or under the 1989 Accession Convention, but only with respect to any territory—

(a)   to which the Brussels Conventions apply; and

(b)   which is excluded from the scope of the Regulation pursuant to Article 299 of the Treaty establishing the European Community;]

['Lugano Contracting State' means—

(a)   one of the original parties to the Lugano Convention, that is to say Austria, Belgium, Denmark, Finland, France, the Federal Republic of Germany, the Hellenic Republic, Iceland, the Republic of Ireland, Italy, Luxembourg, the Netherlands, Norway, Portugal, Spain, Sweden, Switzerland and the United Kingdom; or

(b)   a party who has subsequently acceded to that Convention, that is to say, Poland.]

['Regulation State' in any provision, in the application of that provision in relation to the Regulation, means a 'Member State'].

[(4)   Any question arising as to whether it is the Regulation, any of the Brussels

Conventions, or the Lugano Convention which applies in the circumstances of a particular case shall be determined as follows—
    (a)   in accordance with Article 54B of the Lugano Convention (which determines the relationship between the Brussels Conventions and the Lugano Convention); and
    (b)   in accordance with Article 68 of the Regulation (which determines the relationship between the Brussels Conventions and the Regulation).]

2   The [Brussels Conventions] to have the force of law
    (1)   The [Brussels Conventions] shall have the force of law in the United Kingdom, and judicial notice shall be taken of them.
    (2)   [For convenience of reference there are set out in Schedules 1, 2, 3, 3A, 3B and 3C respectively the English texts of—
    (a)   the 1968 Convention as amended by Titles II and III of the Accession Convention, by Titles II and III of the 1982 Accession Convention, by Titles II and III of, and Annex I(d) to, the 1989 Accession Convention and by Titles II and III of the 1996 Accession Convention;
    (b)   the 1971 Protocol as amended by Title IV of the Accession Convention, by Title IV of the 1982 Accession Convention, by Title IV of the 1989 Accession Convention and by Title IV of the 1996 Accession Convention;
    (c)   Titles V and VI of the Accession Convention (transitional and final provisions) as amended by Title V of the 1989 Accession Convention;
    (d)   Titles V and VI of the 1982 Accession Convention (transitional and final provisions); and
    (e)   Titles VI and VII of the 1989 Accession Convention (transitional and final provisions),
    (f)   Titles V and VI of the 1996 Accession Convention (transitional and final provisions),
being texts prepared from the authentic English texts referred to in Articles 37 and 41 of the Accession Convention [, in Article 17 of the 1982 Accession Convention, in Article 34 of the 1989 Accession Convention and in Article 18 of the 1996 Accession Convention.]

3   Interpretation of the [Brussels Conventions]
    (1)   Any question as to the meaning or effect of any provision of the [Brussels Conventions] shall, if not referred to the European Court in accordance with the 1971 Protocol, be determined in accordance with the principles laid down by and any relevant decision of the European Court.
    (2)   Judicial notice shall be taken of any decision of, or expression of opinion by, the European Court on any such question.
    (3)   Without prejudice to the generality of subsection (1), the following reports (which are reproduced in the Official Journal of the Communities), namely—
    (a)   the reports by Mr P Jenard on the 1968 Convention and the 1971 Protocol; and
    (b)   the report by Professor Peter Schlosser on the Accession Convention; and
    (c)   [the report by Professor Demetrios I Evrigenis and Professor K D Kerameus on the 1982 Accession Convention; and
    (d)   the report by Mr Martinho de Almeida Cruz, Mr Manuel Desantes Real and Mr P Jenard on the 1989 Accession Convention,]
may be considered in ascertaining the meaning or effect of any provision of the [Brussels Conventions] and shall be given such weight as is appropriate in the circumstances.

[3A   The Lugano Convention to have the force of law
    (1)   The Lugano Convention shall have the force of law in the United Kingdom, and judicial notice shall be taken of it.
    (2)   For convenience of reference there is set out in Schedule 3C the English text

of the Lugano Convention [as amended on the accession of Poland to that Convention].]

[3B   Interpretation of the Lugano Convention
   (1)   In determining any question as to the meaning or effect of a provision of the Lugano Convention, a court in the United Kingdom shall, in accordance with Protocol No 2 to that Convention, take account of any principles laid down in any relevant decision delivered by a court of any other Lugano Contracting State concerning provisions of the Convention.
   (2)   Without prejudice to any practice of the courts as to the matters which may be considered apart from this section, the report on the Lugano Convention by Mr P Jenard and Mr G Möller (which is reproduced in the Official Journal of the Communities of 28th July 1990) may be considered in ascertaining the meaning or effect of any provision of the Convention and shall be given such weight as is appropriate in the circumstances.]

Supplementary provisions as to recognition and enforcement of judgments

4   Enforcement of judgments other than maintenance orders
   (1)   A judgment, other than a maintenance order, which is the subject of an application under Article 31 [of the 1968 Convention or of the Lugano Convention] for its enforcement in any part of the United Kingdom shall, to the extent that its enforcement is authorised by the appropriate court, be registered in the prescribed manner in that court.
   In this subsection 'the appropriate court' means the court to which the application is made in pursuance of Article 32 (that is to say, the High Court or the Court of Session).
   (2)   Where a judgment is registered under this section, the reasonable costs or expenses of and incidental to its registration shall be recoverable as if they were sums recoverable under the judgment.
   (3)   A judgment registered under this section shall, for the purposes of its enforcement, be of the same force and effect, the registering court shall have in relation to its enforcement the same powers, and proceedings for or with respect to its enforcement may be taken, [as if it was a judgment which had been originally given] by the registering court and had (where relevant) been entered.
   (4)   Subsection (3) is subject to Article 39 (restriction of enforcement where appeal pending or time for appeal unexpired), to section 7 and to any provision made by rules of court as to the manner in which and conditions subject to which a judgment registered under this section may be enforced.

5   Recognition and enforcement of maintenance orders
   (1)   The function of transmitting to the appropriate court an application under Article 31 [of the 1968 Convention or of the Lugano Convention] for the recognition or enforcement in the United Kingdom of a maintenance order shall be discharged—
      (a)   [as respects England and Wales and Northern Ireland, by the Lord Chancellor; and
      (b)   as respects Scotland, by the Secretary of State.]
   In this subsection 'the appropriate court' means the magistrates' court or sheriff court having jurisdiction in the matter in accordance with the second paragraph of Article 32.
   (2)   Such an application shall be determined in the first instance by the prescribed officer of that court.
   (3)   Where on such an application the enforcement of the order is authorised to any extent, the order shall to that extent be registered in the prescribed manner in that court.
   (4)   A maintenance order registered under this section shall, for the purposes of

its enforcement, be of the same force and effect, the registering court shall have in relation to its enforcement the same powers, and proceedings for or with respect to its enforcement may be taken, as if it was an order which had been originally made by the registering court.

(5) Subsection (4) is subject to Article 39 (restriction on enforcement where appeal pending or time for appeal unexpired), to section 7 and to any provision made by rules of court as to the manner in which and conditions subject to which an order registered under this section may be enforced.

(6) A maintenance order which by virtue of this section is enforceable by a magistrates' court in Northern Ireland [shall, subject to the modifications of Article 98 of the Magistrates' Courts (Northern Ireland) Order 1981 specified in subsection (6A) below, be enforceable as an order made by that court to which that article applies].

(6A) [*Applies to Northern Ireland.*]

(7) The payer under a maintenance order registered under this section in a magistrates' court in England and Wales or Northern Ireland shall give notice of any change of address to the [proper officer] of that court.

A person who without reasonable excuse fails to comply with this subsection shall be guilty of an offence and liable on summary conviction to a fine not exceeding [level 2 on the standard scale].

[(8) In subsection (7) 'proper officer' means—

(a) in relation to a magistrates' court in England and Wales, the [designated officer]

for the court; and

(b) in relation to a magistrates' court in Northern Ireland, the clerk of the court.]

6 Appeals under Article 37, second paragraph and Article 41

(1) The single further appeal on a point of law referred to in the 1968 Convention and the Lugano Convention Article 37, second paragraph and Article 41 in relation to the recognition or enforcement of a judgment other than a maintenance order lies—

(a) in England and Wales or Northern Ireland, to the Court of Appeal or to the House of Lords in accordance with Part II of the Administration of Justice Act 1969 (appeals direct from the High Court to the House of Lords);

(b) in Scotland, to the Inner House of the Court of Session.

(2) Paragraph (a) of subsection (1) has effect notwithstanding section 15(2) of the Administration of Justice Act 1969 (exclusion of direct appeal to the House of Lords in cases where no appeal to that House lies from a decision of the Court of Appeal).

(3) The single further appeal on a point of law referred to in [each of those Conventions] Article 37, second paragraph and Article 41 in relation to the recognition or enforcement of a maintenance order lies—

(a) in England and Wales, to the High Court by way of case stated in accordance with section 111 of the Magistrates' Courts Act 1980;

(b) in Scotland, to the Inner House of the Court of Session;

(c) in Northern Ireland, to the Court of Appeal.

7 Interest on registered judgments

(1) Subject to subsection (4), where in connection with an application for registration of a judgment under section 4 or 5 the applicant shows—

(a) that the judgment provides for the payment of a sum of money; and

(b) that in accordance with the law of the Contracting State in which the judgment was given interest on that sum is recoverable under the judgment from a particular date of time, the rate of interest and the date or time from which it is so recoverable shall be registered with the judgment and, subject to any provision made under subsection (2), the debt resulting, apart from section

4(2), from the registration of the judgment shall carry interest in accordance with the registered particulars.

(2)   Provision may be made by rules of court as to the manner in which and the periods by reference to which any interest payable by virtue of subsection (1) is to be calculated and paid, including provision for such interest to cease to accrue as from a prescribed date.

(3)   Costs or expenses recoverable by virtue of section 4(2) shall carry interest as if they were the subject of an order for the payment of costs or expenses made by the registering court on the date of registration.

(4)   Interest on arrears of sums payable under a maintenance order registered under section 5 in a magistrates' court in England and Wales or Northern Ireland shall not be recoverable in that court, but without prejudice to the operation in relation to any such order of section 2A of the Maintenance Orders Act 1958 or section 11A of the Maintenance and Affiliation Orders Act (Northern Ireland) 1966 (which enable interest to be recovered if the order is re-registered for enforcement in the High Court).

(5)   Except as mentioned in subsection (4), debts under judgments registered under section 4 or 5 shall carry interest only as provided by this section.

8   Currency of payment under registered maintenance orders

(1)   Sums payable in the United Kingdom under a maintenance order by virtue of its registration under section 5, including any arrears so payable, shall be paid in the currency of the United Kingdom.

(2)   Where the order is expressed in any other currency, the amounts shall be converted on the basis of the exchange rate prevailing on the date of registration of the order.

(3)   For the purposes of this section, a written certificate purporting to be signed by an officer of any bank in the United Kingdom and stating the exchange rate prevailing on a specified date shall be evidence, and in Scotland sufficient evidence, of the facts stated.

Other supplementary provisions

9   Provisions supplementary to Title VII of 1968 Convention

(1)   The provisions of Title VII of the 1968 Convention [and, apart from Article 54B, of Title VII of the Lugano Convention] (relationship between [the Convention in question] and other conventions to which Contracting States are or may become parties) shall have effect in relation to—

(a)   any statutory provision, whenever passed or made, implementing any such other convention in the United Kingdom; and

(b)   any rule of law so far as it has the effect of so implementing any such other convention,

as they have effect in relation to that other convention itself.

[...]

(2)   Her Majesty may by Order in Council declare a provision of a convention entered into by the United Kingdom to be a provision where by the United Kingdom assumed an obligation of a kind provided for in Article 59 (which allows a Contracting State to agree with a third State to withhold recognition in certain cases from a judgment given by a court in another Contracting State which took jurisdiction on one of the grounds mentioned in the second paragraph of Article 3).

10   Allocation within UK of jurisdiction with respect to trusts and consumer contracts

(1)   The provisions of this section have effect for the purpose of allocating within the United Kingdom jurisdiction in certain proceedings in respect of which

the 1968 Convention [or the Lugano Convention] confers jurisdiction on the courts of the United Kingdom generally and to which section 16 does not apply.

(2)   Any proceedings which by virtue of Article 5(6) (trusts) are brought in the United Kingdom shall be brought in the courts of the part of the United Kingdom in which the trust is domiciled.

(3)   Any proceedings which by virtue of the first paragraph of Article 14 (consumer contracts) are brought in the United Kingdom by a consumer on the ground that he is himself domiciled there shall be brought in the courts of the part of the United Kingdom in which he is domiciled.

11   Proof and admissibility of certain judgments and related documents

(1)   For the purposes of the 1968 Convention [and the Lugano Convention]—

(a)   a document, duly authenticated, which purports to be a copy of a judgment given by a court of a Contracting State other than the United Kingdom shall without further proof be deemed to be a true copy, unless the contrary is shown; and

(b)   the original or a copy of any such document as is mentioned in Article 46(2) or 47 (supporting documents to be produced by a party seeking recognition or enforcement of a judgment) shall be evidence, and in Scotland sufficient evidence, of any matter to which it relates.

[(2)   A document purporting to be a copy of an authentic instrument drawn up or registered, and enforceable, in a Contracting State other than the United Kingdom is duly authenticated for the purposes of this section if it purports to be certified to be a true copy of such an instrument by a person duly authorised in that Contracting State to do so.]

(3)   Nothing in this section shall prejudice the admission in evidence of any document which is admissible apart from this section.

12   Provision for issue of copies of, and certificated in connection with, UK Judgments

The Court of Session may by Act of Sederunt make provision for enabling any interested party wishing to secure under the 1968 Convention [or the Lugano Convention] the recognition or enforcement in another Contracting State of a judgment within section 18(2)(c) to obtain, subject to any conditions specified in the rules—

(a)   a copy of the judgment; and

(b)   a certificate giving particulars relating to the judgment [...].

13   Modifications to cover authentic instruments and court settlements.

(1)   Her Majesty may by Order in Council provide that—

(a)   any provision of this Act relating to the recognition or enforcement in the United Kingdom or elsewhere of judgments to which the 1968 Convention [or the Lugano Convention] applies; and

(b)   any other statutory provision, whenever passed or made, so relating,

shall apply, with such modifications as may be specified in the Order, in relation to documents and settlements within Title IV of the 1968 Convention [or, as the case may be, Title IV of the Lugano Convention] (authentic instruments and court settlements enforceable in the same manner as judgments) as if they were judgments to which [the Convention in question] applies.

(2)   An Order in Council under this section may make different provision in relation to different descriptions of documents and settlements.

(3)   Any Order in Council under this section shall be subject to annulment in pursuance of a resolution of either House of Parliament.

14   Modifications consequential on revision of the Conventions

(1)   If at any time it appears to Her Majesty in Council that Her Majesty's Government in the United Kingdom have agreed to a revision of [the Lugano Convention or any of the Brussels Conventions], including in particular any revision connected with the accession to [the Lugano Convention or] the 1968 Convention

of one or more further states, Her Majesty may by Order in Council make such modifications of this Act or any other statutory provision, whenever passed or made, as Her Majesty considers appropriate in consequence of the revision.

(2)   An Order in Council under this section shall not be made unless a draft of the Order has been laid before Parliament and approved by a resolution of each House of Parliament.

(3)   In this section 'revision' means an omission from, addition to or alteration of [the Lugano Convention or any of the Brussels Conventions] and includes replacement of any of the Conventions to any extent by another convention, protocol or other description of international agreement.

15   Interpretation of Part I and consequential amendments

(1)   In this Part, unless the context otherwise requires—

'judgment' has the meaning given by Article 25;

'maintenance order' means a maintenance judgment within the meaning of the 1968 Convention [or, as the case may be, the Lugano Convention];

'payer', in relation to a maintenance order, means the person liable to make payments for which the order provides;

'prescribed' means prescribed by rules of court.

(2)   References in this Part to a judgment registered under section 4 or 5 include, to the extent of its registration, references to a judgment so registered to a limited extent only.

(3)   Anything authorised or required by the 1968 Convention, [the Lugano Convention] or this Part to be done by, to or before a particular magistrates' court may be done by, to or before any magistrates' court acting [in the same local justice area (or, in Northern Ireland, for the same] petty sessions district) as that court.

PART II

JURISDICTION, AND RECOGNITION AND ENFORCEMENT OF JUDGMENTS, WITHIN UNITED KINGDOM

16   Allocation within UK of jurisdiction in certain civil proceedings

(1)   The provisions set out in Schedule 4 (which contains a modified version of [Chapter II of the Regulation]) shall have effect for determining, for each part of the United Kingdom, whether the courts of law of that part, or any particular court of law in that part, have or has jurisdiction in proceedings where—

(a)   [the subject-matter of the proceedings is within the scope of the Regulation as determined by Article 1 of the Regulation (whether or not the Regulation has effect in relation to the proceedings); and]

(b)   the defendant or defender is domiciled in the United Kingdom or the proceedings are of a kind mentioned in [Article 22 of the Regulation] (exclusive jurisdiction regardless of domicile).

[...]

(3)   In determining any question as to the meaning or effect of any provision contained in Schedule 4—

(a)   regard shall be had to any relevant principles laid down by the European Court in connection with Title II of the 1998 Convention [or Chapter II of the Regulation] and to any relevant decision of that court as to the meaning or effect of any provision of that Title [or that Chapter]; and

(b)   without prejudice to the generality of paragraph (a), the reports mentioned in section 3(3) may be considered and shall, so far as relevant, be given such weight as is appropriate in the circumstances.

(4)   The provisions of this section and Schedule 4 shall have effect subject to [the Regulation,] the 1968 Convention [and the Lugano Convention] and to the provisions of section 17.

...

17　Exclusion of certain proceedings from Schedule 4

(1)　Schedule 4 shall not apply to proceedings of any description listed in Schedule 5 or to proceedings in Scotland under any enactment which confers jurisdiction on a Scottish court in respect of a specific subject-matter on specific grounds.

(2)　Her Majesty may by Order in Council—

(a)　add to the list in Schedule 5 any description of proceedings in any part of the United Kingdom; and

(b)　remove from that list any description of proceedings in any part of the United Kingdom (whether included in the list as originally enacted or added by virtue of this subsection).

(3)　An Order in Council under subsection (2)—

(a)　may make different provisions for different descriptions of proceedings, for the same description of proceedings in different courts or for different parts of the United Kingdom; and

(b)　may contain such transitional and other incidental provisions as appear to Her Majesty to be appropriate.

(4)　An Order in Council under subsection (2) shall not be made unless a draft of the Order has been laid before parliament and approved by a resolution of each House of Parliament.

18　Enforcement of UK judgments in other parts of UK

(1)　In relation to any judgment to which this section applies—

(a)　Schedule 6 shall have effect for the purpose of enabling any money provisions contained in the judgments to be enforced in a part of the United Kingdom other than the part in which the judgment was given; and

(b)　Schedule 7 shall have effect for the purpose of enabling any non-money provisions so contained to be so enforced.

(2)　In this section 'judgment' means any of the following (references to the giving of a judgment being construed accordingly)—

(a)　any judgment or order (by whatever name called) given or made by a court of law in the United Kingdom;

(b)　any judgment or order not within paragraph (a) which has been entered in England and Wales or Northern Ireland in the High Court or a county court;

(c)　any document which the Scotland has been registered for execution in the Books of Council and Session or in the sheriff court books kept for any sheriffdom;

(d)　any award or order made by a tribunal in any part of the United Kingdom which is enforceable in that part without an order of a court of law;

(e)　an arbitration award which has become enforceable in the part of the United Kingdom in which it was given in the same manner as a judgment given by a court of law in that part;

[(f)　an order made, or a warrant issued, under Part 8 of the Proceeds of Crime Act 2002 for the purposes of a civil recovery investigation within the meaning given by section 341 of that Act;]

and, subject to the following provisions of this section, this section applies to all such judgments.

(3)　Subject to subsection (4), this section does not apply to—

(a)　a judgment given in proceedings in a magistrates' court in England and Wales or Northern Ireland;

(b)　a judgment given in proceedings other the civil proceedings;

[(ba)　a judgment given in the exercise of jurisdiction in relation to insolvency law, within the meaning of section 426 of the Insolvency Act 1986;]

(c)　a judgment given in proceedings relating to—

[...]

(iii)　the obtaining of title to administer the estate of a deceased person;

(d)   an order made under Part 2, 3 or 4 of the Proceeds of Crime Act 2002 (confiscation).

(4)   This section applies, whatever the nature of the proceedings in which it is made, to—

(a)   a decree issued under section 13 of the Court of Exchequer (Scotland) Act 1856 (recovery of certain rent-charges and penalties by process of the Court of Session);

(b)   an order which is enforceable in the same manner as a judgment of the High Court in England and Wales by virtue of section 16 of the Contempt of Court Act 1981 or section 140 of the Supreme Court Act 1981 (which relate to fines for contempt of court and forfeiture of recognisances).

[(4A)   This section does not apply as respects—

(a)   the enforcement in Scotland of orders made by the High Court or a county court in England and Wales under or for the purposes of Part VI of the Criminal Justice Act 1988 or the Drug Trafficking Act 1994 (confiscation of the proceeds of certain offences or of drug trafficking); or

(b)   the enforcement in England and Wales of orders made by the Court of Session or by the sheriff under or for the purposes of the Proceeds of Crime (Scotland) Act 1995.]

(5)   This section does not apply to so much of any judgment as—

(a)   is an order to which section 16 of the Maintenance Orders Act 1950 applies (and is therefore an order for whose enforcement in another part of the United Kingdom provision is made by Part II of that Act);

(b)   concerns the status or legal capacity of an individual;

(c)   relates to the management of the affairs of a person not capable of managing his own affairs;

(d)   is a provisional (including protective) measure other than an order for the making of an interim payment;

and except where otherwise stated references to a judgment to which this section applies are to such a judgment exclusive of any such provisions.

(6)   The following are within subsection (5)(b), but without prejudice to the generality of that provision—

(a)   a decree of judicial separation or of separation;

(b)   [any order which is a Part I order for the purposes of the Family Law Act 1986].

(7)   This section does not apply to a judgment of a court outside the United Kingdom which falls to be treated for the purposes of its enforcement as a judgments of a court of law in the United Kingdom by virtue of registration under Part II of the Administration of Justice Act 1920, Part I of the Foreign Judgments (Reciprocal Enforcement) Act 1933, Part I of the Maintenance Orders (Reciprocal Enforcement) Act 1972 or section 4 or 5 of this Act.

(8)   A judgment to which this section applies, other than a judgment within paragraph (e) of subsection (2), shall not be enforced in another part of the United Kingdom except by way of registration under Schedule 6 or 7.

19   Recognition of UK judgments in other parts of UK

(1)   A judgment to which this section applies given in one part of the United Kingdom shall not be refused recognition in another part of the United Kingdom solely on the ground that, in relation to that judgment, the court which gave it was not a court of competent jurisdiction according to the rules of private international law in force in that other part.

(2)   Subject to subsection (3), this section applies to any judgment to which section 18 applies.

(3)   This section does not apply to—

(a)   the documents mentioned in paragraph (c) of the definition of 'judgment' in section 18(2);

(b)   the awards and orders mentioned in paragraphs (d) and (e) of that definition;

(c)   the decrees and orders referred to in section 18(4).

PART III
JURISDICTION IN SCOTLAND

20   Rules as to jurisdiction in Scotland

(1)   Subject to [the Regulation, to] Parts I and II and to the following provisions of this Part, Schedule 8 has effect to determine in what circumstances a person may be sued in civil proceedings in the Court of Session or in a sheriff court.

(2)   Nothing in Schedule 8 affects the competence as respects subject-matter or value of the Court of Session or of the sheriff court.

(3)   Section 6 of the Sheriff Courts (Scotland) Act 1907 shall cease to have effect to the extent that it determines jurisdiction in relation to any matter to which Schedule 8 applies.

[...]

(5)   In determining any question as to the meaning or effect of any provision contained in Schedule 8—

(a)   regard shall be had to any relevant principles laid down by the European Court in connection with Title II of the 1968 Convention [or Chapter II of the Regulation] and to any relevant decision of that court as to the meaning or effect of any provision of that Title [or that Chapter]; and

(b)   without prejudice to the generality of paragraph (a), the reports mentioned in section 3(3) may be considered and shall, so far as relevant, be given such weight as is appropriate in the circumstances.

21   Continuance of certain existing jurisdictions

(1)   Schedule 8 does not affect—

(a)   the operation of any enactment which confers jurisdiction on a Scottish court in respect of a specific subject-matter on specific grounds;

(b)   without prejudice to the foregoing generality, the jurisdiction of any court in respect of any matter mentioned in Schedule 9.

(2)   Her Majesty may by Order in Council—

(a)   add to the list in Schedule 9 any description of proceedings; and

(b)   remove from that list any description of proceedings (whether included in the list as originally enacted or added by virtue of this subsection).

(3)   An Order in Council under subsection (2) may—

(a)   make different provision for different descriptions of proceedings or for the same description of proceedings in different courts; and

(b)   contain such transitional and other incidental provisions as appear to Her Majesty to be appropriate.

(4)   An Order in Council under subsection (2) shall not be made unless a draft of the Order has been laid before Parliament and approved by a resolution of each House of Parliament.

22   Supplementary provision

(1)   Nothing in Schedule 8 shall prevent a court from declining jurisdiction on the ground of forum non conveniens.

(2)   Nothing in Schedule 8 affects the operation of any enactment or rule of law under which a court may decline to exercise jurisdiction because of the prorogation by parties of the jurisdiction of another court.

(3)   For the avoidance of doubt, it is declared that nothing in Schedule 8 affects the nobile officium of the Court of Session.

(4)   Where a court has jurisdiction in any proceedings by virtue of Schedule 8, that court shall also have jurisdiction to determine any matter which—

(a)   is ancillary or incidental to the proceedings; or

(b) requires to be determined for the purposes of a decision in the proceedings.

23 Savings and consequential amendments
(1) Nothing in Schedule 8 shall affect—
(a) the power of any court to vary or recall a maintenance order granted by the court;
(b) the power of a sheriff court under section 22 of the Maintenance Orders Act 1950 (discharge and variation of maintenance orders registered in sheriff courts) to very or discharge a maintenance order registered in that court under Part II of that Act; or
(c) the power of a sheriff court under section 9 of the Maintenance Orders (Reciprocal Enforcement) Act 1972 (variation and revocation of maintenance orders registered in United Kingdom courts) to vary or revoke a registered order within the meaning of Part I of that Act.
(2) *[Amending provisions.]*

PART IV
MISCELLANEOUS PROVISIONS

Provisions relating to jurisdiction

...

27 Provisional and protective measures in Scotland in the absence of substantive proceedings
(1) The Court of Session may, in any case to which this subsection applies—
(a) subject to subsection (2)(c), grant a warrant for the arrestment of any assets situated in Scotland;
(b) subject to subsection (2)(c), grant a warrant of inhibition over any property situated in Scotland; and
(c) grant interim interdict.
(2) Subsection (1) applies to any case in which—
(a) proceedings have been commenced but not concluded, or, in relation to paragraph (c) of that subsection, are to be commenced, in another [Brussels or Lugano Contracting State], in another Regulation State or in England and Wales or Northern Ireland;
(b) [the subject-matter of the proceedings is within the scope of the Regulation as determined by Article 1 of the Regulation; and]
(c) in relation to paragraphs (a) and (b) of subsection (1), such a warrant could competently have been granted in equivalent proceedings before a Scottish court;
but it shall not be necessary, in determining whether proceedings have been commenced for the purpose of paragraph (a) of this subsection, to show that any document has been served on or notice given to the defender.
(3) Her Majesty may by Order in Council confer on the Court of Session power to do anything mentioned in subsection (1) or in section 28 in relation to proceedings of any of the following descriptions, namely—
(a) proceedings commenced otherwise than in a [Brussels or Lugano Contracting State or Regulation State];
(b) [proceedings whose subject-matter is not within the scope of the Regulation as determined by Article 1 of the Regulation;]
(c) arbitration proceedings;
(d) in relation to subsection (1)(c) or section 28, proceedings which are to be commenced otherwise than in a [Brussels or Lugano Contracting State or Regulation State].
(4) An Order in Council under subsection (3)—

(a)   may confer power to do only certain of the things mentioned in sub-section (1) or in section 28;

(b)   may make different provision for different classes of proceedings, for proceedings pending in different countries or courts outside the United Kingdom or in different parts of the United Kingdom, and for other different circumstances; and

(c)   may impose conditions or restrictions on the exercise of any power conferred by the Order.

(5)   Any Order in Council under subsection (3) shall be subject to annulment in pursuance of a resolution of either House of Parliament.

28   Application of s 1 of Administration of Justice (Scotland) Act 1972

When any proceedings have been brought, or are likely to be brought, in another [Brussels or Lugano Contracting State, in a Regulation State] or in England and Wales or Northern Ireland in respect of any matter which is within the scope of the [Regulation] as determined in Article 1, the Court of Session shall have the like power to make an order under section 1 of the Administration of Justice (Scotland) Act 1972 [as amended by the Law Reform (Miscellaneous Provisions)(Scotland) Act 1985] as if the proceedings in question had been brought, or were likely to be brought, in that court.

30   Proceedings in England and Wales or Northern Ireland for torts to immovable property

(1)   The jurisdiction of any court in England and Wales or Northern Ireland to entertain proceedings for trespass to, or any other tort affecting, immovable property shall extend to cases in which the property in question is situated outside that part of the United Kingdom unless the proceedings are principally concerned with a question of the title to, or the right to possession of, that property.

(2)   Subsection (1) has effect subject to the 1968 Convention [and the Lugano Convention and the Regulation] and to the provisions set out in Schedule 4.

Provisions relating to recognition and enforcement of judgments

31   Overseas judgments given against states, etc

(1)   A judgment given by a court of an overseas country against a state other than the United Kingdom or the state to which that court belongs shall be recognised and enforced in the United Kingdom if, and only if—

(a)   it would be so recognised and enforced if it had not been given against a state; and

(b)   that court would have had jurisdiction in the matter if it had applied rules corresponding to those applicable to such matters in the United Kingdom in accordance with sections 2 to 11 of the State Immunity Act 1978.

(2)   References in subsection (1) to a judgment given against a state include references to judgments of any of the following descriptions given in relation to a state—

(a)   judgments against the government, or a department of the government, of the state but not (except as mentioned in paragraph (c)) judgments against an entity which is distinct from the executive organs of government;

(b)   judgments against the sovereign or head of state in his public capacity;

(c)   judgments against any such separate entity as is mentioned in paragraph (a) given in proceedings relating to anything done by it in the exercise of the sovereign authority of the state.

(3)   Nothing in subsection (1) shall affect the recognition or enforcement in the United Kingdom of a judgment to which Part I of the Foreign Judgments (Reciprocal Enforcement) Act 1933 applies by virtue of section 4 of the Carriage of Goods by Road Act 1965, section 17(4) of the Nuclear Installations Act 1965, section [166(4) of the Merchant Shipping Act 1995, regulation 8 of the Railways (Conven-

tion on International Carriage by Rail Regulations 2005] or section 5 of the Carriage of Passengers by Road Act 1974.

(4) Sections 12, 13 and 14(3) and (4) of the State Immunity Act 1978 (service of process and procedural privileges) shall apply to proceedings for the recognition or enforcement in the United Kingdom of a judgment given by a court of an overseas country (whether or not that judgment is within subsection (1) of this section) as they apply to other proceedings.

(5) In this section 'state', in the case of a federal state, includes any of its constituent territories.

32 Overseas judgments given in proceedings brought in breach of agreement for settlement of disputes

(1) Subject to the following provisions of this section, a judgment given by a court of an overseas country in any proceedings shall not be recognised or enforced in the United Kingdom if—

(a) the bringing of those proceedings in that court was contrary to an agreement under which the dispute in question was to be settled otherwise than by proceedings in the courts of that country; and

(b) those proceedings were not brought in that court by, or with the agreement of, the person against whom the judgment was given; and

(c) that person did not counter claim in the proceedings or otherwise submit to the jurisdiction of that court.

(2) Subsection (1) does not apply where the agreement referred to in paragraph (a) of the subsection was illegal, void or unenforceable or was incapable of being performed for reasons not attributable to the fault of the party bringing the proceedings in which the judgment was given.

(3) In determining whether a judgment given by a court of an overseas country should be recognised or enforced in the United Kingdom, a court in the United Kingdom shall not be bound by any decision of the overseas court relating to any of the matters mentioned in subsection (1) or (2).

(4) Nothing in subsection (1) shall affect the recognition or enforcement in the United Kingdom of—

(a) a judgment which is required to be recognised or enforced there under the 1968 Convention [or the Lugano Convention or the Regulation];

(b) a judgment to which Part I of the Foreign Judgments (Reciprocal Enforcement) Act 1933 applies by virtue of section 4 of the Carriage of Goods by Road Act 1965, section 17(4) of the Nuclear Installations Act 1965, [regulation 8 of the Railways (Convention on International Carriage by Rail) Regulations 2005] or section 5 of the Carriage of Passengers by Road Act 1974 or section 177(4) of the Merchant Shipping Act 1995.

33 Certain steps not to amount to submission to jurisdiction of overseas court

(1) For the purposes of determining whether a judgments given by a court of an overseas country should be recognised or enforced in England and Wales or Northern Ireland, the person against whom the judgment was given shall not be regarded as having submitted to the jurisdiction of the court by reason only of the fact that he appeared (conditionally or otherwise) in the proceedings for all or any one or more of the following purposes, namely—

(a) to contest the jurisdiction of the court;

(b) to ask the court to dismiss or stay the proceedings on the ground that the dispute in question should be submitted to arbitration or to the determination of the courts of another country;

(c) to protect, or obtain the release of, property seized or threatened with seizure in the proceedings.

(2) Nothing in this section shall affect the recognition or enforcement in England and Wales or Northern Ireland of a judgment which is required to be

recognised or enforced there under the 1968 Convention [or the Lugano Convention or the Regulation].

34　Certain judgments a bar to further proceedings on the same cause of action

No proceedings may be brought by a person in England and Wales or Northern Ireland on a cause of action in respect of which a judgment has been given in his favour in proceedings between the same parties, or their privies, in a court in another part of the United Kingdom or in a court of an overseas country, unless that judgment is not enforceable or entitled to recognition in England and Wales or, as the case may be, in Northern Ireland.

35　Minor amendments relating to overseas judgments

(1)　The Foreign Judgments (Reciprocal Enforcement) Act 1933 shall have effect with the amendments specified in Schedule 10, being amendments whose main purpose is to enable Part I of that Act to be applied to judgments of courts other than superior courts, to judgments providing for interim payments and to certain arbitration awards.

...

PART V
SUPPLEMENTARY AND GENERAL PROVISIONS

Domicile

41　Domicile of individuals

(1)　Subject to Article 52 (which contains provisions for determining whether a party is domiciled in a Contracting State), the following provisions of this section determine, for the purposes of the 1968 Convention [, the Lugano Convention] and this Act, whether an individual is domiciled in the United Kingdom or in a particular part of, or place in, the United Kingdom or in a state other than a Contracting State.

(2)　An individual is domiciled in the United Kingdom if and only if—

(a)　he is resident in the United Kingdom; and

(b)　the nature and circumstances of this residence indicate that he has a substantial connection with the United Kingdom.

(3)　Subject to subsection (5), an individual is domiciled in a particular part of the United Kingdom if and only if—

(a)　he is resident in that part; and

(b)　the nature and circumstances of his residence indicate that he has a substantial connection with that part.

(4)　An individual is domiciled in a particular place in the United Kingdom if and only if he—

(a)　is domiciled in the part of the United Kingdom in which that place is situated; and

(b)　is resident in that place.

(5)　An individual who is domiciled in the United Kingdom but in whose case the requirements of subsection (3)(b) are not satisfied in relation to any particular part of the United Kingdom shall be treated as domiciled in the part of the United Kingdom in which he is resident.

(6)　In the case of an individual who—

(a)　is resident in the United Kingdom, or in a particular part of the United Kingdom; and

(b)　has been so resident for the last three months or more,

the requirements of subsection (2)(b) or, as the case may be, subsection (3)(b) shall be presumed to be fulfilled unless the contrary is proved.

(7)　An individual is domiciled in a state other than a Contracting State if and only if—

(a)   he is resident in that state; and

(b)   the nature and circumstances of his residence indicate that he has a substantial connection with that state.

42   Domicile and seat of corporation or association

(1)   For the purposes of this Act the seat of a corporation or association (as determined by this section) shall be treated as its domicile.

(2)   The following provisions of this section determine where a corporation or association has its seat—

(a)   for the purpose of Article 53 (which for the purposes of the 1968 Convention [or, as the case may be, the Lugano Convention] equates the domicile of such a body with its seat); and

(b)   for the purposes of this Act other than the provisions mentioned in section 43(1)(b) and (c).

(3)   A corporation or association has its seat in the United Kingdom, if and only if—

(a)   it was incorporated or formed under the law of a part of the United Kingdom and has its registered office or some other official address in the United Kingdom; or

(b)   its central management and control is exercised in the United Kingdom.

(4)   A corporation or association has its seat in a particular part of the United Kingdom if and only if it has its seat in the United Kingdom and—

(a)   it has its registered office or some other official address in that part; or

(b)   its central management and control is exercised in that part; or

(c)   it has a place of business in that part.

(5)   A corporation or association has its seat in a particular place in the United Kingdom if and only if it has its seat in the part of the United Kingdom in which that place is situated and—

(a)   it has its registered office or some other official address in that place; or

(b)   its central management and control is exercised in that place; or

(c)   it has a place of business in that place.

(6)   Subject to subsection (7), a corporation or association has its seat in a state other than the United Kingdom if and only if—

(a)   it was incorporated or formed under the law of that state and has its registered office or some other official address there; or

(b)   its central management and control is exercised in that state.

(7)   A corporation or association shall not be regarded as having its seat in a Contracting State other than the United Kingdom if it is shown that the courts of that state would not regard it as having its seat there.

(8)   In this section—

'business' includes any activity carried on by a corporation or association, and 'place of business' shall be construed accordingly;

'official address', in relation to a corporation or association, means an address which it is required by law to register, notify or maintain for the purpose of receiving notices or other communications.

43   Seat of corporation or association for purposes of Article 16(2) and related provisions

(1)   The following provisions of this section determine where a corporation or association has its seat for the purposes of—

(a)   Article 16(2) [of the 1968 Convention or of the Lugano Convention] (which confers exclusive jurisdiction over proceedings relating to the formation or dissolution of such bodies, or to the decisions of their organs);

(b)   [rules 4 and 11(b)] in Schedule 4; and

(c)   [rules 2(1) and 5(1)(b)] in Schedule 8.

(2)   A corporation or association has its seat in the United Kingdom if and only if—

(a)   it was incorporated or formed under the law of a part of the United Kingdom; or

(b)   its central management and control is exercised in the United Kingdom.

(3)   A corporation or association has its seat in a particular part of the United Kingdom if and only if it has its seat in the United Kingdom and—

(a)   subject to subsection (5), it was incorporated or formed under the law of that part; or

(b)   being incorporated or formed under the law of a state other than the United Kingdom, its central management and control is exercised in that part.

(4)   A corporation or association has its seat in a particular place in Scotland if and only if it has its seat in Scotland and—

(a)   it has its registered office or some other official address in that place; or

(b)   it has no registered office or other official address in Scotland, but its central management and control is exercised in that place.

(5)   A corporation or association incorporated or formed under—

(a)   an enactment forming part of the law of more than one part of the United Kingdom; or

(b)   an instrument having effect in the domestic law of more than one part of the United Kingdom,

shall, if it has a registered office, be taken to have its seat in the part of the United Kingdom in which that office is situated, and not in any other part of the United Kingdom.

(6)   Subject to subsection (7), a corporation or association has its seat in a Contracting State other than the United Kingdom if and only if—

(a)   it was incorporated or formed under the law of that state; or

(b)   its central management and control is exercised in that state.

(7)   A corporation or association shall not be regarded as having its seat in a Contracting State other than the United Kingdom if—

(a)   it has its seat in the United Kingdom by virtue of subsection (2)(a); or

(b)   it is shown that the courts of that other state would not regard it for the purposes of Article 16(2) as having its seat there.

(8)   In this section 'official address' has the same meaning as in section 42.

44   Persons deemed to be domiciled in the United Kingdom for certain purposes

(1)   This section applies to—

(a)   proceedings within Section 3 of Title II of the 1968 Convention [or Section 3 of Title II of the Lugano Convention] (insurance contracts), and

(b)   proceedings within Section 4 of [Title II of either of those Conventions] (consumer contracts).

(2)   A person who, for the purposes of proceedings to which this section applies arising out of the operations of a branch, agency or other establishment in the United Kingdom, is deemed for the purposes of the 1968 Convention [or, as the case may be, of the Lugano Convention] to be domiciled in the United Kingdom by virtue of—

(a)   Article 8, second paragraph (insurers); or

(b)   Article 13, second paragraph (suppliers of goods, services or credit to consumers),

shall, for the purposes of those proceedings, be treated for the purposes of this Act as so domiciled and as domiciled in the part of the United Kingdom in which the branch, agency or establishment in question is situated.

45   Domicile of trusts

(1)   The following provisions of this section determine, for the purposes of the 1968 Convention [, the Lugano Convention] and this Act, where a trust is domiciled.

(2)   A trust is domiciled in the United Kingdom if and only if it is by virtue of subsection (3) domiciled in a part of the United Kingdom.

(3)   A trust is domiciled in a part of the United Kingdom if and only if the system of law of that part is the system of law with which the trust has its closest and most real connection.

...

Other supplementary provisions

...

49   Saving for powers to stay, sist, strike out or dismiss proceedings
Nothing in this Act shall prevent any court in the United Kingdom from staying, sisting, striking out or dismissing any proceedings before it, on the ground of forum non conveniens or otherwise, where to do so is not inconsistent with the 1968 Convention [or, as the case may be, the Lugano Convention].

General

50   Interpretation: general
In this Act, unless the context otherwise requires—
   ['the Accession Convention', 'the 1982 Accession Convention', 'the 1989 Accession Convention' and 'the 1996 Accession' Convention have the meaning given by section 1(1);]
   'Article' and references to sub-divisions of numbered Articles are to be construed in accordance with section 1(2)(b);
   'association' means an unincorporated body of persons;
   ['Brussels Contracting State' has the meaning given by section 1(3);
   'the Brussels Conventions' has the meaning given by section 1(1);]
   'Contracting State' has the meaning given by section 1(3);
   'the 1968 Convention' has the meaning given by section 1(1), and references to that Convention and to provisions of it are to be construed in accordance with section 1(2)(a);
   'corporation' means a body corporate, and includes a partnership subsisting under the law of Scotland;
   'court', without more, includes a tribunal;
   'court of law', in relation to the United Kingdom, means any of the following courts, namely—
      (a)   the House of Lords,
      (b)   in England and Wales or Northern Ireland, the Court of Appeal, the High Court, the Crown Court, a county court and a magistrates' court,
      (c)   in Scotland, the Court of Session and a sheriff court;
   'the Crown' is to be construed in accordance with section 51(2);
   'enactment' includes an enactment comprised in Northern Ireland legislation;
   'judgment', subject to sections 15(1) and 18(2) and to paragraph 1 of Schedules 6 and 7, means any judgment or order (by whatever name called) given or made by a court in any civil proceedings;
   ['Lugano Contracting State' has the meaning given by section 1(3);
   'the Lugano Convention' has the meaning given by section 1(i);]
   'magistrates' court', in relation to Northern Ireland, means a court of summary jurisdiction;
   'modifications' includes additions, omissions and alterations;
   'overseas country' means any country or territory outside the United Kingdom;
   'part of the United Kingdom' means England and Wales, Scotland or Northern Ireland;
   'the 1971 Protocol' has the meaning given by section 1(1), and references to that Protocol and to provisions of it are to be construed in accordance with section 1(2)(a);

['the Regulation' has the meaning given by section 1(1);
'Regulation State' has the meaning given by section 1(3);]
'rules of court', in relation to any court, means rules, orders or regulations made
by the authority having power to make rules, orders or regulations regulating the
procedure of that court, and includes—
    (a)   in Scotland, Acts of Sederunt;
    (b)   in Northern Ireland, Judgment Enforcement Rules;
'statutory provision' means any provisions contained in an Act, or in any
Northern Ireland legislation, or in—
    (a)   subordinate legislation (as defined in section 21(1) of the Interpretation
Act 1978); or
    (b)   any instrument of a legislative character made under any Northern Ire-
land legislation;
'tribunal' —
    (a)   means a tribunal of any description other than a court of law;
    (b)   in relation to an overseas country, includes, as regards matters relating to
maintenance within the meaning of the 1968 Convention, any authority having
power to give, enforce, vary or revoke a maintenance order.

SCHEDULES

SCHEDULE 2
TEXT OF 1971 PROTOCOL, AS AMENDED

Article 1
The Court of Justice of the European Communities shall have jurisdiction to give
rulings on the interpretation of the Convention on jurisdiction and the enforcement
of judgments in civil and commercial matters and of the Protocol annexed to that
Convention, signed at Brussels on 27th September 1968, and also on the interpretation of the present Protocol.
    The Court of Justice of the European Communities shall also have jurisdiction to
give rulings on the interpretation of the Convention on the accession of the Kingdom of Denmark, Ireland and the United Kingdom of Great Britain and Northern
Ireland to the Convention of 27 September 1968 and to this Protocol.
    The Court of Justice of the European Communities shall also have jurisdiction to
give rulings on the interpretation of the Convention on the accession of the
Hellenic Republic to the Convention of 27 September 1968 and to this Protocol, as
adjusted by the 1978 Convention.
    The Court of Justice of the European Communities shall also have jurisdiction to
give rulings on the interpretation of the Convention on the accession of the Kingdom of Spain and the Portuguese Republic to the Convention of 27 September
1968 and to this Protocol, as adjusted by the 1978 Convention and the 1982 Convention.
    The Court of Justice of the European Communities shall also have jurisdiction to
give rulings on the interpretation of the Convention on the accession of the Republic of Austria, the Republic of Finland and the Kingdom of Sweden to the Convention of 27 September 1968 and to this Protocol, as adjusted by the 1978
Convention, the 1982 Convention and the 1989 Convention.

Article 2
The following courts may request the Court of Justice to give preliminary rulings
on questions of interpretation—
    1.   ... .
    – in the United Kingdom: the House of Lords and courts to which application
has been made under the second paragraph of Article 37 or under Article 41 of
the Convention.

2.   The courts of the Contracting States when they are sitting in an appellate capacity.
3.   In the cases provided for in Article 37 of the Convention, the courts referred to in that Article.

Article 3

1.   Where a question of interpretation of the Convention or of one of the other instruments referred to in Article 1 is raised in a case pending before one of the courts listed in point 1 of Article 2, that court shall, if it considers that a decision on the question is necessary to enable it to give judgment, request the Court of Justice to give a ruling thereon.
2.   Where such a question is raised before any court referred to in point 2 or 3 of Article 2, that court may, under the conditions laid down in paragraph 1, request the Court of Justice to give a ruling thereon.

Article 4

1.   The competent authority of a Contracting State may request the Court of Justice to give a ruling on a question of interpretation of the Convention or of one of the other instruments referred to in Article 1 if judgments given by courts of that State conflict with the with the interpretation given either by the Court of Justice or in a judgment of one of the courts of another Contracting State referred to in point 1 or 2 of Article 2.The provisions of this paragraph shall apply only to judgments which have become res judicata.
2.   The interpretation given by the Court of Justice in response to such a request shall not affect the judgments which gave rise to the request for interpretation.
3.   The Procurators-General of the Courts of Cassation of the Contracting States, or any other authority designated by a Contracting State, shall be entitled to request the Court of Justice for a ruling on interpretation in accordance with paragraph 1.
4.   The Registrar of the Court of Justice shall give notice of the request to the Contracting States, to the Commission and to the Council of the European Communities; they shall then be entitled within two months of the notification to submit statements of case or written observations to the Court.
5.   No fees shall be levied or any costs or expenses awarded in respect of the proceedings provided for in this Article.

Article 5

1.   Except where this Protocol otherwise provides, the provisions of the Treaty establishing the European Economic Community and those of the Protocol on the Statute of the Court of Justice annexed thereto, which are applicable when the Court is requested to give a preliminary ruling, shall also apply to any proceedings for the interpretation of the Convention and the other instruments referred to in Article 1.
2.   The Rules of Procedure of the Court of Justice shall, if necessary, be adjusted and supplemented in accordance with Article 188 of the Treaty establishing the European Economic Community.
   ...

[SCHEDULE 3C
TEXT OF THE LUGANO CONVENTION]

At the date of going to press the Lugano Convention was undergoing revision. The most up-to-date available version of the Convention is reproduced in Part VI: Draft Materials, below at p 300.

SCHEDULE 4
CHAPTER II OF THE REGULATION AS MODIFIED: RULES FOR ALLOCATION OF JURISDICTION WITHIN UK

General

1.   Subject to the rules of this Schedule, persons domiciled in a part of the United Kingdom shall be sued in the courts of that part.

2.   Persons domiciled in a part of the United Kingdom may be sued in the courts of another part of the United Kingdom only by virtue of rules 3 to 13 of this Schedule.

Special jurisdiction

3.   A person domiciled in a part of the United Kingdom may, in another part of the United Kingdom, be sued—
    (a)   in matters relating to a contract, in the courts for the place of performance of the obligation in question;
    (b)   in matters relating to maintenance, in the courts for the place where the maintenance creditor is domiciled or habitually resident or, if the matter is ancillary to proceedings concerning the status of a person, in the court which, according to its own law, has jurisdiction to entertain those proceedings, unless that jurisdiction is based solely on the nationality of one of the parties;
    (c)   in matters relating to tort, delict or quasi-delict, in the courts for the place where the harmful event occurred or may occur;
    (d)   as regards a civil claim for damages or restitution which is based on an act giving rise to criminal proceedings, in the court seised of those proceedings, to the extent that that court has jurisdiction under its own law to entertain civil proceedings;
    (e)   as regards a dispute arising out of the operations of a branch, agency or other establishment, in the courts for the place in which the branch, agency or other establishment is situated;
    (f)   as settlor, trustee or beneficiary of a trust created by the operation of a statute, or by a written instrument, or created orally and evidenced in writing, in the courts of the part of the United Kingdom in which the trust is domiciled;
    (g)   as regards a dispute concerning the payment of remuneration claimed in respect of the salvage of a cargo or freight, in the court under the authority of which the cargo or freight in question—
        (i)   has been arrested to secure such payment; or
        (ii)   could have been so arrested, but bail or other security has been given;
provided that this provision shall apply only if it is claimed that the defendant has an interest in the cargo or freight or had such an interest at the time of salvage;
    (h)   in proceedings—
        (i)   concerning a debt secured on immovable property; or
        (ii)   which are brought to assert, declare or determine proprietary or possessory rights, or rights of security, in or over movable property, or to obtain authority to dispose of movable property;
in the courts of the part of the United Kingdom in which the property is situated.

4.   Proceedings which have as their object a decision of an organ of a company or other legal person or of an association of natural or legal persons may, without prejudice to the other provisions of this Schedule, be brought in the courts of the part of the United Kingdom in which that company, legal person or association has its seat.

5.   A person domiciled in a part of the United Kingdom may, in another part of the United Kingdom, also be sued—

    (a)   where he is one of a number of defendants, in the courts for the place where any one of them is domiciled, provided the claims are so closely connected that it is expedient to hear and determine them together to avoid the risk of irreconcilable judgments resulting from separate proceedings;

    (b)   as a third party in an action on a warranty or guarantee or in any other third party proceedings, in the court seised of the original proceedings, unless these were instituted solely with the object of removing him from the jurisdiction of the court which would be competent in his case;

    (c)   on a counter-claim arising from the same contract or facts on which the original claim was based, in the court in which the original claim is pending;

    (d)   in matters relating to a contract, if the action may be combined with an action against the same defendant in matters relating to rights in rem in immovable property, in the court of the part of the United Kingdom in which the property is situated.

6.   Where by virtue of this Schedule a court of a part of the United Kingdom has jurisdiction in actions relating to liability arising from the use or operation of a ship, that court, or any other court substituted for this purpose by the internal law of that part, shall also have jurisdiction over claims for limitation of such liability.

Jurisdiction over consumer contracts

7.—(1)   In matters relating to a contract concluded by a person, the consumer, for a purpose which can be regarded as being outside his trade or profession, jurisdiction shall be determined by this rule and rules 8 and 9, without prejudice to rule 3(e) and (h)(ii), if—

    (a)   it is a contract for the sale of goods on instalment credit terms; or

    (b)   it is a contract for a loan repayable by instalments, or for any other form of credit, made to finance the sale of goods; or

    (c)   in all other cases, the contract has been concluded with a person who pursues commercial or professional activities in the part of the United Kingdom in which the consumer is domiciled or, by any means, directs such activities to that part or to other parts of the United Kingdom including that part, and the contract falls within the scope of such activities.

(2)   This rule shall not apply to a contract of transport other than a contract which, for an inclusive price, provides for a combination of travel and accommodation, or to a contract of insurance.

8.—(1)   A consumer may bring proceedings against the other party to a contract either in the courts of the part of the United Kingdom in which that party is domiciled or in the courts of the part of the United Kingdom in which the consumer is domiciled.

(2)   Proceedings may be brought against a consumer by the other party to the contract only in the courts of the part of the United Kingdom in which the consumer is domiciled.

(3)   The provisions of this rule shall not affect the right to bring a counter-claim in the court in which, in accordance with this rule and rules 7 and 9, the original claim is pending.

9.   The provisions of rules 7 and 8 may be departed from only by an agreement—

    (a)   which is entered into after the dispute has arisen; or

    (b)   which allows the consumer to bring proceedings in courts other than those indicated in those rules; or

    (c)   which is entered into by the consumer and the other party to the contract, both of whom are at the time of conclusion of the contract domiciled or habitually resident in the same part of the United Kingdom, and which confers jurisdiction on the courts of that part, provided that such an agreement is not contrary to the law of that part.

Jurisdiction over individual contracts of employment

10.—(1) In matters relating to individual contracts of employment, jurisdiction shall be determined by this rule, without prejudice to rule 3(e).

(2)   An employer may be sued—

(a)   in the courts of the part of the United Kingdom in which he is domiciled; or

(b)   in the courts of the part of the United Kingdom where the employee habitually carries out his work or in the courts of that part where he last did so; or

(c)   if the employee does not or did not habitually carry out his work in any one place, in the courts of the part of the United Kingdom where the business which engaged the employee is or was situated.

(3)   An employer may bring proceedings only in the courts of the part of the United Kingdom in which the employee is domiciled.

(4)   The provisions of this rule shall not affect the right to bring a counter-claim in the court in which, in accordance with this rule, the original claim is pending.

(5)   The provisions of this rule may be departed from only by an agreement on jurisdiction—

(a)   which is entered into after the dispute has arisen; or

(b)   which allows the employee to bring proceedings in courts other than those indicated in this rule.

Exclusive jurisdiction

11.   The following courts shall have exclusive jurisdiction, regardless of domicile:—

(a)—(i)   in proceedings which have as their object rights in rem in immovable property or tenancies of immovable property, the courts of the part of the United Kingdom in which the property is situated;

(ii) however, in proceedings which have as their object tenancies of immovable property concluded for temporary private use for a maximum period of six consecutive months, the courts of the part of the United Kingdom in which the defendant is domiciled shall also have jurisdiction, provided that the tenant is a natural person and that the landlord and the tenant are domiciled in the same part of the United Kingdom;

(b)   in proceedings which have as their object the validity of the constitution, the nullity or the dissolution of companies or other legal persons or associations of natural or legal persons, the courts of the part of the United Kingdom in which the company, legal person or association has its seat;

(c)   in proceedings which have as their object the validity of entries in public registers, the courts of the part of the United Kingdom in which the register is kept;

(d)   in proceedings concerned with the enforcement of judgments, the courts of the part of the United Kingdom in which the judgment has been or is to be enforced.

Prorogation of jurisdiction

12.—(1)   If the parties have agreed that a court or the courts of a part of the United Kingdom are to have jurisdiction to settle any disputes which have arisen or which may arise in connection with a particular legal relationship, and, apart from this Schedule, the agreement would be effective to confer jurisdiction under the law of that part, that court or those courts shall have jurisdiction.

(2)   The court or courts of a part of the United Kingdom on which a trust instrument has conferred jurisdiction shall have jurisdiction in any proceedings

brought against a settlor, trustee or beneficiary, if relations between these persons or their rights or obligations under the trust are involved.

(3)   Agreements or provisions of a trust instrument conferring jurisdiction shall have no legal force if they are contrary to the provisions of rule 9, or if the courts whose jurisdiction they purport to exclude have exclusive jurisdiction by virtue of rule 11.

13.—(1)   Apart from jurisdiction derived from other provisions of this Schedule, a court of a part of the United Kingdom before which a defendant enters an appearance shall have jurisdiction.

(2)   This rule shall not apply where appearance was entered to contest the jurisdiction, or where another court has exclusive jurisdiction by virtue of rule 11.

Examination as to jurisdiction and admissibility

14.   Where a court of a part of the United Kingdom is seised of a claim which is principally concerned with a matter over which the courts of another part of the United Kingdom have exclusive jurisdiction by virtue of rule 11, it shall declare of its own motion that it has no jurisdiction.

15.—(1)   Where a defendant domiciled in one part of the United Kingdom is sued in a court of another part of the United Kingdom and does not enter an appearance, the court shall declare of its own motion that it has no jurisdiction unless its jurisdiction is derived from the provisions of this Schedule.

(2)   The court shall stay the proceedings so long as it is not shown that the defendant has been able to receive the document instituting the proceedings or an equivalent document in sufficient time to enable him to arrange for his defence, or that all necessary steps have been taken to this end.

Provisional, including protective, measures

16.   Application may be made to the courts of a part of the United Kingdom for such provisional, including protective, measures as may be available under the law of that part, even if, under this Schedule, the courts of another part of the United Kingdom have jurisdiction as to the substance of the matter.

SCHEDULE 6
ENFORCEMENT OF UK JUDGMENTS (MONEY PROVISIONS)

Preliminary

1.   In this Schedule—
'judgment' means any judgment to which section 18 applies and references to the giving of a judgment shall be construed accordingly;
'money provision' means a provision for the payment of one or more sums of money;
'prescribed' means prescribed by rules of court.

Certificates in respect of judgments

2.—(1)   Any interested party who wishes to secure the enforcement in another part of the United Kingdom of any money provisions contained in a judgment may apply for a certificate under this Schedule.

(2)   The application shall be made in the prescribed manner to the proper officer of the original court, that is to say—
(a)   in relation to a judgment within paragraph (a) of the definition of 'judg-

ment' in section 18(2), the court by which the judgment or order was given or made;

(b)   in relation to a judgment within paragraph (b) of that definition, the court in which the judgment or order is entered;

(c)   in relation to a judgment within paragraph (c) of that definition, the court in whose books the document is registered;

(d)   in relation to a judgment within paragraph (d) of the definition, the tribunal by which the award or order was made;

(e)   in relation to a judgment within paragraph (e) of that definition, the court which gave the judgment or made the order by virtue of which the award has become enforceable as mentioned in that paragraph.

3.   A certificate shall not be issued under this Schedule in respect of a judgment unless under the law of the part of the United Kingdom in which the judgement was given—

(a)   either—

(i)   the time for bringing an appeal against the judgment has expired, no such appeal having been brought within that time; or

(ii)   such an appeal having been brought within that time, that appeal has been finally disposed of; and

(b)   enforcement of the judgment is not for the time being stayed or suspended, and the time available for its enforcement has not expired.

4.—(1)   Subject to paragraph 3, on an application under paragraph 2 the proper officer shall issue to the applicant a certificate in the prescribed form—

(a)   stating the sum or aggregate of the sums (including any costs or expenses) payable under the money provisions contained in the judgment, the rate of interest, if any, payable thereon and the date or time from which any such interest began to accrue;

(b)   stating that the conditions specified in paragraph 3(a) and (b) are satisfied in relation to the judgment; and

(c)   containing such other particulars as may be prescribed.

(2)   More than one certificate may be issued under this Schedule (simultaneously or at different times) in respect of the same judgment.

Registration of certificates

5.—(1)   Where a certificate has been issued under this Schedule in any part of the United Kingdom, any interested party may, within six months from the date of its issue, apply in the prescribed manner to the proper officer of the superior court in any other part of the United Kingdom for the certificate to be registered in that court.

(2)   In this paragraph 'superior court' means, in relation to England and Wales or Northern Ireland, the High Court and, in relation to Scotland, the Court of Session.

(3)   Where an application is duly made under this paragraph to the proper officer of a superior court, he shall register the certificate in that court in the prescribed manner.

General effect of registration

6.—(1)   A certificate registered under this Schedule shall, for the purposes of its enforcement, be of the same force and effect, the registering court shall have in relation to its enforcement the same powers, and proceedings for or with respect to its enforcement may be taken, as if the certificate had been a judgment originally given in the registering court and had (where relevant) been entered.

(2)   Sub-paragraph (1) is subject to the following provisions of this Schedule

and to any provision made by rules of court as to the manner in which and the conditions subject to which a certificate registered under this Schedule may be enforced.

Costs or expenses

7.   Where a certificate is registered under this Schedule, the reasonable costs or expenses of and incidental to the obtaining of the certificate and its registration shall be recoverable as if they were costs or expenses stated in the certificate to be payable under a money provision contained in the original judgment.

Interest

8.—(1)   Subject to any provision made under sub-paragraph (2), the debt resulting, apart from paragraph 7, from the registration of the certificate shall carry interest at the rate, if any, stated in the certificate from the date or time so stated.

(2)   Provision may be made by rules of court as to the manner in which and the periods by reference to which any interest payable by virtue of sub-paragraph (1) is to be calculated and paid, including provision for such interest to cease to accrue as from a prescribed date.

(3)   All such sums as are recoverable by virtue of paragraph 7 carry interest as if they were the subject of an order for costs or expenses made by the registering court on the date of registration of the certificate.

(4)   Except as provided by this paragraph sums payable by virtue of the registration of a certificate under this Schedule shall not carry interest.

Stay or sisting of enforcement in certain cases

9.   Where a certificate in respect of a judgment has been registered under this Schedule, the registering court may, if it is satisfied that any person against whom it is sought to enforce the certificate is entitled and intends to apply under the law of the part of the United Kingdom in which the judgment was given for any remedy which would result in the setting aside or quashing of the judgment, stay (or, in Scotland, sist) proceedings for the enforcement of the certificate, on such terms as it thinks fit, for such period as appears to the court to be reasonably sufficient to enable the application to be disposed of.

Cases in which registration of a certificate must or may be set aside

10.   Where a certificate has been registered under this Schedule, the registering court—

(a)   shall set aside the registration if, on an application made by any interested party, it is satisfied that the registration was contrary to the provisions of this Schedule;

(b)   may set aside the registration if, on an application so made, it is satisfied that the matter in dispute in the proceedings in which the judgment in question was given had previously been the subject of a judgment by another court or tribunal having jurisdiction in the matter.

SCHEDULE 7
ENFORCEMENT OF UK JUDGMENTS (NON-MONEY PROVISIONS)

Preliminary

1.   In this Schedule—
'judgment' means any judgment to which section 18 applies and references to the giving of a judgment shall be construed accordingly;

'non-money provision' means a provision for any relief or remedy not requiring payment of a sum of money;

'prescribed' means prescribed by rules of court.

Certified copy of judgments

2.—(1) Any interested party who wishes to secure the enforcement in another part of the United Kingdom of any non-money provisions contained in a judgment may apply for a certified copy of the judgment.

(2) The application shall be made in the prescribed manner to the proper officer of the original court, that is to say—

(a) in relation to a judgment within paragraph (a) of the definition of 'judgment' in section 18(2), the court by which the judgment or order was given or made;

(b) in relation to a judgment within paragraph (b) of that definition, the court in which the judgment or order is entered;

(c) in relation to a judgment within paragraph (c) of that definition, the court in whose books the document is registered;

(d) in relation to a judgment within paragraph (d) of that definition, the tribunal by which the award for order was made;

(e) in relation to a judgment within paragraph (e) of that definition, the court which gave the judgment or made the order by virtue of which the award has become enforceable as mentioned in that paragraph.

3. A certified copy of a judgment shall not be issued under this Schedule unless under the law of the part of the United Kingdom in which the judgment was given—

(a) either—

(i) the time for bringing an appeal against the judgment has expired, no such appeal having been brought within that time; or

(ii) such an appeal having been brought within that time, that appeal has been finally disposed of; and

(b) enforcement of the judgment is not for the time being stayed or suspended, and the time available for its enforcement has not expired.

4.—(1) Subject to paragraph 3, on an application under paragraph 2 the proper officer shall issue to the applicant—

(a) a certified copy of the judgment (including any money provisions or excepted provisions which it may contain); and

(b) a certificate stating that the conditions specified in paragraph 3(a) and (b) are satisfied in relation to the judgment.

(2) In sub-paragraph (1)(a) 'excepted provision' means any provision of a judgment which is excepted from the application of section 18 by subsection (5) of that section.

(3) There may be issued under this Schedule (simultaneously or at different times)—

(a) more than one certified copy of the same judgment; and

(b) more than one certificate in respect of the same judgment.

Registration of judgments

5.—(1) Where a certified copy of a judgment has been issued under this Schedule in any part of the United Kingdom, any interested party may apply in the prescribed manner to the superior court in any other part of the United Kingdom for the judgment to be registered in that court.

(2) In this paragraph 'superior court' means, in relation to England and Wales

or Northern Ireland, the High Court and, in relation to Scotland, the Court of Session.

(3) An application under this paragraph for the registration of a judgment must be accompanied by—

(a)   a certified copy of the judgment issued under this Schedule; and

(b)   a certificate issued under paragraph 4(1)(b) in respect of the judgment not more than six months before the date of the application.

(4) Subject to sub-paragraph (5), where an application under this paragraph is duly made to a superior court, the court shall order the whole of the judgment as set out in the certified copy to be registered in that court in the prescribed manner.

(5) A judgment shall not be registered under this Schedule by the superior court in any part of the United Kingdom if compliance with the non-money provisions contained in the judgment would involve a breach of the law of that part of the United Kingdom.

General effect of registration

6.—(1) The non-money provisions contained in a judgment registered under this Schedule shall, for the purposes of their enforcement, be of the same force and effect, the registering court shall have in relation to their enforcement the same powers, and proceedings for or with respect to their enforcement may be taken, as if the judgment containing them had been originally given in the registering court and had (where relevant) been entered.

(2) Sub-paragraph (1) is subject to the following provisions of this Schedule and to any provision made by rules of court as to the manner in which and conditions subject to which the non-money provisions contained in a judgment registered under this Schedule may be enforced.

Costs of expenses

7.—(1) Where a judgment is registered under this Schedule, the reasonable costs or expenses of and incidental to—

(a)   the obtaining of the certified copy of the judgment and of the necessary certificate under paragraph 4(1)(b) in respect of it; and

(b)   the registration of the judgment,

shall be recoverable as if on the date of registration there had also been registered in the registering court a certificate under Schedule 6 in respect of the judgment and as if those costs or expenses were costs or expenses stated in that certificate to be payable under a money provision contained in the judgment.

(2) All such sums as are recoverable by virtue of sub-paragraph (1) shall carry interest as if they were the subject of an order for costs or expenses made by the registering court on the date of registration of the judgment.

Stay or sisting of enforcement in certain cases

8. Where a judgment has been registered under this Schedule, the registering court may, if it is satisfied that any person against whom it is sought to enforce the judgment is entitled and intends to apply under the law of the part of the United Kingdom in which the judgment was given for any remedy which would result in the setting aside or quashing of the judgment, stay (or, in Scotland, sist) proceedings for the enforcement of the judgment, on such terms as it thinks fit, for such period as appears to the court to be reasonably sufficient to enable the application to be disposed of.

Cases in which registered judgment may be set aside

9.   Where a judgment has been registered under this Schedule, the registering court—

(a)   shall set aside the registration if, on an application made by any interested party, it is satisfied that the registration was contrary to the provisions of this Schedule;

(b)   may set aside the registration if, on an application so made, it is satisfied that the matter in dispute in the proceedings in which the judgment was given had previously been the subject of a judgment by another court or tribunal having jurisdiction in the matter.

SCHEDULE 8
RULES AS TO JURISDICTION IN SCOTLAND

General

1.   Subject to the following rules, persons shall be sued in the courts for the place where they are domiciled.

Special jurisdiction

2.   Subject to rules 3 (jurisdiction over consumer contracts), 4 (jurisdiction over individual contracts of employment), 5 (exclusive jurisdiction) and 6 (prorogation), a person may also be sued—

(a)   where he has no fixed residence, in a court within whose jurisdiction he is personally cited;

(b)   in matters relating to a contract, in the courts for the place of performance of the obligation in question;

(c)   in matters relating to delict or quasi-delict, in the courts for the place where the harmful event occurred or may occur;

(d)   as regards a civil claim for damages or restitution which is based on an act giving rise to criminal proceedings, in the court seised of those proceedings to the extent that the court has jurisdiction to entertain civil proceedings;

(e)   in matters relating to maintenance, in the courts for the place where the maintenance creditor is domiciled or habitually resident or, if the matter is ancillary to proceedings concerning the status of a person, in the court which has jurisdiction to entertain those proceedings, provided that an action for adherence and aliment or of affiliation and aliment shall be treated as a matter relating to maintenance which is not ancillary to proceedings concerning the status of a person;

(f)   as regards a dispute arising out of the operations of a branch, agency or other establishment, in the courts for the place in which the branch, agency or other establishment is situated;

(g)   in his capacity as settlor, trustee or beneficiary of a trust domiciled in Scotland created by the operation of a statute, or by a written instrument, or created orally and evidenced in writing, in the Court of Session, or the appropriate sheriff court within the meaning of section 24A of the Trusts (Scotland) Act 1921;

(h)   where he is not domiciled in the United Kingdom, in the courts for any place where—

(i)   any movable property belonging to him has been arrested; or

(ii)   any immovable property in which he has any beneficial interest is situated;

(i)   in proceedings which are brought to assert, declare or determine proprietary or possessory rights, or rights of security, in or over movable property,

or to obtain authority to dispose of movable property, in the courts for the place
where the property is situated;

(j)   in proceedings for interdict, in the courts for the place where it is alleged
that the wrong is likely to be committed;

(k)   in proceedings concerning a debt secured over immovable property, in
the courts for the place where the property is situated;

(l)   in proceedings which have as their object a decision of an organ of a
company or other legal person or of an association of natural or legal persons, in
the courts for the place where that company, legal person or association has its
seat;

(m)   in proceedings concerning an arbitration which is conducted in Scotland
or in which the procedure is governed by Scots law, in the Court of Session;

(n)   in proceedings principally concerned with the registration in the United
Kingdom or the validity in the United Kingdom of patents, trade marks, designs
or other similar rights required to be deposited or registered, in the Court of
Session;

(o) (i)   where he is one of a number of defenders, in the courts for the place
where any one of them is domiciled, provided the claims are so closely connected that it is expedient to hear and determine them together to avoid the risk
of irreconcilable judgments resulting from separate proceedings;

(ii)   as a third party in an action on a warranty or guarantee or in any other
third party proceedings, in the court seised of the original proceedings, unless
these were instituted solely with the object of removing him from the jurisdiction of the court which would be competent in his case;

(iii)   on a counterclaim arising from the same contract or facts on which the
original claim was based, in the court in which the original claim is pending;

(p)   in matters relating to a contract, if the action may be combined with an
action against the same defender in matters relating to rights in rem in immovable property, in the courts for the place where the property is situated;

(q)   as regards a claim for limitation of liability arising from the use or operation of a ship, in the court having jurisdiction in the action relating to such
liability.

Jurisdiction over consumer contracts

3.—(1)   In matters relating to a contract concluded by a person, the consumer, for
a purpose which can be regarded as being outside his trade or profession, subject
to rule 5, jurisdiction shall be determined by this rule if—

(a)   it is a contract for the sale of goods on instalment credit terms; or

(b)   it is a contract for a loan repayable by instalments, or for any other form
of credit, made to finance the sale of goods; or

(c)   in all other cases, the contract has been concluded with a person who
pursues commercial or professional activities in Scotland or, by any means,
directs such activities to Scotland or to several places including Scotland, and
the contract falls within the scope of such activities.

(2)   This rule shall not apply to a contract of transport other than a contract
which, for an inclusive price, provides for a combination of travel and accommodation.

(3)   A consumer may bring proceedings against the other party to a contract
only in—

(a)   the courts for the place in which that party is domiciled;

(b)   the courts for the place in which he is himself domiciled; or

(c)   any court having jurisdiction by virtue of rule 2(f) or (i).

(4)   Proceedings may be brought against a consumer by the other party to the
contract only in the courts for the place where the consumer is domiciled or any
court having jurisdiction under rule 2(i).

(5)   The provisions of this rule shall not affect the right to bring a counterclaim in the court in which, in accordance with this rule, the original claim is pending.

(6)   The provisions of this rule may be departed from only by an agreement—

(a)   which is entered into after the dispute has arisen; or

(b)   which allows the consumer to bring proceedings in courts other than those indicated in this rule; or

(c)   which is entered into by the consumer and the other party to the contract, both of whom are at the time of conclusion of the contract domiciled or habitually resident in the same Regulation State, and which confers jurisdiction on the courts of that Regulation State, provided that such an agreement is not contrary to the law of that Regulation State.

Jurisdiction over individual contracts of employment

4.—(1)   In matters relating to individual contracts of employment, jurisdiction shall be determined by this rule, without prejudice to rule 2(f).

(2)   An employer may be sued—

(a)   in the courts for the place where he is domiciled; or

(b)   in the courts for the place where the employee habitually carries out his work or in the courts for the last place where he did so; or

(c)   if the employee does not or did not habitually carry out his work in any one place, in the courts for the place where the business which engaged the employee is or was situated.

(3)   An employer may bring proceedings only in the courts for the place in which the employee is domiciled.

(4)   The provisions of this rule shall not affect the right to bring a counter-claim in the court in which, in accordance with this rule, the original claim is pending.

(5)   The provisions of this rule may be departed from only by an agreement on jurisdiction—

(a)   which is entered into after the dispute has arisen; or

(b)   which allows the employee to bring proceedings in courts other than those indicated in this rule.

Exclusive jurisdiction

5.—(1)   Notwithstanding anything contained in any of rules 1 to 4 above or 6 to 9 below but subject to paragraph (3) below, the following courts shall have exclusive jurisdiction:—

(a)   in proceedings which have as their object rights in rem in, or tenancies of, immovable property, the courts for the place where the property is situated;

(b)   in proceedings which have as their object the validity of the constitution, the nullity or the dissolution of companies or other legal persons or associations of natural or legal persons, the courts for the place where the company, legal person or association has its seat;

(c)   in proceedings which have as their object the validity of entries in public registers, the courts for the place where the register is kept;

(d)   in proceedings concerned with the enforcement of judgments, the courts for the place where the judgment has been or is to be enforced.

(2)   No court shall exercise jurisdiction in a case where immovable property, the seat of a body mentioned in paragraph (1)(b) above, a public register or the place where a judgment has been or is to be enforced is situated outside Scotland and where paragraph (1) would apply if the property, seat, register or, as the case may be, place of enforcement were situated in Scotland.

(3)   In proceedings which have as their object tenancies of immovable property concluded for temporary private use for a maximum period of six consecutive months, the courts for the place in which the defender is domiciled shall also have

jurisdiction, provided that the tenant is a natural person and that the landlord and tenant are domiciled in Scotland.

Prorogation of jurisdiction

6.—(1) If the parties have agreed that a court is to have jurisdiction to settle any disputes which have arisen or which may arise in connection with a particular legal relationship, that court shall have jurisdiction.

(2) Such an agreement conferring jurisdiction shall be either—

(a) in writing or evidenced in writing; or

(b) in a form which accords with practices which the parties have established between themselves; or

(c) in international trade or commerce, in a form which accords with a usage of which the parties are or ought to have been aware and which in such trade or commerce is widely known to, and regularly observed by, parties to contracts of the type involved in the particular trade or commerce concerned.

(3) Any communication by electronic means which provides a durable record of the agreement shall be equivalent to 'writing'.

(4) The court on which a trust instrument has conferred jurisdiction shall have exclusive jurisdiction in any proceedings brought against a settlor, trustee or beneficiary, if relations between these persons or their rights or obligations under the trust are involved.

(5) Where an agreement or a trust instrument confers jurisdiction on the courts of the United Kingdom or of Scotland, proceedings to which paragraph (1) or, as the case may be, (4) above applies may be brought in any court in Scotland.

(6) Agreements or provisions of a trust instrument conferring jurisdiction shall have no legal force if the courts whose jurisdiction they purport to exclude have exclusive jurisdiction by virtue of rule 5 or where rule 5(2) applies.

7.—(1) Apart from jurisdiction derived from other provisions of this Schedule, a court before whom a defender enters an appearance shall have jurisdiction.

(2) This rule shall not apply where appearance was entered to contest jurisdiction, or where another court has exclusive jurisdiction by virtue of rule 5 or where rule 5(2) applies.

Examination as to jurisdiction and admissibility

8. Where a court is seised of a claim which is principally concerned with a matter over which another court has exclusive jurisdiction by virtue of rule 5, or where it is precluded from exercising jurisdiction by rule 5(2), it shall declare of its own motion that it has no jurisdiction.

9. Where in any case a court has no jurisdiction which is compatible with this Schedule, and the defender does not enter an appearance, the court shall declare of its own motion that it has no jurisdiction.

MATRIMONIAL AND FAMILY PROCEEDINGS ACT 1984
(1984 c 42)

PART IV
FINANCIAL PROVISION IN SCOTLAND AFTER OVERSEAS DIVORCE ETC

28 Circumstances in which a Scottish court may entertain application for financial provision

(1) Where parties to a marriage have been divorced in an overseas country, then, subject to subsection (4) below, if the jurisdictional requirements and the conditions set out in subsections (2) and (3) below respectively are satisfied, the court

may entertain an application by one of the parties for an order for financial provision.

(2) The jurisdictional requirements mentioned in subsection (1) above are that—

(a) the applicant was domiciled or habitually resident in Scotland on the date when the application was made; and

(b) the other party to the marriage—

(i) was domiciled or habitually resident in Scotland on the date when the application was made; or

(ii) was domiciled or habitually resident in Scotland when the parties last lived together as husband and wife; or

(iii) on the date when the application was made, was an owner or tenant of, or had a beneficial interest in, property in Scotland which had at some time been a matrimonial home of the parties; and

(c) where the court is the sheriff court, either—

(i) one of the parties was, on the date when the application was made, habitually resident in the sheriffdom; or

(ii) paragraph (b)(iii) above is satisfied in respect of property wholly or partially within the sheriffdom.

(3) The conditions mentioned in subsection (1) above are that—

(a) the divorce falls to be recognised in Scotland;

(b) the other party to the marriage initiated the proceedings for divorce;

(c) the application was made within five years after the date when the divorce took effect;

(d) a court in Scotland would have had jurisdiction to entertain an action for divorce between the parties if such an action had been brought in Scotland immediately before the foreign divorce took effect;

(e) the marriage had a substantial connection with Scotland; and

(f) both parties are living at the time of the application.

(4) Where the jurisdiction of the court to entertain proceedings under this Part of this Act would fall to be determined by reference to the jurisdictional requirements imposed by virtue of Part I of the Civil Jurisdiction and Judgments Act 1982 (implementation of certain European conventions) [or by virtue of Council Regulation (EC) No 44/2001 of 22nd December 2000 on jurisdiction and the recognition and enforcement of judgments in civil and commercial matters or] then—

(a) satisfaction of the requirements of subsection (2) above shall not obviate the need to satisfy the requirements imposed by virtue of [that Regulation or] Part I of that Act; and

(b) satisfaction of the requirements imposed by virtue of [that Regulation or] Part I of that Act shall obviate the need to satisfy the requirements of subsection (2) above;

and the court shall entertain or not entertain the proceedings accordingly.

29 Disposal of application in Scotland

(1) Subject to subsections (2) to (5) below, Scots law shall apply, with any necessary modifications, in relation to an application under section 28 above as it would apply if the application were being made in an action for divorce in Scotland.

(2) In disposing of an application entertained by it under the said section 28, the court shall exercise its powers so as to place the parties, in so far as it is reasonable and practicable to do so, in the financial position in which they would have been if the application had been disposed of, in an action for divorce in Scotland, on the date on which the foreign divorce took effect.

(3) In determining what is reasonable and practicable for the purposes of subsection (2) above, the court shall have regard in particular to—

(a) the parties' resources, present and foreseeable at the date of disposal of the application;

(b)   any order made by a foreign court in or in connection with the divorce proceedings for the making of financial provision in whatever form, or the transfer of property, by one of the parties to the other; and

(c)   subsection (5) below.

(4)   Except where subsection (5) below applies, the court may make an order for an interim award of a periodical allowance where—

(a)   it appears from the applicant's averments that in the disposal of the application an order for financial provision is likely to be made; and

(b)   the court considers that such an interim award is necessary to avoid hardship to the applicant.

(5)   Where but for section 28(2)(b)(iii) above the court would not have jurisdiction to entertain the application, the court may make an order—

(a)   relating to the former matrimonial home or its furniture and plenishings; or

(b)   that the other party to the marriage shall pay to the applicant a capital sum not exceeding the value of that other party's interest in the former matrimonial home and its furniture and plenishings,

but shall not be entitled to make any other order for financial provision.

CHILD ABDUCTION AND CUSTODY ACT 1985
(1985 c 60)

PART I
INTERNATIONAL CHILD ABDUCTION

1   The Hague Convention

(1)   In this Part of this Act 'the Convention' means the Convention on the Civil Aspects of International Child Abduction which was signed at The Hague on 25th October 1980.

(2)   Subject to the provisions of this Part of this Act, the provisions of that Convention set out in Schedule 1 to this Act shall have the force of law in the United Kingdom.

[(3)   But—

(a)   those provisions of the Convention,

(b)   this Part of this Act, and

(c)   rules of court under section 10 of this Act,

are subject to Article 60 of the Council Regulation (by virtue of which the Regulation takes precedence over the Hague Convention, in so far as it concerns matters governed by the Regulation).

(4)   'The Council Regulation' means Council Regulation (EC) No 2201/2003 of 27th November 2003 concerning jurisdiction and the recognition and enforcement of judgments in matrimonial matters and matters of parental responsibility.]

2   Contracting States

(1)   For the purposes of the Convention as it has effect under this Part of this Act the Contracting States other than the United Kingdom shall be those for the time being specified by an Order in Council under this section.

(2)   An Order in Council under this section shall specify the date of the coming into force of the Convention as between the United Kingdom and any State specified in the Order; and, except where the Order otherwise provides, the Convention shall apply as between the United Kingdom and that State only in relation to wrongful removals or retentions occurring on or after that date.

(3)   Where the Convention applies, or applies only, to a particular territory or particular territories specified in a declaration made by a Contracting State under Article 39 or 40 of the Convention references to that State in subsections (1) and (2) above shall be construed as references to that territory or those territories.

3 Central Authorities

(1) Subject to subsection (2) below, the functions under the Convention of a Central Authority shall be discharged—

(a) in England and Wales and in Northern Ireland by the Lord Chancellor; and

(b) in Scotland by the Secretary of State.

(2) Any application made under the Convention by or on behalf of a person outside the United Kingdom may be addressed to the Lord Chancellor as the Central Authority in the United Kingdom.

(3) Where any such application relates to a function to be discharged under subsection (1) above by the Secretary of State it shall be transmitted by the Lord Chancellor to the Secretary of State and where such an application is addressed to the Secretary of State but relates to a function to be discharged under subsection (1) above by the Lord Chancellor the Secretary of State shall transmit it to the Lord Chancellor.

4 Judicial authorities

The courts having jurisdiction to entertain applications under the Convention shall be—

(a) in England and Wales or in Northern Ireland the High Court; and

(b) in Scotland the Court of Session.

5 Interim powers

Where an application has been made to a court in the United Kingdom under the Convention, the court may, at any time before the application is determined, give such interim directions as it thinks fit for the purpose of securing the welfare of the child concerned or of preventing changes in the circumstances relevant to the determination of the application.

6 Reports

Where the Lord Chancellor or the Secretary of State is requested to provide information relating to a child under Article 7(d) of the Convention he may—

(a) request a local authority or [an officer of the Service] to make a report to him in writing with respect to any matter which appears to him to be relevant;

(b) request the Department of Health and Social Services for Northern Ireland to arrange for a suitably qualified person to make such a report to him;

(c) request any court to which a written report relating to the child has been made to send him a copy of the report;

and such a request shall be duly complied with.

7 Proof of documents and evidence

(1) For the purposes of Article 14 of the Convention a decision or determination of a judicial or administrative authority outside the United Kingdom may be proved by a duly authenticated copy of the decision or determination; and any document purporting to be such a copy shall be deemed to be a true copy unless the contrary is shown.

(2) For the purposes of subsection (1) above a copy is duly authenticated if it bears the seal, or is signed by a judge or officer, of the authority in question.

(3) For the purposes of Articles 14 and 30 of the Convention any such document as is mentioned in Article 8 of the Convention, or a certified copy of any such document, shall be sufficient evidence of anything stated in it.

8 Declarations by United Kingdom courts

The High Court or Court of Session may, on an application made for the purposes of Article 15 of the Convention by any person appearing to the court to have an interest in the matter, make a declaration or declarator that the removal of any child from, or his retention outside, the United Kingdom was wrongful within the meaning of Article 3 of the Convention.

9   Suspension of court's powers in cases of wrongful removal
The reference in Article 16 of the Convention to deciding on the merits of rights of custody shall be construed as a reference to—

(a)   making, varying or revoking a custody order, or [a supervision order under section 1(2) of the Children and Young Persons Act 1969 or section 95(1), 97(2), 143(6) or 144 of the Children and Young Persons Act (Northern Ireland) 1968 (not being a custody order)];

[(aa)   enforcing under section 29 of the Family Law Act 1986 a custody order within the meaning of Chapter V of Part I of that Act;]

(b)   registering or enforcing a decision under Part II of this Act;

[...]

[(d)   making, varying or discharging an order under section 86 of the Children (Scotland) Act 1995;]

[...]

PART II
RECOGNITION AND ENFORCEMENT OF CUSTODY DECISIONS

...

24A   Power to order disclosure of child's whereabouts
(1)   Where—

(a)   in proceedings for the return of a child under Part I of this Act; or

(b)   on an application for the recognition, registration or enforcement of a decision in respect of a child under Part II of this Act,

there is not available to the court adequate information as to where the child is, the court may order any person who it has reason to believe may have relevant information to disclose it to the court.

(2)   A person shall not be excused from complying with an order under subsection (1) above by reason that to do so may incriminate him or his spouse [or civil partner] of an offence; but a statement or admission made in compliance with such an order shall not be admissible in evidence against either of them in proceedings for any offence other than perjury.

PART III
SUPPLEMENTARY

25   Termination of existing custody orders, etc
(1)   Where—

(a)   an order is made for the return of a child under Part I of this Act; or

(b)   a decision with respect to a child (other than a decision mentioned in subsection (2) below) is registered under section 16 of this Act,

any custody order relating to him shall cease to have effect.

(2)   The decision referred to in subsection (1)(b) above is a decision which is only a decision relating to custody within the meaning of section 16 of this Act by virtue of being a decision relating to rights of access.

(4)   *[Applies to Northern Ireland.]*

[...]

(7)   *[Applies to Northern Ireland.]*

Section 1(2)   SCHEDULE 1
CONVENTION ON THE CIVIL ASPECTS OF INTERNATIONAL CHILD
ABDUCTION

CHAPTER 1 – SCOPE OF THE CONVENTION

Article 3

The removal or the retention of a child is to be considered wrongful where—

(a)   it is in breach of rights of custody attributed to a person, an institution or any other body, either jointly or alone, under the law of the State in which the child was habitually resident immediately before the removal or retention; and

(b)   at the time of removal or retention those rights were actually exercised, either jointly or alone, or would have been so exercised but for the removal or retention.

The rights of custody mentioned in sub-paragraph (a) above may arise in particular by operation of law or by reason of a judicial or administrative decision, or by reason of an agreement having legal effect under the law of that State.

Article 4

The Convention shall apply to any child who was habitually resident in a Contracting State immediately before any breach of custody or access rights. The Convention shall cease to apply when the child attains the age of sixteen years.

Article 5

For the purposes of this Convention—

(a)   'rights of custody' shall include rights relating to the care of the person of the child and, in particular, the right to determine the child's place of residence;

(b)   'rights of access' shall include the right to take a child for a limited period of time to a place other than the child's habitual residence.

CHAPTER II – CENTRAL AUTHORITIES

Article 7

Central Authorities shall co-operate with each other and promote co-operation amongst the competent authorities in their respective States to secure the prompt return of children and to achieve the other objects of this Convention.

In particular, either directly or through any intermediary, they shall take all appropriate measures—

(a)   to discover the whereabouts of a child who has been wrongfully removed or retained;

(b)   to prevent further harm to the child or prejudice to interested parties by taking or causing to be taken provisional measures;

(c)   to secure the voluntary return of the child or to bring about an amicable resolution of the issues;

(d)   to exchange, where desirable, information relating to the social background of the child;

(e)   to provide information of a general character as to the law of their State in connection with the application of the Convention;

(f)   to initiate or facilitate the institution of judicial or administrative proceedings with a view to obtaining the return of the child and, in a proper case, to make arrangements for organizing or securing the effective exercise of rights of access;

(g)   where the circumstances so require, to provide or facilitate the provision of legal aid and advice, including the participation of legal counsel and advisers;

(h)   to provide such administrative arrangements as may be necessary and appropriate to secure the safe return of the child;

(i)   to keep each other informed with respect to the operation of this Convention and, as far as possible, to eliminate any obstacles to its application.

CHAPTER III – RETURN OF CHILDREN

Article 8

Any person, institution or other body claiming that a child has been removed or retained in breach of custody rights may apply either to the Central Authority of the child's habitual residence or to the Central Authority of any other Contracting State for assistance in securing the return of the child.

The application shall contain—

(a)   information concerning the identity of the applicant, of the child and of the person alleged to have removed or retained the child;

(b)   where available, the date of birth of the child;

(c)   the grounds on which the applicant's claim for return of the child is based;

(d)   all available information relating to the whereabouts of the child and the identity of the person with whom the child is presumed to be.

The application may be accompanied or supplemented by—

(e)   an authenticated copy of any relevant decision or agreement;

(f)   a certificate or an affidavit emanating from a Central Authority, or other competent authority of the State of the child's habitual residence, or from a qualified person, concerning the relevant law of that State;

(g)   any other relevant document.

Article 9

If the Central Authority which receives an application referred to in Article 8 has reason to believe that the child is in another Contracting State, it shall directly and without delay transmit the application to the Central Authority of that Contracting State and inform the requesting Central Authority, or the applicant, as the case may be.

Article 10

The Central Authority of the State where the child is shall take or cause to be taken all appropriate measures in order to obtain the voluntary return of the child.

Article 11

The judicial or administrative authorities of Contracting States shall act expeditiously in proceedings for the return of children.

If the judicial or administrative authority concerned has not reached a decision within six weeks from the date of commencement of the proceedings, the applicant or the Central Authority of the requested State, on its own initiative or if asked by the Central Authority of the requesting State, shall have the right to request a statement of the reasons for the delay. If a reply is received by the Central Authority of the requested State, that Authority shall transmit the reply to the Central Authority of the requesting State, or to the applicant, as the case may be.

Article 12

Where a child has been wrongfully removed or retained in terms of Article 3 and, at the date of the commencement of the proceedings before the judicial or administrative authority of the Contracting State where the child is, a period of less than one year has elapsed from the date of the wrongful removal or retention, the authority concerned shall order the return of the child forthwith.

The judicial or administrative authority, even where the proceedings have been commenced after the expiration of the period of one year referred to in the preceding paragraph, shall also order the return of the child, unless it is demonstrated that the child is now settled in its new environment.

Where the judicial or administrative authority in the requested state has reason to believe that the child has been taken to another State, it may stay the proceedings or dismiss the application for the return of the child.

Article 13
Notwithstanding the provisions of the preceding Article, the judicial or administrative authority of the requested State is not bound to order the return of the child if the person, institution or other body which opposes its return establishes that—

(a) the person, institution or other body having the care of the person of the child was not actually exercising the custody rights at the time of removal or retention, or had consented to or subsequently acquiesced in the removal or retention; or

(b) there is a grave risk that his or her return would expose the child to physical or psychological harm or otherwise place the child in an intolerable situation.

The judicial or administrative authority may also refuse to order the return of the child if it finds that the child objects to being returned and has attained an age and degree of maturity at which it is appropriate to take account of its views.

In considering the circumstances referred to in this Article, the judicial and administrative authorities shall take into account the information relating to the social background of the child provided by the Central Authority or other competent authority of the child's habitual residence.

Article 14
In ascertaining whether there has been a wrongful removal or retention within the meaning of Article 3, the judicial or administrative authorities of the requested State may take notice directly of the law of, and of judicial or administrative decisions, formally recognised or not in the State of the habitual residence of the child, without recourse to the specific procedures for the proof of that law or for the recognition of foreign decisions which would otherwise be applicable.

Article 15
The judicial or administrative authorities of a Contracting State may, prior to the making of an order for the return of the child, request that the applicant obtain from the authorities of the State of the habitual residence of the child a decision or other determination that the removal or retention was wrongful within the meaning of Article 3 of the Convention, where such a decision or determination may be obtained in that State. The Central Authorities of the Contracting States shall so far as practicable assist applicants to obtain such a decision or determination.

Article 16
After receiving notice of a wrongful removal or retention of a child in the sense of Article 3, the judicial or administrative authorities of the Contracting State to which the child has been removed or in which it has been retained shall not decide on the merits of rights of custody until it has been determined that the child is not to be returned under this Convention or unless an application under this Convention is not lodged within a reasonable time following receipt of the notice.

Article 17
The sole fact that a decision relating to custody has been given in or is entitled to recognition in the requested State shall not be a ground for refusing to return a child under this Convention, but the judicial or administrative authorities of the requested State may take account of the reasons for that decision in applying this Convention.

Article 18
The provisions of this Chapter do not limit the power of a judicial or administrative authority to order the return of the child at any time.

Article 19

A decision under this Convention concerning the return of the child shall not be taken to be a determination on the merits of any custody issue.

CHAPTER IV – RIGHTS OF ACCESS

Article 21

An application to make arrangements for organising or securing the effective exercise of rights of access may be presented to the Central Authorities of the Contracting States in the same way as an application for the return of a child.

The Central Authorities are bound by the obligations of co-operation which are set forth in Article 7 to promote the peaceful enjoyment of access rights and the fulfilment of any conditions to which the exercise of those rights may be subject. The Central Authorities shall take steps to remove, as far as possible, all obstacles to the exercise of such rights. The Central Authorities, either directly or through intermediaries, may initiate or assist in the institution of proceedings with a view to organising or protecting these rights and securing respect for the conditions to which the exercise of these rights may be subject.

CHAPTER V – GENERAL PROVISIONS

Article 22

No security, bond or deposit, however described, shall be required to guarantee the payment of costs and expenses in the judicial or administrative proceedings falling within the scope of this Convention.

Article 24

Any application, communication or other document sent to the Central Authority of the requested State shall be in the original language, and shall be accompanied by a translation into the official language or one of the official languages of the requested State or, where that is not feasible, a translation into French or English.

Article 26

Each Central Authority shall bear its own costs in applying this Convention.

Central Authorities and other public services of Contracting States shall not impose any charges in relation to applications submitted under this Convention. In particular, they may not require any payment from the applicant towards the costs and expenses of the proceedings or, where applicable, those arising from the participation of legal counsel or advisers. However, they may require the payment of the expenses incurred or to be incurred in implementing the return of the child.

However, a Contracting State may, by making a reservation in accordance with Article 42, declare that it shall not be bound to assume any costs referred to in the preceding paragraph resulting from the participation of legal counsel or advisers or from court proceedings, except insofar as those costs may be covered by its system of legal aid and advice.

Upon ordering the return of a child or issuing an order concerning rights of access under this Convention, the judicial or administrative authorities may, where appropriate, direct the person who removed or retained the child, or who prevented the exercise of rights of access, to pay necessary expenses incurred by or on behalf of the applicant, including travel expenses, any costs incurred or payments made for locating the child, the costs of legal representation of the applicant, and those of returning the child.

Article 27

When it is manifest that the requirements of this Convention are not fulfilled or that the application is otherwise not well founded, a Central Authority is not bound to accept the application. In that case, the Central Authority shall forthwith inform the applicant or the Central Authority through which the application was submitted, as the case may be, of its reasons.

Article 28
A Central Authority may require that the application be accompanied by a written authorisation empowering it to act on behalf of the applicant, or to designate a representative so to act.

Article 29
This Convention shall not preclude any person, institution or body who claims that there has been a breach of custody or access rights within the meaning of Article 3 or 21 from applying directly to the judicial or administrative authorities of a Contracting State, whether or not under the provisions of this Convention.

Article 30
Any application submitted to the Central Authorities or directly to the judicial or administrative authorities of a Contracting State in accordance with the terms of this Convention, together with documents and any other information appended thereto or provided by a Central Authority, shall be admissible in the courts or administrative authorities of the Contracting States.

Article 31
In relation to a State which in matters of custody of children has two or more systems of law applicable in different territorial units—
    (a)   any reference to habitual residence in that State shall be construed as referring to habitual residence in a territorial unit of that State;
    (b)   any reference to the law of the State of habitual residence shall be construed as referring to the law of the territorial unit in that State where the child habitually resides.

Article 32
In relation to a State which in matters of custody of children has two or more systems of law applicable to different categories of persons, any reference to the law of that State shall be construed as referring to the legal system specified by the law of that State.

BANKRUPTCY (SCOTLAND) ACT 1985
(1985 c 66)

9 Jurisdiction
(1) The Court of Session shall have jurisdiction in respect of the sequestration of the estate of a living debtor or of a deceased debtor if the debtor had an established place of business in Scotland, or was habitually resident there, at the relevant time.

(2) The Court of Session shall have jurisdiction in respect of the sequestration of the estate of any entity which may be sequestrated by virtue of section 6 of this Act, if the entity—
    (a)   had an established place of business in Scotland at the relevant time; or
    (b)   was constituted or formed under Scots law, and at any time carried on business in Scotland.

(3) Notwithstanding that the partner of a firm, whether alive or deceased, does not fall within subsection (1) above, the Court of Session shall have jurisdiction in respect of the sequestration of his estate if a petition has been presented for the sequestration of the estate of the firm of which he is, or was at the relevant time before his decease, a partner and the process of that sequestration is still current.

(4) The provisions of this section shall apply to the sheriff as they apply to the Court of Session but as if for the word 'Scotland' wherever it occurs there were

substituted the words 'the sheriffdom' and in subsection (3) after the word 'presented' there were inserted the words 'in the sheriffdom'.

(5)   In this section 'the relevant time' means at any time in the year immediately preceding the date of presentation of the petition or the date of death, as the case may be.

[(6)   This section is subject to Article 3 of the EC Regulation.]*

10   Concurrent proceedings for sequestration or analogous remedy

(1)   If, in the course of sequestration proceedings, the petitioner for sequestration, the debtor or a creditor concurring in the petition (the petition in such proceedings being hereafter in this section referred to as the 'instant petition') is, or becomes, aware that—

   (a)   another petition for sequestration of the debtor's estate is before a court or such sequestration has been awarded; or

   (b)   a petition for the appointment of a judicial factor on the debtor's estate is before a court or such a judicial factor has been appointed; or

   (c)   [a petition is before a court for the winding up of the debtor under Part IV or V of the Insolvency Act 1986 or section 372 of the Financial Services and Markets Act 2000];

   (d)   an application for an analogous remedy in respect of the debtor's estate is proceeding or such an analogous remedy is in force,

he shall as soon as possible bring that fact to the notice of the court to which the instant petition was presented.

(2)   If a petitioner (not being the debtor) or a creditor concurring in the petition fails to comply with subsection (1) above, he may be made liable for the expenses of presenting the petition for sequestration; and, if the debtor fails to comply with subsection (1) above, he shall be guilty of an offence and liable, on summary conviction, to a fine not exceeding level 5 on the standard scale.

(3)   Where in the course of sequestration proceedings any of the circumstances mentioned in paragraph (a), (b) or (c) of subsection (1) above exists then—

   (a)   the court to which the instant petition was presented may, on its own motion or at the instance of the debtor or any creditor or other person having an interest, allow that petition to proceed or may sist or dismiss it; or

   (b)   without prejudice to paragraph (a) above, the Court of Session may, on its own motion or on application by the debtor or any creditor or other person having an interest, direct the sheriff before whom the instant petition is pending, or the court before which the other petition is pending, to sist or dismiss the instant petition or, as the case may be, the other petition, or may order the petitions to be heard together.

(4)   Where in respect of the same estate—

   (a)   a petition for sequestration is pending before a court; and

   (b)   an application for an analogous remedy is proceeding or an analogous remedy is in force,

the court, on its own motion or at the instance of the debtor or any creditor or other person having an interest, may allow the petition for sequestration to proceed or may sist or dismiss it.

(5)   In this section 'analogous remedy' means a bankruptcy order under the Bankruptcy Act 1914 or under the Insolvency Act 1985 or an administration order under section 112 of the County Courts Act 1984 in England and Wales or under any enactment having the like effect in Northern Ireland or a remedy analogous to either of the aforesaid remedies, or to sequestration, in any other country.

---

*Council Regulation (EC) No 1346/2000 on Insolvency Proceedings; see Part IV at p 188 below.

31   Vesting of estate at date of sequestration*

(1)   Subject to section 33 of this Act [and section 91(3) of the Pensions Act 1995], the whole estate of the debtor shall vest as at the date of sequestration in the permanent trustee for the benefit of the creditors; and—

(a)   the estate shall so vest by virtue of the act and warrant issued on confirmation of the permanent trustee's appointment; and

(b)   the act and warrant shall, in respect of the heritable estate in Scotland of the debtor, have the same effect as if a decree of adjudication in implement of sale, as well as a decree of adjudication for payment and in security of debt, subject to no legal reversion, had been pronounced in favour of the permanent trustee.

[(1A)   *It shall not be competent for—*

(a)   *the trustee; or*

(b)   *any person deriving title from the trustee,*

to complete title to any heritable estate in Scotland vested in the trustee by virtue of his appointment before the expiry of the period mentioned in subsection (1B) below.

(1B)   *That period is the period of 28 days (or such other period as may be prescribed) beginning with the day on which—*

(a)   *the certified copy of the order of the sheriff granting warrant is recorded under subsection (1)(a) of section 14 of this Act; or*

(b)   *the certified copy of the determination of the Accountant in Bankruptcy awarding sequestration is recorded under subsection (1A) of that section,*

in the register of inhibitions.]

(2)   The exercise by the permanent trustee of any power conferred on him by this Act in respect of any heritable estate vested in him by virtue of the act and warrant shall not be challengeable on the ground of any prior inhibition (reserving any effect of such inhibition on ranking).

(3)   Where the debtor has an uncompleted title to any heritable estate in Scotland, the permanent trustee may complete title thereto either in his own name or in the name of the debtor, but completion of title in the name of the debtor shall not validate by accretion any unperfected right in favour of any person other than the permanent trustee.

(4)   Any moveable property, in respect of which but for this subsection—

(a)   delivery or possession; or

(b)   intimation of its assignation,

would be required in order to complete title to it, shall vest in the permanent trustee by virtue of the act and warrant as if at the date of sequestration the permanent trustee had taken delivery or possession of the property or had made intimation of its assignation to him, as the case may be.

(5)   Any non-vested contingent interest which the debtor has shall vest in the permanent trustee as if an assignation of that interest had been executed by the debtor and intimation thereof made at the date of sequestration.

(6)   Any person claiming a right to any estate claimed by the permanent trustee may apply to the court for the estate to be excluded from such vesting, a copy of the application being served on the permanent trustee; and the court shall grant the application if it is satisfied that the estate should not be so vested.

(7)   Where any successor of a deceased debtor whose estate has been sequestrated has made up title to, or is in possession of, any part of that estate, the court may, on the application of the permanent trustee, order the successor to convey such estate to him

(8)   In subsection (1) above [, subject to section 31A of this Act,] the 'whole

---

*Section 31 includes, in *italic* type, amendments made by s 17 of the Bankruptcy and Diligence etc (Scotland) Act 2007. At the date of going to press s 17 was not in force but is expected to come into effect during the lifetime of this edition.

estate of the debtor' means [subject to subsection (9) below] his whole estate at the date of sequestration, wherever situated, including—

(a)	any income or estate vesting in the debtor on that date;

[(aa)	any property of the debtor, title to which has not been completed by another person deriving right from the debtor;]

(b)	the capacity to exercise and to take proceedings for exercising, all such powers in, over, or in respect of any property as might have been exercised by the debtor for his own benefit as at, or on, the date of sequestration or might be exercised on a relevant date (within the meaning of section 32(10) of this Act).

[(9)	Subject to subsection (10) below, the 'whole estate of the debtor' does not include any interest of the debtor as tenant under any of the following tenancies—

(a)	a tenancy which is an assured tenancy within the meaning of Part II of the Housing (Scotland) Act 1988, or

(b)	a protected tenancy within the meaning of the Rent (Scotland) Act 1984 in respect of which, by virtue of any provision of Part VIII of that Act, no premium can lawfully be required as a condition of the assignation, or

(c)	a Scottish secure tenancy within the meaning of the Housing (Scotland) Act 2001 (asp 10).

(10)	On the date on which the permanent trustee serves notice to that effect on the debtor, the interest of this debtor as tenant under any of the tenancies referred to in subsection (9) above shall form part of his estate and vest in the permanent trustee as if it had vested in him under section 32(6) of this Act.]

**[31A	Proceedings under EC Regulation: modified definition of 'estate'**

In the application of this Act to insolvency proceedings under the EC Regulation, a reference to 'estate' is a reference to estate which may be dealt with in those proceedings.]

INSOLVENCY ACT 1986
(1986 c 45)

**72	Cross-border operation of receivership provisions**

(1)	A receiver appointed under the law of either part of Great Britain in respect of the whole or any part of any property or undertaking of a company and in consequence of the company having created a charge which, as created, was a floating charge may exercise his powers in the other part of Great Britain so far as their exercise is not inconsistent with the law applicable there.

(2)	In subsection (1) 'receiver' includes a manager and a person who is appointed both receiver and manager.

**426	Co-operation between courts exercising jurisdiction in relation to insolvency**

(1)	An order made by a court in any part of the United Kingdom in the exercise of jurisdiction in relation to insolvency law shall be enforced in any other part of the United Kingdom as if it were made by a court exercising the corresponding jurisdiction in that other part.

(2)	However, without prejudice to the following provisions of this section, nothing in subsection (1) requires a court in any part of the United Kingdom to enforce, in relation to property situated in that part, any order made by a court in any other part of the United Kingdom.

(3)	The Secretary of State, with the concurrence in relation to property situated in England and Wales of the Lord Chancellor, may by order make provision for securing that a trustee or assignee under the insolvency law of any part of the United Kingdom has, with such modifications as may be specified in the order, the same rights in relation to any property situated in another part of the United Kingdom as he would have in the corresponding circumstances if he were a trustee or assignee under the insolvency law of that other part.

(4)   The courts having jurisdiction in relation to insolvency law in any part of the United Kingdom shall assist the courts having the corresponding jurisdiction in any other part of the United Kingdom or any relevant country or territory.

(5)   For the purposes of subsection (4) a request made to a court in any part of the United Kingdom by a court in any other part of the United Kingdom or in a relevant country or territory is authority for the court to which the request is made to apply, in relation to any matters specified in the request, the insolvency law which is applicable by either court in relation to comparable matters falling within its jurisdiction.

In exercising its discretion under this subsection, a court shall have regard in particular to the rules of private international law.

(6)   Where a person who is a trustee or assignee under the insolvency law of any part of the United Kingdom claims property situated in any other part of the United Kingdom (whether by virtue of an order under subsection (3) or otherwise), the submission of that claim to the court exercising jurisdiction in relation to insolvency law in that other part shall be treated in the same manner as a request made by a court for the purpose of subsection (4).

(7)   Section 38 of the Criminal Law Act 1977 (execution of warrant of arrest throughout the United Kingdom) applies to a warrant which, in exercise of any jurisdiction in relation to insolvency law, is issued in any part of the United Kingdom for the arrest of a person as it applies to a warrant issued in that part of the United Kingdom for the arrest of a person charged with an offence.

(8)   Without prejudice to any power to make rules of court, any power to make provision by subordinate legislation for the purpose of giving effect in relation to companies or individuals to the insolvency law of any part of the United Kingdom includes power to make provision for the purpose of giving effect in that part to any provision made by or under the preceding provisions of this section.

(9)   An order under subsection (3) shall be made by statutory instrument subject to annulment in pursuance of a resolution of either House of Parliament.

(10)   In this section 'insolvency law' means—

(a)   in relation to England and Wales, provision extending to England and Wales and made by or under this Act or sections 1A, 6 to 10, 12 to 15, 19(c) and 20 (with Schedule 1 of the Company Directors Disqualification Act 1986 and sections 1 to 17 of that Act as they apply for the purposes of those provisions of that Act;

(b)   in relation to Scotland, provision extending to Scotland and made by or under this Act, sections 1A, 6 to 10, 12 to 15, 19(c) and 20 (with Schedule 1) of the Company Directors Disqualification Act 1986 [and sections 1 to 17 of that Act as they apply for the purposes of those provisions of that Act], Part XVIII of the Companies Act or the Bankruptcy (Scotland) Act 1985;

(c)   in relation to Northern Ireland, provision made by or under the Bankruptcy Acts (Northern Ireland) 1857 to 1980, Part V, VI or IX of the Companies Act (Northern Ireland) 1960 or Part IV of the Companies (Northern Ireland) Order 1978;

(d)   in relation to any relevant country or territory, so much of the law of that country or territory as corresponds to provisions falling within any of the foregoing paragraphs; and references in this subsection to any enactment include, in relation to any time before the coming into force of that enactment the corresponding enactment in force at that time.

(11)   In this section 'relevant country or territory' means—

(a)   any of the Channel Islands or the Isle of Man, or

(b)   any country or territory designated for the purposes of this section by the Secretary of State by order made by statutory instrument.

FAMILY LAW ACT 1986
(1986 c 55)

PART I
CHILD CUSTODY

CHAPTER III – JURISDICTION OF COURTS IN SCOTLAND

8 Jurisdiction in independent proceedings
A court in Scotland may entertain an application for a Part I order otherwise than in matrimonial [or civil partnership] proceedings only if it has jurisdiction under section 9, 10, 12 or 15(2) of this Act.

9 Habitual residence
Subject to section 11 of this Act, an application for a Part I order otherwise than in matrimonial [or civil partnership] proceedings may be entertained by—
    (a) the Court of Session if, on the date of the application, the child concerned is habitually resident in Scotland;
    (b) the sheriff if, on the date of the application, the child concerned is habitually resident in the sheriffdom.

10 Presence of child
Subject to section 11 of this Act, an application for a Part I order otherwise than in matrimonial [or civil partnership] proceedings may be entertained by—
    (a) the Court of Session if, on the date of the application, the child concerned—
        (i) is present in Scotland; and
        (ii) is not habitually resident in any part of the United Kingdom;
    (b) the sheriff if, on the date of the application,—
        (i) the child is present in Scotland;
        (ii) the child is not habitually resident in any part of the United Kingdom; and
        (iii) either the pursuer or the defender in the application is habitually resident in the sheriffdom.

11 Provisions supplementary to sections 9 and 10
    (1) Subject to subsection (2) below, the jurisdiction of the court to entertain an application for a Part I order with respect to a child by virtue of section 9, 10 or 15(2) of this Act is excluded if, on the date of the application, matrimonial or civil partnership proceedings are continuing in a court in any part of the United Kingdom in respect of the marriage or civil partnership of the parents of the child.
    (2) Subsection (1) above shall not apply in relation to an application for a Part I order if the court in which the matrimonial [or civil partnership] proceedings are continuing has made one of the following orders, that is to say—
    (a) an order under section 2A(4), 13(6) or 19A(4) of this Act (not being an order made by virtue of section 13(6)(a)(ii)); or
    (b) an order under section 5(2), 14(2) or 22(2) of this Act which is recorded as made for the purpose of enabling Part I proceedings with respect to the child concerned to be taken in Scotland or, as the case may be, in another court in Scotland,
and that order is in force.

12 Emergency jurisdiction
Notwithstanding that any other court, whether within or outside Scotland, has jurisdiction to entertain an application for a [Part I order], the Court of Session or the sheriff shall have jurisdiction to entertain such an application if—
    (a) the child concerned is present in Scotland or, as the case may be, in the sheriffdom on the date of the application; and

(b)   the Court of Session or sheriff considers that, for the protection of the child, it is necessary to make such an order immediately.

13   Jurisdiction ancillary to matrimonial proceedings

(1)   The jurisdiction of a court in Scotland to entertain an application for a Part I order in matrimonial or civil partnership proceedings shall be modified by the following provisions of this section.

(2)   A court in Scotland shall not have jurisdiction—

(a)   after the dismissal of matrimonial proceedings or after decree of absolvitor is granted therein; or

(b)   after the dismissal of civil partnership proceedings,

to entertain an application for a Part 1 order in those proceedings unless the application therefor was made on or before such dismissal or the granting of the decree of absolvitor.

(3)   Where, after a decree of separation has been granted, an application is made in the separation process for a Part I order, a court in Scotland shall not have jurisdiction to entertain that application if, on the date of the application, proceedings for divorce or nullity of marriage or proceedings for dissolution or nullity of civil partnership in respect of the marriage or civil partnership concerned are continuing in another court in the United Kingdom.

(4)   A court in Scotland shall not have jurisdiction to entertain an application for the variation of a Part I order made in matrimonial or civil partnership proceedings where the court has refused to grant the principal remedy sought in the proceedings if, on the date of the application, matrimonial or civil partnership proceedings in respect of the marriage or civil partnership concerned are continuing in another court in the United Kingdom.

(5)   Subsections (3) and (4) above shall not apply if the court in which the other proceedings there referred to are continuing has made—

(a)   an order under section 2A(4) or 19A(4) of this Act or under subsection (6) below (not being an order made by virtue of paragraph (a)(ii) of that subsection), or

(b)   an order under section 5(2), 14(2) or 22(2) of this Act which is recorded as made for the purpose of enabling Part I proceedings with respect to the child concerned to be taken in Scotland or, as the case may be, in another court in Scotland,

and that order is in force.

(6)   A court in Scotland which has jurisdiction in matrimonial [or civil partnership] proceedings to entertain an application for a Part I order with respect to a child may make an order declining such jurisdiction if—

(a)   it appears to the court with respect to that child that—

(i)   but for section 11(1) of this Act, another court in Scotland would have jurisdiction to entertain an application for a Part I order, or

(ii)   but for section 3(2), 6(3), 20(2) or 23(3) of this Act, a court in another part of the United Kingdom would have jurisdiction to make a Part I order or an order varying a Part I order; and

(b)   the court considers that it would be more appropriate for Part I matters relating to that child to be determined in that other court or part.

(7)   The court may recall an order made under subsection (6) above.

14   Power of court to refuse application or sist proceedings

(1)   A court in Scotland which has jurisdiction to entertain an application for a Part I order may refuse the application in any case where the matter in question has already been determined in other proceedings.

(2)   Where, at any stage of the proceedings on an application made to a court in Scotland for a Part I order, it appears to the court—

(a)   that proceedings with respect to the matters to which the application relates are continuing outside Scotland or in another court in Scotland;

(b)   that it would be more appropriate for those matters to be determined in proceedings outside Scotland or in another court in Scotland and that such proceedings are likely to be taken there [; or

(c)   that it should exercise its powers under Article 15 of the Council Regulation (transfer to a court better placed to hear the case),]

the court may sist the proceedings on that application [or (as the case may be) exercise its powers under Article 15 of the Council Regulation].

15   Duration, variation and recall of orders

(1)   Where, after the making by a court in Scotland of a Part I order ('the existing order') with respect to a child,—

(a)   a Part I order, or an order varying a Part I order, competently made by another court in any part of the United Kingdom with respect to that child; or

(b)   an order relating to the parental responsibilities or parental rights in relation to that child which is made outside the United Kingdom and recognised in Scotland by virtue of section 26 of this Act [or by virtue of the Council Regulation],

comes into force, the existing order shall cease to have effect so far as it makes provision for any matter for which the same or different provision is made by the order of the other court in the United Kingdom or, as the case may be, the order so recognised.

(2)   Subject to sections 11(1) and 13(3) and (4) of this Act, a court in Scotland which has made a Part I order ('the original order') may, notwithstanding that it would no longer have jurisdiction to make the original order, make an order varying or recalling the original order; but if the original order has by virtue of subsection (1) above ceased to have effect so far as it makes provision for any matter, the court shall not have power to vary that order under this subsection so as to make provision for that matter.

(3)   In subsection (2) above, an order varying an original order means any Part I order made with respect to the same child as the original order was made.

(4)   Where, by virtue of subsection (1) above, a child is to live with a different person, then, if there is in force an order made by a court in Scotland providing for the supervision of that child by a local authority, that order shall cease to have effect.

17   Orders for delivery of child

(1)   An application by one parent of a child for an order for the delivery of the child from the other parent, where the order is not sought to implement a Part I order, may be entertained by the Court of Session or a sheriff if, but only if, the Court of Session or, as the case may be, the sheriff would have jurisdiction under this Chapter to make a Part I order with respect to the child concerned.

[...]

(3)   Subsection (1) above shall apply to an application by one party to a marriage for an order for the delivery of the child concerned from the other party where the child, although not a child of both parties to the marriage, is a child of the family of those parties as it applies to an application by one parent of a child for an order for the delivery of the child from the other parent.

[(4)   In subsection (3) above, 'child of the family' means any child who has been treated by both parties as a child of their family, except a child who has been placed with those parties as foster parents by a local authority or a voluntary organisation.]

[**17A**   The provisions of this Chapter are subject to Sections 2 and 3 of Chapter II of the Council Regulation.]

18   Interpretation of Chapter III

(1)   In this Chapter—

'child' means a person who has not attained the age of sixteen;

['civil partnership proceedings' means proceedings for dissolution or nullity of a civil partnership or for the separation of the partners in a civil partnership;]

'matrimonial proceedings' means proceedings for divorce, nullity of marriage or judicial separation.

(2)   In this Chapter, 'the date of the application' means, where two or more applications are pending, the date of the first of those applications; and, for the purposes of this subsection, an application is pending until a Part I order or, in the case of an application mentioned in section 16(1) of this Act, an order relating to the guardianship of a child, has been granted in pursuance of the application or the court has refused to grant such an order.

CHAPTER V – RECOGNITION AND ENFORCEMENT

25   Recognition of Part I orders: general

(1)   Where a [Part I order] made by a court in any part of the United Kingdom is in force with respect to a child who has not attained the age of sixteen, then, subject to subsection (2) below, the order shall be recognised in any other part of the United Kingdom as having the same effect in that other part as if it had been made by the appropriate court in that other part and as if that court had had jurisdiction to make it.

(2)   Where a [Part I order] includes provision as to the means by which rights conferred by the order are to be enforced, subsection (1) above shall not apply to that provision.

(3)   A court in a part of the United Kingdom in which a [Part I order] is recognised in accordance with subsection (1) above shall not enforce the order unless it has been registered in that part of the United Kingdom under section 27 of this Act and proceedings for enforcement are taken in accordance with section 29 of this Act.

26   Recognition: special Scottish rule

(1)   An order relating to parental responsibilities or parental rights in relation to a child which is made outside the United Kingdom shall be recognised in Scotland if the order was made in the country where the child was habitually resident.

(2)   Subsection (1) above shall not apply to an order as regards which provision as to recognition is made by [Articles 21 to 27, 41(1) and 42(1)] of the Council Regulation.

27   Registration

(1)   Any person on whom any rights are conferred by a [Part I order] may apply to the court which made it for the order to be registered in another part of the United Kingdom under this section.

(2)   An application under this section shall be made in the prescribed manner and shall contain the prescribed information and be accompanied by such documents as may be prescribed.

(3)   On receiving an application under this section the court which made the [Part I order] shall, unless it appears to the court that the order is no longer in force, cause the following documents to be sent to the appropriate court in the part of the United Kingdom specified in the application, namely—

(a)   a certified copy of the order, and

(b)   where the order has been varied, prescribed particulars of any variation which is in force, and

(c)   a copy of the application and of any accompanying documents.

(4)   Where the prescribed officer of the appropriate court receives a certified copy of a [Part I order] under subsection (3) above, he shall forthwith cause the order, together with particulars of any variation, to be registered in that court in the prescribed manner.

(5)   An order shall not be registered under this section in respect of a child who

has attained the age of sixteen, and the registration of an order in respect of a child who has not attained the age of sixteen shall cease to have effect on the attainment by the child of that age.

28 Cancellation and variation of registration

(1) A court which revokes, recalls or varies an order registered under section 27 of this Act shall cause notice of the revocation, recall or variation to be given in the prescribed manner to the prescribed officer of the court in which it is registered and, on receiving the notice, the prescribed officer—

(a) in the case of the revocation or recall of the order, shall cancel the registration, and

(b) in the case of the variation of the order, shall cause particulars of the variation to be registered in the prescribed manner.

(2) Where—

(a) an order registered under section 27 of this Act ceases (in whole or in part) to have effect in the part of the United Kingdom in which it was made, otherwise than because of its revocation, recall or variation, or

(b) an order registered under section 27 of this Act in Scotland ceases (in whole or in part) to have effect there as a result of the making of an order in proceedings outside the United Kingdom.

the court in which the order is registered may, of its own motion or on the application of any person who appears to the court to have an interest in the matter, cancel the registration (or, if the order has ceased to have effect in part, cancel the registration so far as it relates to the provisions which have ceased to have effect).

29 Enforcement

(1) Where a [Part I order] has been registered under section 27 of this Act, the court in which it is registered shall have the same powers for the purpose of enforcing the order as it would have if it had itself made the order and had jurisdiction to make it; and proceedings for or with respect to enforcement may be taken accordingly.

(2) Where an application has been made to any court for the enforcement of an order registered in that court under section 27 of this Act, the court may, at any time before the application is determined, give such interim directions as it thinks fit for the purpose of securing the welfare of the child concerned or of preventing changes in the circumstances relevant to the determination of the application.

(3) The references in subsection (1) above to a [Part I order] do not include references to any provision of the order as to the means by which rights conferred by the order are to be enforced.

30 Staying or sisting of enforcement proceedings

(1) Where in accordance with section 29 of this Act proceedings are taken in any court for the enforcement of an order registered in that court, any person who appears to the court to have an interest in the matter may apply for the proceedings to be stayed or sisted on the ground that he has taken or intends to take other proceedings (in the United Kingdom or elsewhere) as a result of which the order may cease to have effect, or may have a different effect, in the part of the United Kingdom in which it is registered.

(2) If after considering an application under subsection (1) above the court considers that the proceedings for enforcement should be stayed or sisted in order that other proceedings may be taken or concluded, it shall stay or sist the proceedings for enforcement accordingly.

(3) The court may remove a stay or recall a sist granted in accordance with subsection (2) above if it appears to the court—

(a) that there has been unreasonable delay in the taking or prosecution of the other proceedings referred to in that subsection, or

(b)   that those other proceedings are concluded and that the registered order, or a relevant part of it, is still in force.

(4)   Nothing in this section shall affect any power exercisable apart from this section to grant, remove or recall a stay or sist.

31   Dismissal of enforcement proceedings

(1)   Where in accordance with section 29 of this Act proceedings are taken in any court for the enforcement of an order registered in that court, any person who appears to the court to have an interest in the matter may apply for those proceedings to be dismissed on the ground that the order has (in whole or in part) ceased to have effect in the part of the United Kingdom in which it was made.

(2)   Where in accordance with section 29 of this Act proceedings are taken in the Court of Session for the enforcement of an order registered in that court, any person who appears to the court to have an interest in the matter may apply for those proceedings to be dismissed on the ground that the order has (in whole or in part) ceased to have effect in Scotland as a result of the making of an order in proceedings outside the United Kingdom.

(3)   If, after considering an application under subsection (1) or (2) above, the court is satisfied that the registered order has ceased to have effect, it shall dismiss the proceedings for enforcement (or, if it is satisfied that the order has ceased to have effect in part, it shall dismiss the proceedings so far as they relate to the enforcement of provisions which have ceased to have effect).

32   Interpretation of Chapter V

(1)   In this Chapter—

'the appropriate court', in relation to England and Wales or Northern Ireland, means the High Court and, in relation to Scotland, means the Court of Session;

['Part I order'] includes (except where the context otherwise requires) any order within section 1(3) of this Act which, on the assumptions mentioned in subsection (3) below—

(a)   could have been made notwithstanding the provisions of this Part;

(b)   would have been a [Part I order] for the purposes of this Part; and

(c)   would not have ceased to have effect by virtue of section 6, 15 or 23 of this Act.

(2)   In the application of this Chapter to Scotland, ['Part I order'] also includes (except where the context otherwise requires) any order within section 1(3) of this Act which, on the assumptions mentioned in subsection (3) below—

(a)   would have been a [Part I order] for the purposes of this Part; and

(b)   would not have ceased to have effect by virtue of section 6 or 23 of this Act,

and which, but for the provisions of this Part, would be recognised in Scotland under any rule of law.

(3)   The said assumptions are—

(a)   that this Part had been in force at all material times; and

(b)   that any reference in section 1 of this Act to any enactment included a reference to any corresponding enactment previously in force.

CHAPTER VI – MISCELLANEOUS AND SUPPLEMENTAL

33   Power to order disclosure of child's whereabouts

(1)   Where in proceedings for or relating to a Part I order in respect of a child there is not available to the court adequate information as to where the child is, the court may order any person who it has reason to believe may have relevant information to disclose it to the court.

(2)   A person shall not be excused from complying with an order under subsection (1) above by reason that to do so may incriminate him or his spouse [or civil partner] of an offence; but a statement or admission made in compliance with

such an order shall not be admissible in evidence against either of them in proceedings for any offence other than perjury.

(3)   A court in Scotland before which proceedings are pending for the enforcement of an order relating to parental responsibilities or parental rights in relation to a child made outside the United Kingdom which is recognised in Scotland shall have the same powers as it would have under subsection (1) above if the order were its own.

34   Power to order recovery of child

(1)   Where—

(a)   a person is required by a Part I order, or an order for the enforcement of a Part I order, to give up a child to another person ('the person concerned'), and

(b)   the court which made the order imposing the requirement is satisfied that the child has not been given up in accordance with the order,

the court may make an order authorising an officer of the court or a constable to take charge of the child and deliver him to the person concerned.

(2)   The authority conferred by subsection (1) above includes authority—

(a)   to enter and search any premises where the person acting in pursuance of the order has reason to believe the child may be found, and

(b)   to use such force as may be necessary to give effect to the purpose of the order.

(3)   Where by virtue of—

(a)   section 14 of the Children Act 1989, or

(b)   [Article 14 (enforcement of residence orders) of the Children (Northern Ireland) Order 1995,] a Part I order (or a provision of a Part I order) may be enforced as if it were an order requiring a person to give up a child to another person, subsection (1) above shall apply as if the Part I order had included such a requirement.

(4)   This section is without prejudice to any power conferred on a court by or under any other enactment or rule of law.

35   Powers to restrict removal of child from jurisdiction

[...]

(3)   A court in Scotland—

(a)   at any time after the commencement of proceedings in connection with which the court would have jurisdiction to make [a Part I] order, or

(b)   in any proceedings in which it would be competent for the court to grant an interdict prohibiting the removal of a child from its jurisdiction,

may, on an application by any of the persons mentioned in subsection (4) below, grant interdict or interim interdict prohibiting the removal of the child from the United Kingdom or any part of the United Kingdom, or out of the control of the person in [whose care] the child is.

(4)   The said persons are—

(a)   any party to the proceedings,

(b)   the [guardian] of the child concerned, and

(c)   any other person who has or wishes to obtain the [...] care of the child.

(5)   In subsection (3) above 'the court' means the Court of Session or the sheriff; and for the purposes of subsection (3)(a) above, proceedings shall be held to commence—

(a)   in the Court of Session, when a summons is signeted or a petition is presented;

(b)   in the sheriff court, when the warrant of citation is signed.

36   Effect of orders restricting removal

(1)   This section applies to any order made by a court in the United Kingdom prohibiting the removal of a child from the United Kingdom or from any specified part of it.

(2)   An order to which this section applies shall have effect in each part of the United Kingdom other than the part in which it was made—
(a)   as if it had been made by the appropriate court in that other part, and
(b)   in the case of an order which has the effect of prohibiting the child's removal to that other part, as if it had included a prohibition on his further removal to any place except one to which he could be removed consistently with the order.
(3)   The references in subsections (1) and (2) above to prohibitions on a child's removal include references to prohibitions subject to exceptions; and in a case where removal is prohibited except with the consent of the court, nothing in subsection (2) above shall be construed as affecting the identity of the court whose consent is required.
(4)   In this section 'child' means a person who has not attained the age of sixteen; and this section shall cease to apply to an order relating to a child when he attains the age of sixteen.

37   Surrender of passports
(1)   Where there is in force an order prohibiting or otherwise restricting the removal of a child from the United Kingdom or from any specified part of it, the court by which the order was in fact made, or by which it is treated under section 36 of this Act as having been made, may require any person to surrender any United Kingdom passport which has been issued to, or contains particulars of, the child.
(2)   In this section 'United Kingdom passport' means a current passport issued by the Government of the United Kingdom.

38   Automatic restriction on removal of wards of court
(1)   The rule of law which (without any order of the court) restricts the removal of a ward of court from the jurisdiction of the court shall, in a case to which this section applies, have effect subject to the modifications in subsection (3) below.
(2)   This section applies in relation to a ward of court if—
(a)   proceedings for divorce, nullity or judicial separation in respect of the marriage of his parents are continuing in a court in another part of the United Kingdom (that is to say, in a part of the United Kingdom outside the jurisdiction of the court of which he is a ward),
[(aa)   proceedings for dissolution or annulment or legal separation in respect of the civil partnership of his parents are continuing in a court in another part of the United Kingdom (that is to say, in a part of the United Kingdom outside the jurisdiction of the court of which he is a ward), or]
(b)   he is habitually resident in another part of the United Kingdom,
except where that other part is Scotland and he has attained the age of sixteen.
(3)   Where this section applies, the rule referred to in subsection (1) above shall not prevent—
(a)   the removal of the ward of court, without the consent of any court, to the other part of the United Kingdom mentioned in subsection (2) above, or
(b)   his removal to any other place with the consent of either the appropriate court in that other part of the United Kingdom or the court mentioned in subsection (2)(a) [or (aa)] above.

39   Duty to furnish particulars of other proceedings
Parties to proceedings for or relating to a [Part I order] shall, to such extent and in such manner as may be prescribed, give particulars of other proceedings known to them which relate to the child concerned (including proceedings instituted abroad and proceedings which are no longer continuing).

40   Interpretation of Chapter VI
(1)   In this Chapter—
'the appropriate court' has the same meaning as in Chapter V;

['Part I order'] includes (except where the context otherwise requires) any such order as is mentioned in section 32(1) of this Act.

(2)   In the application of this Chapter to Scotland, ['Part I order'] also includes (except where the context otherwise requires) any such order as is mentioned in section 32(2) of this Act.

41   Habitual residence after removal without consent, etc
(1)   Where a child who—
   (a)   has not attained the age of sixteen, and
   (b)   is habitually resident in a part of the United Kingdom,
becomes habitually resident outside that part of the United Kingdom in consequence of circumstances of the kind specified in subsection (2) below, he shall be treated for the purposes of this Part as continuing to be habitually resident in that part of the United Kingdom for the period of one year beginning with the date on which those circumstances arise.

(2)   The circumstances referred to in subsection (1) above exist where the child is removed from or retained outside, or himself leaves or remains outside, the part of the United Kingdom in which he was habitually resident before his change of residence—
   (a)   without the agreement of the person or all the persons having, under the law of that part of the United Kingdom, the right to determine where he is to reside, or
   (b)   in contravention of an order made by a court in any part of the United Kingdom.

(3)   A child shall cease to be treated by virtue of subsection (1) above as habitually resident in a part of the United Kingdom if, during the period there mentioned—
   (a)   he attains the age of sixteen, or
   (b)   he becomes habitually resident outside that part of the United Kingdom with the agreement of the person or persons mentioned in subsection (2)(a) above and not in contravention of an order made by a court in any part of the United Kingdom.

42   General interpretation of Part I
(1)   In this Part—
'certified copy', in relation to an order of any court, means a copy certified by the prescribed officer of the court to be a true copy of the order or of the official record of the order;
['parental responsibilities' and 'parental rights' have the meanings respectively given by sections 1(3) and 2(4) of the Children (Scotland) Act 1995;]
'part of the United Kingdom' means England and Wales, Scotland or Northern Ireland;
'prescribed' means prescribed by rules of court or act of sederunt;
['the Council Regulation' means Council Regulation (EC) No 2201/2003 of 27th November 2003 concerning jurisdiction and the recognition and enforcement of judgments in matrimonial matters and matters of parental responsibility.]

(2)   For the purposes of this Part proceedings in England and Wales or in Northern Ireland for divorce, nullity or judicial separation in respect of the marriage of the parents of a child shall, unless they have been dismissed, be treated as continuing until the child concerned attains the age of eighteen (whether or not a decree has been granted and whether or not, in the case of a decree of divorce or nullity of marriage, that decree has been made absolute).

[(2A)   For the purposes of this Part proceedings in England and Wales or in Northern Ireland for dissolution, annulment or legal separation in respect of the civil partnership of the parents of the child shall, unless they have been dismissed, be treated as continuing until the child concerned attains the age of eighteen (whether or not a dissolution, nullity or separation order has been made and whether or not, in the case of a dissolution or nullity order, that order has been made final).]

(3) For the purposes of this Part, matrimonial proceedings [or civil partnership proceedings] in a court in Scotland which has jurisdiction in those proceedings to make a [Part I order] with respect to a child shall, unless they have been dismissed or decree of absolvitor has been granted therein, be treated as continuing until the child concerned attains the age of sixteen.

(4) Any reference in this Part to proceedings in respect of the marriage of the parents of a child shall, in relation to a child who, although not a child of both parties to the marriage, is a child of the family of those parties, be construed as a reference to proceedings in respect of that marriage; and for this purpose 'child of the family'—

(a)   if the proceedings are in England and Wales, means any child who has been treated by both parties as a child of their family, except a child who [is placed with those parties as foster parents] by a local authority or a voluntary organisation;

(b)   if the proceedings are in Scotland, means any child [who has been treated by both parties as a child of their family, except a child who has been placed with those parties as foster parents by a local authority or a voluntary organisation];

(c)   if the proceedings are in Northern Ireland, means any child who has been treated by both parties as a child of their family, except a child who [is placed with those parties as foster parents by an authority within the meaning of the Children (Northern Ireland) Order 1995] or a voluntary organisation.

[(4A) Any reference in this Part to proceedings in respect of the civil partnership of the parents of a child shall, in relation to a child who, although not a child of the civil partners, is a child of the family of the civil partners, be construed as a reference to proceedings in respect of that civil partnership; and for this purpose 'child of the family' has the meaning given in paragraphs (a) to (c) of subsection (4) (but substituting references to the civil partners for references to the parties to the marriage).]

(5) References in this Part to Part I orders include (except where the context otherwise requires) references to Part I orders as varied.

(6) For the purposes of this Part each of the following orders shall be treated as varying the [Part I order] to which it relates—

(a)   an order which provides for a person [to be allowed contact with or] to be given access to a child who is the subject of a [Part I order], or which makes provision for the education of such a child.

[...]

(7) [In this Part—

(a)   references to Part I proceedings in respect of a child are references to any proceedings for a Part I order or an order corresponding to a Part I order and include, in relation to proceedings outside the United Kingdom, references to proceedings before a tribunal or other authority having power under the law having effect there to determine Part I matters; and

(b)   references to Part I matters are references to matters that might be determined by a Part I order or an order corresponding to a Part I order.]

PART II
RECOGNITION OF DIVORCES, ANNULMENTS AND LEGAL SEPARATIONS
DIVORCES, ANNULMENTS AND JUDICIAL SEPARATIONS GRANTED IN
THE BRITISH ISLANDS

44   Recognition in United Kingdom of divorces, annulments and judicial separations granted in the British Islands

(1) Subject to section 52(4) and (5)(a) of this Act, no divorce or annulment

obtained in any part of the British Islands shall be regarded as effective in any part of the United Kingdom unless granted by a court of civil jurisdiction.

(2) Subject to section 51 of this Act, the validity of any divorce, annulment or judicial separation granted by a court of civil jurisdiction in any part of the British Islands shall be recognised throughout the United Kingdom.

45 Recognition in the United Kingdom of overseas divorces, annulments and legal separations

(1) Subject to subsection (2) of this section and sections 51 and 52 of this Act, the validity of a divorce, annulment or legal separation obtained in a country outside the British Islands (in this Part referred to as an overseas divorce, annulment or legal separation) shall be recognised in the United Kingdom if, and only if, it is entitled to recognition—

(a) by virtue of sections 46 to 49 of this Act, or

(b) by virtue of any enactment other than this Part.

(2) Subsection (1) and the following provisions of this Part do not apply to an overseas divorce, annulment or legal separation as regards which provision as to recognition is made by [Articles 21 to 27, 41(1) and 42(1)] of the Council Regulation.

46 Grounds for recognition

(1) The validity of an overseas divorce, annulment or legal separation obtained by means of proceedings shall be recognised if—

(a) the divorce, annulment or legal separation is effective under the law of the country in which it was obtained; and

(b) at the relevant date either party to the marriage—

(i) was habitually resident in the country in which the divorce, annulment or legal separation was obtained; or

(ii) was domiciled in that country; or

(iii) was a national of that country.

(2) The validity of an overseas divorce, annulment or legal separation obtained otherwise than by means of proceedings shall be recognised if—

(a) the divorce, annulment or legal separation is effective under the law of the country in which it was obtained;

(b) at the relevant date—

(i) each party to the marriage was domiciled in that country; or

(ii) either party to the marriage was domiciled in that country and the other party was domiciled in a country under whose law the divorce, annulment or legal separation is recognised as valid; and

(c) neither party to the marriage was habitually resident in the United Kingdom throughout the period of one year immediately preceding that date.

(3) In this section 'the relevant date' means—

(a) in the case of an overseas divorce, annulment or legal separation obtained by means of proceedings, the date of the commencement of the proceedings;

(b) in the case of an overseas divorce, annulment or legal separation obtained otherwise than by means of proceedings, the date on which it was obtained.

(4) Where in the case of an overseas annulment, the relevant date fell after the death of either party to the marriage, any reference in subsection (1) or (2) above to that date shall be construed in relation to that party as a reference to the date of death.

(5) For the purpose of this section, a party to a marriage shall be treated as domiciled in a country if he was domiciled in that country either according to the law of that country in family matters or according to the law of the part of the United Kingdom in which the question of recognition arises.

47 Cross-proceedings and divorces following legal separations

(1)   Where there have been cross-proceedings, the validity of an overseas divorce, annulment or legal separation obtained either in the original proceedings or in the cross-proceedings shall be recognised if—

(a)   the requirements of section 46(1)(b)(i), (ii) or (iii) of this Act are satisfied in relation to the date of the commencement either of the original proceedings or of the cross-proceedings, and

(b)   the validity of the divorce, annulment or legal separation is otherwise entitled to recognition by virtue of the provisions of this Part.

(2)   Where a legal separation, the validity of which is entitled to recognition by virtue of the provisions of section 46 of this Act or of subsection (1) above is converted, in the country in which it was obtained, into a divorce which is effective under the law of that country, the validity of the divorce shall be recognised whether or not it would itself be entitled to recognition by virtue of those provisions.

48 Proof of facts relevant to recognition

(1)   For the purpose of deciding whether an overseas divorce, annulment or legal separation obtained by means of proceedings is entitled to recognition by virtue of section 46 and 47 of this Act, any finding of fact made (whether expressly or by implication) in the proceedings and on the basis of which jurisdiction was assumed in the proceedings shall—

(a)   if both parties to the marriage took part in the proceedings, be conclusive evidence of the fact found; and

(b)   in any other case, be sufficient proof of that fact unless the contrary is shown.

(2)   In this section 'finding of fact' includes a finding that either party to the marriage—

(a)   was habitually resident in the country in which the divorce, annulment or legal separation was obtained; or

(b)   was under the law of that country domiciled there; or

(c)   was a national of that country.

(3)   For the purposes of subsection (1)(a) above, a party to the marriage who has appeared in judicial proceedings shall be treated as having taken part in them.

49 Modifications of Part II in relation to countries comprising territories having different systems of law

(1)   In relation to a country comprising territories in which different systems of law are in force in matters of divorce, annulment or legal separation, the provisions of this Part mentioned in subsections (2) to (5) below shall have effect subject to the modifications there specified.

(2)   In the case of a divorce, annulment or legal separation the recognition of the validity of which depends on whether the requirements of subsection (1)(b)(i) or (ii) of section 46 of this Act are satisfied, that section and, in the case of a legal separation, section 47(2) of this Act shall have effect as if each territory were a separate country.

(3)   In the case of a divorce, annulment or legal separation the recognition of the validity of which depends on whether the requirements of subsection (1)(b)(iii) of section 46 of this Act are satisfied—

(a)   that section shall have effect as if for paragraph (a) of subsection (1) there were substituted the following paragraph—

'(a)   the divorce, annulment or legal separation is effective throughout the country in which it was obtained;'; and

(b)   in the case of a legal separation, section 47(2) of this Act shall have effect as if for the words 'is effective under the law of that country' there were substituted the words 'is effective throughout that country'.

(4)   In the case of a divorce, annulment or legal separation the recognition of

the validity of which depends on whether the requirements of subsection (2)(b) of section 46 of this Act are satisfied, that section and section 52(3) and (4) of this Act and, in the case of a legal separation, section 47(2) of this Act shall have effect as if each territory were a separate country.

(5) Paragraphs (a) and (b) of section 48(2) of this Act shall each have effect as if each territory were a separate country.

50 Non-recognition of divorce or annulment in another jurisdiction no bar to remarriage

Where, in any part of the United Kingdom—

(a) a divorce or annulment has been granted by a court of civil jurisdiction, or

(b) the validity of a divorce or annulment is recognised by virtue of this Part,

the fact that the divorce or annulment would not be recognised elsewhere shall not preclude either party to the marriage from [forming a subsequent marriage or civil partnership in that part of the United Kingdom or cause the subsequent marriage or civil partnership of either party (wherever it takes place) to be treated as invalid in that part.]

51 Refusal of recognition

(1) Subject to section 52 of this Act, recognition of the validity of—

(a) a divorce, annulment or judicial separation granted by a court of civil jurisdiction in any part of the British Islands, or

(b) an overseas divorce, annulment or legal separation,

may be refused in any part of the United Kingdom if the divorce, annulment or separation was granted or obtained at a time when it was irreconcilable with a decision determining the question of the subsistence or validity of the marriage of the parties previously given (whether before or after the commencement of this Part) by a court of civil jurisdiction in that part of the United Kingdom or by a court elsewhere and recognised or entitled to be recognised in that part of the United Kingdom.

(2) Subject to section 52 of this Act, recognition of the validity of—

(a) a divorce or judicial separation granted by a court of civil jurisdiction in any part of the British Islands, or

(b) an overseas divorce or legal separation,

may be refused in any part of the United Kingdom if the divorce or separation was granted or obtained at a time when, according to the law of that part of the United Kingdom (including its rules of private international law and the provisions of this Part), there was no subsisting marriage between the parties.

(3) Subject to section 52 of this Act, recognition by virtue of section 45 of this Act of the validity of an overseas divorce, annulment or legal separation may be refused if—

(a) in the case of a divorce, annulment or legal separation obtained by means of proceedings, it was obtained—

(i) without such steps having been taken for giving notice of the proceedings to a party to the marriage as, having regard to the nature of the proceedings and all the circumstances, should reasonably have been taken; or

(ii) without a party to the marriage having been given (for any reason other than lack of notice) such opportunity to take part in the proceedings as, having regard to those matters, he should reasonably have been given; or

(b) in the case of a divorce, annulment or legal separation obtained otherwise than by means of proceedings—

(i) there is no official document certifying that the divorce, annulment or legal separation is effective under the law of the country in which it was obtained; or

(ii) where either party to the marriage was domiciled in another country at the relevant date, there is no official document certifying that the divorce, annulment or legal separation is recognised as valid under the law of that other country; or

(c)   in either case, recognition of the divorce, annulment or legal separation would be manifestly contrary to public policy.

(4)   In this section—

'official', in relation to a document certifying that a divorce, annulment or legal separation is effective, or is recognised as valid, under the law of any country, means issued by a person or body appointed or recognised for the purpose under that law;

'the relevant date' has the same meaning as in section 46 of this Act;

and subsection (5) of that section shall apply for the purposes of this section as it applies for the purposes of that section.

(5)   Nothing in this Part shall be construed as requiring the recognition of any finding of fault made in any proceedings for divorce, annulment or separation or of any maintenance, custody or other ancillary order made in any such proceedings.

52   Provisions as to divorces, annulments etc obtained before commencement of Part II

(1)   The provisions of this Part shall apply—

(a)   to a divorce, annulment or judicial separation granted by a court of civil jurisdiction in the British Islands before the date of the commencement of this Part, and

(b)   to an overseas divorce, annulment or legal separation obtained before that date,

as well as to one granted or obtained on or after that date.

(2)   In the case of such a divorce, annulment or separation as is mentioned in subsection (1)(a) or (b) above, the provisions of this Part shall require or, as the case may be, preclude the recognition of its validity in relation to any time before that date as well as in relation to any subsequent time, but those provisions shall not—

(a)   affect any property to which any person became entitled before that date, or

(b)   affect the recognition of the validity of the divorce, annulment or separation if that matter has been decided by any competent court in the British Islands before that date.

(3)   Subsections (1) and (2) above shall apply in relation to any divorce or judicial separation granted by a court of civil jurisdiction in the British Islands before the date of the commencement of this Part whether granted before or after the commencement of section 1 of the Recognition of Divorces and Legal Separations Act 1971.

(4)   The validity of any divorce, annulment or legal separation mentioned in subsection (5) below shall be recognised in the United Kingdom whether or not it is entitled to recognition by virtue of any of the foregoing provisions of this Part.

(5)   The divorces, annulments and legal separations referred to in subsection (4) above are—

(a)   a divorce which was obtained in the British Islands before 1st January 1974 and was recognised as valid under rules of law applicable before that date;

(b)   an overseas divorce which was recognised as valid under the Recognition of Divorces and Legal Separations Act 1971 and was not affected by section 16(2) of the Domicile and Matrimonial Proceedings Act 1973 (proceedings otherwise than in a court of law where both parties resident in United Kingdom);

(c)   a divorce of which the decree was registered under section 1 of the Indian and Colonial Divorce Jurisdiction Act 1926;

(d)   a divorce or annulment which-was recognised as valid under section 4 of the Matrimonial Causes (War Marriages) Act 1944; and

(e)   an overseas legal separation which was recognised as valid under the Recognition of Divorces and Legal Separations Act 1971.

54   Interpretation of Part II

(1)   In this Part—

'annulment' includes any decree or declarator of nullity of marriage, however expressed;

['the Council Regulation' means Council Regulation (EC) No 2201/2003 of 27th November 2003 concerning jurisdiction and the recognition and enforcement of judgments in matrimonial matters and matters of parental responsibility;]

'part of the United Kingdom' means England and Wales, Scotland or Northern Ireland;

'proceedings' means judicial or other proceedings.

(2)   In this Part 'country' includes a colony or other dependent territory of the United Kingdom but for the purposes of this Part a person shall be treated as a national of such a territory only if it has a law of citizenship or nationality separate from that of the United Kingdom and he is a citizen or national of that territory under that law.

<h1 style="text-align:center">RECOGNITION OF TRUSTS ACT 1987
(1987 c 14)</h1>

1   Applicable law and recognition of trusts

(1)   The provisions of the Convention set out in the Schedule to this Act shall have the force of law in the United Kingdom.

(2)   Those provisions shall, so far as applicable, have effect not only in relation to the trusts described in Articles 2 and 3 of the Convention but also in relation to any other trusts of property arising under the law of any part of the United Kingdom or by virtue of a judicial decision whether in the United Kingdom or elsewhere.

(3)   In accordance with Articles 15 and 16 such provisions of the law as are there mentioned shall, to the extent there specified, apply to the exclusion of the other provisions of the Convention.

(4)   In Article 17 the reference to a State includes a reference to any country or territory (whether or not a party to the Convention and whether or not forming part of the United Kingdom) which has its own system of law.

(5)   Article 22 shall not be construed as affecting the law to be applied in relation to anything done or omitted before the coming into force of this Act.

Section 1   SCHEDULE
CONVENTION ON THE LAW APPLICABLE TO TRUSTS AND ON THEIR
RECOGNITION

CHAPTER I – SCOPE

Article 1

This Convention specifies the law applicable to trusts and governs their recognition.

Article 2

For the purposes of this Convention, the term 'trust' refers to the legal relationship created – inter vivos or on death – by a person, the settlor, when assets have been placed under the control of a trustee for the benefit of a beneficiary or for a specified purpose.

A trust has the following characteristics—

(a)   the assets constitute a separate fund and are not a part of the trustee's own estate;

(b)   title to the trust assets stands in the name of the trustee or in the name of another person on behalf of the trustee;

(c)   the trustee has the power and the duty, in respect of which he is accountable, to manage, employ or dispose of the assets in accordance with the terms of the trust and the special duties imposed upon him by law.

The reservation by the settlor of certain rights and powers, and the fact that the trustee may himself have rights as a beneficiary, are not necessarily inconsistent with the existence of a trust.

Article 3

The Convention applies only to trusts created voluntarily and evidenced in writing.

Article 4

The Convention does not apply to preliminary issues relating to the validity of wills or of other acts by virtue of which assets are transferred to the trustee.

Article 5

The Convention does not apply to the extent that the law specified by Chapter II does not provide for trusts or the category of trusts involved.

CHAPTER II – APPLICABLE LAW

Article 6

A trust shall be governed by the law chosen by the settlor. The choice must be express or be implied in the terms of the instrument creating or the writing evidencing the trust, interpreted, if necessary, in the light of the circumstances of the case.

Where the law chosen under the previous paragraph does not provide for trusts or the category of trust involved, the choice shall not be effective and the law specified in Article 7 shall apply.

Article 7

Where no applicable law has been chosen, a trust shall be governed by the law with which it is most closely connected.

In ascertaining the law with which a trust is most closely connected reference shall be made in particular to—

(a)   the place of administration of the trust designated by the settlor;

(b)   the situs of the assets of the trust;

(c)   the place of residence or business of the trustee;

(d)   the objects of the trust and the places where they are to be fulfilled.

Article 8

The law specified by Article 6 or 7 shall govern the validity of the trust, its construction, its effects and the administration of the trust.

In particular that law shall govern—

(a)   the appointment, resignation and removal of trustees, the capacity to act as a trustee, and the devolution of the office of trustee;

(b)   the rights and duties of trustees among themselves;

(c)   the right of trustees to delegate in whole or in part the discharge of their duties or the exercise of their powers;

(d)   the power of trustees to administer or to dispose of trust assets, to create security interests in the trust assets, or to acquire new assets;

(e)   the powers of investment of trustees;

(f)   restrictions upon the duration of the trust, and upon the power to accumulate the income of the trust;

(g)   the relationships between the trustees and the beneficiaries including the personal liability of the trustees to the beneficiaries;

(h)   the variation or termination of the trust;

(i)   the distribution of the trust assets;

(j)   the duty of trustees to account for their administration.

Article 9

In applying this Chapter a severable aspect of the trust, particularly matters of administration, may be governed by a different law.

Article 10

The law applicable to the validity of the trust shall determine whether that law or the law governing a severable aspect of the trust may be replaced by another law.

CHAPTER III – RECOGNITION

Article 11

A trust created in accordance with the law specified by the preceding Chapter shall be recognised as a trust.

Such recognition shall imply, as a minimum, that the trust property constitutes a separate fund, that the trustee may sue and be sued in his capacity as trustee, and that he may appear or act in this capacity before a notary or any person acting in an official capacity.

In so far as the law applicable to the trust requires or provides, such recognition shall imply in particular—

(a)   that personal creditors of the trustee shall have no recourse against the trust assets;

(b)   that the trust assets shall not form part of the trustee's estate upon his insolvency or bankruptcy;

(c)   that the trust assets shall not form part of the matrimonial property of the trustee or his spouse nor part of the trustee's estate upon his death;

(d)   that the trust assets may be recovered when the trustee, in breach of trust, has mingled trust assets with his own property or has alienated trust assets. However, the rights and obligations of any third party holder of the assets shall remain subject to the law determined by the choice of law rules of the forum.

Article 12

Where the trustee desires to register assets, movable or immovable, or documents of title to them, he shall be entitled, in so far as this is not prohibited by or inconsistent with the law of the State where registration is sought, to do so in his capacity as trustee or in such other way that the existence of the trust is disclosed.

Article 14

The Convention shall not prevent the application of rules of law more favourable to the recognition of trusts.

CHAPTER IV – GENERAL CLAUSES

Article 15

The Convention does not prevent the application of provisions of the law designated by the conflicts rules of the forum, in so far as those provisions cannot be derogated from by voluntary act, relating in particular to the following matters—

(a)   the protection of minors and incapable parties;

(b)   the personal and proprietary effects of marriage;

(c)   succession rights, testate and intestate, especially the indefeasible shares of spouses and relatives;

(d)   the transfer of title to property and security interests in property;

(e)   the protection of creditors in matters of insolvency;

(f)   the protection, in other respects, of third parties acting in good faith.

If recognition of a trust is prevented by application of the preceding paragraph, the court shall try to give effect to the objects of the trust by other means.

Article 16

The Convention does not prevent the application of those provisions of the law of the forum which must be applied even to international situations, irrespective of rules of conflict of laws.

Article 17

In the Convention the word 'law' means the rules of law in force in a State other than its rules of conflict of laws.

Article 18

The provisions of the Convention may be disregarded when their application would be manifestly incompatible with public policy.

Article 22

The Convention applies to trusts regardless of the date on which they were created.

CONTRACTS (APPLICABLE LAW) ACT 1990
(1990 c 36)

1   Meaning of 'the Conventions'

In this Act—

(a)   'the Rome Convention' means the Convention on the law applicable to contractual obligations opened for signature in Rome on 19th June 1980 and signed by the United Kingdom on 7th December 1981;

(b)   'the Luxembourg Convention' means the Convention on the accession of the Hellenic Republic to the Rome Convention signed by the United Kingdom in Luxembourg on 10th April 1984; and

(c)   'the Brussels Protocol' means the first Protocol on the interpretation of the Rome Convention by the European Court signed by the United Kingdom in Brussels on 19th December 1988;

[(d)   'the Funchal Convention' means the Convention on the accession of the Kingdom of Spain and the Portuguese Republic to the Rome Convention and the Brussels Protocol, with adjustments made to the Rome Convention by the Luxembourg Convention, signed by the United Kingdom in Funchal on 18th May 1992;]

and these Conventions and this Protocol are together referred to as 'the Conventions'.

2   Conventions to have force of law

(1)   Subject to subsections (2) and (3) below, the Conventions shall have the force of law in the United Kingdom.

[(1A)   The internal law for the purposes of Article 1(3) of the Rome Convention is the provisions of the regulations for the time being in force under section 424(3) of the Financial Services and Markets Act 2000.]

(2)   Articles 7(1) and 10(1)(e) of the Rome Convention shall not have the force of law in the United Kingdom.

(3)   Notwithstanding Article 19(2) of the Rome Convention, the Conventions shall apply in the case of conflicts between the laws of different parts of the United Kingdom.

(4)   For ease of reference there are set out in Schedules 1, 2, 3 and 3A to this Act respectively the English texts of—

(a)   the Rome Convention;

(b)   the Luxembourg Convention;

(c)   the Brussels Protocol; and

(d)   the Funchal Convention.

3   Interpretation of Conventions

(1)   Any question as to the meaning or effect of any provision of the Conventions shall, if not referred to the European Court in accordance with the Brussels Protocol, be determined in accordance with the principles laid down by, and any relevant decision of, the European Court.

(2)   Judicial notice shall be taken of any decision of, or expression of opinion by, the European Court on any such question.

(3)   Without prejudice to any practice of the courts as to the matters which may be considered apart from this subsection—

(a)   the report on the Rome Convention by Professor Mario Giuliano and Professor Paul Lagarde which is reproduced in the Official Journal of the Communities of 31st October 1980 may be considered in ascertaining the meaning or effect of any provision of that Convention; and

(b)   any report on the Brussels Protocol which is reproduced in the Official Journal of the Communities may be considered in ascertaining the meaning or effect of any provision of that Protocol.

4   Revision of Conventions etc

(1)   If at any time it appears to Her Majesty in Council that Her Majesty's Government in the United Kingdom—

(a)   have agreed to a revision of any of the Conventions (including, in particular, any revision connected with the accession to the Rome Convention of any state); or

(b)   have given notification in accordance with Article 22(3) of the Rome Convention that either or both of the provisions mentioned in section 2(2) above shall have the force of law in the United Kingdom,

Her Majesty may by Order in Council make such consequential modifications of this Act or any other statutory provision, whenever passed or made, as Her Majesty considers appropriate.

(2)   An Order in Council under subsection (1) above shall not be made unless a draft of the Order has been laid before Parliament and approved by a resolution of each House.

(3)   In subsection (1) above—

'modifications' includes additions, omissions and alterations;

'revision' means an omission from, addition to or alteration of any of the Conventions and includes replacement of any of the Conventions to any extent by another convention, protocol or other description of international agreement; and

'statutory provision' means any provision contained in an Act, or in any Northern Ireland legislation, or in—

(a)   subordinate legislation (as defined in section 21(1) of the Interpretation Act 1978); or

(b)   any instrument of a legislative character made under any Northern Ireland legislation.

...

6   Application to Crown

This Act binds the Crown.

SCHEDULE 1

THE ROME CONVENTION

The High Contracting Parties to the Treaty establishing the European Economic Community,

Anxious to continue in the field of private international law the work of unification of law which has already been done within the Community, in particular in the field of jurisdiction and enforcement of judgments,

Wishing to establish uniform rules concerning the law applicable to contractual obligations,

Have agreed as follows:

TITLE I – SCOPE OF THE CONVENTION

Article 1. Scope of the Convention

1. The rules of this Convention shall apply to contractual obligations in any situation involving a choice between the laws of different countries.

2. They shall not apply to:

(a) questions involving the status or legal capacity of natural persons, without prejudice to Article 11;

(b) contractual obligations relating to:

– wills and succession,

– rights in property arising out of a matrimonial relationship,

– rights and duties arising out of a family relationship, parentage, marriage or affinity, including maintenance obligations in respect of children who are not legitimate;

(c) obligations arising under bills of exchange, cheques and promissory notes and other negotiable instruments to the extent that the obligations under such other negotiable instruments arise out of their negotiable character;

(d) arbitration agreements and agreements on the choice of court;

(e) questions governed by the law of companies and other bodies corporate or unincorporate such as the creation, by registration or otherwise, legal capacity, internal organisation or winding up of companies and other bodies corporate or unincorporate and the personal liability of officers and members as such for the obligations of the company or body;

(f) the question whether an agent is able to bind a principal, or an organ to bind a company or body corporate or unincorporate, to a third party;

(g) the constitution of trusts and the relationship between settlors, trustees and beneficiaries;

(h) evidence and procedure, without prejudice to Article 14.

3. The rules of this Convention do not apply to contracts of insurance which cover risks situated in the territories of the Member States of the European Economic Community. In order to determine whether a risk is situated in these territories the court shall apply its internal law.

4. The preceding paragraph does not apply to contracts of re-insurance.

Article 2. Application of law of non-contracting States

Any law specified by this Convention shall be applied whether or not it is the law of a Contracting State.

TITLE II – UNIFORM RULES

Article 3. Freedom of choice

1. A contract shall be governed by the law chosen by the parties. The choice must be express or demonstrated with reasonable certainty by the terms of the contract or the circumstances of the case. By their choice the parties can select the law applicable to the whole or a part only of the contract.

2. The parties may at any time agree to subject the contract to a law other than that which previously governed it, whether as a result of an earlier choice under this Article or of other provisions of this Convention. Any variation by the parties of the law to be applied made after the conclusion of the contract shall not prejudice its formal validity under Article 9 or adversely affect the rights of third parties.

3.   The fact that the parties have chosen a foreign law, whether or not accompanied by the choice of a foreign tribunal, shall not, where all the other elements relevant to the situation at the time of the choice are connected with one country only, prejudice the application of rules of the law of that country which cannot be derogated from by contract, hereinafter called 'mandatory rules'.

4.   The existence and validity of the consent of the parties as to the choice of the applicable law shall be determined in accordance with the provisions of Articles 8, 9 and 11.

Article 4. Applicable law in the absence of choice

1.   To the extent that the law applicable to the contract has not been chosen in accordance with Article 3, the contract shall be governed by the law of the country with which it is most closely connected. Nevertheless, a severable part of the contract which has a closer connection with another country may by way of exception be governed by the law of that other country.

2.   Subject to the provisions of paragraph 5 of this Article, it shall be presumed that the contract is most closely connected with the country where the party who is to effect the performance which is characteristic of the contract has, at the time of conclusion of the contract, his habitual residence, or, in the case of a body corporate or unincorporate, its central administration. However, if the contract is entered into in the course of that party's trade or profession, that country shall be the country in which the principal place of business is situated or, where under the terms of the contract the performance is to be effected through a place of business other than the principal place of business, the country in which that other place of business is situated.

3.   Notwithstanding the provisions of paragraph 2 of this Article, to the extent that the subject matter of the contract is a right in immovable property or a right to use immovable property it shall be presumed that the contract is most closely connected with the country where the immovable property is situated.

4.   A contract for the carriage of goods shall not be subject to the presumption in paragraph 2. In such a contract if the country in which, at the time the contract is concluded, the carrier has his principal place of business is also the country in which the place of loading or the place of discharge or the principal place of business of the consignor is situated, it shall be presumed that the contract is most closely connected with that country. In applying this paragraph single voyage charter-parties and other contracts the main purpose of which is the carriage of goods shall be treated as contracts for the carriage of goods.

5.   Paragraph 2 shall not apply if the characteristic performance cannot be determined, and the presumptions in paragraphs 2, 3 and 4 shall be disregarded if it appears from the circumstances as a whole that the contract is more closely connected with another country.

Article 5. Certain consumer contracts

1.   This Article applies to a contract the object of which is the supply of goods or services to a person ('the consumer') for a purpose which can be regarded as being outside his trade or profession, or a contract for the provision of credit for that object.

2.   Notwithstanding the provisions of Article 3, a choice of law made by the parties shall not have the result of depriving the consumer of the protection afforded to him by the mandatory rules of the law of the country in which he has his habitual residence:

  – if in that country the conclusion of the contract was preceded by a specific invitation addressed to him or by advertising, and he had taken in that country all the steps necessary on his part for the conclusion of the contract, or

  – if the other party or his agent received the consumer's order in that country, or

  – if the contract is for the sale of goods and the consumer travelled from that country to another country and there gave his order, provided that the consumer's journey was arranged by the seller for the purpose of inducing the consumer to buy.

3.   Notwithstanding the provisions of Article 4, a contract to which this Article applies shall, in the absence of choice in accordance with Article 3, be governed by the law of the country in which the consumer has his habitual residence if it is entered into in the circumstances described in paragraph 2 of this Article.

4.   This Article shall not apply to:

(a)   a contract of carriage;

(b)   a contract for the supply of services where the services are to be supplied to the consumer exclusively in a country other than that in which he has his habitual residence.

5.   Notwithstanding the provisions of paragraph 4, this Article shall apply to a contract which, for an inclusive price, provides for a combination of travel and accommodation.

Article 6. Individual employment contracts

1.   Notwithstanding the provisions of Article 3, in a contract of employment a choice of law made by the parties shall not have the result of depriving the employee of the protection afforded to him by the mandatory rules of the law which would be applicable under paragraph 2 in the absence of choice.

2.   Notwithstanding the provisions of Article 4, a contract of employment shall, in the absence of choice in accordance with Article 3, be governed:

(a)   by the law of the country in which the employee habitually carries out his work in performance of the contract, even if he is temporarily employed in another country; or

(b)   if the employee does not habitually carry out his work in any one country, by the law of the country in which the place of business through which he was engaged is situated;

unless it appears from the circumstances as a whole that the contract is more closely connected with another country, in which case the contract shall be governed by the law of that country.

Article 7. Mandatory rules

1.   When applying under this Convention the law of a country, effect may be given to the mandatory rules of the law of another country with which the situation has a close connection, if and in so far as, under the law of the latter country, those rules must be applied whatever the law applicable to the contract. In considering whether to give effect to these mandatory rules, regard shall be had to their nature and purpose and to the consequences of their application or non-application.

2.   *Nothing in this Convention shall restrict the application of the rules of the law of the forum in a situation where they are mandatory irrespective of the law otherwise applicable to the contract.**

Article 8. Material validity

1.   The existence and validity of a contract, or of any term of a contract, shall be determined by the law which would govern it under this Convention if the contract or term were valid.

2.   Nevertheless a party may rely upon the law of the country in which he has his habitual residence to establish that he did not consent if it appears from the circumstances that it would not be reasonable to determine the effect of his conduct in accordance with the law specified in the preceding paragraph.

---

* The UK entered a reservation disapplying Arts 7(2) and 10(1)(e) in UK courts.

Article 9. Formal validity

1.   A contract concluded between persons who are in the same country is formally valid if it satisfies the formal requirements of the law which governs it under this Convention or of the law of the country where it is concluded.

2.   A contract concluded between persons who are in different countries is formally valid if it satisfies the formal requirements of the law which governs it under this Convention or of the law of one of those countries.

3.   Where a contract is concluded by an agent, the country in which the agent acts is the relevant country for the purposes of paragraphs 1 and 2.

4.   An act intended to have legal effect relating to an existing or contemplated contract is formally valid if it satisfies the formal requirements of the law which under this Convention governs or would govern the contract or of the law of the country where the act was done.

5.   The provisions of the preceding paragraphs shall not apply to a contract to which Article 5 applies, concluded in the circumstances described in paragraph 2 of Article 5. The formal validity of such a contract is governed by the law of the country in which the consumer has his habitual residence.

6.   Notwithstanding paragraphs 1 to 4 of this Article, a contract the subject matter of which is a right in immovable property or a right to use immovable property shall be subject to the mandatory requirements of form of the law of the country where the property is situated if by that law those requirements are imposed irrespective of the country where the contract is concluded and irrespective of the law governing the contract.

Article 10. Scope of the applicable law

1.   The law applicable to a contract by virtue of Articles 3 to 6 and 12 of this Convention shall govern in particular:

   (a)   interpretation;
   (b)   performance;
   (c)   within the limits of the powers conferred on the court by its procedural law, the consequences of breach, including the assessment of damages in so far as it is governed by rules of law;
   (d)   the various ways of extinguishing obligations, and prescription and limitation of actions;
   (e)   *the consequences of nullity of the contract.**

2.   In relation to the manner of performance and the steps to be taken in the event of defective performance regard shall be had to the law of the country in which performance takes place.

Article 11. Incapacity

In a contract concluded between persons who are in the same country, a natural person who would have capacity under the law of that country may invoke his incapacity resulting from another law only if the other party to the contract was aware of this incapacity at the time of the conclusion of the contract or was not aware thereof as a result of negligence.

Article 12. Voluntary assignment

1.   The mutual obligations of assignor and assignee under a voluntary assignment of a right against another person ('the debtor') shall be governed by the law which under this Convention applies to the contract between the assignor and assignee.

2.   The law governing the right to which the assignment relates shall determine its assignability, the relationship between the assignee and the debtor, the conditions under which the assignment can be invoked against the debtor and any question whether the debtor's obligations have been discharged.

Article 13. Subrogation

1.   Where a person ('the creditor') has a contractual claim upon another ('the

debtor'), and a third person has a duty to satisfy the creditor, or has in fact satisfied the creditor in discharge of that duty, the law which governs the third person's duty to satisfy the creditor shall determine whether the third person is entitled to exercise against the debtor the rights which the creditor had against the debtor under the law governing their relationship and, if so, whether he may do so in full or only to a limited extent.

2.   The same rule applies where several persons are subject to the same contractual claim and one of them has satisfied the creditor.

Article 14. Burden of proof, etc
1.   The law governing the contract under this Convention applies to the extent that it contains, in the law of contract, rules which raise presumptions of law or determine the burden of proof.

2.   A contract or an act intended to have legal effect may be proved by any mode of proof recognised by the law of the forum or by any of the laws referred to in Article 9 under which that contract or act is formally valid, provided that such mode of proof can be administered by the forum.

Article 15. Exclusion of renvoi
The application of the law of any country specified by this Convention means the application of the rules of law in force in that country other than its rules of private international law.

Article 16. 'Ordre public'
The application of a rule of the law of any country specified by this Convention may be refused only if such application is manifestly incompatible with the public policy ('ordre public') of the forum.

Article 17. No retrospective effect
This Convention shall apply in a Contracting State to contracts made after the date on which this Convention has entered into force with respect to that State.

Article 18. Uniform interpretation
In the interpretation and application of the preceding uniform rules, regard shall be had to their international character and to the desirability of achieving uniformity in their interpretation and application.

Article 19. States with more than one legal system
1.   Where a State comprises several territorial units each of which has its own rules of law in respect of contractual obligations, each territorial unit shall be considered as a country for the purposes of identifying the law applicable under this Convention.

2.   A State within which different territorial units have their own rules of law in respect of contractual obligations shall not be bound to apply this Convention to conflicts solely between the laws of such units.

Article 20. Precedence of Community law
This Convention shall not affect the application of provisions which, in relation to particular matters, lay down choice of law rules relating to contractual obligations and which are or will be contained in acts of the institutions of the European Communities or in national laws harmonised in implementation of such acts.

Article 21. Relationship with other conventions
This Convention shall not prejudice the application of international conventions to which a Contracting State is, or becomes, a party.

Article 22. Reservations
1.   Any Contracting State may, at the time of signature, ratification, acceptance or approval, reserve the right not to apply:
    (a)   the provisions of Article 7(1);

(b)   the provisions of Article 10(1)(e).

3.   Any Contracting State may at any time withdraw a reservation which it has made; the reservation shall cease to have effect on the first day of the third calendar month after notification of the withdrawal.

TITLE III – FINAL PROVISIONS

Article 23

1.   If, after the date on which this Convention has entered into force for a Contracting State, that State wishes to adopt any new choice of law rule in regard to any particular category of contract within the scope of this Convention, it shall communicate its intention to the other signatory States through the Secretary-General of the Council of the European Communities.

2.   Any signatory State may, within six months from the date of the communication made to the Secretary-General, request him to arrange consultations between signatory States in order to reach agreement.

3.   If no signatory State has requested consultations within this period or if within two years following the communication made to the Secretary-General no agreement is reached in the course of consultations, the Contracting State concerned may amend its law in the manner indicated. The measures taken by that State shall be brought to the knowledge of the other signatory States through the Secretary-General of the Council of the European Communities.

Article 24

1.   If, after the date on which this Convention has entered into force with respect to a Contracting State, that State wishes to become a party to a multilateral convention whose principal aim or one of whose principal aims is to lay down rules of private international law concerning any of the matters governed by this Convention, the procedure set out in Article 23 shall apply. However, the period of two years, referred to in paragraph 3 of that Article, shall be reduced to one year.

2.   The procedure referred to in the preceding paragraph need not be followed if a Contracting State or one of the European Communities is already a party to the multilateral convention, or if its object is to revise a convention to which the State concerned is already a party, or if it is a convention concluded within the framework of the Treaties establishing the European Communities.

Article 25

If a Contracting State considers that the unification achieved by this Convention is prejudiced by the conclusion of agreements not covered by Article 24(1), that State may request the Secretary-General of the Council of the European Communities to arrange consultations between the signatory States of this Convention.

Article 26

Any Contracting State may request the revision of this Convention. In this event a revision conference shall be convened by the President of the Council of the European Communities.

Article 28

1.   This Convention shall be open from 19 June 1980 for signature by the States party to the Treaty establishing the European Economic Community.

2.   This Convention shall be subject to ratification, acceptance or approval by the signatory States. The instruments of ratification, acceptance or approval shall be deposited with the Secretary-General of the Council of the European Communities.

Article 29

1.   This Convention shall enter into force on the first day of the third month following the deposit of the seventh instrument of ratification, acceptance or approval.

2. This Convention shall enter into force for each signatory State ratifying, accepting or approving at a later date on the first day of the third month following the deposit of its instrument of ratification, acceptance or approval.

Article 30
1. This Convention shall remain in force for 10 years from the date of its entry into force in accordance with Article 29(1), even for States for which it enters into force at a later date.

2. If there has been no denunciation it shall be renewed tacitly every five years.

3. A Contracting State which wishes to denounce shall, not less than six months before the expiration of the period of 10 or five years, as the case may be, give notice to the Secretary-General of the Council of the European Communities.

4. The denunciation shall have effect only in relation to the State which has notified it. The Convention will remain in force as between all other Contracting States.

Article 31
The Secretary-General of the Council of the European Communities shall notify the States party to the Treaty establishing the European Economic Community of:
(a)   the signatures;
(b)   the deposit of each instrument of ratification, acceptance or approval;
(c)   the date of entry into force of this Convention;
(d)   communications made in pursuance of Articles 23, 24, 25, 26 and 30;
(e)   the reservations and withdrawals of reservations referred to in Article 22.

Article 32
The Protocol annexed to this Convention shall form an integral part thereof.

SCHEDULE 3
THE BRUSSELS PROTOCOL

The High Contracting Parties to the Treaty establishing the European Economic Community,

Having regard to the Joint Declaration annexed to the Convention on the law applicable to contractual obligations, opened for signature in Rome on 19 June 1980,

Have decided to conclude a Protocol conferring jurisdiction on the Court of Justice of the European Communities to interpret that Convention, and to this end have designated as their Plenipotentiaries:

(Designation of plenipotentiaries)

Who, meeting within the Council of the European Communities, having exchanged their full powers, found in good and due form,

Have agreed as follows:

Article 1
The Court of Justice of the European Communities shall have jurisdiction to give rulings on the interpretation of—
(a)   the Convention on the law applicable to contractual obligations, opened for signature in Rome on 19 June 1980, hereinafter referred to as 'the Rome Convention';
(b)   the Convention on accession to the Rome Convention by the States which have become Members of the European Communities since the date on which it was opened for signature;
(c)   this Protocol.

Article 2
Any of the courts referred to below may request the Court of Justice to give a preliminary ruling on a question raised in a case pending before it and concerning

interpretation of the provisions contained in the instruments referred to in Article 1 if that court considers that a decision on the question is necessary to enable it to give judgment:

    (a) ...

    – in the United Kingdom:

    the House of Lords and other courts from which no further appeal is possible;

    (b) the courts of the Contracting States when acting as appeal courts.

Article 3

1. The competent authority of a Contracting State may request the Court of Justice to give a ruling on a question of interpretation of the provisions contained in the instruments referred to in Article 1 if judgments given by courts of that State conflict with the interpretation given either by the Court of Justice or in a judgment of one of the courts of another Contracting State referred to in Article 2. The provisions of this paragraph shall apply only to judgments which have become res judicata.

2. The interpretation given by the Court of Justice in response to such a request shall not affect the judgments which gave rise to the request for interpretation.

3. The Procurators-General of the Supreme Courts of Appeal of the Contracting States, or any other authority designated by a Contracting State, shall be entitled to request the Court of Justice for a ruling on interpretation in accordance with paragraph 1.

4. The Registrar of the Court of Justice shall give notice of the request to the Contracting States, to the Commission and to the Council of the European Communities; they shall then be entitled within two months of the notification to submit statements of case or written observations to the Court.

5. No fees shall be levied or any costs or expenses awarded in respect of the proceedings provided for in this Article.

...

Article 9

This Protocol shall have effect for as long as the Rome Convention remains in force under the conditions laid down in Article 30 of that Convention.

Article 10

Any Contracting State may request the revision of this Protocol. In this event, a revision conference shall be convened by the President of the Council of the European Communities.

FOREIGN CORPORATIONS ACT 1991
(1991 c 44)

1 Recognition of corporate status of certain foreign corporations

    (1) If at any time—

    (a) any question arises whether a body which purports to have or, as the case may be, which appears to have lost corporate status under the laws of a territory which is not at that time a recognised State should or should not be regarded as having legal personality as a body corporate under the law of any part of the United Kingdom, and

    (b) it appears that the laws of that territory are at that time applied by a settled court system in that territory,

that question and any other material question relating to the body shall be determined (and account shall be taken of those laws) as if that territory were a recognised State.

    (2) For the purposes of subsection (1) above—

(a)   'a recognised State' is a territory which is recognised by Her Majesty's Government in the United Kingdom as a State;

(b)   the laws of a territory which is so recognised shall be taken to include the laws of any part of the territory which are ac-knowledged by the federal or other central government of the territory as a whole; and

(c)   a material question is a question (whether as to capacity, constitution or otherwise) which, in the case of a body corporate, falls to be determined by reference to the laws of the territory under which the body is incorporated.

(3)   Any registration or other thing done at a time before the coming into force of this section shall be regarded as valid if it would have been valid at that time, had subsections (1) and (2) above then been in force.

CHILDREN (SCOTLAND) ACT 1995
(1995 c 36)

14   Jurisdiction and choice of law in relation to certain matters

(1)   The Court of Session shall have jurisdiction to entertain an application for an order relating to the administration of a child's property if the child is habitually resident in, or the property is situated in, Scotland.

(2)   A sheriff shall have jurisdiction to entertain such an application if the child is habitually resident in, or the property is situated in, the sheriffdom.

(3)   Subject to subsection (4) below, any question arising under this Part of this Act—

(a)   concerning—

(i)   parental responsibilities or parental rights; or

(ii)   the responsibilities or rights of a guardian,

in relation to a child shall, in so far as it is not also a question such as is mentioned in paragraph (b) below, be determined by the law of the place of the child's habitual residence at the time when the question arises;

(b)   concerning the immediate protection of a child shall be determined by the law of the place where the child is when the question arises; and

(c)   as to whether a person is validly appointed or constituted guardian of a child's shall be determined by the law of the place of the child's habitual residence on the date when the appointment was made (the date of death of the testator being taken to be the date of appointment where an appointment was made by will), or the event constituting the guardianship occurred.

(4)   Nothing in any provision of law in accordance with which, under subsection (3) above, a question which arises in relation to an application for, or the making of, an order under subsection (1) of section 11 of this Act falls to be determined, shall affect the application of subsection (7) of that section.

[(5)   The provisions of sections 9, 11, 13 and this section are subject to Sections 2 and 3 of Chapter II of Council Regulation (EC) No 2201/2003 of 27th November 2003 concerning jurisdiction and the recognition and enforcement of judgments in matrimonial matters and matters of parental responsibility.]

PRIVATE INTERNATIONAL LAW (MISCELLANEOUS PROVISIONS) ACT 1995
(1995 c 42)

PART II
VALIDITY OF MARRIAGES UNDER A LAW WHICH PERMITS POLYGAMY

7   Validity and effect in Scots law of potentially polygamous marriages

(1)   A person domiciled in Scotland does not lack capacity to enter into a marriage by reason only that the marriage is entered into under a law which permits polygamy.

(2)   For the avoidance of doubt, a marriage valid by the law of Scotland and entered into—

(a)   under a law which permits polygamy; and

(b)   at a time when neither party to the marriage is already married,

has, so long as neither party marries a second spouse during the subsistence of the marriage, the same effects for all purposes of the law of Scotland as a marriage entered into under a law which does not permit polygamy.

PART III

CHOICE OF LAW IN TORT AND DELICT

9   Purpose of Part III

(1)   The rules in this Part apply for choosing the law (in this Part referred to as 'the applicable law') to be used for determining issues relating to tort or (for the purposes of the law of Scotland) delict.

(2)   The characterisation for the purposes of private international law of issues arising in a claim as issues relating to tort or delict is a matter for the courts of the forum.

(3)   The rules in this Part do not apply in relation to issues arising in any claim excluded from the operation of this Part by section 13 below.

(4)   The applicable law shall be used for determining the issues arising in a claim, including in particular the question whether an actionable tort or delict has occurred.

(5)   The applicable law to be used for determining the issues arising in a claim shall exclude any choice of law rules forming part of the law of the country or countries concerned.

(6)   For the avoidance of doubt (and without prejudice to the operation of section 14 below) this Part applies in relation to events occurring in the forum as it applies in relation to events occurring in any other country.

(7)   In this Part as it extends to any country within the United Kingdom, 'the forum' means England and Wales, Scotland or Northern Ireland, as the case may be.

(8)   In this Part 'delict' includes quasi-delict.

10   Abolition of certain common law rules

The rules of the common law, in so far as they—

(a)   require actionability under both the law of the forum and the law of another country for the purpose of determining whether a tort or delict is actionable; or

(b)   allow (as an exception from the rules falling within paragraph (a) above) for the law of a single country to be applied for the purpose of determining the issues, or any of the issues, arising in the case in question,

are hereby abolished so far as they apply to any claim in tort or delict which is not excluded from the operation of this Part by section 13 below.

11   Choice of applicable law: the general rule

(1)   The general rule is that the applicable law is the law of the country in which the events constituting the tort or delict in question occur.

(2)   Where elements of those events occur in different countries, the applicable law under the general rule is to be taken as being—

(a)   for a cause of action in respect of personal injury caused to an individual or death resulting from personal injury, the law of the country where the individual was when he sustained the injury;

(b)   for a cause of action in respect of damage to property, the law of the country where the property was when it was damaged; and

(c)   in any other case, the law of the country in which the most significant element or elements of those events occurred.

(3)   In this section 'personal injury' includes disease or any impairment of physical or mental condition.

12   Choice of applicable law: displacement of general rule

(1)   If it appears, in all the circumstances, from a comparison of—

(a)   the significance of the factors which connect a tort or delict with the country whose law would be the applicable law under the general rule; and

(b)   the significance of any factors connecting the tort or delict with another country,

that it is substantially more appropriate for the applicable law for determining the issues arising in the case, or any of those issues, to be the law of the other country, the general rule is displaced and the applicable law for determining those issues or that issue (as the case may be) is the law of that other country.

(2)   The factors that may be taken into account as connecting a tort or delict with a country for the purposes of this section include, in particular, factors relating to the parties, to any of the events which constitute the tort or delict in question or to any of the circumstances or consequences of those events.

13   Exclusion of defamation claims from Part III

(1)   Nothing in this Part applies to affect the determination of issues arising in any defamation claim.

(2)   For the purposes of this section 'defamation claim' means —

(a)   any claim under the law of any part of the United Kingdom for libel or slander or for slander of title, slander of goods or other malicious falsehood and any claim under the law of Scotland for verbal injury; and

(b)   any claim under the law of any other country corresponding to or otherwise in the nature of a claim mentioned in paragraph (a) above.

14   Transitional provision and savings

(1)   Nothing in this Part applies to acts or omissions giving rise to a claim which occur before the commencement of this Part.

(2)   Nothing in this Part affects any rules of law (including rules of private international law) except those abolished by section 10 above.

(3)   Without prejudice to the generality of subsection (2) above, nothing in this Part—

(a)   authorises the application of the law of a country outside the forum as the applicable law for determining issues arising in any claim in so far as to do so—

(i)   would conflict with principles of public policy; or

(ii)   would give effect to such a penal, revenue or other public law as would not otherwise be enforceable under the law of the forum; or

(b)   affects any rules of evidence, pleading or practice or authorises questions of procedure in any proceedings to be determined otherwise than in accordance with the law of the forum.

(4)   This Part has effect without prejudice to the operation of any rule of law which either has effect notwithstanding the rules of private international law applicable in the particular circumstances or modifies the rules of private international law that would otherwise be so applicable.

15   Crown application

(1)   This Part applies in relation to claims by or against the Crown as it applies in relation to claims to which the Crown is not a party.

(2)   In subsection (1) above a reference to the Crown does not include a reference to Her Majesty in Her private capacity or to Her Majesty in right of Her Duchy of Lancaster or to the Duke of Cornwall.

(3)   Without prejudice to the generality of section 14(2) above, nothing in this section affects any rule of law as to whether proceedings of any description may be brought against the Crown.

SCOTLAND ACT 1998
(1998 c 46)

PART I
THE SCOTTISH PARLIAMENT

Legislation

29 Legislative competence

(1)   An Act of the Scottish Parliament is not law so far as any provision of the Act is outside the legislative competence of the Parliament.

(2)   A provision is outside that competence so far as any of the following paragraphs apply—

(a)   it would form part of the law of a country or territory other than Scotland, or confer or remove functions exercisable otherwise than in or as regards Scotland,

(b)   it relates to reserved matters,

(c)   it is in breach of the restrictions in Schedule 4,

(d)   it is incompatible with any of the Convention rights or with Community law,

(e)   it would remove the Lord Advocate from his position as head of the systems of criminal prosecution and investigation of deaths in Scotland.

(3)   For the purposes of this section, the question whether a provision of an Act of the Scottish Parliament relates to a reserved matter is to be determined, subject to subsection (4), by reference to the purpose of the provision, having regard (among other things) to its effect in all the circumstances.

(4)   A provision which—

(a)   would otherwise not relate to reserved matters, but

(b)   makes modifications of Scots private law, or Scots criminal law, as it applies to reserved matters,

is to be treated as relating to reserved matters unless the purpose of the provision is to make the law in question apply consistently to reserved matters and otherwise.

30 Legislative competence; supplementary

(1)   Schedule 5 (which defines reserved matters) shall have effect.

(2)   Her Majesty may by Order in Council make any modifications of Schedule 4 or 5 which She considers necessary or expedient.

(3)   Her Majesty may by Order in Council specify functions which are to be treated, for such purposes of this Act as may be specified, as being, or as not being, functions which are exercisable in or as regards Scotland.

(4)   An Order in Council under this section may also make such modifications of—

(a)   any enactment or prerogative instrument (including any enactment comprised in or made under this Act), or

(b)   any other instrument or document,

as Her Majesty considers necessary or expedient in connection with other provision made by the Order.

PART II
THE SCOTTISH ADMINISTRATION

Ministerial functions

57 Community law and Convention rights

(1)   Despite the transfer to the Scottish Ministers by virtue of section 53 of functions in relation to observing and implementing obligations under Community

law, any function of a Minister of the Crown in relation to any matter shall continue to be exercisable by him as regards Scotland for the purposes specified in section 2(2) of the European Communities Act 1972.

(2)   A member of the Scottish Executive has no power to make any subordinate legislation, or to do any other act, so far as the legislation or act is incompatible with any of the Convention rights or with Community law.

(3)   Subsection (2) does not apply to an act of the Lord Advocate—

(a)   in prosecuting any offence, or

(b)   in his capacity as head of the systems of criminal prosecution and investigation of deaths in Scotland,

which, because of subsection (2) of section 6 of the Human Rights Act 1998, is not unlawful under subsection (1) of that section.

PART VI
SUPPLEMENTARY

Final provisions

126   Interpretation
...

(4)   References in this Act to Scots private law are to the following areas of the civil law of Scotland—

(a)   the general principles of private law (including private international law),

(b)   the law of persons (including natural persons, legal persons and unincorporated bodies),

(c)   the law of obligations (including obligations arising from contract, unilateral promise, delict, unjustified enrichment and negotiorum gestio),

(d)   the law of property (including heritable and moveable property, trusts and succession), and

(e)   the law of actions (including jurisdiction, remedies, evidence, procedure, diligence, recognition and enforcement of court orders, limitation of actions and arbitration), and include references to judicial review of administrative action.
...

(9)   In this Act—

(a)   all those rights, powers, liabilities, obligations and restrictions from time to time created or arising by or under the Community Treaties, and

(b)   all those remedies and procedures from time to time provided for by or under the Community Treaties,

are referred to as 'Community law.'

(10)   In this Act, 'international obligations' means any international obligations of the United Kingdom other than obligations to observe and implement Community law or the Convention rights.
...

SCHEDULE 5
RESERVED MATTERS

Foreign affairs etc

7.—(1)   International relations, including relations with territories outside the United Kingdom, the European Communities (and their institutions) and other international organisations, regulation of international trade, and international development assistance and co-operation are reserved matters.

(2)   Sub-paragraph (1) does not reserve—

(a)   observing and implementing international obligations, obligations under the Human Rights Convention and obligations under Community law,

(b)   assisting Ministers of the Crown in relation to any matter to which that sub-paragraph applies.

ADOPTION (INTERCOUNTRY ASPECTS) ACT 1999
(1999 c 18)

Implementation of Convention

1   Regulations giving effect to Convention
(1)   Subject to the provisions of this Act, regulations made by the Secretary of State may make provision for giving effect to the Convention on Protection of Children and Co-operation in respect of Intercountry Adoption, concluded at the Hague on 29th May 1993 ('the Convention').
(2)   The text of the Convention (so far as material) is set out in Schedule 1 to this Act.
(3)   Regulations under this section may—
    (a)   apply, with or without modifications, any provision of the enactments relating to adoption;
    (b)   provide that any person who contravenes or fails to comply with any provision of the regulations is to be guilty of an offence and liable on summary conviction to imprisonment for a term not exceeding three months, or a fine not exceeding level 5 on the standard scale, or both;
    (c)   make different provision for different purposes or areas; and
    (d)   make such incidental, supplementary, consequential or transitional provision as appears to the Secretary of State to be expedient.
(4)   Regulations under this section shall be made by statutory instrument which shall be subject to annulment in pursuance of a resolution of either House of Parliament.
(5)   Subject to subsection (6), any power to make subordinate legislation under or for the purposes of the enactments relating to adoption includes power to do so with a view to giving effect to the provisions of the Convention.
(6)   Subsection (5) does not apply in relation to any power which is exercisable by the National Assembly for Wales.

2   Central Authorities and accredited bodies
(1)   The functions under the Convention of the Central Authority are to be discharged—
    (a)   separately in relation to England and Scotland by the Secretary of State; and
    (b)   in relation to Wales by the National Assembly for Wales.
(2)   [A communication may be sent to the Central Authority in relation to any part of Great Britain by sending it (for forwarding if necessary) to the Central Authority in relation to England.]
[(2A)   A registered adoption society is an accredited body for the purposes of the Convention if, in accordance with the conditions of the registration, the society may provide facilities in respect of Convention adoptions and adoptions effected by Convention adoption orders.
(2B)   A registered adoption service is an accredited body for the purpose of the Convention if, in accordance with the conditions of its registration, the service may provide facilities in respect of Convention adoptions and adoptions effected by Convention adoption orders.]
(3)   An approved adoption society is an accredited body for the purposes of the Convention if the approval extends to the provision of facilities in respect of Convention adoptions and adoptions effected by Convention adoption orders.
(4)   The functions under Article 9(a) to (c) of the Convention are to be discharged by local authorities and accredited bodies on behalf of the Central Authority.

[(5)   In this section, 'registered adoption society' has the same meaning as in section 2 of the Adoption and Children Act 2002 (basic definitions); and expressions used in this section in its application to England and Wales which are also used in that Act have the same meanings as in that Act.]

(6)   [In this section in its application to Scotland, 'registered adoption service' means an adoption service provided as mentioned in section 2(11)(b) of the Regulation of Care (Scotland) Act 2001 (asp 8) and registered under Part 1 of that Act; and 'registration' shall be construed accordingly.]

Miscellaneous and supplemental

17   Savings for adoptions etc under 1965 Convention

(1)   In relation to—
   (a)   a 1965 Convention adoption order or an application for such an order; or
   (b)   a 1965 Convention adoption,
the 1976 and 1978 Acts shall have effect without the amendments made by sections 3 to 6 and 8 and Schedule 2 to this Act and the associated repeals made by Schedule 3 to this Act.

(2)   In subsection (1) in its application to the 1976 or 1978 Act—
'1965 Convention adoption order' has the meaning which 'Convention adoption order' has in that Act as it has effect without the amendments and repeals mentioned in that subsection;
'1965 Convention adoption' has the meaning which 'regulated adoption' has in that Act as it so has effect.

18   Short title, interpretation, commencement and extent

(1)   This Act may be cited as the Adoption (Intercountry Aspects) Act 1999.

(2)   In this Act—
'the 1976 Act' means the Adoption Act 1976;
'the 1978 Act' means the Adoption (Scotland) Act 1978;
'the Convention' means the Convention on Protection of Children and Co-operation in respect of Intercountry Adoption, concluded at the Hague on 29th May 1993.

(3)   This Act, except this section, shall come into force on such day as the Secretary of State may by order made by statutory instrument appoint and different days may be appointed for different purposes.

(4)   Subject to subsection (5), this Act extends to Great Britain only.

(5)   Any amendment of an enactment which extends to any other part of the British Islands or any colony also extends to that part or colony.

SCHEDULE 1   Section 1
CONVENTION ON PROTECTION OF CHILDREN AND CO-OPERATION IN
RESPECT OF INTERCOUNTRY ADOPTION

The States signatory to the present Convention.

Recognizing that the child, for the full and harmonious development of his or her personality, should grow up in a family environment, in an atmosphere of happiness, love and understanding,

Recalling that each State should take, as a matter of priority, appropriate measures to enable the child to remain in the care of his or her family of origin,

Recognizing that intercountry adoption may offer the advantage of a permanent family to a child for whom a suitable family cannot be found in his or her State of origin,

Convinced of the necessity to take measures to ensure that intercountry adoptions are made in the best interests of the child and with respect for his or her fundamental rights, and to prevent the abduction, the sale of, or traffic in children,

Desiring to establish common provisions to this effect, taking into account the principles set forth in international instruments, in particular the United Nations Convention on the Rights of the Child, of 20 November 1989, and the United Nations Declaration on Social and Legal Principles relating to the Protection and Welfare of Children, with Special Reference to Foster Placement and Adoption Nationally and Internationally (General Assembly Resolution 41/85, of 3 December 1986),

Have agreed upon the following provisions—

CHAPTER 1 – SCOPE OF THE CONVENTION

Article 1

The objects of the present Convention are—

(a)   to establish safeguards to ensure that intercountry adoptions take place in the best interests of the child and with respect for his or her fundamental rights as recognised in international law;

(b)   to establish a system of co-operation amongst Contracting States to ensure that those safeguards are respected and thereby prevent the abduction, the sale of, or traffic in children;

(c)   to secure the recognition in Contracting States of adoptions made in accordance with the Convention.

Article 2

1.   The Convention shall apply where a child habitually resident in one Contracting State ('the State of origin') has been, is being, or is to be moved to another Contracting State ('the receiving State') either after his or her adoption in the State of origin by spouses or a person habitually resident in the receiving State, or for the purposes of such an adoption in the receiving State or in the State of origin.

2.   The Convention covers only adoptions which create a permanent parent-child relationship.

Article 3

The Convention ceases to apply if the agreements mentioned in Article 17, sub-paragraph (c), have not been given before the child attains the age of eighteen years.

CHAPTER II – REQUIREMENTS FOR INTERCOUNTRY ADOPTIONS

Article 4

An adoption within the scope of the Convention shall take place only if the competent authorities of the State of origin—

(a)   have established that the child is adoptable;

(b)   have determined, after possibilities for placement of the child within the State of origin have been given due consideration, that an intercountry adoption is in the child's best interests;

(c)   have ensured that—

(i)   the persons, institutions and authorities whose consent is necessary for adoption, have been counselled as may be necessary and duly informed of the effects of their consent, in particular whether or not an adoption will result in the termination of the legal relationship between the child and his or her family of origin,

(ii)   such persons, institutions and authorities have given their consent freely, in the required legal form, and expressed or evidenced in writing,

(iii)   the consents have not been induced by payment or compensation of any kind and have not been withdrawn, and

(iv)   the consent of the mother, where required, has been given only after the birth of the child; and

(d)   have ensured, having regard to the age and degree of maturity of the child, that—

(i)   he or she has been counselled and duly informed of the effects of the adoption and of his or her consent to the adoption, where such consent is required,

  (ii)   consideration has been given to the child's wishes and opinions,

  (iii) the child's consent to the adoption, where such consent is required, has been given freely, in the required legal form, and expressed or evidenced in writing, and

  (iv)   such consent has not been induced by payment or compensation of any kind.

Article 5

An adoption within the scope of the Convention shall take place only if the competent authorities of the receiving State—

  (a)   have determined that the prospective adoptive parents are eligible and suited to adopt;

  (b)   have ensured that the prospective adoptive parents have been counselled as may be necessary; and

  (c)   have determined that the child is or will be authorised to enter and reside permanently in that State.

CHAPTER III – CENTRAL AUTHORITIES AND ACCREDITED BODIES

Article 6

1.   A Contracting State shall designate a Central Authority to discharge the duties which are imposed by the Convention upon such authorities.

2.   Federal States, States with more than one system of law or States having autonomous territorial units shall be free to appoint more than one Central Authority and to specify the territorial or personal extent of their functions. Where a State has appointed more than one Central Authority, it shall designate the Central Authority to which any communication may be addressed for transmission to the appropriate Central Authority within that State.

Article 7

1.   Central Authorities shall co-operate with each other and promote co-operation amongst the competent authorities in their States to protect children and to achieve the other objects of the Convention.

2.   They shall take directly all appropriate measures to—

  (a)   provide information as to the laws of their States concerning adoption and other general information, such as statistics and standard forms;

  (b)   keep one another informed about the operation of the Convention and, as far as possible, eliminate any obstacles to its application.

Article 8

Central Authorities shall take, directly or through public authorities, all appropriate measures to prevent improper financial or other gain in connection with an adoption and to deter all practices contrary to the objects of the Convention.

Article 9

Central Authorities shall take, directly or through public authorities or other bodies duly accredited in their State, all appropriate measures, in particular to—

  (a)   collect, preserve and exchange information about the situation of the child and the prospective adoptive parents, so far as is necessary to complete the adoption;

  (b)   facilitate, follow and expedite proceedings with a view to obtaining the adoption;

  (c)   promote the development of adoption counselling and post-adoption services in their States;

  (d)   provide each other with general evaluation reports about experience with intercountry adoption;

(e)   reply, in so far as is permitted by the law of their State, to justified requests from other Central Authorities or public authorities for information about a particular adoption situation.

Article 10
Accreditation shall only be granted to and maintained by bodies demonstrating their competence to carry out properly the tasks with which they may be entrusted.

Article 11
An accredited body shall—
(a)   pursue only non-profit objectives according to such conditions and within such limits as may be established by the competent authorities of the State of accreditation;
(b)   be directed and staffed by persons qualified by their ethical standards and by training or experience to work in the field of intercountry adoption; and
(c)   be subject to supervision by competent authorities of that State as to its composition, operation and financial situation.

Article 12
A body accredited in one Contracting State may act in another Contracting State only if the competent authorities of both States have authorised it to do so.

Article 13
The designation of the Central Authorities and, where appropriate, the extent of their functions, as well as the names and addresses of the accredited bodies shall be communicated by each Contracting State to the Permanent Bureau of the Hague Conference on Private International Law.

CHAPTER IV – PROCEDURAL REQUIREMENTS IN INTERCOUNTRY
ADOPTION

Article 14
Persons habitually resident in a Contracting State, who wish to adopt a child habitually resident in another Contracting State, shall apply to the Central Authority in the State of their habitual residence.

Article 15
1.   If the Central Authority of the receiving State is satisfied that the applicants are eligible and suited to adopt, it shall prepare a report including information about their identity, eligibility and suitability to adopt, background, family and medical history, social environment, reasons for adoption, ability to undertake an intercountry adoption, as well as the characteristics of the children for whom they would be qualified to care.
2.   It shall transmit the report to the Central Authority of the State of origin.

Article 16
1.   If the Central Authority of the State of origin is satisfied that the child is adoptable, it shall—
(a)   prepare a report including information about his or her identity, adoptability, background, social environment, family history, medical history including that of the child's family, and any special needs of the child;
(b)   give due consideration to the child's upbringing and to his or her ethnic, religious and cultural background;
(c)   ensure that consents have been obtained in accordance with Article 4; and
(d)   determine, on the basis in particular of the reports relating to the child and the prospective adoptive parents, whether the envisaged placement is in the best interests of the child.

2.   It shall transmit to the Central Authority of the receiving State its report on the child, proof that the necessary consents have been obtained and the reasons for its determination on the placement, taking care not to reveal the identity of the mother and the father if, in the State of origin, these identities may not be disclosed.

Article 17
Any decision in the State of origin that a child should be entrusted to prospective adoptive parents may only be made if—
(a)   the Central Authority of that State has ensured that the prospective adoptive parents agree;
(b)   the Central Authority of the receiving State has approved such decision, where such approval is required by the law of that State or by the Central Authority of the State of origin;
(c)   the Central Authorities of both States have agreed that the adoption may proceed; and
(d)   it has been determined, in accordance with Article 5, that the prospective adoptive parents are eligible and suited to adopt and that the child is or will be authorised to enter and reside permanently in the receiving State.

Article 18
The Central Authorities of both States shall take all necessary steps to obtain permission for the child to leave the State of origin and to enter and reside permanently in the receiving State.

Article 19
1.   The transfer of the child to the receiving State may only be carried out if the requirements of Article 17 have been satisfied.
2.   The Central Authorities of both States shall ensure that this transfer takes place in secure and appropriate circumstances and, if possible, in the company of the adoptive or prospective adoptive parents.
3.   If the transfer of the child does not take place, the reports referred to in Articles 15 and 16 are to be sent back to the authorities who forwarded them.

Article 20
The Central Authorities shall keep each other informed about the adoption process and the measures taken to complete it, as well as about the progress of the placement if a probationary period is required.

Article 21
1.   Where the adoption is to take place after the transfer of the child to the receiving State and it appears to the Central Authority of that State that the continued placement of the child with the prospective adoptive parents is not in the child's best interests, such Central Authority shall take the measures necessary to protect the child, in particular—
(a)   to cause the child to be withdrawn from the prospective adoptive parents and to arrange temporary care;
(b)   in consultation with the Central Authority of the State of origin, to arrange without delay a new placement of the child with a view to adoption or, if this is not appropriate, to arrange alternative long-term care; an adoption shall not take place until the Central Authority of the State of origin has been duly informed concerning the new prospective adoptive parents;
(c)   as a last resort, to arrange the return of the child, if his or her interests so require.
2.   Having regard in particular to the age and degree of maturity of the child, he or she shall be consulted and, where appropriate, his or her consent obtained in relation to measures to be taken under this Article.

Article 22

1.   The functions of a Central Authority under this Chapter may be performed by public authorities or by bodies accredited under Chapter III, to the extent permitted by the law of its State.

2.   Any Contracting State may declare to the depositary of the Convention that the functions of the Central Authority under Articles 15 to 21 may be performed in that State, to the extent permitted by the law and subject to the supervision of the competent authorities of that State, also by bodies or persons who—

(a)   meet the requirements of integrity, professional competence, experience and accountability of that State; and

(b)   are qualified by their ethical standards and by training or experience to work in the field of intercountry adoption.

3.   A Contracting State which makes the declaration provided for in paragraph 2 shall keep the Permanent Bureau of the Hague Conference on Private International Law informed of the names and addresses of these bodies and persons.

4.   Any Contracting State may declare to the depositary of the Convention that adoptions of children habitually resident in its territory may only take place if the functions of the Central Authorities are performed in accordance with paragraph 1.

5.   Notwithstanding any declaration made under paragraph 2, the reports provided for in Articles 15 and 16 shall, in every case, be prepared under the responsibility of the Central Authority or other authorities or bodies in accordance with paragraph 1.

CHAPTER V – RECOGNITION AND EFFECTS OF THE ADOPTION

Article 23

1.   An adoption certified by the competent authority of the State of the adoption as having been made in accordance with the Convention shall be recognised by operation of law in the other Contracting States. The certificate shall specify when and by whom the agreements under Article 17, sub-paragraph c, were given.

2.   Each Contracting State shall, at the time of signature, ratification, acceptance, approval or accession, notify the depositary of the Convention of the identity and the functions of the authority or the authorities which, in that State, are competent to make the certification. It shall also notify the depositary of any modification in the designation of these authorities.

Article 24

The recognition of an adoption may be refused in a contracting State only if the adoption is manifestly contrary to its public policy, taking into account the best interests of the child.

Article 25

Any Contracting State may declare to the depositary of the convention that it will not be bound under this Convention to recognise adoptions made in accordance with an agreement concluded by application of Article 39, paragraph 2.

Article 26

1.   The recognition of an adoption includes recognition of—

(a)   The legal parent-child relationship between the child and his or her adoptive parents;

(b)   parental responsibility of the adoptive parents for the child;

(c)   the termination of a pre-existing legal relationship between the child and his or her mother and father, if the adoption has this effect in the Contracting State where it was made.

2.   In the case of an adoption having the effect of terminating a pre-existing legal parent-child relationship, the child shall enjoy in the receiving State, and in

any other Contracting State where the adoption is recognised, rights equivalent to those resulting from adoptions having this effect in each such State.

3.   The preceding paragraphs shall not prejudice the application of any provision more favourable for the child, in force in the Contracting State which recognises the adoption.

Article 27

1.   Where an adoption granted in the State of origin does not have the effect of terminating a pre-existing legal parent-child relationship, it may, in the receiving State which recognises the adoption under the Convention, be converted into an adoption having such an effect—

(a)   if the law of the receiving State so permits; and

(b)   if the consents referred to in Article 4, sub-paragraphs c and d, have been or are given for the purpose of such an adoption.

2.   Article 23 applies to the decision converting the adoption.

CHAPTER VI – GENERAL PROVISIONS

Article 28

The Convention does not affect any law of a State of origin which requires that the adoption of a child habitually resident within that State take place in that State or which prohibits the child's placement in, or transfer to, the receiving State prior to adoption.

Article 29

There shall be no contact between the prospective adoptive parents and the child's parents or any other person who has care of the child until the requirements of Article 4, sub-paragraphs a to c, and Article 5, sub-paragraph a, have been met, unless the adoption takes place within a family or unless the contact is in compliance with the conditions established by the competent authority of the State of origin.

Article 30

1.   The competent authorities of a Contracting State shall ensure that information held by them concerning the child's origin, in particular information concerning the identity of his or her parents, as well as the medical history, is preserved.

2.   They shall ensure that the child or his or her representative has access to such information, under appropriate guidance, in so far as is permitted by the law of that State.

Article 31

Without prejudice to Article 30, personal data gathered or transmitted under the Convention, especially data referred to in Articles 15 and 16, shall be used only for the purposes for which they were gathered or transmitted.

Article 32

1.   No one shall derive improper financial or other gain from an activity related to an intercountry adoption.

2.   Only costs and expenses, including reasonable professional fees of persons involved in the adoption, may be charged or paid.

3.   The directors, administrators and employees of bodies involved in an adoption shall not receive remuneration which is unreasonably high in relation to services rendered.

Article 33

A competent authority which finds that any provision of the Convention has not been respected or that there is a serious risk that it may not be respected, shall immediately inform the Central Authority of its State. This Central Authority shall be responsible for ensuring that appropriate measures are taken.

Article 34
If the competent authority of the State of destination of a document so requests, a translation certified as being in conformity with the original must be furnished. Unless otherwise provided, the costs of such translation are to be borne by the prospective adoptive parents.

Article 35
The competent authorities of the contracting States shall act expeditiously in the process of adoption.

Article 36
In relation to a State which has two or more systems of law with regard to adoption applicable in different territorial units—
    (a)   any reference to habitual residence in that State shall be construed as referring to habitual residence in a territorial unit of that State;
    (b)   any reference to the law of that State shall be construed as referring to the law in force in the relevant territorial unit;
    (c)   any reference to the competent authorities or to the public authorities of that State shall be construed as referring to those authorised to act in the relevant territorial unit;
    (d)   any reference to the accredited bodies of that State shall be construed as referring to bodies accredited in the relevant territorial unit.

Article 37
In relation to a State which with regard to adoption has two or more systems of law applicable to different categories of persons, any reference to the law of that State shall be construed as referring to the legal system specified by the law of that State.

Article 38
A State within which different territorial units have their own rules of law in respect of adoption shall not be bound to apply the Convention where a State with a unified system of law would not be bound to do so.

Article 39
    1.   The convention does not affect any international instrument to which Contracting States are Parties and which contains provisions on matters governed by the Convention, unless a contrary declaration is made by the States parties to such instrument.
    2.   Any Contracting State may enter into agreements with one or more other Contracting States, with a view to improving the application of the Convention in their mutual relations. These agreements may derogate only from the provisions of Articles 14 to 16 and 18 to 21. The States which have concluded such an agreement shall transmit a copy to the depositary of the Convention.

Article 40
No reservation to the Convention shall be permitted.

Article 41
The Convention shall apply in every case where an application pursuant to Article 14 has been received after the Convention has entered into force in the receiving State and the State of origin.

Article 42
The Secretary General of the Hague Conference on Private International Law shall at regular intervals convene a Special Commission in order to review the practical operation of the Convention.

ADOPTION AND CHILDREN ACT 2002
(2002 c 38)

83 Restriction on bringing children in

(1) This section applies where a person who is habitually resident in the British Islands (the 'British resident')—

(a) brings, or causes another to bring, a child who is habitually resident outside the British Islands into the United Kingdom for the purpose of adoption by the British resident, or

(b) at any time brings, or causes another to bring, into the United Kingdom a child adopted by the British resident under an external adoption effected within the period of six months ending with that time.

The references to adoption, or to a child adopted, by the British resident include a reference to adoption, or to a child adopted, by the British resident and another person.

(2) But this section does not apply if the child is intended to be adopted under a Convention adoption order.

(3) An external adoption means an adoption, other than a Convention adoption, of a child effected under the law of any country or territory outside the British Islands, whether or not the adoption is—

(a) an adoption within the meaning of Chapter 4, or

(b) a full adoption (within the meaning of section 88(3)).

(4) Regulations may require a person intending to bring, or to cause another to bring, a child into the United Kingdom in circumstances where this section applies—

(a) to apply to an adoption agency (including a Scottish or Northern Irish adoption agency) in the prescribed manner for an assessment of his suitability to adopt the child, and

(b) to give the agency any information it may require for the purpose of the assessment.

(5) Regulations may require prescribed conditions to be met in respect of a child brought into the United Kingdom in circumstances where this section applies.

(6) In relation to a child brought into the United Kingdom for adoption in circumstances where this section applies, regulations may—

(a) provide for any provision of Chapter 3 to apply with modifications or not to apply,

(b) if notice of intention to adopt has been given, impose functions in respect of the child on the local authority to which the notice was given.

(7) If a person brings, or causes another to bring, a child into the United Kingdom at any time in circumstances where this section applies, he is guilty of an offence if—

(a) he has not complied with any requirement imposed by virtue of subsection (4), or

(b) any condition required to be met by virtue of subsection (5) is not met, before that time, or before any later time which may be prescribed.

(8) A person guilty of an offence under this section is liable—

(a) on summary conviction to imprisonment for a term not exceeding six months, or a fine not exceeding the statutory maximum, or both,

(b) on conviction on indictment, to imprisonment for a term not exceeding twelve months, or a fine, or both.

(9) In this section, 'prescribed' means prescribed by regulations and 'regulations' means regulations made by the Secretary of State, after consultation with the Assembly.

84 Giving parental responsibility prior to adoption abroad

(1) The High Court may, on an application by persons who the court is satis-

fied intend to adopt a child under the law of a country or territory outside the British Islands, make an order giving parental responsibility for the child to them.

(2)   An order under this section may not give parental responsibility to persons who the court is satisfied meet those requirements as to domicile, or habitual residence, in England and Wales which have to be met if an adoption order is to be made in favour of those persons.

(3)   An order under this section may not be made unless any requirements prescribed by regulations are satisfied.

(4)   An application for an order under this section may not be made unless at all times during the preceding ten weeks the child's home was with the applicant or, in the case of an application by two people, both of them.

(5)   Section 46(2) to (4) has effect in relation to an order under this section as it has effect in relation to adoption orders.

(6)   Regulations may provide for any provision of this Act which refers to adoption orders to apply, with or without modifications, to orders under this section.

(7)   In this section, 'regulations' means regulations made by the Secretary of State, after consultation with the Assembly.

85   Restriction on taking children out

(1)   A child who—

(a)   is a Commonwealth citizen, or

(b)   is habitually resident in the United Kingdom,

must not be removed from the United Kingdom to a place outside the British Islands for the purpose of adoption unless the condition in subsection (2) is met.

(2)   The condition is that—

(a)   the prospective adopters have parental responsibility for the child by virtue of an order under section 84, or

(b)   the child is removed under the authority of an order under section 49 of the Adoption (Scotland) Act 1978 (c 28) or Article 57 of the Adoption (Northern Ireland) Order 1987 (SI 1987/2203 (NI 22)).

(3)   Removing a child from the United Kingdom includes arranging to do so; and the circumstances in which a person arranges to remove a child from the United Kingdom include those where he—

(a)   enters into an arrangement for the purpose of facilitating such a removal of the child,

(b)   initiates or takes part in any negotiations of which the purpose is the conclusion of an arrangement within paragraph (a), or

(c)   causes another person to take any step mentioned in paragraph (a) or (b).

An arrangement includes an agreement (whether or not enforceable).

(4)   A person who removes a child from the United Kingdom in contravention of subsection (1) is guilty of an offence.

(5)   A person is not guilty of an offence under subsection (4) of causing a person to take any step mentioned in paragraph (a) or (b) of subsection (3) unless it is proved that he knew or had reason to suspect that the step taken would contravene subsection (1).

But this subsection only applies if sufficient evidence is adduced to raise an issue as to whether the person had the knowledge or reason mentioned.

(6)   A person guilty of an offence under this section is liable—

(a)   on summary conviction to imprisonment for a term not exceeding six months, or a fine not exceeding the statutory maximum, or both,

(b)   on conviction on indictment, to imprisonment for a term not exceeding twelve months, or a fine, or both.

(7)   In any proceedings under this section—

(a)   a report by a British consular officer or a deposition made before a British consular officer and authenticated under the signature of that officer is admissible, upon proof that the officer or the deponent cannot be found in the United Kingdom, as evidence of the matters stated in it, and

(b)   it is not necessary to prove the signature or official character of the person who appears to have signed any such report or deposition.

86   Power to modify sections 83 and 85

(1)   Regulations may provide for section 83 not to apply if—

(a)   the adopters or (as the case may be) prospective adopters are natural parents, natural relatives or guardians of the child in question (or one of them is), or

(b)   the British resident in question is a partner of a parent of the child, and any prescribed conditions are met.

(2)   Regulations may provide for section 85(1) to apply with modifications, or not to apply, if—

(a)   the prospective adopters are parents, relatives or guardians of the child in question (or one of them is), or

(b)   the prospective adopter is a partner of a parent of the child, and any prescribed conditions are met.

(3)   On the occasion of the first exercise of the power to make regulations under this section—

(a)   the statutory instrument containing the regulations is not to be made unless a draft of the instrument has been laid before, and approved by a resolution of, each House of Parliament, and

(b)   accordingly section 140(2) does not apply to the instrument.

(4)   In this section, 'prescribed' means prescribed by regulations and 'regulations' means regulations made by the Secretary of State after consultation with the Assembly.

87   Overseas adoptions

(1)   In this Act, 'overseas adoption'—

(a)   means an adoption of a description specified in an order made by the Secretary of State, being a description of adoptions effected under the law of any country or territory outside the British Islands, but

(b)   does not include a Convention adoption.

(2)   Regulations may prescribe the requirements that ought to be met by an adoption of any description effected after the commencement of the regulations for it to be an overseas adoption for the purposes of this Act.

(3)   At any time when such regulations have effect, the Secretary of State must exercise his powers under this section so as to secure that subsequently effected adoptions of any description are not overseas adoptions for the purposes of this Act if he considers that they are not likely within a reasonable time to meet the prescribed requirements.

(4)   In this section references to this Act include the Adoption Act 1976 (c 36).

(5)   An order under this section may contain provision as to the manner in which evidence of any overseas adoption may be given.

(6)   In this section—

'adoption' means an adoption of a child or of a person who was a child at the time the adoption was applied for,

'regulations' means regulations made by the Secretary of State after consultation with the Assembly.

88   Modification of section 67 for Hague Convention adoptions

(1)   If the High Court is satisfied, on an application under this section, that each of the following conditions is met in the case of a Convention adoption, it may direct that section 67(3) does not apply, or does not apply to any extent specified in the direction.

(2)   The conditions are—

(a)   that under the law of the country in which the adoption was effected, the adoption is not a full adoption,

(b)   that the consents referred to in Article 4(c) and (d) of the Convention have not been given for a full adoption or that the United Kingdom is not the receiving State (within the meaning of Article 2 of the Convention),

(c)   that it would be more favourable to the adopted child for a direction to be given under subsection (1).

(3)   A full adoption is an adoption by virtue of which the child is to be treated in law as not being the child of any person other than the adopters or adopter.

(4)   In relation to a direction under this section and an application for it, sections 59 and 60 of the Family Law Act 1986 (c 55) (declarations under Part 3 of that Act as to marital status) apply as they apply in relation to a direction under that Part and an application for such a direction.

89   Annulment etc of overseas or Hague Convention adoptions

(1)   The High Court may, on an application under this subsection, by order annul a Convention adoption or Convention adoption order on the ground that the adoption is contrary to public policy.

(2)   The High Court may, on an application under this subsection—

(a)   by order provide for an overseas adoption or a determination under section 91 to cease to be valid on the ground that the adoption or determination is contrary to public policy or that the authority which purported to authorise the adoption or make the determination was not competent to entertain the case, or

(b)   decide the extent, if any, to which a determination under section 91 has been affected by a subsequent determination under that section.

(3)   The High Court may, in any proceedings in that court, decide that an overseas adoption or a determination under section 91 is to be treated, for the purposes of those proceedings, as invalid on either of the grounds mentioned in subsection (2)(a).

(4)   Subject to the preceding provisions, the validity of a Convention adoption, Convention adoption order or overseas adoption or a determination under section 91 cannot be called in question in proceedings in any court in England and Wales.

91   Overseas determinations and orders

(1)   Subsection (2) applies where any authority of a Convention country (other than the United Kingdom) or of the Channel Islands, the Isle of Man or any British overseas territory has power under the law of that country or territory—

(a)   to authorise, or review the authorisation of, an adoption order made in that country or territory, or

(b)   to give or review a decision revoking or annulling such an order or a Convention adoption.

(2)   If the authority makes a determination in the exercise of that power, the determination is to have effect for the purpose of effecting, confirming or terminating the adoption in question or, as the case may be, confirming its termination.

(3)   Subsection (2) is subject to section 89 and to any subsequent determination having effect under that subsection.

105   Effect of certain Scottish orders and provisions

(1)   A Scottish adoption order or an order under section 25 of the Adoption (Scotland) Act 1978 (c 28) (interim adoption orders) has effect in England and Wales as it has in Scotland, but as if references to the parental responsibilities and the parental rights in relation to a child were to parental responsibility for the child.

(2)   An order made under section 18 of the Adoption (Scotland) Act 1978 (freeing orders), and the revocation or variation of such an order under section 20 or 21 of that Act, have effect in England and Wales as they have effect in Scotland, but

as if references to the parental responsibilities and the parental rights in relation to a child were to parental responsibility for the child.

(3)   Any person who—

(a)   contravenes section 27(1) of that Act (removal where adoption agreed etc.), or

(b)   contravenes section 28(1) or (2) of that Act (removal where applicant provided home),

is guilty of an offence and liable on summary conviction to imprisonment for a term not exceeding three months, or a fine not exceeding level 5 on the standard scale, or both.

(4)   Orders made under section 29 of that Act (order to return or not to remove child) are to have effect in England and Wales as if they were orders of the High Court under section 41 of this Act.

CIVIL PARTNERSHIP ACT 2004
(2004 c 33)

PART 1
INTRODUCTION

1   Civil partnership

(1)   A civil partnership is a relationship between two people of the same sex ('civil partners')—

(a)   which is formed when they register as civil partners of each other—

(i)   in England or Wales (under Part 2),

(ii)   in Scotland (under Part 3),

(iii)   in Northern Ireland (under Part 4), or

(iv)   outside the United Kingdom under an Order in Council made under Chapter 1 of Part 5 (registration at British consulates etc. or by armed forces personnel), or

(b)   which they are treated under Chapter 2 of Part 5 as having formed (at the time determined under that Chapter) by virtue of having registered an overseas relationship.

(2)   Subsection (1) is subject to the provisions of this Act under or by virtue of which a civil partnership is void.

(3)   A civil partnership ends only on death, dissolution or annulment.

(4)   The references in subsection (3) to dissolution and annulment are to dissolution and annulment having effect under or recognised in accordance with this Act.

(5)   References in this Act to an overseas relationship are to be read in accordance with Chapter 2 of Part 5.

PART 3
CIVIL PARTNERSHIP: SCOTLAND

CHAPTER 1 – FORMATION AND ELIGIBILITY

85   Formation of civil partnership by registration

(1)   For the purposes of section 1, two people are to be regarded as having registered as civil partners of each other once each of them has signed the civil partnership schedule, in the presence of—

(a)   each other,

(b)   two witnesses both of whom have attained the age of 16, and

(c)   the authorised registrar,

(all being present at a registration office or at a place agreed under section 93).

(2)   But the two people must be eligible to be so registered.

(3)   Subsection (1) applies regardless of whether subsection (4) is complied with.

(4)   After the civil partnership schedule has been signed under subsection (1), it must also be signed, in the presence of the civil partners and each other by-
  (a)   each of the two witnesses, and
  (b)   the authorised registrar.

86   Eligibility

(1)   Two people are not eligible to register in Scotland as civil partners of each other if—
  (a)   they are not of the same sex,
  (b)   they are related in a forbidden degree,
  (c)   either has not attained the age of 16,
  (d)   either is married or already in civil partnership, or
  (e)   either is incapable of-
      (i)   understanding the nature of civil partnership, or
      (ii)   validly consenting to its formation.

(2)   Subject to subsection (3), a man is related in a forbidden degree to another man if related to him in a degree specified in column 1 of Schedule 10 and a woman is related in a forbidden degree to another woman if related to her in a degree specified in column 2 of that Schedule.

(3)   A man and any man related to him in a degree specified in column 1 of paragraph 2 of Schedule 10, or a woman and any woman related to her in a degree specified in column 2 of that paragraph, are not related in a forbidden degree if—
  (a)   both persons have attained the age of 21, and
  (b)   the younger has not at any time before attaining the age of 18 lived in the same household as the elder and been treated by the elder as a child of the elder's family.

(4)   Paragraph 2 of Schedule 10 has effect subject to the modifications specified in subsection (5) in the case of a person (here the 'relevant person') whose gender has become the acquired gender under the Gender Recognition Act 2004 (c 7).

(5)   The reference in that paragraph to—
  (a)   a former wife of the relevant person includes any former husband of the relevant person, and
  (b)   a former husband of the relevant person includes any former wife of the relevant person.

[...]

(8)   References in this section and in Schedule 10 to relationships and degrees of relationship are to be construed in accordance with section 1(1) of the Law Reform (Parent and Child) (Scotland) Act 1986 (c 9).

(9)   For the purposes of this section, a degree of relationship specified in paragraph 1 of Schedule 10 exists whether it is of the full blood or the half blood.

(10)   Amend section 41(1) of the Adoption (Scotland) Act 1978 (c 28) (application to determination of forbidden degrees of provisions of that Act relating to the status conferred by adoption) as follows—
  (a)   after first 'marriage' insert ', to the eligibility of persons to register as civil partners of each other', and
  (b)   for 'and incest' substitute ', to such eligibility and to incest'.

CHAPTER 5 – DISSOLUTION, SEPARATION AND NULLITY

Dissolution and separation

117   Dissolution

(1)   An action for the dissolution of a civil partnership may be brought in the Court of Session or in the sheriff court.

(2)   In such an action the court may grant decree, if, but only if, it is established that—
  (a)   the civil partnership has broken down irretrievably, or
  (b)   an interim gender recognition certificate under the Gender Recognition Act 2004 (c 7) has, after the date of registration of the civil partnership, been issued to either of the civil partners.
(3)   The irretrievable breakdown of a civil partnership is taken to be established if—
  (a)   since the date of registration of the civil partnership the defender has at any time behaved (whether or not as a result of mental abnormality and whether such behaviour has been active or passive) in such a way that the pursuer cannot reasonably be expected to cohabit with the defender,
  [...]
  (c)   there has been no cohabitation between the civil partners at any time during a continuous period of one year after the date of registration of the civil partnership and immediately preceding the bringing of the action and the defender consents to the granting of decree of dissolution of the civil partnership, or
  (d)   there has been no cohabitation between the civil partners at any time during a continuous period of two years after that date and immediately preceding the bringing of the action.
(4)   Provision is to be made by act of sederunt—
  (a)   for the purpose of ensuring that, in an action to which paragraph (c) of subsection (3) relates, the defender has been given such information as enables that civil partner to understand—
    (i)   the consequences of consenting to the granting of decree, and
    (ii)   the steps which must be taken to indicate such consent, and
  (b)   as to the manner in which the defender in such an action is to indicate such consent, and any withdrawal of such consent,
and where the defender has indicated (and not withdrawn) such consent in the prescribed manner, that indication is sufficient evidence of such consent.
(5)   Provision is to be made by act of sederunt for the purpose of ensuring that, where in an action for the dissolution of a civil partnership the defender is suffering from mental illness, the court appoints a curator ad litem to the defender.
  [...]
(8)   In an action for dissolution of a civil partnership the standard of proof required to establish the ground of action is on balance of probability.

120   Separation
(1)   An action for the separation of the civil partners in a civil partnership may be brought in the Court of Session or in the sheriff court.
(2)   In such an action the court may grant decree if satisfied that the circumstances set out in any of paragraphs (a) to (d) of section 117(3) are established.

121   Dissolution following on decree of separation
(1)   The court may grant decree in an action for the dissolution of a civil partnership even though decree of separation has previously been granted to the pursuer on the same, or substantially the same, facts as those averred in support of that action; and in any such action the court may treat an extract decree of separation lodged in process as sufficient proof of the facts under which that decree was granted.
(2)   Nothing in this section entitles a court to grant decree of dissolution of a civil partnership without receiving evidence from the pursuer.

123   Nullity
[(1)]   Where two people register in Scotland as civil partners of each other, the civil partnership is void if, and only if—
  (a)   they were not eligible to do so,

(b) though they were so eligible, either of them did not consent to its formation, [or

(c) at the time of registration one of them who was capable of consenting to the formation of the civil partnership purported to give consent but did so by reason only of duress or error.]

[(2) In this section 'error' means—

(a) error as to the nature of civil partnership, or

(b) a mistaken belief held by a person ('A') that the other person with whom A purported to register a civil partnership was the person with whom A had agreed to register a civil partnership.]

124   Validity of civil partnerships registered outside Scotland

(1) Where two people register as civil partners of each other in England and Wales—

(a) the civil partnership is void if it would be void in England and Wales under section 49, and

(b) the civil partnership is voidable if it would be voidable there under section 50(1)(a), (b), (c) or (e).

(2) Where two people register as civil partners of each other in Northern Ireland, the civil partnership is—

(a) void, if it would be void in Northern Ireland under section 173, and

(b) voidable, if it would be voidable there under section 174(1)(a), (b), (c) or (e).

(3) Subsection (4) applies where two people register as civil partners of each other under an Order in Council under—

(a) section 210 (registration at British consulates etc), or

(b) section 211 (registration by armed forces personnel),

('the relevant section').

(4) The civil partnership is—

(a) void, if—

(i) the condition in subsection (2)(a) or (b) of the relevant section is not met, or

(ii) a requirement prescribed for the purposes of this paragraph by an Order in Council under the relevant section is not complied with, and

(b) voidable, if—

(i) the appropriate part of the United Kingdom is England and Wales and the circumstances fall within section 50(1)(a), (b), (c) or (e), or

(ii) the appropriate part of the United Kingdom is Northern Ireland and the circumstances fall within section 174(1)(a), (b), (c) or (e).

(5) The appropriate part of the United Kingdom is the part by reference to which the condition in subsection (2)(b) of the relevant section is met.

(6) Subsections (7) and (8) apply where two people have registered an apparent or alleged overseas relationship.

(7) The civil partnership is void if—

(a) the relationship is not an overseas relationship, or

(b) (even though the relationship is an overseas relationship), the parties are not treated under Chapter 2 of Part 5 as having formed a civil partnership.

(8) The civil partnership is voidable if—

(a) the overseas relationship is voidable under the relevant law,

(b) where either of the parties was domiciled in England and Wales at the time when the overseas relationship was registered, the circumstances fall within section 50(1)(a), (b), (c) or (e), or

(c) where either of the parties was domiciled in Northern Ireland at the time when the overseas relationship was registered, the circumstances fall within section 174(1)(a), (b), (c) or (e).

(9) Section 51 or (as the case may be) section 175 applies for the purposes of—

(a)   subsections (1)(b), (2)(b) and (4)(b),

(b)   subsection (8)(a), in so far as applicable in accordance with the relevant law, and

(c)   subsection (8)(b) and (c).

(10)   In subsections (8)(a) and (9)(b) 'the relevant law' means the law of the country or territory where the overseas relationship was registered (including its rules of private international law).

(11)   For the purposes of subsections (8) and (9)(b) and (c), references in sections 50 and 51 or (as the case may be) sections 174 and 175 to the formation of the civil partnership are to be read as references to the registration of the overseas relationship.

125   Financial provision after overseas dissolution or annulment

Schedule 11 relates to applications for financial provision in Scotland after a civil partnership has been dissolved or annulled in a country or territory outside the British Islands.

128   Promise or agreement to enter into civil partnership

No promise or agreement to enter into civil partnership creates any rights or obligations under the law of Scotland; and no action for breach of such a promise or agreement may be brought in any court in Scotland, whatever the law applicable to the promise or agreement.

131   Succession: legal rights arising by virtue of civil partnership

(1)   Where a person dies survived by a civil partner then, unless the circumstance is as mentioned in subsection (2), the civil partner has right to half of the moveable net estate belonging to the deceased at the time of death.

(2)   That circumstance is that the person is also survived by issue, in which case the civil partner has right to a third of that moveable net estate and those issue have right to another third of it.

(3)   In this section—

'issue' means issue however remote, and

'net estate' has the meaning given by section 36(1) (interpretation) of the Succession (Scotland) Act 1964 (c 41).

(4)   Every testamentary disposition executed after the commencement of this section by which provision is made in favour of the civil partner of the testator and which does not contain a declaration to the effect that the provision so made is in full and final satisfaction of the right to any share in the testator's estate to which the civil partner is entitled by virtue of subsection (1) or (2), has effect (unless the disposition contains an express provision to the contrary) as if it contained such a declaration.

(5)   In section 36(1) of the Succession (Scotland) Act 1964 (c 41), in the definition of 'legal rights', for 'and legitim' substitute 'legitim and rights under section 131 of the Civil Partnership Act 2004'.

PART 5

CIVIL PARTNERSHIP FORMED OR DISSOLVED ABROAD ETC

CHAPTER 1 – REGISTRATION OUTSIDE UK UNDER ORDER IN COUNCIL

210   Registration at British consulates etc

(1)   Her Majesty may by Order in Council make provision for two people to register as civil partners of each other—

(a)   in prescribed countries or territories outside the United Kingdom, and

(b)   in the presence of a prescribed officer of Her Majesty's Diplomatic Service,

in cases where the officer is satisfied that the conditions in subsection (2) are met.

(2)   The conditions are that—

(a)   at least one of the proposed civil partners is a United Kingdom national,

(b)   the proposed civil partners would have been eligible to register as civil partners of each other in such part of the United Kingdom as is determined in accordance with the Order,

(c)   the authorities of the country or territory in which it is proposed that they register as civil partners will not object to the registration, and

(d)   insufficient facilities exist for them to enter into an overseas relationship under the law of that country or territory.

(3)   An officer is not required to allow two people to register as civil partners of each other if in his opinion the formation of a civil partnership between them would be inconsistent with international law or the comity of nations.

(4)   An Order in Council under this section may make provision for appeals against a refusal, in reliance on subsection (3), to allow two people to register as civil partners of each other.

(5)   An Order in Council under this section may provide that two people who register as civil partners of each other under such an Order are to be treated for the purposes of sections 221(1)(c)(i) and (2)(c)(i), 222(c), 224(b), 225(1)(c)(i) and (3)(c)(i), 229(1)(c)(i) and (2)(c)(i), 230(c) and 232(b) and section 1(3)(c)(i) of the Presumption of Death (Scotland) Act 1977 (c 27) as if they had done so in the part of the United Kingdom determined as mentioned in subsection (2)(b).

211   Registration by armed forces personnel

(1)   Her Majesty may by Order in Council make provision for two people to register as civil partners of each other—

(a)   in prescribed countries or territories outside the United Kingdom, and

(b)   in the presence of an officer appointed by virtue of the Registration of Births, Deaths and Marriages (Special Provisions) Act 1957 (c 58),

in cases where the officer is satisfied that the conditions in subsection (2) are met.

(2)   The conditions are that—

(a)   at least one of the proposed civil partners—

(i)   is a member of a part of Her Majesty's forces serving in the country or territory,

(ii)   is employed in the country or territory in such other capacity as may be prescribed, or

(iii)   is a child of a person falling within sub-paragraph (i) or (ii) and has his home with that person in that country or territory,

(b)   the proposed civil partners would have been eligible to register as civil partners of each other in such part of the United Kingdom as is determined in accordance with the Order, and

(c)   such other requirements as may be prescribed are complied with.

(3)   In determining for the purposes of subsection (2) whether one person is the child of another, a person who is or was treated by another as a child of the family in relation to—

(a)   a marriage to which the other is or was a party, or

(b)   a civil partnership in which the other is or was a civil partner,

is to be regarded as the other's child.

(4)   An Order in Council under this section may provide that two people who register as civil partners of each other under such an Order are to be treated for the purposes of section 221(1)(c)(i) and (2)(c)(i), 222(c), 224(b), 225(1)(c)(i) and (3)(c)(i), 229(1)(c)(i) and (2)(c)(i), 230(c) and 232(b) and section 1(3)(c)(i) of the Presumption of Death (Scotland) Act 1977 (c 27) as if they had done so in the part of the United Kingdom determined in accordance with subsection (2)(b).

(5)   Any references in this section—

(a)   to a country or territory outside the United Kingdom,

(b)   to forces serving in such a country or territory, and

(c)   to persons employed in such a country or territory,

include references to ships which are for the time being in the waters of a country or territory outside the United Kingdom, to forces serving in any such ship and to persons employed in any such ship.

212 Meaning of 'overseas relationship'

(1) For the purposes of this Act an overseas relationship is a relationship which—

(a) is either a specified relationship or a relationship which meets the general conditions, and

(b) is registered (whether before or after the passing of this Act) with a responsible authority in a country or territory outside the United Kingdom, by two people—

(i) who under the relevant law are of the same sex at the time when they do so, and

(ii) neither of whom is already a civil partner or lawfully married.

(2) In this Chapter, 'the relevant law' means the law of the country or territory where the relationship is registered (including its rules of private international law).

213 Specified relationships

(1) A specified relationship is a relationship which is specified for the purposes of section 212 by Schedule 20.

(2) The Secretary of State may by order amend Schedule 20 by—

(a) adding a relationship,

(b) amending the description of a relationship, or

(c) omitting a relationship.

(3) No order may be made under this section without the consent of the Scottish Ministers and the Department of Finance and Personnel.

(4) The power to make an order under this section is exercisable by statutory instrument.

(5) An order which contains any provision (whether alone or with other provisions) amending Schedule 20 by—

(a) amending the description of a relationship, or

(b) omitting a relationship,

may not be made unless a draft of the statutory instrument containing the order is laid before, and approved by a resolution of, each House of Parliament.

(6) A statutory instrument containing any other order under this section is subject to annulment in pursuance of a resolution of either House of Parliament.

214 The general conditions

The general conditions are that, under the relevant law—

(a) the relationship may not be entered into if either of the parties is already a party to a relationship of that kind or lawfully married,

(b) the relationship is of indeterminate duration, and

(c) the effect of entering into it is that the parties are-

(i) treated as a couple either generally or for specified purposes, or

(ii) treated as married.

215 Overseas relationships treated as civil partnerships: the general rule

(1) Two people are to be treated as having formed a civil partnership as a result of having registered an overseas relationship if, under the relevant law, they—

(a) had capacity to enter into the relationship, and

(b) met all requirements necessary to ensure the formal validity of the relationship.

(2) Subject to subsection (3), the time when they are to be treated as having formed the civil partnership is the time when the overseas relationship is registered (under the relevant law) as having been entered into.

(3)   If the overseas relationship is registered (under the relevant law) as having been entered into before this section comes into force, the time when they are to be treated as having formed a civil partnership is the time when this section comes into force.

(4)   But if—

(a)   before this section comes into force, a dissolution or annulment of the overseas relationship was obtained outside the United Kingdom, and

(b)   the dissolution or annulment would be recognised under Chapter 3 if the overseas relationship had been treated as a civil partnership at the time of the dissolution or annulment,

subsection (3) does not apply and subsections (1) and (2) have effect subject to subsection (5).

(5)   The overseas relationship is not to be treated as having been a civil partnership for the purposes of any provisions except—

(a)   Schedules 7, 11 and 17 (financial relief in United Kingdom after dissolution or annulment obtained outside the United Kingdom);

(b)   such provisions as are specified (with or without modifications) in an order under section 259;

(c)   Chapter 3 (so far as necessary for the purposes of paragraphs (a) and (b)).

(6)   This section is subject to sections 216, 217 and 218.

216   The same-sex requirement

(1)   Two people are not to be treated as having formed a civil partnership as a result of having registered an overseas relationship if, at the critical time, they were not of the same sex under United Kingdom law.

(2)   But if a full gender recognition certificate is issued under the 2004 Act to a person who has registered an overseas relationship which is within subsection (4), after the issue of the certificate the relationship is no longer prevented from being treated as a civil partnership on the ground that, at the critical time, the parties were not of the same sex.

(3)   However, subsection (2) does not apply to an overseas relationship which is within subsection (4) if either of the parties has formed a subsequent civil partnership or lawful marriage.

(4)   An overseas relationship is within this subsection if (and only if), at the time mentioned in section 215(2)—

(a)   one of the parties ('A') was regarded under the relevant law as having changed gender (but was not regarded under United Kingdom law as having done so), and

(b)   the other party was (under United Kingdom law) of the gender to which A had changed under the relevant law.

(5)   In this section—

'the critical time' means the time determined in accordance with section 215(2) or (as the case may be) (3);

'the 2004 Act' means the Gender Recognition Act 2004 (c 7);

'United Kingdom law' means any enactment or rule of law applying in England and Wales, Scotland and Northern Ireland.

(6)   Nothing in this section prevents the exercise of any enforceable Community right.

217   Person domiciled in a part of the United Kingdom

(1)   Subsection (2) applies if an overseas relationship has been registered by a person who was at the time mentioned in section 215(2) domiciled in England and Wales.

(2)   The two people concerned are not to be treated as having formed a civil partnership if, at the time mentioned in section 215(2)—

(a)   either of them was under 16, or

(b)   they would have been within prohibited degrees of relationship under Part 1 of Schedule 1 if they had been registering as civil partners of each other in England and Wales.

(3)   Subsection (4) applies if an overseas relationship has been registered by a person who at the time mentioned in section 215(2) was domiciled in Scotland.

(4)   The two people concerned are not to be treated as having formed a civil partnership if, at the time mentioned in section 215(2), they were not eligible by virtue of paragraph (b), (c) or (e) of section 86(1) to register in Scotland as civil partners of each other.

(5)   Subsection (6) applies if an overseas relationship has been registered by a person who at the time mentioned in section 215(2) was domiciled in Northern Ireland.

(6)   The two people concerned are not to be treated as having formed a civil partnership if, at the time mentioned in section 215(2)—

(a)   either of them was under 16, or

(b)   they would have been within prohibited degrees of relationship under Schedule 12 if they had been registering as civil partners of each other in Northern Ireland.

218   The public policy exception

Two people are not to be treated as having formed a civil partnership as a result of having entered into an overseas relationship if it would be manifestly contrary to public policy to recognise the capacity, under the relevant law, of one or both of them to enter into the relationship.

219   Power to make provision corresponding to EC Regulation 2201/2003

(1)   The Lord Chancellor may by regulations make provision—

(a)   as to the jurisdiction of courts in England and Wales or Northern Ireland in proceedings for the dissolution or annulment of a civil partnership or for legal separation of the civil partners in cases where a civil partner—

(i)   is or has been habitually resident in a member State,

(ii)   is a national of a member State, or

(iii)   is domiciled in a part of the United Kingdom or the Republic of Ireland, and

(b)   as to the recognition in England and Wales or Northern Ireland of any judgment of a court of another member State which orders the dissolution or annulment of a civil partnership or the legal separation of the civil partners.

(2)   The Scottish Ministers may by regulations make provision—

(a)   as to the jurisdiction of courts in Scotland in proceedings for the dissolution or annulment of a civil partnership or for legal separation of the civil partners in such cases as are mentioned in subsection (1)(a), and

(b)   as to the recognition in Scotland of any such judgment as is mentioned in subsection (1)(b).

(3)   The regulations may in particular make provision corresponding to that made by Council Regulation (EC) No 2201/2003 of 27th November 2003 in relation to jurisdiction and the recognition and enforcement of judgments in matrimonial matters.

(4)   The regulations may provide that for the purposes of this Part and the regulations 'member State' means—

(a)   all member States with the exception of such member States as are specified in the regulations, or

(b)   such member States as are specified in the regulations.

(5)   The regulations may make provision under subsections (1)(b) and (2)(b) which applies even if the date of the dissolution, annulment or legal separation is earlier than the date on which this section comes into force.

(6)   Regulations under subsection (1) are to be made by statutory instrument

and may only be made if a draft has been laid before and approved by resolution
of each House of Parliament.

(7)   Regulations under subsection (2) are to be made by statutory instrument
and may only be made if a draft has been laid before and approved by resolution
of the Scottish Parliament.

(8)   In this Part 'section 219 regulations' means regulations made under this
section.

225   Jurisdiction of Scottish courts

(1)   The Court of Session has jurisdiction to entertain an action for the dissolution of a civil partnership or for separation of civil partners if (and only if)—

(a)   the court has jurisdiction under section 219 regulations,

(b)   no court has, or is recognised as having, jurisdiction under section 219
regulations and either civil partner is domiciled in Scotland on the date when
the proceedings are begun, or

(c)   the following conditions are met—

(i)   the two people concerned registered as civil partners of each other in
Scotland,

(ii)   no court has, or is recognised as having, jurisdiction under section 219
regulations, and

(iii)   it appears to the court to be in the interests of justice to assume jurisdiction in the case.

(2)   The sheriff has jurisdiction to entertain an action for the dissolution of a
civil partnership or for separation of civil partners if (and only if) the requirements
of paragraph (a) or (b) of subsection (1) are met and either civil partner—

(a)   was resident in the sheriffdom for a period of 40 days ending with the
date when the action is begun, or

(b)   had been resident in the sheriffdom for a period of not less than 40 days
ending not more than 40 days before that date and has no known residence in
Scotland at that date.

(3)   The Court of Session has jurisdiction to entertain an action for declarator of
nullity of a civil partnership if (and only if)—

(a)   the Court has jurisdiction under section 219 regulations,

(b)   no court has, or is recognised as having, jurisdiction under section 219
regulations and either of the ostensible civil partners—

(i)   is domiciled in Scotland on the date when the proceedings are begun,
or

(ii)   died before that date and either was at death domiciled in Scotland or
had been habitually resident in Scotland throughout the period of 1 year
ending with the date of death, or

(c)   the following conditions are met—

(i)   the two people concerned registered as civil partners of each other in
Scotland,

(ii)   no court has, or is recognised as having, jurisdiction under section 219
regulations, and

(iii)   it appears to the court to be in the interests of justice to assume jurisdiction in the case.

(4)   At any time when proceedings are pending in respect of which a court has
jurisdiction by virtue of any of subsections (1) to (3) (or this subsection) it also has
jurisdiction to entertain other proceedings, in respect of the same civil partnership
(or ostensible civil partnership), for dissolution, separation or (but only where the
court is the Court of Session) declarator of nullity, even though that jurisdiction
would not be exercisable under any of subsections (1) to (3).

226   Sisting of proceedings

(1)   Rules of court may make provision in relation to civil partnerships corresponding to the provision made in relation to marriages by Schedule 3 to the

Domicile and Matrimonial Proceedings Act 1973 (c 45) (sisting of Scottish consistorial actions).

(2)   The rules may in particular make provision—

(a)   for the provision of information by the pursuer and by any other person who has entered appearance in an action where proceedings relating to the same civil partnership (or ostensible civil partnership) are continuing in another jurisdiction, and

(b)   for an action to be sisted where there are concurrent proceedings elsewhere in respect of the same civil partnership (or ostensible civil partnership).

227   Scottish ancillary and collateral orders

(1)   This section applies where after the commencement of this Act an application is competently made to the Court of Session or the sheriff for the making, or the variation or recall, of an order which is ancillary or collateral to an action for—

(a)   the dissolution of a civil partnership,

(b)   the separation of civil partners, or

(c)   declarator of nullity of a civil partnership.

(2)   And the section applies whether the application is made in the same proceedings or in other proceedings and whether it is made before or after the pronouncement of a final decree in the action.

(3)   If the court has or, as the case may be, had jurisdiction to entertain the action, it has jurisdiction to entertain the application unless—

(a)   jurisdiction to entertain the action was under section 219 regulations, and

(b)   to make, vary or recall the order to which the application relates would contravene the regulations.

(4)   Where the Court of Session has jurisdiction by virtue of this section to entertain an application for the variation or recall, as respects any person, of an order made by it and the order is one to which section 8 (variation and recall by the sheriff of certain orders made by the Court of Session) of the Law Reform (Miscellaneous Provisions) (Scotland) Act 1966 (c 19) applies, then for the purposes of any application under that section for the variation or recall of the order in so far as it relates to the person, the sheriff (as defined in that section) has jurisdiction to exercise the power conferred on him by that section.

(5)   The reference in subsection (1) to an order which is ancillary or collateral is to an order relating to children, aliment, financial provision or expenses.

PART 5
CIVIL PARTNERSHIP FORMED OR DISSOLVED ABROAD ETC

CHAPTER 3 – DISSOLUTION ETC: JURISDICTION AND RECOGNITION

Recognition of dissolution, annulment and separation

233   Effect of dissolution, annulment or separation obtained in the UK

(1)   No dissolution or annulment of a civil partnership obtained in one part of the United Kingdom is effective in any part of the United Kingdom unless obtained from a court of civil jurisdiction.

(2)   Subject to subsections (3) and (4), the validity of a dissolution or annulment of a civil partnership or a legal separation of civil partners which has been obtained from a court of civil jurisdiction in one part of the United Kingdom is to be recognised throughout the United Kingdom.

(3)   Recognition of the validity of a dissolution, annulment or legal separation obtained from a court of civil jurisdiction in one part of the United Kingdom may be refused in any other part if the dissolution, annulment or separation was obtained at a time when it was irreconcilable with a decision determining the question of the subsistence or validity of the civil partnership—

(a)   previously given by a court of civil jurisdiction in the other part, or

(b)   previously given by a court elsewhere and recognised or entitled to be recognised in the other part.

(4)   Recognition of the validity of a dissolution or legal separation obtained from a court of civil jurisdiction in one part of the United Kingdom may be refused in any other part if the dissolution or separation was obtained at a time when, according to the law of the other part, there was no subsisting civil partnership.

234   Recognition in the UK of overseas dissolution, annulment or separation

(1)   Subject to subsection (2), the validity of an overseas dissolution, annulment or legal separation is to be recognised in the United Kingdom if, and only if, it is entitled to recognition by virtue of sections 235 to 237.

(2)   This section and sections 235 to 237 do not apply to an overseas dissolution, annulment or legal separation as regards which provision as to recognition is made by section 219 regulations.

(3)   For the purposes of subsections (1) and (2) and sections 235 to 237, an overseas dissolution, annulment or legal separation is a dissolution or annulment of a civil partnership or a legal separation of civil partners which has been obtained outside the United Kingdom (whether before or after this section comes into force).

235   Grounds for recognition

(1)   The validity of an overseas dissolution, annulment or separation obtained by means of proceedings is to be recognised if—

(a)   the dissolution, annulment or separation is effective under the law of the territory in which it was obtained, and at the relevant date either civil partner was habitually resident or domiciled in that territory; or

(b)   the dissolution, annulment or separation is effective throughout the country in which it was obtained and at the relevant date either civil partner was a national of that country.

[(1A)   The validity of an overseas dissolution, annulment or separation obtained by means of proceedings shall also be recognised if—

(a)   the dissolution, annulment or separation is effective under the law of the country in which it was obtained;

(b)   at the relevant date neither civil partner—

(i)   was habitually resident in the country in which the dissolution, annulment or separation was obtained;

(ii)   was domiciled in that country; or

(iii)   was a national of that country; and

(c)   the party seeking the dissolution, annulment or separation was either habitually resident or domiciled in a country whose law does not recognise relationships between people of the same sex and does not provide for dissolution, annulment or separation as regards such relationships.

(1B)   References in paragraph (1A) to 'country' shall include, where appropriate, a territory which comprises part of a country in which different systems of law are in force in matters relating to the dissolution or annulment of a civil partnership or the separation of civil partners.]

(2)   The validity of an overseas dissolution, annulment or separation obtained otherwise than by means of proceedings is to be recognised if—

(a)   the dissolution, annulment or separation is effective under the law of the territory in which it was obtained,

(b)   at the relevant date—

(i)   each civil partner was domiciled in that territory, or

(ii)   either civil partner was domiciled in that territory and the other was domiciled in a country or territory under whose law the dissolution, annulment or separation is recognised as valid, and

(c)   neither civil partner was habitually resident in the United Kingdom throughout the period of 1 year immediately preceding that date.

[(2A) The validity of an overseas dissolution, annulment or separation obtained by otherwise than by means of proceedings shall also be recognised if—

(a)   the dissolution, annulment or separation is effective under the law of the country in which it was obtained;

(b)   at the relevant date one civil partner was domiciled in that country and the other was domiciled in a country whose law does not recognise relationships between people of the same sex and does not provide for recognition of the validity of dissolutions, annulments or separations as regards such relationships; and

(c)   neither civil partner was habitually resident in the United Kingdom throughout the period of 1 year immediately preceding that date.

(2B)   References in paragraph (2A) to 'country' shall include a territory which comprises part of a country in which different systems of law are in force in matters relating to the dissolution or annulment of a civil partnership or the separation of civil partners.]

(3)   In this section 'the relevant date' means—

(a)   in the case of an overseas dissolution, annulment or legal separation obtained by means of proceedings, the date of the commencement of the proceedings;

(b)   in the case of an overseas dissolution, annulment or legal separation obtained otherwise than by means of proceedings, the date on which it was obtained.

(4)   Where in the case of an overseas annulment the relevant date fell after the death of either civil partner, any reference in subsection (1) or (2) to that date is to be read in relation to that civil partner as a reference to the date of death.

236   Refusal of recognition

(1)   Recognition of the validity of an overseas dissolution, annulment or legal separation may be refused in any part of the United Kingdom if the dissolution, annulment or separation was obtained at a time when it was irreconcilable with a decision determining the question of the subsistence or validity of the civil partnership—

(a)   previously given by a court of civil jurisdiction in that part of the United Kingdom, or

(b)   previously given by a court elsewhere and recognised or entitled to be recognised in that part of the United Kingdom.

(2)   Recognition of the validity of an overseas dissolution or legal separation may be refused in any part of the United Kingdom if the dissolution or separation was obtained at a time when, according to the law of that part of the United Kingdom, there was no subsisting civil partnership.

(3)   Recognition of the validity of an overseas dissolution, annulment or legal separation may be refused if—

(a)   in the case of a dissolution, annulment or legal separation obtained by means of proceedings, it was obtained—

(i)   without such steps having been taken for giving notice of the proceedings to a civil partner as, having regard to the nature of the proceedings and all the circumstances, should reasonably have been taken, or

(ii)   without a civil partner having been given (for any reason other than lack of notice) such opportunity to take part in the proceedings as, having regard to those matters, he should reasonably have been given, or

(b)   in the case of a dissolution, annulment or separation obtained otherwise than by means of proceedings—

(i)   there is no official document certifying that the dissolution, annulment or separation is effective under the law of the territory in which it was obtained, or

(ii)   where either civil partner was domiciled in another country or territory at the relevant date, there is no official document certifying that the dissolution, annulment or separation is recognised as valid under the law of that other country or territory, or

(c)   in either case, recognition of the dissolution, annulment or legal separation would be manifestly contrary to public policy.

(4)   In this section—

'official', in relation to a document certifying that a dissolution, annulment or separation is effective, or is recognised as valid, under the law of any country or territory, means issued by a person or body appointed or recognised for the purpose under that law;

'the relevant date' has the same meaning as in section 235.

237   Supplementary provisions relating to recognition of dissolution etc

(1)   For the purposes of sections 235 and 236—

(a)   where a civil partner has obtained an overseas dissolution, annulment or separation in a territory, he is to be treated as domiciled in that territory if he was domiciled there—

(i)   according to the law of that territory in family matters, or

(ii)   according to the law of Scotland;

(b)   in all other cases a civil partner is to be treated as domiciled in a country or territory if he was domiciled in that country or territory—

(i)   according to the law of that country or territory in family matters, or

(ii)   according to the law of Scotland.

(2)   The Lord Chancellor or the Scottish Ministers may by regulations make provision—

(a)   applying sections 235 and 236 and subsection (1) with modifications in relation to any country whose territories have different systems of law in force in matters of dissolution, annulment or legal separation;

(b)   applying sections 235 and 236 with modifications in relation to—

(i)   an overseas dissolution, annulment or legal separation in the case of an overseas relationship (or an apparent or alleged overseas relationship);

(ii)   any case where a civil partner is domiciled in a country or territory whose law does not recognise legal relationships between two people of the same sex;

(c)   with respect to recognition of the validity of an overseas dissolution, annulment or legal separation in cases where there are cross-proceedings;

(d)   with respect to cases where a legal separation is converted under the law of the country or territory in which it is obtained into a dissolution which is effective under the law of that country or territory;

(e)   with respect to proof of findings of fact made in proceedings in any country or territory outside the United Kingdom.

(3)   The power to make regulations under subsection (2) is exercisable by statutory instrument.

(4)   A statutory instrument containing such regulations—

(a)   if made by the Lord Chancellor, is subject to annulment in pursuance of a resolution of either House of Parliament;

(b)   if made by the Scottish Ministers, is subject to annulment in pursuance of a resolution of the Scottish Parliament.

(5)   In this section (except subsection (4)) and sections 233 to 236 and 238—

'annulment' includes any order annulling a civil partnership, however expressed;

'part of the United Kingdom' means England and Wales, Scotland or Northern Ireland;

'proceedings' means judicial or other proceedings.

(6)   Nothing in this Chapter is to be read as requiring the recognition of any finding of fault made in proceedings for dissolution, annulment or legal separation

or of any maintenance, custody or other ancillary order made in any such proceedings.

238   Non-recognition elsewhere of dissolution or annulment

(1)   This section applies where, in any part of the United Kingdom—

(a)   a dissolution or annulment of a civil partnership has been granted by a court of civil jurisdiction, or

(b)   the validity of a dissolution or annulment of a civil partnership is recognised by virtue of this Chapter.

(2)   The fact that the dissolution or annulment would not be recognised outside the United Kingdom does not—

(a)   preclude either party from forming a subsequent civil partnership or marriage in that part of the United Kingdom, or

(b)   cause the subsequent civil partnership or marriage of either party (wherever it takes place) to be treated as invalid in that part.

240   Certificates of no impediment to overseas relationships

(1)   Her Majesty may by Order in Council make provision for the issue of certificates of no impediment to—

(a)   United Kingdom nationals, and

(b)   such other persons falling within subsection (2) as may be prescribed,

who wish to enter into overseas relationships in prescribed countries or territories outside the United Kingdom with persons who are not United Kingdom nationals and who do not fall within subsection (2).

(2)   A person falls within this subsection if under any enactment for the time being in force in any country mentioned in Schedule 3 to the British Nationality Act 1981 (c 61) (Commonwealth countries) that person is a citizen of that country.

(3)   A certificate of no impediment is a certificate that, after proper notices have been given, no legal impediment to the recipient entering into the overseas relationship has been shown to the person issuing the certificate to exist.

SCHEDULE 20
MEANING OF OVERSEAS RELATIONSHIP: SPECIFIED RELATIONSHIPS

A relationship is specified for the purposes of section 213 (meaning of 'overseas relationship') if it is registered in a country or territory given in the first column of the table and fits the description given in relation to that country or territory in the second column—

Country or territory	Description
[Andorra]	[uni estable de parella]
[Australia: Tasmania]	[significant relationship]
Belgium	[the relationship referred to as cohabitation légale, wettelijke samenwoning or gesetzliches zusammenwohnen]
Belgium	marriage
[Canada]	[marriage]
Canada: Nova Scotia	domestic partnership
Canada: Quebec	[the relationship referred to as union civile or as civil union]
Denmark	registreret partnerskab [...]
Finland	[the relationship referred to as rekisteröity parisuhde or as registrerad partnerskap]
France	[pacte civil de solidarité]
Germany	Lebenspartnerschaft (life partnership)
Iceland	staofesta samvist [...]
[Luxembourg]	[the relationship referred to as partenariat enregistré or eingetragene partnerschaft]
Netherlands	[geregistreerd partnerschap]
Netherlands	marriage
[New Zealand]	[civil union]
Norway	registrert partnerskap [...]
[Spain]	[marriage]
Sweden	registrerat partnerskap [...]
[United States of America: California	domestic partnership
United States of America: Connecticut	civil union
United States of America: Maine	domestic partnership
United States of America: Massachusetts	marriage
United States of America: New Jersey	domestic partnership]
United States of America: Vermont	civil union

FAMILY LAW (SCOTLAND) ACT 2006
(2006 asp 2)

2   Void marriages

After section 20 of the Marriage (Scotland) Act 1977 (c 15) there shall be inserted—

Void marriages

'**20A   Grounds on which marriage void**

(1)   Where subsection (2) or (3) applies in relation to a marriage solemnised in Scotland, the marriage shall be void.

(2)   This subsection applies if at the time of the marriage ceremony a party to the marriage who was capable of consenting to the marriage purported to give consent but did so by reason only of duress or error.

(3)   This subsection applies if at the time of the marriage ceremony a party to the marriage was incapable of—

(a)   understanding the nature of marriage; and

(b)   consenting to the marriage.

(4)   If a party to a marriage purported to give consent to the marriage other than by reason only of duress or error, the marriage shall not be void by reason only of that party's having tacitly withheld consent to the marriage at the time when it was solemnised.

(5)   In this section 'error' means—

(a)   error as to the nature of the ceremony; or

(b)   a mistaken belief held by a person ('A') that the other party at the ceremony with whom A purported to enter into a marriage was the person whom A had agreed to marry.'.

22   Domicile of persons under 16

(1)   Subsection (2) applies where—

(a)   the parents of a child are domiciled in the same country as each other; and

(b)   the child has a home with a parent or a home (or homes) with both of them.

(2)   The child shall be domiciled in the same country as the child's parents.

(3)   Where subsection (2) does not apply, the child shall be domiciled in the country with which the child has for the time being the closest connection.

(4)   In this section, 'child' means a person under 16 years of age.

29   Application to court by survivor for provision on intestacy

(1)   This section applies where—

(a)   a cohabitant (the 'deceased') dies intestate; and

(b)   immediately before the death the deceased was—

(i)   domiciled in Scotland; and

(ii)   cohabiting with another cohabitant (the 'survivor').

(2)   Subject to subsection (4), on the application of the survivor, the court may—

(a)   after having regard to the matters mentioned in subsection (3), make an order—

(i)   for payment to the survivor out of the deceased's net intestate estate of a capital sum of such amount as may be specified in the order;

(ii)   for transfer to the survivor of such property (whether heritable or moveable) from that estate as may be so specified;

(b)   make such interim order as it thinks fit.

(3)   Those matters are—

(a)   the size and nature of the deceased's net intestate estate;

(b)   any benefit received, or to be received, by the survivor—

(i)   on, or in consequence of, the deceased's death; and

(ii)   from somewhere other than the deceased's net intestate estate;

(c)   the nature and extent of any other rights against, or claims on, the deceased's net intestate estate; and

(d)   any other matter the court considers appropriate.

(4)   An order or interim order under subsection (2) shall not have the effect of awarding to the survivor an amount which would exceed the amount to which the survivor would have been entitled had the survivor been the spouse or civil partner of the deceased.

(5)   An application under this section may be made to—

(a)   the Court of Session;

(b)   a sheriff in the sheriffdom in which the deceased was habitually resident at the date of death;

(c)   if at the date of death it is uncertain in which sheriffdom the deceased was habitually resident, the sheriff at Edinburgh.

(6)   Any application under this section shall be made before the expiry of the period of 6 months beginning with the day on which the deceased died.

(7)   In making an order under paragraph (a)(i) of subsection (2), the court may specify that the capital sum shall be payable—

(a)   on such date as may be specified;

(b)   in instalments.

(8)   In making an order under paragraph (a)(ii) of subsection (2), the court may specify that the transfer shall be effective on such date as may be specified.

(9)   If the court makes an order in accordance with subsection (7), it may, on an application by any party having an interest, vary the date or method of payment of the capital sum.

(10)   In this section—

'intestate' shall be construed in accordance with section 36(1) of the Succession (Scotland) Act 1964 (c 41);

'legal rights' has the meaning given by section 36(1) of the Succession (Scotland) Act 1964 (c 41);

'net intestate estate' means so much of the intestate estate as remains after provision for the satisfaction of—

(a)   inheritance tax;

(b)   other liabilities of the estate having priority over legal rights and the prior rights of a surviving spouse or surviving civil partner; and

(c)   the legal rights, and the prior rights, of any surviving spouse or surviving civil partner; and

'prior rights' has the meaning given by section 36(1) of the Succession (Scotland) Act 1964 (c 41).

37   Jurisdiction: actions for declarator of recognition of certain foreign decrees

(1)   The Domicile and Matrimonial Proceedings Act 1973 (c 45) shall be amended in accordance with subsections (2) and (3).

(2)   In section 7 (jurisdiction of Court of Session in certain consistorial causes)—

(a)   in subsection (1)—

(i)   for '(2) to (8)' there shall be substituted '(2A) to (10)'; and

(ii)   at the end there shall be inserted—

'(aa)   an action for declarator of recognition, or non-recognition, of a relevant foreign decree.';

(b)   in subsection (3A), after 'marriage', where it first occurs, there shall be inserted 'or for declarator of recognition, or non-recognition, of a relevant foreign decree'; and

(c)   after subsection (8) there shall be added—

'(9)   In this section, 'relevant foreign decree' means a decree of divorce, nullity or separation granted outwith a member state of the European Union.

(10) References in subsection (3A) to a marriage shall, in the case of an action for declarator of recognition, or non-recognition, of a relevant foreign decree, be construed as references to the marriage to which the relevant foreign decree relates.'.

(3) In section 8 (jurisdiction of sheriff court in certain consistorial causes)—
(a) in subsection (1)—
(i) for '(4)' there shall be substituted '(6)';
(ii) the words from 'an' to the end shall become paragraph (a) of that subsection; and
(iii) at the end there shall be added

'and
(b) an action for declarator of recognition, or non-recognition, of a relevant foreign decree.';

(b) in subsection (2), after 'divorce' there shall be inserted 'or for declarator of recognition, or non-recognition, of a relevant foreign decree'; and
(c) after subsection (4) there shall be added—

'(5) In this section, 'relevant foreign decree' has the meaning given by section 7(9).
(6) References in subsection (2) to a marriage shall, in the case of an action for declarator of recognition, or non-recognition, of a relevant foreign decree, be construed as references to the marriage to which the relevant foreign decree relates.'.

38 Validity of marriages

(1) Subject to the Foreign Marriage Act 1892 (c 23), the question whether a marriage is formally valid shall be determined by the law of the place where the marriage was celebrated.
(2) The question whether a person who enters into a marriage—
(a) had capacity; or
(b) consented,
to enter into it shall, subject to subsections (3) and (4) and to section 50 of the Family Law Act 1986 (c 55) (non-recognition of divorce or annulment in another jurisdiction no bar to remarriage), be determined by the law of the place where, immediately before the marriage, that person was domiciled.
(3) If a marriage entered into in Scotland is void under a rule of Scots internal law, then, notwithstanding subsection (2), that rule shall prevail over any law under which the marriage would be valid.
(4) The capacity of the person to enter into the marriage shall not be determined under the law of the place where, immediately before the marriage, the person was domiciled in so far as it would be contrary to public policy in Scotland for such capacity to be so determined.
(5) If the law of the place in which a person is domiciled requires a person under a certain age to obtain parental consent before entering into a marriage, that requirement shall not be taken to affect the capacity of a person to enter into a marriage in Scotland unless failure to obtain such consent would render invalid any marriage that the person purported to enter into in any form anywhere in the world.

39 Matrimonial property

(1) Any question in relation to the rights of spouses to each other's immoveable property arising by virtue of the marriage shall be determined by the law of the place in which the property is situated.
(2) Subject to subsections (4) and (5), if spouses are domiciled in the same country, any question in relation to the rights of the spouses to each other's move-

able property arising by virtue of the marriage shall be determined by the law of that country.

(3) Subject to subsections (4) and (5), if spouses are domiciled in different countries then, for the purposes of any question in relation to the rights of the spouses to each other's moveable property arising by virtue of the marriage, the spouses shall be taken to have the same rights to such property as they had immediately before the marriage.

(4) Any question in relation to—
    (a) the use or occupation of a matrimonial home which is moveable; or
    (b) the use of the contents of a matrimonial home (whether the home is moveable or immoveable),
shall be determined by the law of the country in which the home is situated.

(5) A change of domicile by a spouse (or both spouses) shall not affect a right in moveable property which, immediately before the change, has vested in either spouse.

(6) This section shall not apply—
    (a) in relation to the law on aliment, financial provision on divorce, transfer of property on divorce or succession;
    (b) to the extent that spouses agree otherwise.

(7) In this section, 'matrimonial home' has the same meaning as in section 22 of the 1981 Act.

40 Aliment
Subject to the Maintenance Orders (Reciprocal Enforcement) Act 1972 (c 18), a court in Scotland shall apply Scots internal law in any action for aliment which comes before it.

41 Effect of parents' marriage in determining status to depend on law of domicile
Any question arising as to the effect on a person's status of—
    (a) the person's parents being, or having been, married to each other; or
    (b) the person's parents not being, or not having been, married to each other,
shall be determined by the law of the country in which the person is domiciled at the time at which the question arises.

ADOPTION AND CHILDREN (SCOTLAND) ACT 2007*
(2007 asp 4)

PART 1
ADOPTION

CHAPTER 6 – ADOPTIONS WITH A FOREIGN ELEMENT

Restrictions on movement of children

39 Meaning of 'adoption' in Chapter 3
(1) In this Chapter, 'adoption' means—
    (a) adoption by an adoption order,
    (b) adoption by an adoption order as defined in section 46(1) of the 2002 Act,
    (c) adoption by an order made, or having effect as if made, under Article 12 of the Northern Ireland Order,

---

* At the date of going to press this Act was not in force, but is expected to come into effect during the lifetime of this edition.

    (d)   adoption by an order made in the Isle of Man or any of the Channel Islands,

    (e)   a Convention adoption,

    (f)   an overseas adoption, or

    (g)   an adoption recognised by the law of Scotland and effected under the law of any other country;

and related expressions are to be interpreted accordingly.

(2)   References in this Chapter to adoption do not include an adoption effected before the day on which this Chapter comes into force.

(3)   Any reference in an enactment to an adopted person within the meaning of this Chapter includes a reference to an adopted child within the meaning of Part IV of the Adoption (Scotland) Act 1978 (c 28).

40 Status conferred by adoption

(1)   An adopted person is to be treated in law as if born as the child of the adopters or adopter.

(2)   If an adopted person is adopted—

    (a)   by a relevant couple, or

    (b)   by virtue of section 30(3), by a member of a relevant couple,

the adopted person is to be treated as the child of the couple concerned.

(3)   An adopted person adopted by virtue of section 30(3) by a member of a relevant couple is to be treated in law as not being the child of any person other than the adopter and the other member of the couple.

(4)   Otherwise, an adopted person is to be treated in law as not being the child of any person other than the adopters or adopter.

(5)   Subsections (3) and (4) do not affect any reference in this Act to a person's natural parent or to any other natural relationship.

(6)   Subsection (7) applies where, in the case of a person adopted under a Convention adoption, the Court of Session is satisfied, on an application under this section—

    (a)   that under the law of the country in which the adoption was effected the adoption is not a full adoption,

    (b)   that—

        (i)   the consents mentioned in Article 4(c) and (d) of the Convention have not been given for a full adoption, or

        (ii)   the United Kingdom is not the receiving State (within the meaning of Article 2 of the Convention), and

    (c)   that it would be more favourable to the person for a direction to be given under that subsection.

(7)   The court may direct that subsection (4)—

    (a)   is not to apply, or

    (b)   is not to apply to such extent as may be specified in the direction.

(8)   In subsection (6), 'full adoption' means an adoption by virtue of which the person falls to be treated in law as if the person were not the child of any person other than the adopters or adopter.

(9)   This section has effect from the date of the adoption.

(10)   Subject to the provisions of this Chapter, this section—

    (a)   applies for the interpretation of enactments or instruments passed or made before as well as after the adoption and so applies subject to any contrary indication, and

    (b)   has effect as respects things done, or events occurring, on or after the adoption.

58 Restriction on bringing children into the United Kingdom

(1)   This section applies where a person who is habitually resident in the British Islands (the 'British resident')—

    (a)   brings, or causes another to bring, a child who is habitually resident outwith the British Islands into the United Kingdom for the purpose of adoption by the British resident, or

(b)   at any time brings, or causes another to bring, into the United Kingdom a child adopted by the British resident under an external adoption effected within the period of 12 months ending with that time.

(2)   In subsection (1), the references to adoption, or a child adopted, by the British resident include a reference to adoption, or a child adopted, by the British resident and another person.

(3)   This section does not apply if the child is intended to be adopted under a Convention adoption order.

(4)   An external adoption means an adoption, other than a Convention adoption, of a child effected under the law of any country or territory outwith the British Islands, whether or not the adoption is—

(a)   an adoption within the meaning of Chapter 3, or

(b)   a full adoption (as defined in section 40(8)).

(5)   Regulations may require a person intending to bring, or to cause another to bring, a child into the United Kingdom in circumstances where this section applies—

(a)   to apply to an adoption agency in the prescribed manner for an assessment of the person's suitability to adopt the child, and

(b)   to give the agency any information it may require for the purpose of the assessment.

(6)   Regulations may require prescribed conditions to be met in respect of a child brought into the United Kingdom in circumstances where this section applies.

(7)   In relation to a child brought into the United Kingdom for adoption in circumstances where this section applies, regulations may provide for any provision of Chapter 2 to apply with modifications or not to apply.

(8)   Regulations may provide for this section not to apply if—

(a)   the adopters or, as the case may be, prospective adopters of the child in question are—

(i)   natural parents,

(ii)   natural relatives, or

(iii)   guardians,

of the child (or one of them is), or

(b)   the British resident in question is a step-parent of the child,

and any prescribed conditions are met.

(9)   On the occasion of the first exercise of the power to make regulations under subsection (8)—

(a)   the regulations must not be made unless a draft of the regulations has been approved by a resolution of the Scottish Parliament, and

(b)   accordingly section 117(4) does not apply to the statutory instrument containing the regulations.

(10)   In this section, 'prescribed' means prescribed by regulations and 'regulations' means regulations made by the Scottish Ministers.

59   Preliminary order where child to be adopted abroad

(1)   The appropriate court may, on an application by persons ('the prospective adopters') who the court is satisfied intend to adopt a child under the law of a country or territory outwith the British Islands, make an order vesting parental responsibilities and parental rights in relation to the child in the prospective adopters.

(2)   If the court is satisfied that the prospective adopters would meet the requirements as to domicile, or habitual residence, in Scotland which they would require to meet if an adoption order were to be made on their application, the court may not make an order under this section.

(3)   An order under this section may not be made unless any requirements prescribed by regulations by the Scottish Ministers are satisfied.

(4)   An application for an order under this section may not be made unless at all times during the period of 10 weeks immediately preceding the application the child's home was with the prospective adopters.

(5)   Section 35 has effect in relation to an order under this section as it has effect in relation to adoption orders.

(6)   The Scottish Ministers may by regulations provide for any provision of this Act which relates to adoption orders to apply, with or without modifications, to orders under this section.

60   Restriction on removal of children for adoption outwith Great Britain

(1)   A person who takes or sends a protected child out of Great Britain to any place outwith the British Islands with a view to the adoption of the child by any person commits an offence.

(2)   A person who makes or takes part in any arrangements for transferring the care of a protected child to another person, knowing that the other person intends to take or send the child out of Great Britain in circumstances which would constitute an offence under subsection (1), commits an offence.

(3)   No offence is committed under subsection (1) if the child is taken or sent out of Great Britain under the authority of an order under—
  (a)   section 59,
  (b)   section 84 of the 2002 Act, or
  (c)   Article 57 of the Northern Ireland Order.

(4)   A person is deemed to take part in arrangements for transferring the care of a child to another person for the purpose mentioned in subsection (2) if the person—
  (a)   facilitates the placing of the child in the care of the other person,
  (b)   initiates or takes part in negotiations the purpose or effect of which is—
    (i)   the making of such arrangements, or
    (ii)   the conclusion of an agreement to transfer the care of the child,
for the purpose mentioned in that subsection, or
  (c)   causes any person to initiate or take part in any such negotiations.

(5)   The Scottish Ministers may by regulations provide for subsections (1) to (3) to apply with modifications, or not to apply, if—
  (a)   the prospective adopters are—
    (i)   parents,
    (ii)   relatives, or
    (iii)   guardians,
of the child (or one of them is), or
  (b)   the prospective adopter is a step-parent of the child,
and any conditions prescribed by the regulations are met.

(6)   On the occasion of the first exercise of the power to make regulations under subsection (5)—
  (a)   the regulations must not be made unless a draft of the regulations has been approved by a resolution of the Scottish Parliament, and
  (b)   accordingly section 117(4) does not apply to the statutory instrument containing the regulations.

(7)   In any proceedings under this section—
  (a)   a report by a British consular officer or a deposition made before, and authenticated under the signature of, such an officer is (if proved that the officer or deponent cannot be found in the United Kingdom) sufficient evidence of the matters stated in the report or deposition, and
  (b)   it is not necessary to prove the signature or official character of the person who bears to have signed the report or deposition.

(8)   A person who commits an offence under this section is liable on summary

conviction to imprisonment for a term not exceeding 3 months or a fine not exceeding level 5 on the standard scale or both.

(9)　In subsections (1) and (2), 'protected child' means a child who is—

(a)　habitually resident in the United Kingdom, or

(b)　a Commonwealth citizen.

61　Regulations under section 58: offences

(1)　If a person brings, or causes another to bring, a child into the United Kingdom at any time in circumstances where section 58 applies, the person commits an offence—

(a)　if the person has not complied with any requirement imposed by virtue of subsection (5) of that section, or

(b)　if the person has not met any condition which the person is required to meet by virtue of subsection (6) of that section,

before that time, or before any later time which may be prescribed by regulations made by the Scottish Ministers.

(2)　A person who commits an offence under subsection (1) is liable—

(a)　on summary conviction to imprisonment for a term not exceeding 6 months or a fine not exceeding the statutory maximum or both,

(b)　on conviction on indictment to imprisonment for a term not exceeding 12 months, or a fine or both.

62　Declaration of special restrictions on adoptions from abroad

(1)　This section applies if the Scottish Ministers have reason to believe that, because of practices taking place in a country or territory outwith the British Islands (the 'relevant country') in connection with the adoption of children, it would be contrary to public policy to further the bringing of children into the United Kingdom in the cases mentioned in subsection (2).

(2)　Those cases are—

(a)　that a British resident wishes to bring, or cause another to bring, a child who is not a British resident into the United Kingdom for the purpose of adoption by the British resident and, in connection with the proposed adoption, there have been, or would have to be, proceedings in the relevant country or dealings with authorities or agencies there, or

(b)　that a British resident wishes to bring, or cause another to bring, into the United Kingdom a child adopted by the British resident under an adoption effected, within the period of 12 months ending with the date of the bringing in, under the law of the relevant country.

(3)　The Scottish Ministers may by order declare, in relation to any relevant country, that special restrictions are to apply for the time being in relation to the bringing in of children in the cases mentioned in subsection (2).

(4)　The Scottish Ministers must, as respects each relevant country in relation to which such a declaration has effect for the time being (a 'restricted country'), publish reasons for making the declaration in relation to the country.

(5)　The Scottish Ministers must publish a list of restricted countries ('the restricted list') and keep the list up to date.

(6)　The reasons and the restricted list are to be published in whatever way the Scottish Ministers think appropriate for bringing them to the attention of adoption agencies and members of the public.

(7)　In this section, 'British resident' means a person habitually resident in the British Islands.

(8)　Any reference in this section to adoption by a British resident includes adoption by a British resident and another person.

63　Review

(1)　The Scottish Ministers must keep under review, in relation to each restricted country, whether it should continue to be a restricted country.

(2)   If the Scottish Ministers determine, in relation to a restricted country, that there is no longer a reason to believe what is mentioned in subsection (1) of section 62, they must by order revoke the order containing the declaration made in relation to it under subsection (3) of that section.

(3)   In this section, 'restricted country' has the same meaning as in section 62.

64   The special restrictions

(1)   The special restrictions mentioned in subsection (3) of section 62 are that the Scottish Ministers are not to take any step which they might otherwise have taken in connection with furthering the bringing of a child into the United Kingdom in the cases mentioned in subsection (2) of that section (whether or not that step is provided for by virtue of any enactment).

(2)   Nothing in subsection (1) prevents the Scottish Ministers from taking those steps if, in any particular case, the prospective adopters or, as the case may be, the adopters satisfy the Scottish Ministers that they should take those steps despite the special restrictions.

(3)   The Scottish Ministers may make regulations providing for—

(a)   the procedure to be followed by them in determining whether or not they are satisfied as mentioned in subsection (2),

(b)   matters which they are to take into account when making such a determination (whether or not they also take other matters into account).

65   Imposition of extra conditions in certain cases

(1)   The Scottish Ministers may make regulations providing—

(a)   for them to specify in the restricted list, in relation to any restricted country, a step which is not otherwise provided for by virtue of any enactment but which, by virtue of the arrangements between the United Kingdom and that country, the Scottish Ministers normally take in connection with the bringing in of a child where that country is concerned, and

(b)   that, if such a step has been so specified in relation to a restricted country, one or more conditions specified in the regulations are to be met in respect of a child brought into the United Kingdom in either of the cases mentioned in section 62(2) (reading the reference there to the 'relevant country' as being to the restricted country in question).

(2)   Those conditions are in addition to any provided for by virtue of—

(a)   section 58, or

(b)   any other enactment.

(3)   A person who brings, or causes another to bring, a child into the United Kingdom commits an offence if the person has not met any condition which the person is required to meet by virtue of subsection (1)(b).

(4)   Subsection (3) does not apply if the step specified in the restricted list in relation to any country had already been taken before the publication of the restricted list.

(5)   A person who commits an offence under subsection (3) is liable—

(a)   on summary conviction to imprisonment for a term not exceeding 6 months or a fine not exceeding the statutory maximum or both,

(b)   on conviction on indictment to imprisonment for a term not exceeding 12 months or a fine or both.

(6)   In this section, 'restricted country' and 'restricted list' have the same meanings as in section 62.

66   Power to charge

(1)   This section applies to adoptions to which—

(a)   section 58 applies, or

(b)   regulations made under section 1 of the Adoption (Intercountry Aspects) Act 1999 (c 18) apply.

(2)   The Scottish Ministers may charge a fee to adopters for services provided or to be provided by them in relation to adoptions to which this section applies.

(3)   The Scottish Ministers may determine the level of fee as they see fit and may, in particular—

(a)   charge a flat fee or charge different fees in different cases or descriptions of case,

(b)   in any case or description of case, waive a fee.

(4)   The Scottish Ministers must secure that, taking one financial year with another, the income from fees under this section does not exceed the total cost to them of providing the services in relation to which the fees are imposed.

(5)   In this section, 'financial year' means a period of 12 months ending with 31 March.

(6)   Any references in this section—

(a)   to adoptions include prospective adoptions, and

(b)   to adopters include prospective adopters.

67   Meaning of 'overseas adoption'

(1)   In this Act, 'overseas adoption'—

(a)   means an adoption of a description specified in regulations made by the Scottish Ministers (being a description of adoptions effected under the law of any country or territory outwith the British Islands), but

(b)   does not include a Convention adoption.

(2)   The Scottish Ministers may by regulations prescribe the requirements that ought to be met by an adoption of any description effected after the coming into force of the regulations for it to be an overseas adoption for the purposes of this Act.

(3)   At any time when regulations under subsection (2) are in force, the Scottish Ministers must exercise their power under subsection (1) so as to secure that adoptions of any description effected after the coming into force of the regulations are not overseas adoptions for the purposes of this Act if they consider that such adoptions are not likely, within a reasonable time, to meet the requirements prescribed under subsection (2).

(4)   Regulations under subsection (1) may contain provision as to the manner in which evidence of any overseas adoption may be given.

(5)   In this section, 'adoption' means the adoption of a child or of a person who was a child at the time the adoption was applied for.

68   Annulment and recognition

(1)   The Court of Session may, on an application under this subsection, by order annul a Convention adoption or a Convention adoption order on the ground that the adoption or, as the case may be, order is contrary to public policy.

(2)   The Court of Session may, on an application under this subsection—

(a)   order that an overseas adoption or a determination is to cease to be valid in Great Britain on the ground that the adoption or, as the case may be, determination is contrary to public policy or that the authority which purported to authorise the adoption or make the determination was not competent to entertain the case,

(b)   decide the extent, if any, to which a determination has been affected by a subsequent determination.

(3)   The Court of Session may, in any proceedings in that court, decide that an overseas adoption or a determination is, for the purposes of those proceedings, to be treated as invalid in Great Britain on either of the grounds mentioned in subsection (2)(a).

(4)   An order or decision of the High Court on an application under section 89(2) of the 2002 Act is to be recognised and to have effect as if it were an order or decision of the Court of Session on an application under subsection (2).

(5)   Except as provided by this section, the validity of a Convention adoption, a

Convention adoption order, an overseas adoption or a determination is not to be questioned in proceedings in any court in Scotland.

(6)   In this section 'determination' means such a determination as is mentioned in section 70.

69   Section 68: supplementary provision

(1)   Any application for—
(a)   an order under section 68, or
(b)   a decision under subsection (2)(b) of that section,
is to be made in the manner prescribed in regulations made by the Scottish Ministers and within such period as may be so prescribed.

(2)   No application is to be made under section 68(1) in respect of an adoption unless immediately before the application is made—
(a)   the person adopted was habitually resident in Scotland, or
(b)   the persons on whose application the adoption order was made were habitually resident there.

(3)   In deciding in pursuance of section 68 whether such an authority as is mentioned in section 70 was competent to hear a particular case, a court is to be bound by any finding of fact made by the authority and stated by the authority to be so made for the purpose of determining whether the authority was competent to hear the case.

70   Effect of determinations and orders made outwith Scotland

(1)   Subsection (2) applies where—
(a)   an authority of a Convention country (other than the United Kingdom) having power under the law of that country—
(i)   to authorise, or review the authorisation of, a Convention adoption, or
(ii)   to give or review a decision revoking or annulling such an adoption or a Convention adoption order, or
(b)   an authority of a relevant territory having power under the law of that territory—
(i)   to authorise, or review the authorisation of, a Convention adoption or an adoption effected in that territory, or
(ii)   to give or review a decision revoking or annulling such an adoption or a Convention adoption order,
makes a determination ('the relevant determination') in the exercise of that power.

(2)   Subject to section 68 and any subsequent determination having effect under this subsection, the relevant determination has effect in Scotland for the purpose of effecting, confirming or terminating the adoption in question or confirming its termination as the case may be.

(3)   In subsection (1), 'relevant territory' means—
(a)   any of the Channel Islands,
(b)   the Isle of Man, or
(c)   any British overseas territory (within the meaning of the British Nationality Act 1981 (c 61)).

(4)   Section 35 applies in relation to an order under Article 17 (freeing child for adoption with parental agreement) or 18 (freeing child for adoption without parental agreement) of the Northern Ireland Order as if it were an adoption order.

(5)   Sections 35(2) and (3) and 43 apply in relation to a child who is the subject of an order which—
(a)   is similar to an order under section 59, and
(b)   is made (whether before or after this Act has effect) in a part of the British Islands,
as those sections apply in relation to a child who is the subject of an adoption order.

119   Interpretation

(1)   In this Act, unless the context otherwise requires—

...

'the Convention' means the Convention on Protection of Children and Co-operation in respect of Intercountry Adoption, concluded at the Hague on 29th May 1993,

'Convention adoption' means an adoption effected under the law of a Convention country outwith the British Islands and certified in pursuance of Article 23(1) of the Convention,

'Convention adoption order' means an adoption order which, by virtue of regulations under section 1 of the Adoption (Intercountry Aspects) Act 1999 (c 18), is made as a Convention adoption order,

'Convention country' means any country or territory in which the Convention is in force,

(2)   In this Act, unless the context otherwise requires, references to adoption are to the adoption of children, wherever they may be habitually resident, effected under the law of any country or territory, whether within or outwith the British Islands.

PART II

STATUTORY INSTRUMENTS

ADOPTION (DESIGNATION OF OVERSEAS ADOPTIONS) ORDER 1973
(SI 1973/19)

1.   This Order may be cited as the Adoption (Designation of Overseas Adoptions) Order 1973 and shall come into operation on 1st February 1973.

2.   The Interpretation Act 1889 shall apply to the interpretation of this Order as it applies to the interpretation of an Act of Parliament.

3.—(1)   An adoption of an infant is hereby specified as an overseas adoption if it is an adoption effected in a place in relation to which this Article applies and under the law in force in that place.

(2)   [Subject to paragraphs (2A) and (2B) of this Article] as respects any adoption effected before the date on which this Order comes into operation, this Article applies in relation to any place which, at that date, forms part of a country or territory described in Part I or II of the Schedule to this Order and as respects any adoption effected on or after that date, this Article applies in relation to any place which, at the time the adoption is effected, forms part of a country or territory which at that time is a country or territory described in Part I or II of the Schedule to this Order.

[(2A)   This Article applies, as respects any adoption effected on or after 10th July 1995, in relation to any place which, at the time the adoption is effected, forms part of the People's Republic of China.

(2B)   Paragraph (2A) above extends only to Scotland.]

(3)   In this Article the expression—
'infant' means a person who at the time when the application for adoption was made had
not attained the age of 18 years and had not been married;
'law' does not include customary or common law.

4.—(1)   Evidence that an overseas adoption has been effected may be given by the production of a document purporting to be—

(a)   a certified copy of an entry made, in accordance with the law of the country or territory concerned, in a public register relating to the recording of adoptions and showing that the adoption has been effected; or

(b)   a certificate that the adoption has been effected, signed or purporting to be signed by a person authorised by the law of the country or territory concerned to sign such a certificate, or a certified copy of such certificate.

(2)   Where a document produced by virtue of paragraph (1) of this Article is not in English, the Registrar General or the Registrar General of Births, Deaths and Marriages for Scotland, as the case may be, may require the production of an English translation of the document before satisfying himself of the matters specified in section 8 of the Adoption Act 1968.

(3)   Nothing in this Article shall be construed as precluding proof, in accordance with the Evidence (Foreign, Dominion and Colonial Documents) Act 1933, or the Oaths and Evidence (Overseas Authorities and Countries) Act 1963 or otherwise, that an overseas adoption has been effected.

SCHEDULE

PART I
COMMONWEALTH COUNTRIES AND UNITED KINGDOM DEPENDENT
TERRITORIES

Australia
Bahamas
Barbados
Bermuda
Botswana
British Honduras
British Virgin Islands
Canada
Cayman Islands
The Republic of Cyprus
Dominica
Fiji
Ghana
Gibraltar
Guyana
Hong Kong
Jamaica
Kenya
Lesotho
Malawi
Malaysia
Malta
Mauritius
Montserrat
New Zealand
Nigeria
Pitcairn
St Christopher, Nevis and Anguilla
St Vincent
Seychelles
Singapore
Southern Rhodesia
Sri Lanka
Swaziland
Tanzania
Tonga
Trinidad and Tobago
Uganda
Zambia

PART II
OTHER COUNTRIES AND TERRITORIES

Austria
Belgium
Denmark (including Greenland and the Faroes)
Finland
France (including Réunion, Martinique, Guadeloupe and French Guyana)
The Federal Republic of Germany and Land Berlin (West Berlin)
Greece

Iceland
The Republic of Ireland
Israel
Italy
Luxembourg
The Netherlands (including Surinam and the Antilles)
Norway
Portugal (including the Azores and Madeira)
South Africa and South West Africa
Spain (including the Balearics and the Canary Islands)
Sweden
Switzerland
Turkey
The United States of America
Yugoslavia

CIVIL JURISDICTION AND JUDGMENTS ACT 1982 (PROVISIONAL AND PROTECTIVE MEASURES) (SCOTLAND) ORDER 1997
(SI 1997/2780)

2.   The Court of Session shall have power to do anything mentioned in section 27(1) or 28 of the Civil Jurisdiction and Judgments Act 1982 in relation to proceedings of the following descriptions, namely:—
    (a)   proceedings commenced otherwise than in a Brussels or Lugano Contracting State;
    (b)   proceedings whose subject-matter is not within the scope of the 1968 Convention as determined by Article 1 thereof.

3.   The Court of Session shall have power—
    (a)   to grant interim interdict under subsection (1)(c) of section 27 of the Civil Jurisdiction and Judgments Act 1982;
    (b)   to act as described in section 28 of that Act,
in relation to proceedings which are to be commenced otherwise than in a Brussels or Lugano Contracting State.

CIVIL JURISDICTION AND JUDGMENTS ORDER 2001
(SI 2001/3929)
Interpretation
2.—(1)   In this Order—
    'the Act' means the Civil Jurisdiction and Judgments Act 1982;
    ['the 2005 Agreement' means the Agreement made on 19th October 2005 between the European Community and the Kingdom of Denmark on jurisdiction and the recognition and enforcement of judgments in civil and commercial matters;]
    ['the Regulation' means Council Regulation (EC) No 44/2001 of 22nd December 2000 on jurisdiction and the recognition and enforcement of judgments in civil and commercial matters as amended from time to time and as applied by the 2005 Agreement;
    'Regulation State' in any provision, in the application of that provision in relation to the Regulation, means a Member State.]

The Regulation
3.   Schedule 1 to this Order (which applies certain provisions of the Act with modifications for the purposes of the Regulation) shall have effect.

[The 2005 Agreement
3A.   The Regulation shall have effect as regards Denmark in accordance with the
2005 Agreement.]
SCHEDULE 1
THE REGULATION

Interpretation

1.—(1)   In this Schedule—
'court', without more, includes a tribunal;
'judgment' has the meaning given by Article 32 of the Regulation;
'maintenance order' means a maintenance judgment within the meaning of the
Regulation;
'part of the United Kingdom' means England and Wales, Scotland or Northern
Ireland;
'payer', in relation to a maintenance order, means the person liable to make the
payments for which the order provides;
'prescribed' means prescribed by rules of court.

Enforcement of judgments other than maintenance orders (section 4)

2.—(1)   Where a judgment is registered under the Regulation, the reasonable costs
or expenses of and incidental to its registration shall be recoverable as if they were
sums recoverable under the judgment.
   (2)   A judgment registered under the Regulation shall, for the purposes of its
enforcement, be of the same force and effect, the registering court shall have in
relation to its enforcement the same powers, and proceedings for or with respect to
its enforcement may be taken, as if the judgment had been originally given by the
registering court and had (where relevant) been entered.
   (3)   Sub-paragraph (2) is subject to Article 47 (restriction on enforcement where
appeal pending or time for appeal unexpired), to paragraph 5 and to any provision made by rules of court as to the manner in which and conditions subject to
which a judgment registered under the Regulation may be enforced.

Recognition and enforcement of maintenance orders (section 5)

3.—(1)   The Secretary of State's function (under Article 39 and Annex II) of transmitting an application for the recognition or enforcement in the United Kingdom
of a maintenance order (made under Article 38) to a magistrates' court shall be
discharged—
      (a)   as respects England and Wales and Northern Ireland, by the Lord Chan-
   cellor;
      (b)   as respects Scotland, by the Scottish Ministers.
   (2)   Such an application shall be determined in the first instance by the prescribed officer of the court having jurisdiction in the matter.
   (3)   A maintenance order registered under the Regulation shall, for the purposes of its enforcement, be of the same force and effect, the registering court shall
have in relation to its enforcement the same powers, and proceedings for or with
respect to its enforcement may be taken, as if the order had been originally made
by the registering court.

Appeals under Article 44 and Annex IV (section 6)

4.—(1)   The single further appeal on a point of law referred to under Article 44
and Annex IV in relation to the recognition or enforcement of a judgment other
than a maintenance order lies—

(a)   in England and Wales or Northern Ireland, to the Court of Appeal or to the House of Lords in accordance with Part II of the Administration of Justice Act 1969 (appeals direct from the High Court to the House of Lords);

(b)   in Scotland, to the Inner House of the Court of Session.

(2)   Paragraph (a) of sub-paragraph (1) has effect notwithstanding section 15(2) of the Administration of Justice Act 1969 (exclusion of direct appeal to the House of Lords in cases where no appeal to that House lies from a decision of the Court of Appeal).

(3)   The single further appeal on a point of law referred to in Article 44 and Annex IV in relation to the recognition or enforcement of a maintenance order lies—

(a)   in England and Wales, to the High Court by way of case stated in accordance with section 111 of the Magistrates' Courts Act 1980;

(b)   in Scotland, to the Inner House of the Court of Session;

(c)   in Northern Ireland, to the Court of Appeal.

...

Allocation within United Kingdom of jurisdiction with respect to trusts and consumer contracts (section 10)

7.—(1)   The provisions of this paragraph have effect for the purpose of allocating within the United Kingdom jurisdiction in certain proceedings in respect of which the Regulation confers jurisdiction on the courts of the United Kingdom generally and to which section 16 of the Act does not apply.

(2)   Any proceedings which by virtue of Article 5(6) (trusts) are brought in the United Kingdom shall be brought in the courts of the part of the United Kingdom in which the trust is domiciled.

(3)   Any proceedings which by virtue of the Article 16(1) (consumer contracts) are brought in the United Kingdom by a consumer on the ground that he is himself domiciled there shall be brought in the courts of the part of the United Kingdom in which he is domiciled.

Proof and admissibility of certain judgments and related documents (section 11)

8.—(1)   For the purposes of the Regulation—

(a)   a document, duly authenticated, which purports to be a copy of a judgment given by a court of a Regulation State other than the United Kingdom shall without further proof be deemed to be a true copy, unless the contrary is shown; and

(b)   a certificate obtained in accordance with Article 54 and Annex V shall be evidence, and in Scotland sufficient evidence, that the judgment is enforceable in the Regulation State of origin.

(2)   A document purporting to be a copy of a judgment given by any such court as is mentioned in sub-paragraph (1)(a) is duly authenticated for the purposes of this paragraph if it purports—

(a)   to bear the seal of that court; or

(b)   to be certified by any person in his capacity as a judge or officer of that court to be a true copy of a judgment given by that court.

(3)   Nothing in this paragraph shall prejudice the admission in evidence of any document which is admissible apart from this paragraph.

Domicile of individuals (section 41)

9.—(1)   Subject to Article 59 (which contains provisions for determining whether a party is domiciled in a Regulation State), the following provisions of this paragraph determine, for the purposes of the Regulation, whether an individual is domiciled in the United Kingdom or in a particular part of, or place in, the United Kingdom or in a state other than a Regulation State.

(2) An individual is domiciled in the United Kingdom if and only if—
    (a) he is resident in the United Kingdom; and
    (b) the nature and circumstances of his residence indicate that he has a substantial connection with the United Kingdom.

(3) Subject to sub-paragraph (5), an individual is domiciled in a particular part of the United Kingdom if and only if—
    (a) he is resident in that part; and
    (b) the nature and circumstances of his residence indicate that he has a substantial connection with that part.

(4) An individual is domiciled in a particular place in the United Kingdom if and only if he—
    (a) is domiciled in the part of the United Kingdom in which that place is situated; and
    (b) is resident in that place.

(5) An individual who is domiciled in the United Kingdom but in whose case the requirements of sub-paragraph (3)(b) are not satisfied in relation to any particular part of the United Kingdom shall be treated as domiciled in the part of the United Kingdom in which he is resident.

(6) In the case of an individual who—
    (a) is resident in the United Kingdom, or in a particular part of the United Kingdom; and
    (b) has been so resident for the last three months or more,
the requirements of sub-paragraph (2)(b) or, as the case may be, sub-paragraph (3)(b) shall be presumed to be fulfilled unless the contrary is proved.

(7) An individual is domiciled in a state other than a Regulation State if and only if—
    (a) he is resident in that state; and
    (b) the nature and circumstances of his residence indicate that he has a substantial connection with that state.

Seat of company, or other legal person or association for purposes of Article 22(2)
(section 43)

10.—(1) The following provisions of this paragraph determine where a company, legal person or association has its seat for the purposes of Article 22(2) (which confers exclusive jurisdiction over proceedings relating to the formation or dissolution of such bodies, or to the decisions of their organs).

(2) A company, legal person or association has its seat in the United Kingdom if and only if—
    (a) it was incorporated or formed under the law of a part of the United Kingdom; or
    (b) its central management and control is exercised in the United Kingdom.

(3) Subject to sub-paragraph (4), a company, legal person or association has its seat in a Regulation State other than the United Kingdom if and only if—
    (a) it was incorporated or formed under the law of that state; or
    (b) its central management and control is exercised in that state.

(4) A company, legal person or association shall not be regarded as having its seat in a Regulation State other than the United Kingdom if—
    (a) it has its seat in the United Kingdom by virtue of sub-paragraph (2)(a); or
    (b) it is shown that the courts of that other state would not regard it for the purposes of Article 22(2) as having its seat there.

Persons deemed to be domiciled in the United Kingdom for certain purposes (section 44)

11.—(1)   This paragraph applies to—
  (a)   proceedings within Section 3 of Chapter II of the Regulation (insurance contracts),
  (b)   proceedings within Section 4 of Chapter II of the Regulation (consumer contracts), and
  (c)   proceedings within Section 5 of Chapter II of the Regulation (employment contracts).
  (2)   A person who, for the purposes of proceedings to which this paragraph applies arising out of the operations of a branch, agency or other establishment in the United Kingdom, is deemed for the purposes of the Regulation to be domiciled in the United Kingdom by virtue of—
  (a)   Article 9(2) (insurers); or
  (b)   Article 15(2) (suppliers of goods, services or credit to consumers), or
  (c)   Article 18(2) (employers),
shall, for the purposes of those proceedings, be treated as so domiciled and as domiciled in the part of the United Kingdom in which the branch, agency or establishment in question is situated.

Domicile of trusts (section 45)

12.—(1)   The following provisions of this paragraph determine for the purposes of the Regulation where a trust is domiciled.
  (2)   A trust is domiciled in the United Kingdom if and only if it is by virtue of sub-paragraph (3) domiciled in a part of the United Kingdom.
  (3)   A trust is domiciled in a part of the United Kingdom if and only if the system of law of that part is the system of law with which the trust has its closest and most real connection.

CONTRACTS (APPLICABLE LAW) ACT 1990 (COMMENCEMENT NO 2) ORDER 2004
(SI 2004/3448)

2.   The following provisions of the Contracts (Applicable Law) Act 1990 shall come into force on 1st March 2005:
  (a)   section 2(1) insofar as it relates to the Brussels Protocol as defined in section 1;
  (b)   section 3(1), (2) and (3)(b).

EXPLANATORY NOTE

(This note is not part of the Order.)

This Order brings into force on 1st March 2005 the following provisions of the Contracts (Applicable Law) Act 1990 ('the 1990 Act'): section 2(1), insofar as it relates to the 1988 Brussels Protocol referred to in section 1, and section 3(1), (2) and (3)(b). It thereby brings that Protocol into force for the United Kingdom.

By commencing these provisions, this Order brings the remainder of the 1990 Act into force for all remaining purposes.

This Protocol defines the scope of the jurisdiction of the European Court of Justice in relation to the 1980 Rome Convention on the Law Applicable to Contractual Obligations and the conditions under which that jurisdiction is to be exercised. This convention determines which country's law is to govern contracts which have a connection with more than one country. It was implemented in the United Kingdom by the 1990 Act and came into force on 8th March 1991.

The United Kingdom ratified the Brussels Protocol on 29th January 1991, but has until recently been unable to bring it into force in this country because that depended on the ratification of another protocol to the convention by all those Member States of the European Union which were parties to it. This second protocol confers jurisdiction on the Court of Justice. The commencement of the Brussels Protocol became possible following the second protocol's ratification by Belgium on 5th May 2004; it came into operation, on an international level, on 1st August 2004.

CROSS–BORDER INSOLVENCY REGULATIONS 2006
(SI 2006/1030)

Co-operation between courts exercising jurisdiction in relation to cross-border insolvency

7.—(1)   An order made by a court in either part of Great Britain in the exercise of jurisdiction in relation to the subject matter of these Regulations shall be enforced in the other part of Great Britain as if it were made by a court exercising the corresponding jurisdiction in that other part.

(2)   However, nothing in paragraph (1) requires a court in either part of Great Britain to enforce, in relation to property situated in that part, any order made by a court in the other part of Great Britain.

(3)   The courts having jurisdiction in relation to the subject matter of these Regulations in either part of Great Britain shall assist the courts having the corresponding jurisdiction in the other part of Great Britain.

PART III

SCOTTISH STATUTORY INSTRUMENTS

INTERCOUNTRY ADOPTION (HAGUE CONVENTION) (SCOTLAND) REGULATIONS 2003
(SSI 2003/19)

PART 1
GENERAL

Citation, commencement and extent

1.—(1) These Regulations may be cited as the Intercountry Adoption (Hague Convention) (Scotland) Regulations 2003 and shall come into force on 1st June 2003.

(2) These Regulations extend to Scotland only.

Interpretation

2.   In these Regulations—

'the Act' means the Adoption (Intercountry Aspects) Act 1999;

'the 1978 Act' means the Adoption (Scotland) Act 1978;

'the 2001 Regulations' means the Adoption of Children from Overseas (Scotland) Regulations 2001;

'the Adoption Agencies Regulations' means the Adoption Agencies (Scotland) Regulations 1996 subject to the modifications set out in Schedule 4;

'adoption agency' means a local authority or an approved adoption society which is an accredited body for the purposes of the Convention;

'adoption panel' has the same meaning as in the Adoption Agencies Regulations;

'contact order' has the same meaning as in section 11(2) of the Children (Scotland) Act 1995;

'eligible to adopt', except in regulations 6(7)(a) and 9(1) has the meaning given in regulation 5;

'local authority' in Part 3 means a local authority acting in its capacity as an adoption agency;

'prospective adopter' in Part 2 means a person who makes an application under regulation 3;

'receiving State' has the same meaning as in the Convention;

'relevant local authority' in Part 2 has the meaning given in regulation 13;

'RSCA' means, in relation to a Convention country other than the United Kingdom, the Central Authority of the receiving State;

'SOCA' means, in relation to a Convention country other than the United Kingdom, the Central Authority of the State of origin;

'State of origin' has the same meaning as in Article 2 of the Convention.

Application for assessment of suitability to be an adoptive parent

3.—(1) A person habitually resident in the British Islands who wishes to adopt a child habitually resident in a Convention country outside the British Islands shall apply to an adoption agency for assessment of that person's suitability to be an adoptive parent.

(2) An application under this regulation shall be made in writing and shall include such information as the agency may require.

Requirement to provide information

4.—(1)   Where an application for assessment is made in accordance with regulation 3, the adoption agency shall—

(a)   explain to the prospective adopter the legal implications of adoption and the procedure in relation to adopting a child under the Convention; and

(b)   provide the prospective adopter with written information about the matters referred to in sub-paragraph (a).

(2)   Paragraph (1) does not apply if the adoption agency is satisfied that the requirements set out in paragraph (1) have been carried out in respect of the prospective adopter by another adoption agency.

PART 2
PROCEDURE IN SCOTLAND WHERE THE UNITED KINGDOM IS THE RECEIVING STATE

Eligibility requirements

5.   An adoption agency shall not consider a person eligible to adopt unless—

(a)   in the case of an application for assessment under regulation 3 by a married couple, they have both attained the age of 21 years and the requirement prescribed in regulation 30(2)(a) is complied with; or

(b)   in the case of an application for assessment under regulation 3 by any other person, that person has attained the age of 21 years and the requirement prescribed in regulation 30(2)(a) is complied with.

...

Article 16 report from SOCA and Article 17 Agreement

10.—(1)   Where the Central Authority receive from SOCA the report and additional information specified in Article 16 of the Convention relating to the child whom SOCA considers should be placed for adoption with the prospective adopter, the Central Authority shall send that report and the additional information ('the documents') to the adoption agency.

(2)   The adoption agency shall consider the documents and shall—

(a)   send the report about the child to the prospective adopter; and

(b)   meet with the prospective adopter to—

(i)   discuss the report and the proposed placement; and

(ii)   offer such counselling as may be necessary in connection with the proposed adoption.

(3)   The prospective adopter (or where the prospective adopter is a married couple and there are exceptional circumstances, one of them) shall visit the child in the State of origin before the prospective adopter may give notice to the adoption agency that the prospective adopter wishes to proceed with the proposed adoption.

(4)   Following any agreement under Article 17(c) of the Convention and the placement of the child with the prospective adopter by SOCA, the prospective adopter or, in exceptional circumstances, a nominee of the prospective adopter who has been approved by the adoption agency shall accompany the child on entering the United Kingdom.

(5)   Where—

(a)   the procedure set out in paragraph (2) has been followed; and

(b)   the prospective adopter has informed the adoption agency in writing that—

(i)   the prospective adopter (or where the prospective adopter is a married couple and there are exceptional circumstances, one of them) has visited the child in the State of origin; and

(ii)   the prospective adopter wishes to proceed to adopt the child,

the adoption agency shall notify the Central Authority accordingly and at the same time confirm that it is satisfied that there are no impediments to the adoption proceeding.

(6)   Where the Central Authority has received notification from the adoption agency under paragraph (5), the Central Authority shall—

(a)   notify SOCA that—

(i)   the prospective adopter wishes to proceed to adopt the child;

(ii)   the Central Authority is prepared to agree with SOCA that the adoption may proceed; and

(b)   confirm to SOCA that—

(i)   in the case where the requirements specified in section 1(5A) of the British Nationality Act 1981 are met that the child will be authorised to enter and reside permanently in the United Kingdom; and

(ii)   in any other case, if entry clearance and leave to enter and remain, as may be necessary, is granted and not revoked or curtailed and a Convention adoption order or a Convention adoption is made, the child will be authorised to enter and reside permanently in the United Kingdom.

(7)   The Central Authority shall inform the adoption agency and the prospective adopter when the agreement under Article 17(c) of the Convention has been made.

(8)   If, at any stage before the agreement under Article 17(c) of the Convention is made, SOCA notifies the Central Authority that it has decided the proposed placement should not proceed, then—

(a)   the Central Authority shall inform the adoption agency of SOCA's decision;

(b)   the adoption agency shall then inform the prospective adopter of that decision and return the documents to the Central Authority; and

(c)   the Central Authority shall then return the documents to SOCA.

(9)   If, at any stage before the child is placed with the prospective adopter, the prospective adopter notifies the adoption agency that the prospective adopter does not wish to proceed with the adoption of the child, the adoption agency shall inform the Central Authority and return the documents to that Central Authority who shall in turn notify SOCA of the prospective adopter's decision and return the documents to SOCA.

Duty of adoption agency before child's arrival in Scotland

11.   Where the adoption agency is informed by the Central Authority that the agreement under Article 17(c) of the Convention has been made and the adoption may proceed, the adoption agency shall—

(a)   send a written report of the child's health history and current state of health, so far as it is known, to the prospective adopter's registered medical practitioner, if any, together with particulars of the placement;

(b)   in a case where the adoption agency is not the local authority within whose area the prospective adopter has their home, notify that authority of the particulars of the placement; and

(c)   notify the local education authority within whose area the prospective adopter has their home in writing of the particulars of the placement if the child is of compulsory school age within the meaning of section 31 of the Education Act (Scotland) 1980 or if the adoption agency's medical adviser considers the child either—

(i)   to have a problem of medical significance;

(ii)   to have [additional support needs within the meaning of the Education (Additional Support for Learning) (Scotland) Act 2004 (asp 4)]; or

(iii)   to be disabled.

Child placed with prospective adopter but no Convention adoption is made in the State of origin

12.   Regulations 13 to 17 apply where, following agreement between the Central

Authority and SOCA under Article 17(c) of the Convention that the adoption may proceed, no Convention adoption is made, or applied for, in the State of origin but the child is placed with the prospective adopter by SOCA and the prospective adopter (or the nominee appointed in terms of regulation 10(4)) then returns to Scotland with the child.

Duty of prospective adopter to notify local authority
13.   A prospective adopter to whom regulation 12 applies shall, within the period of fourteen days beginning with the date on which that person (or the nominee) brings the child into the United Kingdom, give notice to the local authority within whose area that person has their home ('the relevant local authority') of—
    (a)   that person's intention to apply for an adoption order to be made as a Convention adoption order in accordance with section 22 of the 1978 Act; or
    (b)   that person's intention not to proceed with the adoption.

Duty of prospective adopters where child is placed with them
14.—(1)   The prospective adopter with whom the child is placed shall not be obliged to allow the child to visit or stay with any person, or otherwise to allow contact between the child and any person, except under and in terms of a contact order.
    (2)   Subject to paragraphs (3) and (4), the prospective adopter shall not cause or permit—
    (a)   the child to be known by a new surname; or
    (b)   the child to be removed from the United Kingdom,
unless the court gives leave or the relevant local authority agrees.
    (3)   Paragraph (2)(a) does not apply if the competent authority of the State of origin has agreed that the child may be known by a new surname.
    (4)   Paragraph (2)(b) does not prevent the removal of the child for a period of less than one month by the prospective adopter.

...

Convention adoptions subject to a probationary period
18.—(1)   This regulation applies where—
    (a)   the child has been placed with the prospective adopters by the competent authority of the State of origin;
    (b)   a Convention adoption has been applied for by the prospective adopter in the State of origin but the child's placement with the prospective adopter is subject to a probationary period before the Convention adoption is made; and
    (c)   either the prospective adopter returns to Scotland with the child or the child travels to Scotland with a nominee appointed in terms of regulation 10(4), before that probationary period is completed and before the Convention adoption is made in the State of origin.
    (2)   The relevant local authority shall, if requested by the competent authority of the State of origin, submit a report about the placement to that authority and such a report must be prepared within such timescale and shall contain such information as the competent authority may reasonably require.

Procedural requirements following a Convention adoption order or Convention adoption
19.—(1)   Where a Convention adoption order is made by a court in Scotland, the court shall send a copy of that order to the Central Authority.
    (2)   On receipt of an order sent under paragraph (1), the Central Authority shall issue a certificate in the form set out in Schedule 2 certifying that the adoption has been made in accordance with the Convention.
    (3)   A copy of the certificate issued under paragraph (2) shall be sent to—
    (a)   SOCA;
    (b)   the adoptive parents; and

(c)   the adoption agency and, if different, the relevant local authority.

(4)   Where the Central Authority receive a certificate under Article 23 of the Convention in respect of a Convention adoption made in that Convention country, the Central Authority shall send a copy of that certificate to—

(a)   the adoptive parents; and

(b)   the adoption agency.

Refusal of court in Scotland to make a Convention adoption order

20.—(1)   Where an application for a Convention adoption order is refused by the court the prospective adopter shall surrender the child to the relevant local authority within the period determined by the court for that purpose.

(2)   Subject to paragraph (3), where an application for a Convention adoption order is withdrawn and the prospective adopter notifies the adoption agency that the prospective adopter does not intend to submit a fresh application for a Convention adoption order, then the prospective adopter shall surrender the child to the relevant local authority within 7 days after such notification.

(3)   Notwithstanding paragraph (2), where an application for a Convention adoption order is withdrawn and a fresh application for a Convention adoption order has not been submitted to the court within 28 days after the date of such withdrawal or such longer period as the relevant local authority may agree in writing, the prospective adopter shall surrender the child to the relevant local authority within 7 days of the expiry of that period.

Annulment of a Convention adoption order or a Convention adoption

21.   Where a Convention adoption order or a Convention adoption is annulled under section 53(1) of the 1978 Act the court shall send a copy of the order to—

(a)   the Central Authority for onward transmission to SOCA;

(b)   the adoptive parents; and

(c)   the adoption agency and, if different, the relevant local authority.

PART 3

PROCEDURE IN SCOTLAND WHERE THE UNITED KINGDOM IS THE
STATE OF ORIGIN

Duty of adoption agency in respect of assessment of child

22.—(1)   This regulation applies where—

(a)   a local authority—

(i)   has decided that adoption is in the best interests of a child under regulation 11(1) of the Adoption Agencies Regulations;

(ii)   has considered the possibilities for placement of that child within the British Islands; and

(iii)   considers that adoption by a person habitually resident in a Convention country outside the British Islands may be in the child's best interests; and

(b)   the child is free for adoption by virtue of an order made under section 18 of the 1978 Act, section 18 of the Adoption Act 1976 or Article 17(1) or 18(1) of the Adoption (Northern Ireland) Order 1987.

(2)   The local authority shall refer the case of the child to the adoption panel together with—

(a)   the documents referred to in regulation 8 of the Adoption Agencies Regulations originally sent to the adoption panel; and

(b)   a report from the child's social worker—

(i)   explaining why that social worker considers that adoption by a person habitually resident in a Convention country outside the British Islands may be in the child's best interests; and

(ii)   if appropriate, having regard to the child's age and understanding, setting out the child's views and wishes in relation to adoption.

Function of the adoption panel in assessing the child
23.—(1) The adoption panel shall consider the case of the child and make a recommendation to the local authority as to whether adoption by a person habitually resident in a Convention country outside the British Islands is in the best interests of the child.

(2) In considering what recommendation to make, the adoption panel shall have regard to the duties imposed upon the local authority by sections 6, 6A and 7 of the 1978 Act (duty to promote the welfare of the child and religious upbringing of adopted child) and shall—

(a) consider and take into account all of the information and the reports passed to it under regulation 22(2);

(b) request the local authority to obtain any other relevant information which the panel considers necessary; and

(c) obtain legal advice in relation to the case as may be necessary.

Decision and notification
24.—(1) The local authority shall make a decision on the matter referred to the adoption panel within 14 days after the date of recommendation by the adoption panel and shall do so only after taking into account the recommendation of the adoption panel.

(2) No member of an adoption panel shall take part in any decision made by the local authority under paragraph (1).

(3) The local authority shall, within 7 days of making its decision, notify the Central Authority of—

(a) the name and age of the child;

(b) the reasons why they consider that the child may be suitable for adoption by a person habitually resident in a Convention country outside the British Islands;

(c) the date on which the freeing order under section 18 of the Adoption Act 1976, section 18 of the 1978 Act or Article 17(1) or 18(1) of the Adoption (Northern Ireland) Order 1987 was made; and

(d) any other information that Authority may require.

(4) The Central Authority shall maintain a list of children who are notified to it under paragraph (3).

(5) The Central Authority shall make the contents of the Convention list available for inspection by the other central authorities within the British Islands on request.

(6) In the event that a local authority either completes an alternative placement for a child who is the subject of a notification in terms of paragraph (3) or otherwise determines that adoption by a person habitually resident in a Convention Country outside the British Islands is no longer in the best interests of such a child, that local authority shall notify the Central Authority of that fact and the Central Authority shall amend the Convention list accordingly.

(7) Subject to paragraph (8), within 7 days of the decision under paragraph (1), the local authority shall notify in writing the parents of the child including, where the local authority considers this to be in the child's best interests, the father or mother of the child who is a parent in terms of section 15(1) of the Children (Scotland) Act 1995 but who does not have parental responsibilities, or the guardian of the child if their whereabouts are known to the local authority, that the child has been approved in principle for adoption in a Convention country outside the British Islands.

(8) No notification shall be given in terms of paragraph (7) to a person who has made a declaration under section 18(6) or 19(4) of the 1978 Act (declaration as to no further involvement with the child) and has not withdrawn that declaration under section 19 of the 1978 Act.

(9) In this regulation and in regulation 25 'Convention list' means—

(a)   in relation to the Central Authority, a list of children notified to that authority in accordance with paragraph (3); or

(b)   in relation to any other central authority within the British Islands, a list of children notified to that Authority in accordance with provisions which correspond to paragraph (3).

Receipt of Article 15 report from RSCA

25.—(1)   This regulation applies where—

(a)   the Central Authority receives a report ('the Article 15 report') from the RSCA which has been prepared for the purposes of Article 15 of the Convention;

(b)   the Article 15 report relates to a prospective adopter who is habitually resident in the receiving State and has applied for a determination as to suitability and eligibility to adopt in terms of Article 5 of the Convention (a 'Convention prospective adopter'); and

(c)   the Convention prospective adopter wishes to adopt a child who is habitually resident in Scotland.

(2)   If the Central Authority is satisfied that the Convention prospective adopter meets those requirements as to age and marital status which are required to be met if an adoption order were to be made in Scotland in favour of that person, the Central Authority shall consult the Convention list and, if the Central Authority considers it appropriate, consult any Convention list maintained by another central authority within the British Islands.

(3)   The Central Authority may pass a copy of the Article 15 report to the other Central authorities within the British Islands for the purpose of enabling those authorities to consult their Convention list.

(4)   Where the Central Authority identifies a child who may be suitable to be adopted by the Convention prospective adopter, it shall send the Article 15 report to the local authority which referred the child's details to the Central Authority.

(5)   The local authority shall consider the report and where it considers that it may be appropriate to place the child for adoption with the Convention prospective adopter it shall refer the proposed placement for adoption to the adoption panel together with—

(a)   the Article 15 report;

(b)   the documents referred to in regulation 22(2);

(c)   its observations on the proposed placement; and

(d)   any other relevant information about the child.

Function of adoption panel in assessing proposed placement

26.—(1)   The adoption panel shall consider the proposed placement referred to it by the local authority under regulation 25(5) and make a recommendation to the local authority, as to whether—

(a)   the Convention prospective adopter is a suitable adoptive parent for the child; and

(b)   the proposed placement is in the best interests of the child.

(2)   In considering what recommendation to make under paragraph (1), the adoption panel—

(a)   shall have regard to the child's upbringing and the child's ethnic, religious and cultural background;

(b)   shall have regard to the duties imposed upon it by sections 6, 6A and 7 of the 1978 Act (duty to promote welfare of child and religious upbringing of adopted child);

(c)   shall have regard to the documents referred to it under regulation 25(5);

(d)   may ask the local authority to obtain any other relevant information which the panel considers necessary; and

(e)   may obtain legal advice as it considers necessary in relation to the case.

(3)   The local authority shall make a decision about the proposed placement

within 14 days after the date of decision by the adoption panel and shall do so only after having taken into account the recommendations of the adoption panel.

(4)   No member of an adoption panel shall take part in any decision made by the local authority under paragraph (3).

(5)   Subject to paragraph (6), within 7 days of the decision under paragraph (3), the local authority shall notify in writing the parents of the child including, where the local authority considers this to be in the child's best interests, the father or mother of the child who is a parent in terms of section 15(1) of the Children (Scotland) Act 1995 but who does not have parental responsibilities, or the guardian of the child if their whereabouts are known to the local authority, that the child has been placed for adoption in a Convention country outside the British Islands.

(6)   No notification shall be given in terms of paragraph (5) to a person who has made a declaration under section 18(6) or 19(4) of the Act (declaration as to no further involvement with the child) and has not withdrawn that declaration under section 19 of the Act.

Preparation of the Article 16 report for RSCA

27.—(1)   Where the local authority decides under regulation 26 that the proposed placement is in the best interests of the child and the adoption may proceed, it shall prepare a report for the purposes of Article 16 of the Convention ('the Article 16 report') which shall include—

(a)   information about the child's identity, suitability for adoption, background, social environment, family history, medical history including that of the child's family, and any special needs of the child; and

(b)   the reasons for its decision.

(2)   The local authority shall, within 14 days of the date of the decision under paragraph 26(3), send the Article 16 report to the Central Authority together with the evidence that a freeing order has been made in respect of the child.

(3)   The Central Authority shall send the Article 16 report and other information referred to it in paragraph (2) to the RSCA.

(4)   The Central Authority may notify the RSCA that it is prepared to agree that the adoption may proceed:

Provided that the RSCA has confirmed that—

(a)   the Convention prospective adopter has agreed to adopt the child and has received such counselling as may be necessary;

(b)   the Convention prospective adopter has confirmed that either—

(i)   the Convention prospective adopter will accompany the child to the receiving State; or

(ii)   in exceptional circumstances, the child will be accompanied by a nominee of the Convention prospective adopter who has been approved by the local authority;

(c)   it is content for the adoption to proceed; and

(d)   the child is or will be authorised to enter and reside permanently in the Convention country if a Convention adoption is made in that Convention country or a Convention adoption order is made in the United Kingdom.

(5)   The Central Authority may not make an agreement under Article 17(c) of the Convention with the RSCA unless the local authority have confirmed that—

(a)   it has met the Convention prospective adopter;

(b)   the Convention prospective adopter (or, where the Convention Prospective adopter is a married couple and there are exceptional circumstances, one of them) has visited the child; and

(c)   it is content for the adoption to proceed.

(6)   A local authority shall not place a child for adoption with a Convention prospective adopter unless the agreement under Article 17(c) of the Convention has been made and the relevant Central Authority shall advise the local authority when that agreement has been made.

Procedural requirements following a Convention adoption order or Convention adoption

28.—(1)   Where a Convention adoption order is made by a court in Scotland, the court shall send a copy of that order to the Central Authority.

(2)   On receipt of an order under paragraph (1), the Central Authority shall issue a certificate in the form set out in Schedule 2 certifying that the Convention adoption order has been made in accordance with the Convention.

(3)   A copy of the certificate shall be sent to—
(a)   the RSCA; and
(b)   the local authority.

Procedural requirements following receipt of Article 23 certificate

29.   Where the Central Authority receives a certificate in terms of Article 23 of the Convention from the RSCA, it shall send a copy of that certificate to—
(a)   the local authority; and
(b)   the Registrar General for Scotland.

PART 4
MISCELLANEOUS

Requirements prescribed for the purposes of section 17 of the 1978 Act

30.—(1)   The requirements which must be complied with for the purposes of section 17 of the 1978 Act are those prescribed in paragraphs (2) and (3).

(2)   Where the United Kingdom is the receiving State the requirements are that—
(a)   both spouses (in the case of an application by a married couple) or the applicant (in the case of an application by one person) have been habitually resident in part of the British Islands for a period of not less than 1 year ending with the date of the application;
(b)   the child to be adopted—
(i)   has not attained the age of 18 years on the date of the application for a Convention adoption order;
(ii)   was, on the date on which the agreement under Article 17(c) was made, habitually resident in a Convention country outside the British Islands; and
(iii)   has, if over the age of twelve years, consented to the making of the Convention adoption order except where the court is satisfied that the child is incapable of giving consent to the making of the order; and
(c)   in a case where the applicant (in the case of an application by one person) or one of the spouses (in the case of an application by a married couple) is not a British citizen by virtue of section 1 of the British Nationality Act 1981, the Home Office has confirmed that the child is authorised to enter and reside permanently in the United Kingdom.

(3)   Where the United Kingdom is the State of origin the requirements are that—
(a)   both spouses (in the case of an application by a married couple) or the applicant (in the case of an application by one person) are habitually resident in a Convention country outside the British Islands on the date of the application; and
(b)   the child to be adopted—
(i)   has not attained the age of 18 years on the date of the application for a Convention adoption order;
(ii)   is free for adoption by virtue of an order made under section 18 of the 1978 Act, section 18 of the Adoption Act 1976, or Article 17(1) or 18(1) of the Adoption (Northern Ireland) Order 1987; and
(iii)   is habitually resident in part of the British Islands on the date of the application.

REGISTRATION OF FOREIGN ADOPTIONS (SCOTLAND) REGULATIONS 2003
(SSI 2003/67)

Citation and commencement
1. These Regulations may be cited as the Registration of Foreign Adoptions (Scotland) Regulations 2003, and shall come into force on 1st June 2003.

Interpretation
2. In these Regulations—
'the 1978 Act' means the Adoption (Scotland) Act 1978;
'the Adopted Children Register' has the same meaning as in section 45 of the 1978 Act;
'central authority' has the same meaning as in the Convention;
'the Convention' means the Convention on Protection of Children and Co-operation in respect of Intercountry Adoption, concluded at the Hague on 29th May 1993;
'Convention adoption' means an adoption effected under the law of any country or territory outside the British Islands in which the Convention is in force, and certified in pursuance of Article 23(1) of the Convention; and
'overseas adoption' has the same meaning as in section 65(2) of the 1978 Act.

Requirements for registration
7.—(1) An application for an entry to be made in the Adopted Children Register in respect of a Convention adoption may be made only if the person making the application provides—
   (a) the Article 23 certificate made under the Convention by the central authority of the appropriate Convention country or territory in respect of the adoption, or a copy of that certificate certified as a true copy of the original by a notary public or equivalent officer; and
   (b) where appropriate, a translation of that certificate into English certified by the translator as a correct translation.
(2) An application for an entry to be made in the Adopted Children Register in respect of an overseas adoption may be made only if the person making the application provides—
   (a) either—
     (i) a certified copy of the adoption order made in respect of the adopted child; or
     (ii) a certified copy of an entry made in respect of the adopted child, in accordance with the law of the country or territory concerned, in a public register relating to the recording of adoptions, and showing that the adoption has been effected; and
   (b) where appropriate, a translation of that order or entry into English certified by the translator as a correct translation.
(3) In paragraph (2)(a) above a copy is certified if it is certified as a true copy of the original order or entry by the court or other competent authority that made that order or entry.

EUROPEAN COMMUNITIES (MATRIMONIAL AND PARENTAL RESPONSIBILITY JURISDICTION AND JUDGMENTS) (SCOTLAND) REGULATIONS 2005
(SSI 2005/42)

Citation, commencement and extent
1.—(1) These Regulations may be cited as the European Communities (Matrimonial and Parental Responsibility Jurisdiction and Judgments) (Scotland) Regulations 2005 and shall come into force on 1st March 2005.

(2)   These Regulations extend to Scotland only.

...

Transitional
6.   Proceedings started under Council Regulation (EC) No 1347/2000 of 29th May 2000 on jurisdiction and the recognition and enforcement of judgments in matrimonial matters and in matters of parental responsibility for children of both spouses may continue under that Regulation until decree as if these Regulations had not been made.

...

Application
7.   The amendments to—
(a)   the Domicile and Matrimonial Proceedings Act 1973 made by regulation 2;
(b)   the Family Law Act 1986 made by regulation 4; and
(c)   the Children (Scotland) Act 1995 made by regulation 5,
shall apply only in respect of proceedings commenced on or after 1st March 2005.

CIVIL PARTNERSHIP (SUPPLEMENTARY PROVISIONS RELATING TO THE RECOGNITION OF OVERSEAS DISSOLUTIONS, ANNULMENTS OR SEPARATIONS) (SCOTLAND) REGULATIONS 2005
(SSI 2005/567)

Citation, commencement, interpretation and extent
1.—(1)   These Regulations may be cited as the Civil Partnership (Supplementary Provisions relating to the Recognition of Overseas Dissolutions, Annulments or Separations) (Scotland) Regulations 2005 and shall come into force on 5th December 2005.
(2)   In these Regulations 'the Act' means the Civil Partnership Act 2004.
(3)   These Regulations extend to Scotland only.

...

Cross-proceedings
4.   Where there have been cross-proceedings, the validity of an overseas dissolution, annulment or separation obtained either in the original proceedings or in the cross-proceedings shall be recognised if—
(a)   the requirements of section 235(1)(b)(i), (ii) or (iii) of the Act or of regulation 3 above are satisfied in relation to the date of the commencement either of the original proceedings or of the cross-proceedings; and
(b)   the validity of the dissolution, annulment or separation is otherwise entitled to recognition by virtue of sections 235 and 236 of the Act.

Dissolutions following separations
5.—(1)   Where a separation, the validity of which is entitled to recognition either by virtue of section 235 of the Act or by virtue of regulation 3 or 4 above, is converted, under the law of the country in which it was obtained, into a dissolution which is effective under the law of that country, the validity of that dissolution shall be recognised whether or not that dissolution would itself be entitled to recognition by virtue of any of those provisions.
(2)   In cases where a country comprises territories in which different systems of law are in force in matters concerning the dissolution or annulment of a civil partnership or the separation of civil partners, for the words in paragraph (1) above 'under the law of the country in which it was obtained, into a dissolution which is effective under the law of that country' there shall be substituted the words 'under the law of the territory in which it was obtained, into a dissolution which is effective throughout the country of which that territory forms a part'.

Proof of facts relevant to recognition

6.—(1)   For the purpose of deciding whether an overseas dissolution, annulment or separation obtained by means of proceedings is entitled to recognition by virtue of section 235 of the Act or regulation 3, 4 or 5 above, any finding of fact made (whether expressly or by implication) in the proceedings and on the basis of which jurisdiction was assumed in the proceedings shall—

(a)   if both parties to the civil partnership took part in the proceedings, be conclusive evidence of the fact found; and

(b)   in any other case, be sufficient proof of that fact unless the contrary is shown.

(2)   In this regulation 'finding of fact' includes a finding that either party to the civil partnership—

(a)   was habitually resident in the country in which the dissolution, annulment or separation was obtained;

(b)   was under the law of that country domiciled there; or

(c)   was a national of that country.

(3)   For the purposes of paragraph (1)(a) above, a party to the civil partnership who has appeared in judicial proceedings shall be treated as having taken part in them.

(4)   References in this regulation to 'country' include references to a territory which comprises part of a country in which different systems of law are in force in matters relating to the dissolution or annulment of a civil partnership or the separation of civil partners.

**CIVIL PARTNERSHIP ACT 2004 (OVERSEAS RELATIONSHIPS)
(SCOTLAND) ORDER 2005
(SSI 2005/573)**

Citation, commencement, interpretation and extent

1.—(1)   This Order may be cited as the Civil Partnership (Overseas Relationships) (Scotland) Order 2005 and shall come into force on 5th December 2005.

(2)   In this Order—

'the Act' means the Civil Partnership Act 2004; and

'recognised overseas relationship' means an overseas relationship which is treated as a civil partnership pursuant to chapter 2 of Part 5 of the Act.

(3)   This Order shall extend to Scotland only.

Overseas relationships dissolved etc. before commencement treated as civil partnerships

2.   The following provisions are specified for the purpose of section 215(5)(b) of the Act (overseas relationships treated as civil partnerships: the general rule)—

(a)   section 2 (Marriage of related persons) and section 3 (Notice of intention to marry) of and Schedule 1 (Degrees of Relationship) to the Marriage (Scotland) Act 1977;

(b)   the Damages (Scotland) Act 1976; and

(c)   section 86 (Eligibility) and section 88 (Notice of proposed civil partnership) of and Schedule 10 (Forbidden Degrees of Relationship: Scotland) to the Act.

Transitional provision relating to overseas relationships

3.   Section 212 of the Act shall apply for the purpose of determining whether a relationship entered into before 5th December 2005 is an overseas relationship as though for the words in subsection (1)(b) from 'and' to the end of the subsection there were substituted—

'(ii)   neither of whom is lawfully married or a party to a recognised overseas relationship registered under the relevant law before the relationship concerned was entered into; and

(iii) neither of whom is on 5th December a party to a marriage which on the date of its celebration was valid according to the law of Scotland (including its rules of private international law).'.

CIVIL PARTNERSHIP (JURISDICTION AND RECOGNITION OF JUDGMENTS) (SCOTLAND) REGULATIONS 2005
(SSI 2005/629)

Citation, commencement and extent

1. These Regulations may be cited as the Civil Partnership (Jurisdiction and Recognition of Judgments) (Scotland) Regulations 2005 and come into force on 5th December 2005.

2. These Regulations extend to Scotland only.

Application

3.—(1) These Regulations apply to proceedings for the dissolution or annulment of an overseas relationship entitled to be treated as a civil partnership, or for the separation of the parties to the same, as they apply to proceedings for the dissolution or annulment of a civil partnership or the separation of civil partners.

(2) Regulations 6 and 7, in respect of recognition and non-recognition of a judgment, apply to all judgments even if the date of the judgment is earlier than the date on which section 219 of the Civil Partnership Act 2004 and these Regulations come into force.

PART 1
JURISDICTION

Jurisdiction

4. The courts in Scotland shall have jurisdiction in relation to proceedings for the dissolution or annulment of a civil partnership or for the separation of civil partners where—

(a) both civil partners are habitually resident in Scotland;

(b) both civil partners were last habitually resident in Scotland and one of the civil partners continues to reside there;

(c) the defender is habitually resident in Scotland;

(d) the pursuer is habitually resident in Scotland and has resided there for at least one year immediately preceding the date on which the action is begun; or

(e) the pursuer is domiciled and habitually resident in Scotland and has resided there for at least six months immediately preceding the date on which the action is begun.

PART 2
RECOGNITION AND REFUSAL OF RECOGNITION OF JUDGMENTS

Definitions for Part 2

5.—(1) In this Part 'judgment' means an order for the dissolution or annulment of a civil partnership or the separation of civil partners pronounced by a court of a member State, however termed by that State.

(2) A 'court of a member State' referred to in paragraph (1) means all the authorities, whether judicial or administrative, in member States with jurisdiction in those matters falling within the scope of these Regulations.

(3) The 'member States' referred to in paragraph 1 are any of the following States—

Austria, Belgium, Cyprus, Czech Republic, Denmark, Estonia, Finland, France, Germany, Greece, Hungary, Ireland, Italy, Latvia, Lithuania, Luxembourg, Malta, Netherlands, Poland, Portugal, Slovakia, Slovenia, Spain and Sweden.

Recognition of a judgment

6.—(1) Subject to regulation 7, where a judgment is (or has been) given in respect of a civil partnership, that judgment shall be recognised in Scotland.

(2) Any interested party may apply to the Court of Session for a declarator of recognition or non recognition of a judgment.

(3) Where the recognition of a judgment is raised as an incidental issue in proceedings before a court, that court may determine the issue.

Refusal of recognition of a judgment

7.—(1) Recognition of the validity of a judgment may be refused in Scotland if the judgment was obtained at a time when it was irreconcilable with a decision determining the question of the subsistence or validity of the civil partnership—

(a) previously given by a court of civil jurisdiction in Scotland; or

(b) previously given by a court elsewhere and recognised or entitled to be recognised in Scotland.

(2) Recognition of the validity of a judgment may be refused in Scotland if the judgment was obtained at a time when, according to the law of Scotland, there was no subsisting civil partnership.

(3) Recognition of the validity of a judgment may be refused if—

(a) in the case of a judgment obtained by means of proceedings, it was obtained—

(i) without such steps having been taken for giving notice of the proceeding to a civil partner as, having regard to the nature of the proceedings and all the circumstances, should reasonably have been taken, or

(ii) without a civil partner having been given (for any reason other than lack of notice) such opportunity to take part in the proceedings as, having regard to those matters, he should reasonably have been given; or

(b) in the case of a judgment obtained otherwise than by means of proceedings—

(i) there is no official document certifying the judgment is effective under the law of the country in which it was obtained, or

(ii) where either civil partner was domiciled in another country at the relevant date, there is no official document certifying that the judgment is recognised as valid under the law of that other country; or

(c) in either case, recognition of the judgment would be manifestly contrary to public policy.

(4) In this regulation—

'official', in relation to a document certifying that a judgment is effective, or is recognised as valid, under the law of any country, means issued by a person or a body appointed or recognised for the purpose under that law; and

'the relevant date' means—

(a) in the case of a judgment obtained by means of proceedings, the date of commencement of proceedings; or

(b) in the case of a judgment obtained otherwise than by means of proceedings, the date on which it was obtained.

Jurisdiction and review

8. The court may not review the jurisdiction of the court which issued the judgment.

9. A judgment may not be reviewed as to its substance.

Differences in applicable law

10. The recognition of a judgment may not be refused because the law of Scotland would not allow dissolution, annulment or separation on the same facts.

Sist of proceedings

11.   Where recognition is sought of a judgment given in a member State and an appeal against that judgment has been lodged in that member State, the court may sist the proceedings.

FAMILY LAW (SCOTLAND) ACT 2006 (COMMENCEMENT, TRANSITIONAL PROVISIONS AND SAVINGS) ORDER 2006 (SSI 2006/212)

Citation and interpretation

1.   ....
  (2)   In this Order—
    (a)   'the Act' means the Family Law (Scotland) Act 2006;
    (b)   'the 1986 Act' means the Law Reform (Parent and Child) (Scotland) Act 1986; and
    (c)   references to sections, subsections and schedules are, unless otherwise stated, references to sections and subsections of, and schedules to, the Act.

2.   Subject to the transitional provisions and savings contained in articles 3 to 13, the provisions of the Act shall come into force on 4th May 2006.

Transitional provisions

3.   In so far as they relate to periods of non-cohabitation, the provisions of sections 5, 6 and 8, and paragraphs 3 to 5 and 7 of schedule 1 shall not apply where spouses or, as the case may be, civil partners cease to cohabit before 4th May 2006.

4.   The provisions of sections 12, 16, 21, 22, 32, and 37 to 42 and paragraph 1 of schedule 2 shall not apply in relation to any proceedings which commenced before 4th May 2006.

5.   The provisions of section 19 and paragraph 11 of schedule 1 shall not apply where spouses are divorced or any marriage is annulled or, as the case may be, any civil partnership is dissolved or annulled before 4th May 2006.

6.   The provisions of section 28 shall not apply in respect of cohabitants who cease to cohabit before 4th May 2006.

7.   The provisions of section 29 shall not apply where a cohabitant dies before 4th May 2006.

8.   The provisions of section 35 shall not apply in respect of deaths which occur before 4th May 2006.

Savings provisions

9.   Notwithstanding commencement of the amendment in section 21(2)(c) adding subsection (6) of section 1 of the 1986 Act, it shall continue to be competent to bring an action for declarator of legitimacy, legitimation or illegitimacy for the purposes of the determination of any question mentioned in subsection (4) of that section.

10.   Notwithstanding commencement of the amendment to section 7 of the 1986 Act in paragraph 6(2) of schedule 2, that section shall continue to have effect on and after 4th May 2006 as it had effect immediately before that date in relation to actions for declarator of legitimacy, legitimation or illegitimacy brought for the purposes of the determination of any question mentioned in section 1(4) of the 1986 Act.

11.   Notwithstanding commencement of its repeal in schedule 3, the Legitimation (Scotland) Act 1968 shall continue to have effect on and after 4th May 2006 as it had effect immediately before that date for the purposes of the determination of any question as to the succession to or devolution of any title, honour or dignity.

12. Notwithstanding commencement of the repeal in schedule 3 of the words 'legitimacy, legitimation, illegitimacy' in section 8(2) of the Civil Evidence (Scotland) Act 1988, that section shall continue to have effect on and after 4th May 2006 as it had effect immediately before that date in relation to actions for declarator of legitimacy, legitimation or illegitimacy brought for the purposes of the determination of any question mentioned in section 1(4) or 9(1)(c) or (ca) of the 1986 Act.

DIVORCE (RELIGIOUS BODIES) (SCOTLAND) REGULATIONS 2006
(SSI 2006/253)

Citation and commencement
1. These Regulations may be cited as the Divorce (Religious Bodies) (Scotland) Regulations 2006 and shall come into force on 3rd June 2006.

Religious body
2. Any Hebrew Congregation is prescribed as a religious body for the purposes of section 3A(7) of the Divorce (Scotland) Act 1976.

PART IV

EC MATERIALS

TREATY ESTABLISHING THE EUROPEAN COMMUNITY (AMSTERDAM CONSOLIDATED VERSION)

OJ 1997 C340/173

TITLE IV(ex Title IIIa) VISAS, ASYLUM, IMMIGRATION AND OTHER POLICIES RELATED TO FREE MOVEMENT OF PERSONS

Article 61 (ex Article 73i)
In order to establish progressively an area of freedom, security and justice, the Council shall adopt:
...
(c)   measures in the field of judicial cooperation in civil matters as provided for in Article 65;

...

Article 65 (ex Article 73m)
Measures in the field of judicial cooperation in civil matters having cross-border implications, to be taken in accordance with Article 67 and insofar as necessary for the proper functioning of the internal market, shall include:
(a)   improving and simplifying:
– the system for cross-border service of judicial and extrajudicial documents;
– cooperation in the taking of evidence;
– the recognition and enforcement of decisions in civil and commercial cases, including decisions in extrajudicial cases;
(b)   promoting the compatibility of the rules applicable in the Member States concerning the conflict of laws and of jurisdiction;
(c)   eliminating obstacles to the good functioning of civil proceedings, if necessary by promoting the compatibility of the rules on civil procedure applicable in the Member States.

...

Article 67 (ex Article 73o)
1.   During a transitional period of five years following the entry into force of the Treaty of Amsterdam, the Council shall act unanimously on a proposal from the Commission or on the initiative of a Member State and after consulting the European Parliament.
2.   After this period of five years:
– the Council shall act on proposals from the Commission; the Commission shall examine any request made by a Member State that it submit a proposal to the Council;
– the Council, acting unanimously after consulting the European Parliament, shall take a decision with a view to providing for all or parts of the areas covered by this Title to be governed by the procedure referred to in Article 251 and adapting the provisions relating to the powers of the Court of Justice.
3.   By derogation from paragraphs 1 and 2, measures referred to in Article 62(2)(b)(i) and (iii) shall, from the entry into force of the Treaty of Amsterdam, be

adopted by the Council acting by a qualified majority on a proposal from the Commission and after consulting the European Parliament.

4.   By derogation from paragraph 2, measures referred to in Article 62(2)(b) (ii) and (iv) shall, after a period of five years following the entry into force of the Treaty of Amsterdam, be adopted by the Council acting in accordance with the procedure referred to in Article 251.

Article 68 (ex Article 73p)

1.   Article 234 shall apply to this Title under the following circumstances and conditions: where a question on the interpretation of this Title or on the validity or interpretation of acts of the institutions of the Community based on this Title is raised in a case pending before a court or a tribunal of a Member State against whose decisions there is no judicial remedy under national law, that court or tribunal shall, if it considers that a decision on the question is necessary to enable it to give judgment, request the Court of Justice to give a ruling thereon.

...

3.   The Council, the Commission or a Member State may request the Court of Justice to give a ruling on a question of interpretation of this Title or of acts of the institutions of the Community based on this Title. The ruling given by the Court of Justice in response to such a request shall not apply to judgments of courts or tribunals of the Member States which have become res judicata.

Article 69 (ex Article 73q)

The application of this Title shall be subject to the provisions of the Protocol on the position of the United Kingdom and Ireland and to the Protocol on the position of Denmark and without prejudice to the Protocol on the application of certain aspects of Article 14 of the Treaty establishing the European Community to the United Kingdom and to Ireland.

TREATY OF AMSTERDAM AMENDING THE TREATY ON EUROPEAN UNION, THE TREATIES ESTABLISHING THE EUROPEAN COMMUNITIES AND CERTAIN RELATED ACTS—PROTOCOL ON THE POSITION OF THE UNITED KINGDOM AND IRELAND

Official Journal C 340, 10/11/1997 p 99

THE HIGH CONTRACTING PARTIES,

DESIRING to settle certain questions relating to the United Kingdom and Ireland,

HAVING REGARD to the Protocol on the application of certain aspects of Article 7a of the Treaty establishing the European Community to the United Kingdom and to Ireland,

HAVE AGREED UPON the following provisions which shall be annexed to the Treaty establishing the European Community and to the Treaty on European Union,

Article 1

Subject to Article 3, the United Kingdom and Ireland shall not take part in the adoption by the Council of proposed measures pursuant to Title IIIa of the Treaty establishing the European Community. By way of derogation from Article 148(2) of the Treaty establishing the European Community, a qualified majority shall be defined as the same proportion of the weighted votes of the members of the Council concerned as laid down in the said Article 148(2). The unanimity of the members of the Council, with the exception of the representatives of the governments of the United Kingdom and Ireland, shall be necessary for decisions of the Council which must be adopted unanimously.

Article 2

In consequence of Article 1 and subject to Articles 3, 4 and 6, none of the provisions of Title IIIa of the Treaty establishing the European Community, no measure adopted pursuant to that Title, no provision of any international agreement concluded by the Community pursuant to that Title, and no decision of the Court of Justice interpreting any such provision or measure shall be binding upon or applicable in the United Kingdom or Ireland and no such provision, measure or decision shall in any way affect the competences, rights and obligations of those States and no such provision, measure or decision shall in any way affect the acquis communautaire nor form part of Community law as they apply to the United Kingdom or Ireland.

Article 3

1. The United Kingdom or Ireland may notify the President of the Council in writing, within three months after a proposal or initiative has been presented to the Council pursuant to Title IIIa of the Treaty establishing the European Community, that it wishes to take part in the adoption and application of any such proposed measure, whereupon that State shall be entitled to do so. By way of derogation from Article 148(2) of the Treaty establishing the European Community, a qualified majority shall be defined as the same proportion of the weighted votes of the members of the Council concerned as laid down in the said Article 148(2).

The unanimity of the members of the Council, with the exception of a member which has not made such a notification, shall be necessary for decisions of the Council which must be adopted unanimously. A measure adopted under this paragraph shall be binding upon all Member States which took part in its adoption.

2. If after a reasonable period of time a measure referred to in paragraph 1 cannot be adopted with the United Kingdom or Ireland taking part, the Council may adopt such measure in accordance with Article 1 without the participation of the United Kingdom or Ireland. In that case Article 2 applies.

Article 4

The United Kingdom or Ireland may at any time after the adoption of a measure by the Council pursuant to Title IIIa of the Treaty establishing the European Community notify its intention to the Council and to the Commission that it wishes to accept that measure. In that case, the procedure provided for in Article 5a(3) of the Treaty establishing the European Community shall apply mutatis mutandis.

Article 5

A Member State which is not bound by a measure adopted pursuant to Title IIIa of the Treaty establishing the European Community shall bear no financial consequences of that measure other than administrative costs entailed for the institutions.

Article 6

Where, in cases referred to in this Protocol, the United Kingdom or Ireland is bound by a measure adopted by the Council pursuant to Title IIIa of the Treaty establishing the European Community, the relevant provisions of that Treaty, including Article 73p, shall apply to that State in relation to that measure.

Article 7

Articles 3 and 4 shall be without prejudice to the Protocol integrating the Schengen acquis into the framework of the European Union.

Article 8

Ireland may notify the President of the Council in writing that it no longer wishes to be covered by the terms of this Protocol. In that case, the normal treaty provisions will apply to Ireland.

COUNCIL REGULATION (EC) NO 1346/2000 OF 29 MAY 2000 ON INSOLVENCY PROCEEDINGS

Official Journal L 160, 30/06/2000 p 1

THE COUNCIL OF THE EUROPEAN UNION,

Having regard to the Treaty establishing the European Community, and in particular Articles 61 (c) and 67(1) thereof,
   Having regard to the initiative of the Federal Republic of Germany and the Republic of Finland,
   Having regard to the opinion of the European Parliament,
   Having regard to the opinion of the Economic and Social Committee,

Whereas:
   (1)   The European Union has set out the aim of establishing an area of freedom, security and justice.
   (2)   The proper functioning of the internal market requires that cross-border insolvency proceedings should operate efficiently and effectively and this Regulation needs to be adopted in order to achieve this objective which comes within the scope of judicial cooperation in civil matters within the meaning of Article 65 of the Treaty.
   (3)   The activities of undertakings have more and more cross-border effects and are therefore increasingly being regulated by Community law. While the insolvency of such undertakings also affects the proper functioning of the internal market, there is a need for a Community act requiring coordination of the measures to be taken regarding an insolvent debtor's assets.
   (4)   It is necessary for the proper functioning of the internal market to avoid incentives for the parties to transfer assets or judicial proceedings from one Member State to another, seeking to obtain a more favourable legal position (forum shopping).
   (5)   These objectives cannot be achieved to a sufficient degree at national level and action at Community level is therefore justified.
   (6)   In accordance with the principle of proportionality this Regulation should be confined to provisions governing jurisdiction for opening insolvency proceedings and judgments which are delivered directly on the basis of the insolvency proceedings and are closely connected with such proceedings. In addition, this Regulation should contain provisions regarding the recognition of those judgments and the applicable law which also satisfy that principle.
   (7)   Insolvency proceedings relating to the winding-up of insolvent companies or other legal persons, judicial arrangements, compositions and analogous proceedings are excluded from the scope of the 1968 Brussels Convention on jurisdiction and the Enforcement of judgments in Civil and Commercial Matters, as amended by the Conventions on Accession to this Convention.
   (8)   In order to achieve the aim of improving the efficiency and effectiveness of insolvency proceedings having crossborder effects, it is necessary, and appropriate, that the provisions on jurisdiction, recognition and applicable law in this area should be contained in a Community law measure which is binding and directly applicable in Member States.
   (9)   This Regulation should apply to insolvency proceedings, whether the debtor is a natural person or a legal person, a trader or an individual. The insolvency proceedings to which this Regulation applies are listed in the Annexes. Insolvency proceedings concerning insurance undertakings, credit institutions, investment undertakings holding funds or securities for third parties and collective investment undertakings should be excluded from the scope of this Regulation. Such undertakings should not be covered by this Regulation since they are subject

to special arrangements and, to some extent, the national supervisory authorities have extremely wide-ranging powers of intervention.

(10) Insolvency proceedings do not necessarily involve the intervention of a judicial authority; the expression 'court' in this Regulation should be given a broad meaning and include a person or body empowered by national law to open insolvency proceedings. In order for this Regulation to apply, proceedings (comprising acts and formalities set down in law) should not only have to comply with the provisions of this Regulation, but they should also be officially recognised and legally effective in the Member State in which the insolvency proceedings are opened and should be collective insolvency proceedings which entail the partial or total divestment of the debtor and the appointment of a liquidator.

(11) This Regulation acknowledges the fact that as a result of widely differing substantive laws it is not practical to introduce insolvency proceedings with universal scope in the entire Community. The application without exception of the law of the State of opening of proceedings would, against this background, frequently lead to difficulties. This applies, for example, to the widely differing laws on security interests to be found in the Community. Furthermore, the preferential rights enjoyed by some creditors in the insolvency proceedings are, in some cases, completely different. This Regulation should take account of this in two different ways. On the one hand, provision should be made for special rules on applicable law in the case of particularly significant rights and legal relationships (eg rights in rem and contracts of employment). On the other hand, national proceedings covering only assets situated in the State of opening should also be allowed alongside main insolvency proceedings with universal scope.

(12) This Regulation enables the main insolvency proceedings to be opened in the Member State where the debtor has the centre of his main interests. These proceedings have universal scope and aim at encompassing all the debtor's assets. To protect the diversity of interests, this Regulation permits secondary proceedings to be opened to run in parallel with the main proceedings. Secondary proceedings may be opened in the Member State where the debtor has an establishment. The effects of secondary proceedings are limited to the assets located in that State. Mandatory rules of coordination with the main proceedings satisfy the need for unity in the Community.

(13) The 'centre of main interests' should correspond to the place where the debtor conducts the administration of his interests on a regular basis and is therefore ascertainable by third parties.

(14) This Regulation applies only to proceedings where the centre of the debtor's main interests is located in the Community.

(15) The rules of jurisdiction set out in this Regulation establish only international jurisdiction, that is to say, they designate the Member State the courts of which may open insolvency proceedings. Territorial jurisdiction within that Member State must be established by the national law of the Member State concerned.

(16) The court having jurisdiction to open the main insolvency proceedings should be enabled to order provisional and protective measures from the time of the request to open proceedings. Preservation measures both prior to and after the commencement of the insolvency proceedings are very important to guarantee the effectiveness of the insolvency proceedings. In that connection this Regulation should afford different possibilities. On the one hand, the court competent for the main insolvency proceedings should be able also to order provisional protective measures covering assets situated in the territory of other Member States. On the other hand, a liquidator temporarily appointed prior to the opening of the main insolvency proceedings should be able, in the Member States in which an establishment belonging to the debtor is to be found, to apply for the preservation measures which are possible under the law of those States.

(17) Prior to the opening of the main insolvency proceedings, the right to

request the opening of insolvency proceedings in the Member State where the debtor has an establishment should be limited to local creditors and creditors of the local establishment or to cases where main proceedings cannot be opened under the law of the Member State where the debtor has the centre of his main interest. The reason for this restriction is that cases where territorial insolvency proceedings are requested before the main insolvency proceedings are intended to be limited to what is absolutely necessary. If the main insolvency proceedings are opened, the territorial proceedings become secondary.

(18)   Following the opening of the main insolvency proceedings, the right to request the opening of insolvency proceedings in a Member State where the debtor has an establishment is not restricted by this Regulation. The liquidator in the main proceedings or any other person empowered under the national law of that Member State may request the opening of secondary insolvency proceedings.

(19)   Secondary insolvency proceedings may serve different purposes, besides the protection of local interests. Cases may arise where the estate of the debtor is too complex to administer as a unit or where differences in the legal systems concerned are so great that difficulties may arise from the extension of effects deriving from the law of the State of the opening to the other States where the assets are located. For this reason the liquidator in the main proceedings may request the opening of secondary proceedings when the efficient administration of the estate so requires.

(20)   Main insolvency proceedings and secondary proceedings can, however, contribute to the effective realisation of the total assets only if all the concurrent proceedings pending are coordinated. The main condition here is that the various liquidators must cooperate closely, in particular by exchanging a sufficient amount of information. In order to ensure the dominant role of the main insolvency proceedings, the liquidator in such proceedings should be given several possibilities for intervening in secondary insolvency proceedings which are pending at the same time. For example, he should be able to propose a restructuring plan or composition or apply for realisation of the assets in the secondary insolvency proceedings to be suspended.

(21)   Every creditor, who has his habitual residence, domicile or registered office in the Community, should have the right to lodge his claims in each of the insolvency proceedings pending in the Community relating to the debtor's assets. This should also apply to tax authorities and social insurance institutions. However, in order to ensure equal treatment of creditors, the distribution of proceeds must be coordinated. Every creditor should be able to keep what he has received in the course of insolvency proceedings but should be entitled only to participate in the distribution of total assets in other proceedings if creditors with the same standing have obtained the same proportion of their claims.

(22)   This Regulation should provide for immediate recognition of judgments concerning the opening, conduct and closure of insolvency proceedings which come within its scope and of judgments handed down in direct connection with such insolvency proceedings. Automatic recognition should therefore mean that the effects attributed to the proceedings by the law of the State in which the proceedings were opened extend to all other Member States. Recognition of judgments delivered by the courts of the Member States should be based on the principle of mutual trust. To that end, grounds for non-recognition should be reduced to the minimum necessary. This is also the basis on which any dispute should be resolved where the courts of two Member States both claim competence to open the main insolvency proceedings. The decision of the first court to open proceedings should be recognised in the other Member States without those Member States having the power to scrutinise the court's decision.

(23)   This Regulation should set out, for the matters covered by it, uniform rules on conflict of laws which replace, within their scope of application, national rules of private international law. Unless otherwise stated, the law of the Member State

of the opening of the proceedings should be applicable (lex concursus). This rule on conflict of laws should be valid both for the main proceedings and for local proceedings; the lex concursus determines all the effects of the insolvency proceedings, both procedural and substantive, on the persons and legal relations concerned. It governs all the conditions for the opening, conduct and closure of the insolvency proceedings.

(24)   Automatic recognition of insolvency proceedings to which the law of the opening State normally applies may interfere with the rules under which transactions are carried out in other Member States. To protect legitimate expectations and the certainty of transactions in Member States other than that in which proceedings are opened, provisions should be made for a number of exceptions to the general rule.

(25)   There is a particular need for a special reference diverging from the law of the opening State in the case of rights in rem, since these are of considerable importance for the granting of credit. The basis, validity and extent of such a right in rem should therefore normally be determined according to the lex situs and not be affected by the opening of insolvency proceedings. The proprietor of the right in rem should therefore be able to continue to assert his right to segregation or separate settlement of the collateral security. Where assets are subject to rights in rem under the lex situs in one Member State but the main proceedings are being carried out in another Member State, the liquidator in the main proceedings should be able to request the opening of secondary proceedings in the jurisdiction where the rights in rem arise if the debtor has an establishment there. If a secondary proceeding is not opened, the surplus on sale of the asset covered by rights in rem must be paid to the liquidator in the main proceedings.

(26)   If a set-off is not permitted under the law of the opening State, a creditor should nevertheless be entitled to the setoff if it is possible under the law applicable to the claim of the insolvent debtor. In this way, set-off will acquire a kind of guarantee function based on legal provisions on which the creditor concerned can rely at the time when the claim arises.

(27)   There is also a need for special protection in the case of payment systems and financial markets. This applies for example to the position-closing agreements and netting agreements to be found in such systems as well as to the sale of securities and to the guarantees provided for such transactions as governed in particular by Directive 98/26/EC of the European Parliament and of the Council of 19 May 1998 on settlement finality in payment and securities settlement systems (5). For such transactions, the only law which is material should thus be that applicable to the system or market concerned. This provision is intended to prevent the possibility of mechanisms for the payment and settlement of transactions provided for in the payment and set-off systems or on the regulated financial markets of the Member States being altered in the case of insolvency of a business partner. Directive 98/26/EC contains special provisions which should take precedence over the general rules in this Regulation.

(28)   In order to protect employees and jobs, the effects of insolvency proceedings on the continuation or termination of employment and on the rights and obligations of all parties to such employment must be determined by the law applicable to the agreement in accordance with the general rules on conflict of law. Any other insolvency law questions, such as whether the employees' claims are protected by preferential rights and what status such preferential rights may have, should be determined by the law of the opening State.

(29)   For business considerations, the main content of the decision opening the proceedings should be published in the other Member States at the request of the liquidator. If there is an establishment in the Member State concerned, there may be a requirement that publication is compulsory. In neither case, however, should publication be a prior condition for recognition of the foreign proceedings.

(30)   It may be the case that some of the persons concerned are not in fact

aware that proceedings have been opened and act in good faith in a way that conflicts with the new situation. In order to protect such persons who make a payment to the debtor because they are unaware that foreign proceedings have been opened when they should in fact have made the payment to the foreign liquidator, it should be provided that such a payment is to have a debt-discharging effect.

(31)   This Regulation should include Annexes relating to the organisation of insolvency proceedings. As these Annexes relate exclusively to the legislation of Member States, there are specific and substantiated reasons for the Council to reserve the right to amend these Annexes in order to take account of any amendments to the domestic law of the Member States.

(32)   The United Kingdom and Ireland, in accordance with Article 3 of the Protocol on the position of the United Kingdom and Ireland annexed to the Treaty on European Union and the Treaty establishing the European Community, have given notice of their wish to take part in the adoption and application of this Regulation.

(33)   Denmark, in accordance with Articles 1 and 2 of the Protocol on the position of Denmark annexed to the Treaty on European Union and the Treaty establishing the European Community, is not participating in the adoption of this Regulation, and is therefore not bound by it nor subject to its application,

HAS ADOPTED THIS REGULATION:

CHAPTER I
GENERAL PROVISIONS

Article 1. Scope
1.   This Regulation shall apply to collective insolvency proceedings which entail the partial or total divestment of a debtor and the appointment of a liquidator.
2.   This Regulation shall not apply to insolvency proceedings concerning insurance undertakings, credit institutions, investment undertakings which provide services involving the holding of funds or securities for third parties, or to collective investment undertakings.

Article 2. Definitions
For the purposes of this Regulation:
(a)   'insolvency proceedings' shall mean the collective proceedings referred to in Article 1 (1). These proceedings are listed in Annex A;
(b)   'liquidator' shall mean any person or body whose function is to administer or liquidate assets of which the debtor has been divested or to supervise the administration of his affairs. Those persons and bodies are listed in Annex C;
(c)   'winding-up proceedings' shall mean insolvency proceedings within the meaning of point (a) involving realising the assets of the debtor, including where the proceedings have been closed by a composition or other measure terminating the insolvency, or closed by reason of the insufficiency of the assets. Those proceedings are listed in Annex B;
(d)   'court' shall mean the judicial body or any other competent body of a Member State empowered to open insolvency proceedings or to take decisions in the course of such proceedings;
(e)   'judgment' in relation to the opening of insolvency proceedings or the appointment of a liquidator shall include the decision of any court empowered to open such proceedings or to appoint a liquidator;
(f)   'the time of the opening of proceedings' shall mean the time at which the judgment opening proceedings becomes effective, whether it is a final judgment or not;
(g)   'the Member State in which assets are situated' shall mean, in the case of:
– tangible property, the Member State within the territory of which the property is situated,

– property and rights ownership of or entitlement to which must be entered in a public register, the Member State under the authority of which the register is kept,

– claims, the Member State within the territory of which the third party required to meet them has the centre of his main interests, as determined in Article 3(1);

(h) 'establishment' shall mean any place of operations where the debtor carries out a non-transitory economic activity with human means and goods.

Article 3. International jurisdiction

1. The courts of the Member State within the territory of' which the centre of a debtor's main interests is situated shall have jurisdiction to open insolvency proceedings. In the case of a company or legal person, the place of the registered office shall be presumed to be the centre of its main interests in the absence of proof to the contrary.

2. Where the centre of a debtor's main interests is situated within the territory of a Member State, the courts of another Member State shall have jurisdiction to open insolvency proceedings against that debtor only if he possesses an establishment within the territory of that other Member State. The effects of those proceedings shall be restricted to the assets of the debtor situated in the territory of the latter Member State.

3. Where insolvency proceedings have been opened under paragraph 1, any proceedings opened subsequently under paragraph 2 shall be secondary proceedings. These latter proceedings must be winding-up proceedings.

4. Territorial insolvency proceedings referred to in paragraph 2 may be opened prior to the opening of main insolvency proceedings in accordance with paragraph 1 only:

(a) where insolvency proceedings under paragraph 1 cannot be opened because of the conditions laid down by the law of the Member State within the territory of which the centre of the debtor's main interests is situated; or

(b) where the opening of territorial insolvency proceedings is requested by a creditor who has his domicile, habitual residence or registered office in the Member State within the territory of which the establishment is situated, or whose claim arises from the operation of that establishment.

Article 4. Law applicable

1. Save as otherwise provided in this Regulation, the law applicable to insolvency proceedings and their effects shall be that of the Member State within the territory of which such proceedings are opened, hereafter referred to as the 'State of the opening of proceedings'.

2. The law of the State of the opening of proceedings shall determine the conditions for the opening of those proceedings, their conduct and their closure. It shall determine in particular:

(a) against which debtors insolvency proceedings may be brought on account of their capacity;

(b) the assets which form part of the estate and the treatment of assets acquired by or devolving on the debtor after the opening of the insolvency proceedings;

(c) the respective powers of the debtor and the liquidator;

(d) the conditions under which set-offs may be invoked;

(e) the effects of insolvency proceedings on current contracts to which the debtor is party;

(f) the effects of the insolvency proceedings on proceedings brought by individual creditors, with the exception of lawsuits pending;

(g) the claims which are to be lodged against the debtor's estate and the treatment of claims arising after the opening of insolvency proceedings;

(h) the rules governing the lodging, verification and admission of claims;

(i)   the rules governing the distribution of proceeds from the realisation of assets, the ranking of claims and the rights of creditors who have obtained partial satisfaction after the opening of insolvency proceedings by virtue of a right in rem or through a set-off;

(j)   the conditions for and the effects of closure of insolvency proceedings, in particular by composition;

(k)   creditors' rights after the closure of insolvency proceedings;

(l)   who is to bear the costs and expenses incurred in the insolvency proceedings;

(m)   the rules relating to the voidness, voidability or unenforceability of legal acts detrimental to all the creditors.

Article 5. Third parties' rights in rem

1.   The opening of insolvency proceedings shall not affect the rights in rem of creditors or third parties in respect of tangible or intangible, moveable or immoveable assets—both specific assets and collections of indefinite assets as a whole which change from time to time—belonging to the debtor which are situated within the territory of another Member State at the time of the opening of proceedings.

2.   The rights referred to in paragraph 1 shall in particular mean:

(a)   the right to dispose of assets or have them disposed of and to obtain satisfaction from the proceeds of or income from those assets, in particular by virtue of a lien or a mortgage;

(b)   the exclusive right to have a claim met, in particular a right guaranteed by a lien in respect of the claim or by assignment of the claim by way of a guarantee;

(c)   the right to demand the assets from, and/or to require restitution by, anyone having possession or use of them contrary to the wishes of the party so entitled;

(d)   a right in rem to the beneficial use of assets.

3.   The right, recorded in a public register and enforceable against third parties, under which a right in rem within the meaning of paragraph 1 may be obtained, shall be considered a right in rem.

4.   Paragraph 1 shall not preclude actions for voidness, voidability or unenforceability as referred to in Article 4(2)(m).

Article 6. Set-off

1.   The opening of insolvency proceedings shall not affect the right of creditors to demand the set-off of their claims against the claims of the debtor, where such a set-off is permitted by the law applicable to the insolvent debtor's claim.

2.   Paragraph 1 shall not preclude actions for voidness, voidability or unenforceability as referred to in Article 4(2)(m).

Article 7. Reservation of title

1.   The opening of insolvency proceedings against the purchaser of an asset shall not affect the seller's rights based on a reservation of title where at the time of the opening of proceedings the asset is situated within the territory of a Member State other than the State of opening of proceedings.

2.   The opening of insolvency proceedings against the seller of an asset, after delivery of the asset, shall not constitute grounds for rescinding or terminating the sale and shall not prevent the purchaser from acquiring title where at the time of the opening of proceedings the asset sold is situated within the territory of a Member State other than the State of the opening of proceedings.

3.   Paragraphs 1 and 2 shall not preclude actions for voidness, voidability or unenforceability as referred to in Article 4(2)(m).

Article 8. Contracts relating to immoveable property

The effects of insolvency proceedings on a contract conferring the right to acquire or make use of immoveable property shall be governed solely by the law of the Member State within the territory of which the immoveable property is situated.

Article 9. Payment systems and financial markets
1. Without prejudice to Article 5, the effects of insolvency proceedings on the rights and obligations of the parties to a payment or settlement system or to a financial market shall be governed solely by the law of the Member State applicable to that system or market.

2. Paragraph 1 shall not preclude any action for voidness, voidability or unenforceability which may be taken to set aside payments or transactions under the law applicable to the relevant payment system or financial market.

Article 10. Contracts of employment
The effects of insolvency proceedings on employment contracts and relationships shall be governed solely by the law of the Member State applicable to the contract of employment.

Article 11. Effects on rights subject to registration
The effects of insolvency proceedings on the rights of the debtor in immoveable property, a ship or an aircraft subject to registration in a public register shall be determined by the law of the Member State under the authority of which the register is kept.

Article 12. Community patents and trade marks
For the purposes of this Regulation, a Community patent, a Community trade mark or any other similar right established by Community law may be included only in the proceedings referred to in Article 3(1).

Article 13. Detrimental acts
Article 4(2)(m) shall not apply where the person who benefited from an act detrimental to all the creditors provides proof that:
– the said act is subject to the law of a Member State other than that of the State of the opening of proceedings, and
– that law does not allow any means of challenging that act in the relevant case.

Article 14. Protection of third-party purchasers
Where, by an act concluded after the opening of insolvency proceedings, the debtor disposes, for consideration, of
– an immoveable asset, or
– a ship or an aircraft subject to registration in a public register, or
– securities whose existence presupposes registration in a register laid down by law,
the validity of that act shall be governed by the law of the State within the territory of which the immoveable asset is situated or under the authority of which the register is kept.

Article 15. Effects of insolvency proceedings on lawsuits pending
The effects of insolvency proceedings on a lawsuit pending concerning an asset or a right of which the debtor has been divested shall be governed solely by the law of the Member State in which that lawsuit is pending.

CHAPTER II
RECOGNITION OF INSOLVENCY PROCEEDINGS

Article 16. Principle
1. Any judgment opening insolvency proceedings handed down by a court of a Member State which has jurisdiction pursuant to Article 3 shall be recognised in all the other Member States from the time that it becomes effective in the State of the opening of proceedings.

This rule shall also apply where, on account of his capacity, insolvency proceedings cannot be brought against the debtor in other Member States.

2.   Recognition of the proceedings referred to in Article 3(1) shall not preclude the opening of the proceedings referred to in Article 3(2) by a court in another Member State. The latter proceedings shall be secondary insolvency proceedings within the meaning of Chapter III.

Article 17. Effects of recognition

1.   The judgment opening the proceedings referred to in Article 3(1) shall, with no further formalities, produce the same effects in any other Member State as under this law of the State of the opening of proceedings, unless this Regulation provides otherwise and as long as no proceedings referred to in Article 3(2) are opened in that other Member State.

2.   The effects of the proceedings referred to in Article 3(2) may not be challenged in other Member States. Any restriction of the creditors' rights, in particular a stay or discharge, shall produce effects vis-a-vis assets situated within the territory of another Member State only in the case of those creditors who have given their consent.

Article 18. Powers of the liquidator

1.   The liquidator appointed by a court which has jurisdiction pursuant to Article 3(1) may exercise all the powers conferred on him by the law of the State of the opening of proceedings in another Member State, as long as no other insolvency proceedings have been opened there nor any preservation measure to the contrary has been taken there further to a request for the opening of insolvency proceedings in that State. He may in particular remove the debtor's assets from the territory of the Member State in which they are situated, subject to Articles 5 and 7.

2.   The liquidator appointed by a court which has jurisdiction pursuant to Article 3(2) may in any other Member State claim through the courts or out of court that moveable property was removed from the territory of the State of the opening of proceedings to the territory of that other Member State after the opening of the insolvency proceedings. He may also bring any action to set aside which is in the interests of the creditors.

3.   In exercising his powers, the liquidator shall comply with the law of the Member State within the territory of which he intends to take action, in particular with regard to procedures for the realisation of assets. Those powers may not include coercive measures or the right to rule on legal proceedings or disputes.

Article 19. Proof of the liquidator's appointment

The liquidator's appointment shall be evidenced by a certified copy of the original decision appointing him or by any other certificate issued by the court which has jurisdiction.

A translation into the official language or one of the official languages of the Member State within the territory of which he intends to act may be required. No legalisation or other similar formality shall be required.

Article 20. Return and imputation

1.   A creditor who, after the opening of the proceedings referred to in Article 3(1) obtains by any means, in particular through enforcement, total or partial satisfaction of his claim on the assets belonging to the debtor situated within the territory of another Member State, shall return what he has obtained to the liquidator, subject to Articles 5 and 7.

2.   In order to ensure equal treatment of creditors a creditor who has, in the course of insolvency proceedings, obtained a dividend on his claim shall share in distributions made in other proceedings only where creditors of the same ranking or category have, in those other proceedings, obtained an equivalent dividend.

Article 21. Publication

1. The liquidator may request that notice of the judgment opening insolvency proceedings and, where appropriate, the decision appointing him, be published in any other Member State in accordance with the publication procedures provided for in that State. Such publication shall also specify the liquidator appointed and whether the jurisdiction rule applied is that pursuant to Article 3(1) or Article 3(2).

2. However, any Member State within the territory of which the debtor has an establishment may require mandatory publication. In such cases, the liquidator or any authority empowered to that effect in the Member State where the proceedings referred to in Article 3(1) are opened shall take all necessary measures to ensure such publication.

Article 22. Registration in a public register

1. The liquidator may request that the judgment opening the proceedings referred to in Article 3(1) be registered in the land register, the trade register and any other public register kept in the other Member States.

2. However, any Member State may require mandatory registration. In such cases, the liquidator or any authority empowered to that effect in the Member State where the proceedings referred to in Article 3(1) have been opened shall take all necessary measures to ensure such registration.

Article 23. Costs

The costs of the publication and registration provided for in Articles 21 and 22 shall be regarded as costs and expenses incurred in the proceedings.

Article 24. Honouring of an obligation to a debtor

1. Where an obligation has been honoured in a Member State for the benefit of a debtor who is subject to insolvency proceedings opened in another Member State, when it should have been honoured for the benefit of the liquidator in those proceedings, the person honouring the obligation shall be deemed to have discharged it if he was unaware of the opening of proceedings.

2. Where such an obligation is honoured before the publication provided for in Article 21 has been effected, the person honouring the obligation shall be presumed, in the absence of proof to the contrary, to have been unaware of the opening of insolvency proceedings; where the obligation is honoured after such publication has been effected, the person honouring the obligation shall be presumed, in the absence of proof to the contrary, to have been aware of the opening of proceedings.

Article 25. Recognition and enforceability of other judgments

1. Judgments handed down by a court whose judgment concerning the opening of proceedings is recognised in accordance with Article 16 and which concern the course and closure of insolvency proceedings, and compositions approved by that court shall also be recognised with no further formalities. Such judgments shall be enforced in accordance with Articles 31 to 51, with the exception of Article 34(2), of the Brussels Convention on jurisdiction and the Enforcement of judgments in Civil and Commercial Matters, as amended by the Conventions of Accession to this Convention.

The first subparagraph shall also apply to judgments deriving directly from the insolvency proceedings and which are closely linked with them, even if they were handed down by another court.

The first subparagraph shall also apply to judgments relating to preservation measures taken after the request for the opening of insolvency proceedings.

2. The recognition and enforcement of judgments other than those referred to in paragraph 1 shall be governed by the Convention referred to in paragraph 1, provided that that Convention is applicable.

3. The Member States shall not be obliged to recognise or enforce a judgment

referred to in paragraph 1 which might result in a limitation of personal freedom or postal secrecy.

Article 26. Public policy
Any Member State may refuse to recognise insolvency proceedings opened in another Member State or to enforce a judgment handed down in the context of such proceedings where the effects of such recognition or enforcement would be manifestly contrary to that State's public policy, in particular its fundamental principles or the constitutional rights and liberties of the individual.

CHAPTER III
SECONDARY INSOLVENCY PROCEEDINGS

Article 27. Opening of proceedings
The opening of the proceedings referred to in Article 3(1) by a court of a Member State and which is recognised in another Member State (main proceedings) shall permit the opening in that other Member State, a court of which has jurisdiction pursuant to Article 3(2), of secondary insolvency proceedings without the debtor's insolvency being examined in that other State. These latter proceedings must be among the proceedings listed in Annex B. Their effects shall be restricted to the assets of the debtor situated within the territory of that other Member State.

Article 28. Applicable law
Save as otherwise provided in this Regulation, the law applicable to secondary proceedings shall be that of the Member State within the territory of which the secondary proceedings are opened.

Article 29. Right to request the opening of proceedings
The opening of secondary proceedings may be requested by:
    (a)   the liquidator in the main proceedings;
    (b)   any other person or authority empowered to request the opening of insolvency proceedings under the law of the Member State within the territory of which the opening of secondary proceedings is requested.

Article 30. Advance payment of costs and expenses
Where the law of the Member State in which the opening of secondary proceedings is requested requires that the debtor's assets be sufficient to cover in whole or in part the costs and expenses of the proceedings, the court may, when it receives such a request, require the applicant to make an advance payment of costs or to provide appropriate security.

Article 31. Duty to cooperate and communicate information
    1.   Subject to the rules restricting the communication of information, the liquidator in the main proceedings and the liquidators in the secondary proceedings shall be duty bound to communicate information to each other. They shall immediately communicate any information which may be relevant to the other proceedings, in particular the progress made in lodging and verifying claims and all measures aimed at terminating the proceedings.
    2.   Subject to the rules applicable to each of the proceedings, the liquidator in the main proceedings and the liquidators in the secondary proceedings shall be duty bound to cooperate with each other.
    3.   The liquidator in the secondary proceedings shall give the liquidator in the main proceedings an early opportunity of submitting proposals on the liquidation or use of the assets in the secondary proceedings.

Article 32. Exercise of creditors' rights
    1.   Any creditor may lodge his claim in the main proceedings and in any secondary proceedings.
    2.   The liquidators in the main and any secondary proceedings shall lodge in

other proceedings claims which have already been lodged in the proceedings for which they were appointed, provided that the interests of creditors in the latter proceedings are served thereby, subject to the right of creditors to oppose that or to withdraw the lodgement of their claims where the law applicable so provides.

3. The liquidator in the main or secondary proceedings shall be empowered to participate in other proceedings on the same basis as a creditor, in particular by attending creditors' meetings.

Article 33. Stay of liquidation

1. The court, which opened the secondary proceedings, shall stay the process of liquidation in whole or in part on receipt of a request from the liquidator in the main proceedings, provided that in that event it may require the liquidator in the main proceedings to take any suitable measure to guarantee the interests of the creditors in the secondary proceedings and of individual classes of creditors. Such a request from the liquidator may be rejected only if it is manifestly of no interest to the creditors in the main proceedings. Such a stay of the process of liquidation may be ordered for up to three months. It may be continued or renewed for similar periods.

2. The court referred to in paragraph 1 shall terminate the stay of the process of liquidation:
– at the request of the liquidator in the main proceedings,
– of its own motion, at the request of a creditor or at the request of the liquidator in the secondary proceedings if that measure no longer appears justified, in particular, by the interests of creditors in the main proceedings or in the secondary proceedings.

Article 34. Measures ending secondary insolvency proceedings

1. Where the law applicable to secondary proceedings allows for such proceedings to be closed without liquidation by a rescue plan, a composition or a comparable measure, the liquidator in the main proceedings shall be empowered to propose such a measure himself

Closure of the secondary proceedings by a measure referred to in the first subparagraph shall not become final without the consent of the liquidator in the main proceedings; failing his agreement, however, it may become final if the financial interests of the creditors in the main proceedings are not affected by the measure proposed.

2. Any restriction of creditors' rights arising from a measure referred to in paragraph 1 which is proposed in secondary proceedings, such as a stay of payment or discharge of debt, may not have effect in respect of the debtor's assets not covered by those proceedings without the consent of all the creditors having an interest.

3. During a stay of the process of liquidation ordered pursuant to Article 33, only the liquidator in the main proceedings or the debtor, with the former's consent, may propose measures laid down in paragraph 1 of this Article in the secondary proceedings; no other proposal for such a measure shall be put to the vote or approved.

Article 35. Assets remaining in the secondary proceedings

If by the liquidation of assets in the secondary proceedings it is possible to meet all claims allowed under those proceedings, the liquidator appointed in those proceedings shall immediately transfer any assets remaining to the liquidator in the main proceedings.

Article 36. Subsequent opening of the main proceedings

Where the proceedings referred to in Article 3(1) are opened following the opening of the proceedings referred to in Article 3(2) in another Member State, Articles 31 to 35 shall apply to those opened first, in so far as the progress of those proceedings so permits.

Article 37. Conversion of earlier proceedings

The liquidator in the main proceedings may request that proceedings listed in Annex A previously opened in another Member State be converted into winding-up proceedings if this proves to be in the interests of the creditors in the main proceedings.

The court with jurisdiction under Article 3(2) shall order conversion into one of the proceedings listed in Annex B.

Article 38. Preservation measures

Where the court of a Member State which has jurisdiction pursuant to Article 3(1) appoints a temporary administrator in order to ensure the preservation of the debtor's assets, that temporary administrator shall be empowered to request any measures to secure and preserve any of the debtor's assets situated in another Member State, provided for under the law of that State, for the period between the request for the opening of insolvency proceedings and the judgment opening the proceedings.

CHAPTER IV
PROVISION OF INFORMATION FOR CREDITORS AND LODGEMENT OF THEIR CLAIMS

Article 39. Right to lodge claims

Any creditor who has his habitual residence, domicile or registered office in a Member State other than the State of the opening of proceedings, including the tax authorities and social security authorities of Member States, shall have the right to lodge claims in the insolvency proceedings in writing.

Article 40. Duty to inform creditors

1.   As soon as insolvency proceedings are opened in a Member State, the court of that State having jurisdiction or the liquidator appointed by it shall immediately inform known creditors who have their habitual residences, domiciles or registered offices in the other Member States.

2.   That information, provided by an individual notice, shall in particular include time limits, the penalties laid down in regard to those time limits, the body or authority empowered to accept the lodgement of claims and the other measures laid down. Such notice shall also indicate whether creditors whose claims are preferential or secured in rem need lodge their claims.

Article 41. Content of the lodgement of a claim

A creditor shall send copies of supporting documents, if any, and shall indicate the nature of the claim, the date on which it arose and its amount, as well as whether he alleges preference, security in rem or a reservation of title in respect of the claim and what assets are covered by the guarantee he is invoking.

Article 42. Languages

1.   The information provided for in Article 40 shall be provided in the official language or one of the official languages of the State of the opening of proceedings. For that purpose a form shall be used bearing the heading 'Invitation to lodge a claim. Time limits to be observed' in all the official languages of the institutions of the European Union.

2.   Any creditor who has his habitual residence, domicile or registered office in a Member State other than the State of the opening of proceedings may lodge his claim in the official language or one of the official languages of that other State. In that event, however, the lodgement of his claim shall bear the heading 'Lodgement of claim' in the official language or one of the official languages of the State of the opening of proceedings. In addition, he may be required to provide a translation into the official language or one of the official languages of the State of the opening of proceedings.

CHAPTER V
TRANSITIONAL AND FINAL PROVISIONS

Article 43. Applicability in time

The provisions of this Regulation shall apply only to insolvency proceedings opened after its entry into force. Acts done by a debtor before the entry into force of this Regulation shall continue to be governed by the law which was applicable to them at the time they were done.

Article 44. Relationship to Conventions

...

3.   This Regulation shall not apply:

...

   (b)   in the United Kingdom of Great Britain and Northern Ireland, to the extent that is irreconcilable with the obligations arising in relation to bankruptcy and the winding-up of insolvent companies from any arrangements with the Commonwealth existing at the time this Regulation enters into force.

...

Article 46. Reports

No later than 1 June 2012, and every five years thereafter, the Commission shall present to the European Parliament, the Council and the Economic and Social Committee a report on the application of this Regulation. The report shall be accompanied if need be by a proposal for adaptation of this Regulation.

Article 47. Entry into force

This Regulation shall enter into force on 31 May 2002.

   This Regulation shall be binding in its entirety and directly applicable in the Member States in accordance with the Treaty establishing the European Community.

Done at Brussels, 29 May 2000.

ANNEX A

Insolvency proceedings referred to in Article 2(a)

...

UNITED KINGDOM

   – winding up by or subject to the supervision of the court
   – creditors' voluntary winding up (with confirmation by the court)
   – administration
   – voluntary arrangements under insolvency legislation
   – bankruptcy or sequestration

COUNCIL REGULATION (EC) NO 1348/2000 OF 29 MAY 2000 ON THE SERVICE IN THE MEMBER STATES OF JUDICIAL AND EXTRAJUDICIAL DOCUMENTS IN CIVIL OR COMMERCIAL MATTERS*

Official Journal L 160, 30/06/2000 p 37

THE COUNCIL OF THE EUROPEAN UNION,

Having regard to the Treaty establishing the European Community, and in particular Article 61(c) and Article 67(1) thereof,

Having regard to the proposal from the Commission,

Having regard to the opinion of the European Parliament,

Having regard to the opinion of the Economic and Social Committee,

Whereas:

(1) The Union has set itself the objective of maintaining and developing the Union as an area of freedom, security and justice, in which the free movement of persons is assured. To establish such an area, the Community is to adopt, among others, the measures relating to judicial cooperation in civil matters needed for the proper functioning of the internal market.

(2) The proper functioning of the internal market entails the need to improve and expedite the transmission of judicial and extrajudicial documents in civil or commercial matters for service between the Member States.

(3) This is a subject now falling within the ambit of Article 65 of the Treaty.

(4) In accordance with the principles of subsidiarity and proportionality as set out in Article 5 of the Treaty, th objectives of this Regulation cannot be sufficiently achieved by the Member States and can therefore be better achieved by the Community. This Regulation does not go beyond what is necessary to achieve those objectives.

(5) The Council, by an Act dated 26 May 1997, drew up a Convention on the service in the Member States of the European Union of judicial and extrajudicial documents in civil or commercial matters and recommended it for adoption by the Member States in accordance with their respective constitutional rules. That Convention has not entered into force. Continuity in the results of the negotiations for conclusion of the Convention should ensured. The main content of this Regulation is substantially taken over from it.

(6) Efficiency and speed in judicial procedures in civil matters means that the transmission of judicial and extrajudicial documents is to be made direct and by rapid means between local bodies designated by the Member States. However, the Member States may indicate their intention of designating only one transmitting or receiving agency or one agency to perform both functions for a period of five years. This designation may, however, be renewed every five years.

(7) Speed in transmission warrants the use of all appropriate means, provided that certain conditions as to the legibility and reliability of the document received are observed. Security in transmission requires that the document to be transmitted be accompanied by a pre-printed form, to be completed in the language of the place where service is to be effected, or in another language accepted by the Member State in question.

(8) To secure the effectiveness of this Regulation, the possibility of refusing service of documents is confined to exceptional situations.

(9) Speed of transmission warrants documents being served within days of reception of the document. However, if service has not been effected after one month has elapsed, the receiving agency should inform the transmitting agency.

*At the date of going to press there is an Amended Proposal for a Regulation of the European Parliament and of the Council on the Service of Documents (2005/0126 (COD)). Negotiations continue.

The expiry of this period should not imply that the request be returned to the transmitting agency where it is clear that service is feasible within a reasonable period.

(10) For the protection of the addressee's interests, service should be effected in the official language or one of the official languages of the place where it is to be effected or in another language of the originating Member State which the addressee understands.

(11) Given the differences between the Member States as regards their rules of procedure, the material date for the purposes of service varies from one Member State to another. Having regard to such situations and the possible difficulties that may arise, this Regulation should provide for a system where it is the law of the receiving Member State which determines the date of service. However, if the relevant documents in the context of proceedings to be brought or pending in the Member State of origin are to be served within a specified period, the date to be taken into consideration with respect to the applicant shall be that determined according to the law of the Member State of origin. A Member State is, however, authorised to derogate from the aforementioned provisions for a transitional period of five years, for appropriate reasons. Such a derogation may be renewed by a Member State at five-year intervals due to reasons related to its legal system.

(12) This Regulation prevails over the provisions contained in bilateral or multilateral agreements or arrangements having the same scope, concluded by the Member States, and in particular the Protocol annexed to the Brussels Convention of 27 September 1968 and the Hague Convention of 15 November 1965 in relations between the Member States party thereto. This Regulation does not preclude Member States from maintaining or concluding agreements or arrangements to expedite or simplify the transmission of documents, provided that they are compatible with the Regulation.

(13) The information transmitted pursuant to this Regulation should enjoy suitable protection. This matter falls within the scope of Directive 95/46/EC of the European Parliament and of the Council of 24 October 1995 on the protection of individuals with regard to the processing of personal data and on the free movement of such data, and of Directive 97/66/EC of the European Parliament and of the Council of 15 December 1997 concerning the processing of personal data and the protection of privacy in the telecommunications sector.

(14) The measures necessary for the implementation of this Regulation should be adopted in accordance with Council Decision 1999/468/EC of 28 June 1999 laying down the procedures for the exercise of implementing powers conferred on the Commission.

(15) These measures also include drawing up and updating the manual using appropriate modem means.

(16) No later than three years after the date of entry into force of this Regulation, the Commission should review its application and propose such amendments as may appear necessary.

(17) The United Kingdom and Ireland, in accordance with Article 3 of the Protocol on the position of the United Kingdom and Ireland annexed to the Treaty on European Union and the Treaty establishing the European Community, have given notice of their wish to take part in the adoption and application of this Regulation.

(18) Denmark, in accordance with Articles 1 and 2 of the Protocol on the position of Denmark annexed to the Treaty on European Union and the Treaty establishing the European Community, is not participating in the adoption of this Regulation, and is therefore not bound by it nor subject to its application,

HAS ADOPTED THIS REGULATION:

CHAPTER I
GENERAL PROVISIONS

Article 1: Scope

1.   This Regulation shall apply in civil and commercial matters where a judicial or extrajudicial document has to be transmitted from one Member State to another for service there.

2.   This Regulation shall not apply where the address of the person to be served with the document is not known.

Article 2. Transmitting and receiving agencies

1.   Each Member State shall designate the public officers, authorities or other persons, hereinafter referred to as 'transmitting agencies', competent for the transmission of judicial or extrajudicial documents to be served in another Member State.

2.   Each Member State shall designate the public officers, authorities or other persons, hereinafter referred to as 'receiving agencies', competent for the receipt of judicial or extrajudicial documents from another Member State.

3.   A Member State may designate one transmitting agency and one receiving agency or one agency to perform both functions. A federal State, a State in which several legal systems apply or a State with autonomous territorial units shall be free to designate more than one such agency. The designation shall have effect for a period of five years and may be renewed at five-year intervals.

4.   Each Member State shall provide the Commission with the following information:

(a)   the names and addresses of the receiving agencies referred to in paragraphs 2 and 3;

(b)   the geographical areas in which they have jurisdiction;

(c)   the means of receipt of documents available to them; and

(d)   the languages that may be used for the completion of the standard form in the Annex.

Member States shall notify the Commission of any subsequent modification of such information.

Article 3. Central body

Each Member State shall designate a central body responsible for:

(a)   supplying information to the transmitting agencies;

(b)   seeking solutions to any difficulties which may arise during transmission of documents for service;

(c)   forwarding, in exceptional cases, at the request of a transmitting agency, a request for service to the competent receiving agency.

A federal State, a State in which several legal systems apply or a State with autonomous territorial units shall be free to designate more than one central body.

CHAPTER II
JUDICIAL DOCUMENTS

Section 1
Transmission and service of Judicial documents

Article 4. Transmission of documents

1.   Judicial documents shall be transmitted directly and as soon as possible between the agencies designated on the basis of Article 2.

2.   The transmission of documents, requests, confirmations, receipts, certificates and any other papers between transmitting agencies and receiving agencies may be carried out by any appropriate means, provided that the content of the document received is true and faithful to that of the document forwarded and that all information in it is easily legible.

3. The document to be transmitted shall be accompanied by a request drawn up using the standard form in the Annex. The form shall be completed in the official language of the Member State addressed or, if there are several official languages in that Member State, the official language or one of the official languages of the place where service is to be effected, or in another language which that Member State has indicated it can accept. Each Member State shall indicate the official language or languages of the European Union other than its own which is or are acceptable to it for completion of the form.

4. The documents and all papers that are transmitted shall be exempted from legalisation or any equivalent formality.

5. When the transmitting agency wishes a copy of the document to be returned together with the certificate referred to in Article 10, it shall send the document in duplicate.

Article 5. Translation of documents

1. The applicant shall be advised by the transmitting agency to which he or she forwards the document for transmission that the addressee may refuse to accept it if it is not in one of the languages provided for in Article 8.

2. The applicant shall bear any costs of translation prior to the transmission of the document, without prejudice to any possible subsequent decision by the court or competent authority on liability for such costs.

Article 6. Receipt of documents by receiving agency

1. On receipt of a document, a receiving agency shall, as soon as possible and in any event within seven days of receipt, send a receipt to the transmitting agency by the swiftest possible means of transmission using the standard form in the Annex.

2. Where the request for service cannot be fulfilled on the basis of the information or documents transmitted, the receiving agency shall contact the transmitting agency by the swiftest possible means in order to secure the missing information or documents.

3. If the request for service is manifestly outside the scope of this Regulation or if non-compliance with the formal conditions required makes service impossible, the request and the documents transmitted shall be returned, on receipt, to the transmitting agency, together with the notice of return in the standard form in the Annex.

4. A receiving agency receiving a document for service but not having territorial jurisdiction to serve it shall forward it, as well as the request, to the receiving agency having territorial jurisdiction in the same Member State if the request complies with the conditions laid down in Article 4(3) and shall inform the transmitting agency accordingly, using the standard form in the Annex. That receiving agency shall inform the transmitting agency when it receives the document, in the manner provided for in paragraph 1.

Article 7. Service of documents

1. The receiving agency shall itself serve the document or have it served, either in accordance with the law of the Member State addressed or by a particular form requested by the transmitting agency, unless such a method is incompatible with the law of that Member State.

2. All steps required for service of the document shall be effected as soon as possible. In any event, if it has not been possible to effect service within one month of receipt, the receiving agency shall inform the transmitting agency by means of the certificate in the standard form in the Annex, which shall be drawn up under the conditions referred to in Article 10(2). The period shall be calculated in accordance with the law of the Member State addressed.

Article 8. Refusal to accept a document

1. The receiving agency shall inform the addressee that he or she may refuse to

accept the document to be served if it is in a language other than either of the following languages:

(a)   the official language of the Member State addressed or, if there are several official languages in that Member State, the official language or one of the official languages of the place where service is to be effected; or

(b)   a language of the Member State of transmission which the addressee understands.

2.   Where the receiving agency is informed that the addressee refuses to accept the document in accordance with paragraph 1, it shall immediately inform the transmitting agency by means of the certificate provided for in Article 10 and return the request and the documents of which a translation is requested.

Article 9. Date of service

1.   Without prejudice to Article 8, the date of service of a document pursuant to Article 7 shall be the date on which it is served in accordance with the law of the Member State addressed.

2.   However, where a document shall be served within a particular period in the context of proceedings to be brought or pending in the Member State of origin, the date to be taken into account with respect to the applicant shall be that fixed by the law of that Member State.

3.   A Member State shall be authorised to derogate from the provisions of paragraphs 1 and 2 for a transitional period of five years, for appropriate reasons.

This transitional period may be renewed by a Member State at five-yearly intervals due to reasons related to its legal system. That Member State shall inform the Commission of the content of such a derogation and the circumstances of the case.

Article 10. Certificate of service and copy of the document served

1.   When the formalities concerning the service of the document have been completed, a certificate of completion of those formalities shall be drawn up in the standard form in the Annex and addressed to the transmitting agency, together with, where Article 4(5) applies, a copy of the document served.

2.   The certificate shall be completed in the official language or one of the official languages of the Member State of origin or in another language which the Member State of origin has indicated that it can accept. Each Member State shall indicate the official language or languages of the European Union other than its own which is or are acceptable to it for completion of the form.

Article 11. Costs of service

1.   The service of judicial documents coming from a Member State shall not give rise to any payment or reimbursement of taxes or costs for services rendered by the Member State addressed.

2.   The applicant shall pay or reimburse the costs occasioned by:

(a)   the employment of a judicial officer or of a person competent under the law of the Member State addressed;

(b)   the use of a particular method of service.

Section 2
Other means of transmission and service of judicial documents

Article 12. Transmission by consular or diplomatic channels

Each Member State shall be free, in exceptional circumstances, to use consular or diplomatic channels to forward judicial documents, for the purpose of service, to those agencies of another Member State which are designated pursuant to Article 2 or 3.

Article 13. Service by diplomatic or consular agents

1.   Each Member State shall be free to effect service of judicial documents on

persons residing in another Member State, without application of any compulsion, directly through its diplomatic or consular agents.

2.   Any Member State may make it known, in accordance with Article 23(1), that it is opposed to such service within its territory, unless the documents are to be served on nationals of the Member State in which the documents originate.

Article 14. Service by post

1.   Each Member State shall be free to effect service of judicial documents directly by post to persons residing in another Member State.

2.   Any Member State may specify, in accordance with Article 23(1), the conditions under which it will accept service of judicial documents by post.

Article 15. Direct service

1.   This Regulation shall not interfere with the freedom of any person interested in a judicial proceeding to effect service of judicial documents directly through the judicial officers, officials or other competent persons of the Member State addressed.

2.   Any Member State may make it known, in accordance with Article 23(1), that it is opposed to the service of judicial documents in its territory pursuant to paragraph 1.

CHAPTER III
EXTRAJUDICIAL DOCUMENTS

Article 16. Transmission

Extrajudicial documents may be transmitted for service in another Member State in accordance with the provisions of this Regulation.

CHAPTER IV
FINAL PROVISIONS

...

Article 19. Defendant not entering an appearance

1.   Where a writ of summons or an equivalent document has had to be transmitted to another Member State for the purpose of service, under the provisions of this Regulation, and the defendant has not appeared, judgment shall not be given until it is established that:

(a)   the document was served by a method prescribed by the internal law of the Member State addressed for the service of documents in domestic actions upon persons who are within its territory; or

(b)   the document was actually delivered to the defendant or to his residence by another method provided for by this Regulation;

and that in either of these cases the service or the delivery was effected in sufficient time to enable the defendant to defend.

2.   Each Member State shall be free to make it known, in accordance with Article 23(1), that the judge, notwithstanding the provisions of paragraph 1, may give judgment even if no certificate of service or delivery has been received, if all the following conditions are fulfilled:

(a)   the document was transmitted by one of the methods provided for in this Regulation;

(b)   a period of time of not less than six months, considered adequate by the judge in the particular case, has elapsed since the date of the transmission of the document;

(c)   no certificate of any kind has been received, even though every reasonable effort has been made to obtain it through the competent authorities or bodies of the Member State addressed.

3. Notwithstanding paragraphs 1 and 2, the judge may order, in case of urgency, any provisional or protective measures.

4. When a writ of summons or an equivalent document has had to be transmitted to another Member State for the purpose of service, under the provisions of this Regulation, and a judgment has been entered against a defendant who has not appeared, the judge shall have the power to relieve the defendant from the effects of the expiration of the time for appeal from the judgment if the following conditions are

(a) the defendant, without any fault on his part, did not have knowledge of the document in sufficient time to defend, or knowledge of the judgment in sufficient time to appeal; and

(b) the defendant has disclosed a prima facie defence to the action on the merits.

An application for relief may be filed only within a reasonable time after the defendant has knowledge of the judgment.

Each Member State may make it known, in accordance with Article 23(1), that such application will not be entertained if it is filed after the expiration of a time to be stated by it in that communication, but which shall in no case be less than one year following the date of the judgment.

5. Paragraph 4 shall not apply to judgments concerning status or capacity of persons.

Article 20. Relationship with agreements or arrangements to which Member States are Parties

1. This Regulation shall, in relation to matters to which it applies, prevail over other provisions contained in bilateral or multilateral agreements or arrangements concluded by the Member States, and in particular Article IV of the Protocol to the Brussels Convention of 1968 and the Hague Convention of 15 November 1965.

2. This Regulation shall not preclude individual Member States from maintaining or concluding agreements or arrangements to expedite further or simplify the transmission of documents, provided that they are compatible with this Regulation.

3. Member States shall send to the Commission:

(a) a copy of the agreements or arrangements referred to in paragraph 2 concluded between the Member States as well as drafts of such agreements or arrangements which they intend to adopt; and

(b) any denunciation of, or amendments to, these agreements or arrangements.

Article 22. Protection of information transmitted

1. Information, including in particular personal data, transmitted under this Regulation shall be used by the receiving agency only for the purpose for which it was transmitted.

2. Receiving agencies shall ensure the confidentiality of such information, in accordance with their national law.

3. Paragraphs 1 and 2 shall not affect national laws enabling data subjects to be informed of the use made of information transmitted under this Regulation.

4. This Regulation shall be without prejudice to Directives 95/46/EC and 97/66/EC.

...

Article 24. Review

No later than 1 June 2004, and every five years thereafter, the Commission shall present to the European Parliament, the Council and the Economic and Social Committee a report on the application of this Regulation, paying special attention to the effectiveness of the bodies designated pursuant to Article 2 and to the practical application of point (c) of Article 3 and Article 9. The report shall be accompanied if need be by proposals for adaptations of this Regulation in line with the evolution of notification systems.

Article 25. Entry into force
This Regulation shall enter into force on 31 May 2001.

This Regulation shall be binding in its entirety and directly applicable in the Member States in accordance with the Treaty establishing the European Community.

Done at Brussels, 29 May 2000.

COUNCIL REGULATION (EC) NO 44/2001 OF 22 DECEMBER 2000 ON JURISDICTION AND THE RECOGNITION AND ENFORCEMENT OF JUDGMENTS IN CIVIL AND COMMERCIAL MATTERS ('BRUSSELS I REGULATION')

Official Journal L 12, 16/01/2001 p 1

THE COUNCIL OF THE EUROPEAN UNION,

Having regard to the Treaty establishing the European Community, and in particular Article 61(c) and Article 67(1) thereof,

Having regard to the proposal from the Commission,

Having regard to the opinion of the European Parliament,

Having regard to the opinion of the Economic and Social Committee,

Whereas:

(1) The Community has set itself the objective of maintaining and developing an area of freedom, security and justice, in which the free movement of persons is ensured. In order to establish progressively such an area, the Community should adopt, amongst other things, the measures relating to judicial cooperation in civil matters which are necessary for the sound operation of the internal market.

(2) Certain differences between national rules governing jurisdiction and recognition of judgments hamper the sound operation of the internal market. Provisions to unify the rules of conflict of jurisdiction in civil and commercial matters and to simplify the formalities with a view to rapid and simple recognition and enforcement of judgments from Member States bound by this Regulation are essential.

(3) This area is within the field of judicial cooperation in civil matters within the meaning of Article 65 of the Treaty.

(4) In accordance with the principles of subsidiarity and proportionality as set out in Article 5 of the Treaty, the objectives of this Regulation cannot be sufficiently achieved by the Member States and can therefore be better achieved by the Community. This Regulation confines itself to the minimum required in order to achieve those objectives and does not go beyond what is necessary for that purpose.

(5) On 27 September 1968 the Member States, acting under Article 293, fourth indent, of the Treaty, concluded the Brussels Convention on Jurisdiction and the Enforcement of Judgments in Civil and Commercial Matters, as amended by Conventions on the Accession of the New Member States to that Convention (hereinafter referred to as the 'Brussels Convention'). On 16 September 1988 Member States and EFTA States concluded the Lugano Convention on Jurisdiction and the Enforcement of Judgments in Civil and Commercial Matters, which is a parallel Convention to the 1968 Brussels Convention. Work has been undertaken for the revision of those Conventions, and the Council has approved the content of the revised texts. Continuity in the results achieved in that revision should be ensured.

(6) In order to attain the objective of free movement of judgments in civil and commercial matters, it is necessary and appropriate that the rules governing juris-

diction and the recognition and enforcement of judgments be governed by a Community legal instrument which is binding and directly applicable.

(7) The scope of this Regulation must cover all the main civil and commercial matters apart from certain well-defined matters.

(8) There must be a link between proceedings to which this Regulation applies and the territory of the Member States bound by this Regulation. Accordingly common rules on jurisdiction should, in principle, apply when the defendant is domiciled in one of those Member States.

(9) A defendant not domiciled in a Member State is in general subject to national rules of jurisdiction applicable in the territory of the Member State of the court seised, and a defendant domiciled in a Member State not bound by this Regulation must remain subject to the Brussels Convention.

(10) For the purposes of the free movement of judgments, judgments given in a Member State bound by this Regulation should be recognised and enforced in another Member State bound by this Regulation, even if the judgment debtor is domiciled in a third State.

(11) The rules of jurisdiction must be highly predictable and founded on the principle that jurisdiction is generally based on the defendant's domicile and jurisdiction must always be available on this ground save in a few well-defined situations in which the subject-matter of the litigation or the autonomy of the parties warrants a different linking factor. The domicile of a legal person must be defined autonomously so as to make the common rules more transparent and avoid conflicts of jurisdiction.

(12) In addition to the defendant's domicile, there should be alternative grounds of jurisdiction based on a close link between the court and the action or in order to facilitate the sound administration of justice.

(13) In relation to insurance, consumer contracts and employment, the weaker party should be protected by rules of jurisdiction more favourable to his interests than the general rules provide for.

(14) The autonomy of the parties to a contract, other than an insurance, consumer or employment contract, where only limited autonomy to determine the courts having jurisdiction is allowed, must be respected subject to the exclusive grounds of jurisdiction laid down in this Regulation.

(15) In the interests of the harmonious administration of justice it is necessary to minimise the possibility of concurrent proceedings and to ensure that irreconcilable judgments will not be given in two Member States. There must be a clear and effective mechanism for resolving cases of lis pendens and related actions and for obviating problems flowing from national differences as to the determination of the time when a case is regarded as pending. For the purposes of this Regulation that time should be defined autonomously.

(16) Mutual trust in the administration of justice in the Community justifies judgments given in a Member State being recognised automatically without the need for any procedure except in cases of dispute.

(17) By virtue of the same principle of mutual trust, the procedure for making enforceable in one Member State a judgment given in another must be efficient and rapid. To that end, the declaration that a judgment is enforceable should be issued virtually automatically after purely formal checks of the documents supplied, without there being any possibility for the court to raise of its own motion any of the grounds for non-enforcement provided for by this Regulation.

(18) However, respect for the rights of the defence means that the defendant should be able to appeal in an adversarial procedure, against the declaration of enforceability, if he considers one of the grounds for non-enforcement to be present. Redress procedures should also be available to the claimant where his application for a declaration of enforceability has been rejected.

(19) Continuity between the Brussels Convention and this Regulation should be ensured, and transitional provisions should be laid down to that end. The same

need for continuity applies as regards the interpretation of the Brussels Convention by the Court of Justice of the European Communities and the 1971 Protocol should remain applicable also to cases already pending when this Regulation enters into force.

(20) The United Kingdom and Ireland, in accordance with Article 3 of the Protocol on the position of the United Kingdom and Ireland annexed to the Treaty on European Union and to the Treaty establishing the European Community, have given notice of their wish to take part in the adoption and application of this Regulation.

(21) Denmark, in accordance with Articles 1 and 2 of the Protocol on the position of Denmark annexed to the Treaty on European Union and to the Treaty establishing the European Community, is not participating in the adoption of this Regulation, and is therefore not bound by it nor subject to its application.*

(22) Since the Brussels Convention remains in force in relations between Denmark and the Member States that are bound by this Regulation, both the Convention and the 1971 Protocol continue to apply between Denmark and the Member States bound by this Regulation.

(23) The Brussels Convention also continues to apply to the territories of the Member States which fall within the territorial scope of that Convention and which are excluded from this Regulation pursuant to Article 299 of the Treaty.

(24) Likewise for the sake of consistency, this Regulation should not affect rules governing jurisdiction and the recognition of judgments contained in specific Community instruments.

(25) Respect for international commitments entered into by the Member States means that this Regulation should not affect conventions relating to specific matters to which the Member States are parties.

(26) The necessary flexibility should be provided for in the basic rules of this Regulation in order to take account of the specific procedural rules of certain Member States. Certain provisions of the Protocol annexed to the Brussels Convention should accordingly be incorporated in this Regulation.

(27) In order to allow a harmonious transition in certain areas which were the subject of special provisions in the Protocol annexed to the Brussels Convention, this Regulation lays down, for a transitional period, provisions taking into consideration the specific situation in certain Member States.

(28) No later than five years after entry into force of this Regulation the Commission will present a report on its application and, if need be, submit proposals for adaptations.

(29) The Commission will have to adjust Annexes I to IV on the rules of national jurisdiction, the courts or competent authorities and redress procedures available on the basis of the amendments forwarded by the Member State concerned; amendments made to Annexes V and VI should be adopted in accordance with Council Decision 1999/468/EC of 28 June 1999 laying down the procedures for the exercise of implementing powers conferred on the Commission,

HAS ADOPTED THIS REGULATION:

CHAPTER I
SCOPE

Article 1

1. This Regulation shall apply in civil and commercial matters whatever the nature of the court or tribunal. It shall not extend, in particular, to revenue, customs or administrative matters.

---

*But see Agreement made on 19 October 2005 between the European Community and the Kingdom of Denmark on jurisdiction and the recognition and enforcement of judgments in civil and commercial matters; see p 262 below.

2.   The Regulation shall not apply to:
   (a)   the status or legal capacity of natural persons, rights in property arising out of a matrimonial relationship, wills and succession;
   (b)   bankruptcy, proceedings relating to the winding-up of insolvent companies or other legal persons, judicial arrangements, compositions and analogous proceedings;
   (c)   social security;
   (d)   arbitration.
3.   In this Regulation, the term 'Member State' shall mean Member States with the exception of Denmark.

CHAPTER II
JURISDICTION

Section 1
General provisions

Article 2
1.   Subject to this Regulation, persons domiciled in a Member State shall, whatever their nationality, be sued in the courts of that Member State.
2.   Persons who are not nationals of the Member State in which they are domiciled shall be governed by the rules of jurisdiction applicable to nationals of that State.

Article 3
1.   Persons domiciled in a Member State may be sued in the courts of another Member State only by virtue of the rules set out in Sections 2 to 7 of this Chapter.
2.   In particular the rules of national jurisdiction set out in Annex I shall not be applicable as against them.

Article 4
1.   If the defendant is not domiciled in a Member State, the jurisdiction of the courts of each Member State shall, subject to Articles 22 and 23, be determined by the law of that Member State.
2.   As against such a defendant, any person domiciled in a Member State may, whatever his nationality, avail himself in that State of the rules of jurisdiction there in force, and in particular those specified in Annex I, in the same way as the nationals of that State.

Section 2
Special jurisdiction

Article 5
A person domiciled in a Member State may, in another Member State, be sued:
1. (a)   in matters relating to a contract, in the courts for the place of performance of the obligation in question;
   (b)   for the purpose of this provision and unless otherwise agreed, the place of performance of the obligation in question shall be:
   – in the case of the sale of goods, the place in a Member State where, under the contract, the goods were delivered or should have been delivered,
   – in the case of the provision of services, the place in a Member State where, under the contract, the services were provided or should have been provided,
   (c)   if subparagraph (b) does not apply then subparagraph (a) applies;
2.   in matters relating to maintenance, in the courts for the place where the maintenance creditor is domiciled or habitually resident or, if the matter is ancillary to proceedings concerning the status of a person, in the court which, according to its own law, has jurisdiction to entertain those proceedings, unless that jurisdiction is based solely on the nationality of one of the parties;

3.   in matters relating to tort, delict or quasi-delict, in the courts for the place where the harmful event occurred or may occur;

4.   as regards a civil claim for damages or restitution which is based on an act giving rise to criminal proceedings, in the court seised of those proceedings, to the extent that that court has jurisdiction under its own law to entertain civil proceedings;

5.   as regards a dispute arising out of the operations of a branch, agency or other establishment, in the courts for the place in which the branch, agency or other establishment is situated;

6.   as settlor, trustee or beneficiary of a trust created by the operation of a statute, or by a written instrument, or created orally and evidenced in writing, in the courts of the Member State in which the trust is domiciled;

7.   as regards a dispute concerning the payment of remuneration claimed in respect of the salvage of a cargo or freight, in the court under the authority of which the cargo or freight in question:

(a)   has been arrested to secure such payment, or

(b)   could have been so arrested, but bail or other security has been given;

provided that this provision shall apply only if it is claimed that the defendant has an interest in the cargo or freight or had such an interest at the time of salvage.

Article 6

A person domiciled in a Member State may also be sued:

1.   where he is one of a number of defendants, in the courts for the place where any one of them is domiciled, provided the claims are so closely connected that it is expedient to hear and determine them together to avoid the risk of irreconcilable judgments resulting from separate proceedings;

2.   as a third party in an action on a warranty or guarantee or in any other third party proceedings, in the court seised of the original proceedings, unless these were instituted solely with the object of removing him from the jurisdiction of the court which would be competent in his case;

3.   on a counter-claim arising from the same contract or facts on which the original claim was based, in the court in which the original claim is pending;

4.   in matters relating to a contract, if the action may be combined with an action against the same defendant in matters relating to rights in rem in immovable property, in the court of the Member State in which the property is situated.

Article 7

Where by virtue of this Regulation a court of a Member State has jurisdiction in actions relating to liability from the use or operation of a ship, that court, or any other court substituted for this purpose by the internal law of that Member State, shall also have jurisdiction over claims for limitation of such liability.

Section 3
Jurisdiction in matters relating to insurance

Article 8

In matters relating to insurance, jurisdiction shall be determined by this Section, without prejudice to Article 4 and point 5 of Article 5.

Article 9

1.   An insurer domiciled in a Member State may be sued:

(a)   in the courts of the Member State where he is domiciled, or

(b)   in another Member State, in the case of actions brought by the policyholder, the insured or a beneficiary, in the courts for the place where the plaintiff is domiciled,

(c)   if he is a co-insurer, in the courts of a Member State in which proceedings are brought against the leading insurer.

2.   An insurer who is not domiciled in a Member State but has a branch, agency or other establishment in one of the Member States shall, in disputes arising out of the operations of the branch, agency or establishment, be deemed to be domiciled in that Member State.

Article 10
In respect of liability insurance or insurance of immovable property, the insurer may in addition be sued in the courts for the place where the harmful event occurred. The same applies if movable and immovable property are covered by the same insurance policy and both are adversely affected by the same contingency.

Article 11
1.   In respect of liability insurance, the insurer may also, if the law of the court permits it, be joined in proceedings which the injured party has brought against the insured.
2.   Articles 8, 9 and 10 shall apply to actions brought by the injured party directly against the insurer, where such direct actions are permitted.
3.   If the law governing such direct actions provides that the policyholder or the insured may be joined as a party to the action, the same court shall have jurisdiction over them.

Article 12
1.   Without prejudice to Article 11(3), an insurer may bring proceedings only in the courts of the Member State in which the defendant is domiciled, irrespective of whether he is the policyholder, the insured or a beneficiary.
2.   The provisions of this Section shall not affect the right to bring a counterclaim in the court in which, in accordance with this Section, the original claim is pending.

Article 13
The provisions of this Section may be departed from only by an agreement:
1.   which is entered into after the dispute has arisen, or
2.   which allows the policyholder, the insured or a beneficiary to bring proceedings in courts other than those indicated in this Section, or
3.   which is concluded between a policyholder and an insurer, both of whom are at the time of conclusion of the contract domiciled or habitually resident in the same Member State, and which has the effect of conferring jurisdiction on the courts of that State even if the harmful event were to occur abroad, provided that such an agreement is not contrary to the law of that State, or
4.   which is concluded with a policyholder who is not domiciled in a Member State, except in so far as the insurance is compulsory or relates to immovable property in a Member State, or
5.   which relates to a contract of insurance in so far as it covers one or more of the risks set out in Article 14.

Article 14
The following are the risks referred to in Article 13(5):
1.   any loss of or damage to:
    (a)   seagoing ships, installations situated offshore or on the high seas, or aircraft, arising from perils which relate to their use for commercial purposes;
    (b)   goods in transit other than passengers' baggage where the transit consists of or includes carriage by such ships or aircraft.
2.   any liability, other than for bodily injury to passengers or loss of or damage to their baggage:
    (a)   arising out of the use or operation of ships, installations or aircraft as referred to in point 1(a) in so far as, in respect of the latter, the law of the Member State in which such aircraft are registered does not prohibit agreements on jurisdiction regarding insurance of such risks;

(b)   for loss or damage caused by goods in transit as described in point 1(b).

3.   any financial loss connected with the use or operation of ships, installations or aircraft as referred to in point 1(a), in particular loss of freight or charter-hire;

4.   any risk or interest connected with any of those referred to in points 1 to 3;

5.   notwithstanding points 1 to 4, all 'large risks' as defined in Council Directive 73/239/EEC, as amended by Council Directives 88/357/EEC and 90/618/EEC, as they may be amended.

Section 4
Jurisdiction over consumer contracts

Article 15

1.   In matters relating to a contract concluded by a person, the consumer, for a purpose which can be regarded as being outside his trade or profession, jurisdiction shall be determined by this Section, without prejudice to Article 4 and point 5 of Article 5, if:

(a)   it is a contract for the sale of goods on instalment credit terms; or

(b)   it is a contract for a loan repayable by instalments, or for any other form of credit, made to finance the sale of goods; or

(c)   in all other cases, the contract has been concluded with a person who pursues commercial or professional activities in the Member State of the consumer's domicile or, by any means, directs such activities to that Member State or to several States including that Member State, and the contract falls within the scope of such activities.

2.   Where a consumer enters into a contract with a party who is not domiciled in the Member State but has a branch, agency or other establishment in one of the Member States, that party shall, in disputes arising out of the operations of the branch, agency or establishment, be deemed to be domiciled in that State.

3.   This Section shall not apply to a contract of transport other than a contract which, for an inclusive price, provides for a combination of travel and accommodation.

Article 16

1.   A consumer may bring proceedings against the other party to a contract either in the courts of the Member State in which that party is domiciled or in the courts for the place where the consumer is domiciled.

2.   Proceedings may be brought against a consumer by the other party to the contract only in the courts of the Member State in which the consumer is domiciled.

3.   This Article shall not affect the right to bring a counter-claim in the court in which, in accordance with this Section, the original claim is pending.

Article 17

The provisions of this Section may be departed from only by an agreement:

1.   which is entered into after the dispute has arisen; or

2.   which allows the consumer to bring proceedings in courts other than those indicated in this Section; or

3.   which is entered into by the consumer and the other party to the contract, both of whom are at the time of conclusion of the contract domiciled or habitually resident in the same Member State, and which confers jurisdiction on the courts of that Member State, provided that such an agreement is not contrary to the law of that Member State.

Section 5
Jurisdiction over individual contracts of employment

Article 18

1.   In matters relating to individual contracts of employment, jurisdiction shall be determined by this Section, without prejudice to Article 4 and point 5 of Article 5.

2.   Where an employee enters into an individual contract of employment with an employer who is not domiciled in a Member State but has a branch, agency or other establishment in one of the Member States, the employer shall, in disputes arising out of the operations of the branch, agency or establishment, be deemed to be domiciled in that Member State.

Article 19
An employer domiciled in a Member State may be sued:
   1.   in the courts of the Member State where he is domiciled; or
   2.   in another Member State:
    (a)   in the courts for the place where the employee habitually carries out his work or in the courts for the last place where he did so, or
    (b)   if the employee does not or did not habitually carry out his work in any one country, in the courts for the place where the business which engaged the employee is or was situated.

Article 20
   1.   An employer may bring proceedings only in the courts of the Member State in which the employee is domiciled.
   2.   The provisions of this Section shall not affect the right to bring a counterclaim in the court in which, in accordance with this Section, the original claim is pending.

Article 21
The provisions of this Section may be departed from only by an agreement on jurisdiction:
   1.   which is entered into after the dispute has arisen; or
   2.   which allows the employee to bring proceedings in courts other than those indicated in this Section.

Section 6
Exclusive jurisdiction

Article 22
The following courts shall have exclusive jurisdiction, regardless of domicile:
   1.   in proceedings which have as their object rights in rem in immovable property or tenancies of immovable property, the courts of the Member State in which the property is situated.
   However, in proceedings which have as their object tenancies of immovable property concluded for temporary private use for a maximum period of six consecutive months, the courts of the Member State in which the defendant is domiciled shall also have jurisdiction, provided that the tenant is a natural person and that the landlord and the tenant are domiciled in the same Member State;
   2.   in proceedings which have as their object the validity of the constitution, the nullity or the dissolution of companies or other legal persons or associations of natural or legal persons, or of the validity of the decisions of their organs, the courts of the Member State in which the company, legal person or association has its seat. In order to determine that seat, the court shall apply its rules of private international law;
   3.   in proceedings which have as their object the validity of entries in public registers, the courts of the Member State in which the register is kept;
   4.   in proceedings concerned with the registration or validity of patents, trade marks, designs, or other similar rights required to be deposited or registered, the courts of the Member State in which the deposit or registration has been applied for, has taken place or is under the terms of a Community instrument or an international convention deemed to have taken place.
   Without prejudice to the jurisdiction of the European Patent Office under the Convention on the Grant of European Patents, signed at Munich on 5 October

1973, the courts of each Member State shall have exclusive jurisdiction, regardless of domicile, in proceedings concerned with the registration or validity of any European patent granted for that State;

5.   in proceedings concerned with the enforcement of judgments, the courts of the Member State in which the judgment has been or is to be enforced.

Section 7
Prorogation of jurisdiction

Article 23

1.   If the parties, one or more of whom is domiciled in a Member State, have agreed that a court or the courts of a Member State are to have jurisdiction to settle any disputes which have arisen or which may arise in connection with a particular legal relationship, that court or those courts shall have jurisdiction. Such jurisdiction shall be exclusive unless the parties have agreed otherwise. Such an agreement conferring jurisdiction shall be either:

(a)   in writing or evidenced in writing; or

(b)   in a form which accords with practices which the parties have established between themselves; or

(c)   in international trade or commerce, in a form which accords with a usage of which the parties are or ought to have been aware and which in such trade or commerce is widely known to, and regularly observed by, parties to contracts of the type involved in the particular trade or commerce concerned.

2.   Any communication by electronic means which provides a durable record of the agreement shall be equivalent to 'writing'.

3.   Where such an agreement is concluded by parties, none of whom is domiciled in a Member State, the courts of other Member States shall have no jurisdiction over their disputes unless the court or courts chosen have declined jurisdiction.

4.   The court or courts of a Member State on which a trust instrument has conferred jurisdiction shall have exclusive jurisdiction in any proceedings brought against a settlor, trustee or beneficiary, if relations between these persons or their rights or obligations under the trust are involved.

5.   Agreements or provisions of a trust instrument conferring jurisdiction shall have no legal force if they are contrary to Articles 13, 17 or 21, or if the courts whose jurisdiction they purport to exclude have exclusive jurisdiction by virtue of Article 22.

Article 24

Apart from jurisdiction derived from other provisions of this Regulation, a court of a Member State before which a defendant enters an appearance shall have jurisdiction. This rule shall not apply where appearance was entered to contest the jurisdiction, or where another court has exclusive jurisdiction by virtue of Article 22.

Section 8
Examination as to jurisdiction and admissibility

Article 25

Where a court of a Member State is seised of a claim which is principally concerned with a matter over which the courts of another Member State have exclusive jurisdiction by virtue of Article 22, it shall declare of its own motion that it has no jurisdiction.

Article 26

1.   Where a defendant domiciled in one Member State is sued in a court of another Member State and does not enter an appearance, the court shall declare of its own motion that it has no jurisdiction unless its jurisdiction is derived from the provisions of this Regulation.

2.   The court shall stay the proceedings so long as it is not shown that the defendant has been able to receive the document instituting the proceedings or an equivalent document in sufficient time to enable him to arrange for his defence, or that all necessary steps have been taken to this end.

3.   Article 19 of Council Regulation (EC) No 1348/2000 of 29 May 2000 on the service in the Member States of judicial and extrajudicial documents in civil or commercial matters shall apply instead of the provisions of paragraph 2 if the document instituting the proceedings or an equivalent document had to be transmitted from one Member State to another pursuant to this Regulation.

4.   Where the provisions of Regulation (EC) No 1348/2000 are not applicable, Article 15 of the Hague Convention of 15 November 1965 on the Service Abroad of Judicial and Extrajudicial Documents in Civil or Commercial Matters shall apply if the document instituting the proceedings or an equivalent document had to be transmitted pursuant to that Convention.

Section 9
Lis pendens—related actions

Article 27
1.   Where proceedings involving the same cause of action and between the same parties are brought in the courts of different Member States, any court other than the court first seised shall of its own motion stay its proceedings until such time as the jurisdiction of the court first seised is established.

2.   Where the jurisdiction of the court first seised is established, any court other than the court first seised shall decline jurisdiction in favour of that court.

Article 28
1.   Where related actions are pending in the courts of different Member States, any court other than the court first seised may stay its proceedings.

2.   Where these actions are pending at first instance, any court other than the court first seised may also, on the application of one of the parties, decline jurisdiction if the court first seised has jurisdiction over the actions in question and its law permits the consolidation thereof.

3.   For the purposes of this Article, actions are deemed to be related where they are so closely connected that it is expedient to hear and determine them together to avoid the risk of irreconcilable judgments resulting from separate proceedings.

Article 29
Where actions come within the exclusive jurisdiction of several courts, any court other than the court first seised shall decline jurisdiction in favour of that court.

Article 30
For the purposes of this Section, a court shall be deemed to be seised:
1.   at the time when the document instituting the proceedings or an equivalent document is lodged with the court, provided that the plaintiff has not subsequently failed to take the steps he was required to take to have service effected on the defendant, or

2.   if the document has to be served before being lodged with the court, at the time when it is received by the authority responsible for service, provided that the plaintiff has not subsequently failed to take the steps he was required to take to have the document lodged with the court.

Section 10
Provisional, including protective, measures

Article 31
Application may be made to the courts of a Member State for such provisional, including protective, measures as may be available under the law of that State,

even if, under this Regulation, the courts of another Member State have jurisdiction as to the substance of the matter.

CHAPTER III
RECOGNITION AND ENFORCEMENT

Article 32
For the purposes of this Regulation, 'judgment' means any judgment given by a court or tribunal of a Member State, whatever the judgment may be called, including a decree, order, decision or writ of execution, as well as the determination of costs or expenses by an officer of the court.

Section 1
Recognition

Article 33
1.   A judgment given in a Member State shall be recognised in the other Member States without any special procedure being required.
2.   Any interested party who raises the recognition of a judgment as the principal issue in a dispute may, in accordance with the procedures provided for in Sections 2 and 3 of this Chapter, apply for a decision that the judgment be recognised.
3.   If the outcome of proceedings in a court of a Member State depends on the determination of an incidental question of recognition that court shall have jurisdiction over that question.

Article 34
A judgment shall not be recognised:
1.   if such recognition is manifestly contrary to public policy in the Member State in which recognition is sought;
2.   where it was given in default of appearance, if the defendant was not served with the document which instituted the proceedings or with an equivalent document in sufficient time and in such a way as to enable him to arrange for his defence, unless the defendant failed to commence proceedings to challenge the judgment when it was possible for him to do so;
3.   if it is irreconcilable with a judgment given in a dispute between the same parties in the Member State in which recognition is sought;
4.   if it is irreconcilable with an earlier judgment given in another Member State or in a third State involving the same cause of action and between the same parties, provided that the earlier judgment fulfils the conditions necessary for its recognition in the Member State addressed.

Article 35
1.   Moreover, a judgment shall not be recognised if it conflicts with Sections 3, 4 or 6 of Chapter II, or in a case provided for in Article 72.
2.   In its examination of the grounds of jurisdiction referred to in the foregoing paragraph, the court or authority applied to shall be bound by the findings of fact on which the court of the Member State of origin based its jurisdiction.
3.   Subject to the paragraph 1, the jurisdiction of the court of the Member State of origin may not be reviewed. The test of public policy referred to in point 1 of Article 34 may not be applied to the rules relating to jurisdiction.

Article 36
Under no circumstances may a foreign judgment be reviewed as to its substance.

Article 37
1.   A court of a Member State in which recognition is sought of a judgment given in another Member State may stay the proceedings if an ordinary appeal against the judgment has been lodged.

2. A court of a Member State in which recognition is sought of a judgment given in Ireland or the United Kingdom may stay the proceedings if enforcement is suspended in the State of origin, by reason of an appeal.

Section 2
Enforcement

Article 38
1. A judgment given in a Member State and enforceable in that State shall be enforced in another Member State when, on the application of any interested party, it has been declared enforceable there.
2. However, in the United Kingdom, such a judgment shall be enforced in England and Wales, in Scotland, or in Northern Ireland when, on the application of any interested party, it has been registered for enforcement in that part of the United Kingdom.

Article 39
1. The application shall be submitted to the court or competent authority indicated in the list in Annex II.
2. The local jurisdiction shall be determined by reference to the place of domicile of the party against whom enforcement is sought, or to the place of enforcement.

Article 40
1. The procedure for making the application shall be governed by the law of the Member State in which enforcement is sought.
2. The applicant must give an address for service of process within the area of jurisdiction of the court applied to. However, if the law of the Member State in which enforcement is sought does not provide for the furnishing of such an address, the applicant shall appoint a representative ad litem.
3. The documents referred to in Article 53 shall be attached to the application.

Article 41
The judgment shall be declared enforceable immediately on completion of the formalities in Article 53 without any review under Articles 34 and 35. The party against whom enforcement is sought shall not at this stage of the proceedings be entitled to make any submissions on the application.

Article 42
1. The decision on the application for a declaration of enforceability shall forthwith be brought to the notice of the applicant in accordance with the procedure laid down by the law of the Member State in which enforcement is sought.
2. The declaration of enforceability shall be served on the party against whom enforcement is sought, accompanied by the judgment, if not already served on that party.

Article 43
1. The decision on the application for a declaration of enforceability may be appealed against by either party.
2. The appeal is to be lodged with the court indicated in the list in Annex III.
3. The appeal shall be dealt with in accordance with the rules governing procedure in contradictory matters.
4. If the party against whom enforcement is sought fails to appear before the appellate court in proceedings concerning an appeal brought by the applicant, Article 26(2) to (4) shall apply even where the party against whom enforcement is sought is not domiciled in any of the Member States.
5. An appeal against the declaration of enforceability is to be lodged within one month of service thereof. If the party against whom enforcement is sought is domiciled in a Member State other than that in which the declaration of enforce-

ability was given, the time for appealing shall be two months and shall run from the date of service, either on him in person or at his residence. No extension of time may be granted on account of distance.

Article 44
The judgment given on the appeal may be contested only by the appeal referred to in Annex IV.

Article 45
1. The court with which an appeal is lodged under Article 43 or Article 44 shall refuse or revoke a declaration of enforceability only on one of the grounds specified in Articles 34 and 35. It shall give its decision without delay.
2. Under no circumstances may the foreign judgment be reviewed as to its substance.

Article 46
1. The court with which an appeal is lodged under Article 43 or Article 44 may, on the application of the party against whom enforcement is sought, stay the proceedings if an ordinary appeal has been lodged against the judgment in the Member State of origin or if the time for such an appeal has not yet expired; in the latter case, the court may specify the time within which such an appeal is to be lodged.
2. Where the judgment was given in Ireland or the United Kingdom, any form of appeal available in the Member State of origin shall be treated as an ordinary appeal for the purposes of paragraph 1.
3. The court may also make enforcement conditional on the provision of such security as it shall determine.

Article 47
1. When a judgment must be recognised in accordance with this Regulation, nothing shall prevent the applicant from availing himself of provisional, including protective, measures in accordance with the law of the Member State requested without a declaration of enforceability under Article 41 being required.
2. The declaration of enforceability shall carry with it the power to proceed to any protective measures.
3. During the time specified for an appeal pursuant to Article 43(5) against the declaration of enforceability and until any such appeal has been determined, no measures of enforcement may be taken other than protective measures against the property of the party against whom enforcement is sought.

Article 48
1. Where a foreign judgment has been given in respect of several matters and the declaration of enforceability cannot be given for all of them, the court or competent authority shall give it for one or more of them.
2. An applicant may request a declaration of enforceability limited to parts of a judgment.

Article 49
A foreign judgment which orders a periodic payment by way of a penalty shall be enforceable in the Member State in which enforcement is sought only if the amount of the payment has been finally determined by the courts of the Member State of origin.

Article 50
An applicant who, in the Member State of origin has benefited from complete or partial legal aid or exemption from costs or expenses, shall be entitled, in the procedure provided for in this Section, to benefit from the most favourable legal aid or the most extensive exemption from costs or expenses provided for by the law of the Member State addressed.

Article 51
No security, bond or deposit, however described, shall be required of a party who in one Member State applies for enforcement of a judgment given in another Member State on the ground that he is a foreign national or that he is not domiciled or resident in the State in which enforcement is sought.

Article 52
In proceedings for the issue of a declaration of enforceability, no charge, duty or fee calculated by reference to the value of the matter at issue may be levied in the Member State in which enforcement is sought.

Section 3
Common provisions

Article 53
   1. A party seeking recognition or applying for a declaration of enforceability shall produce a copy of the judgment which satisfies the conditions necessary to establish its authenticity.
   2. A party applying for a declaration of enforceability shall also produce the certificate referred to in Article 54, without prejudice to Article 55.

Article 54
The court or competent authority of a Member State where a judgment was given shall issue, at the request of any interested party, a certificate using the standard form in Annex V to this Regulation.

Article 55
   1. If the certificate referred to in Article 54 is not produced, the court or competent authority may specify a time for its production or accept an equivalent document or, if it considers that it has sufficient information before it, dispense with its production.
   2. If the court or competent authority so requires, a translation of the documents shall be produced. The translation shall be certified by a person qualified to do so in one of the Member States.

Article 56
No legalisation or other similar formality shall be required in respect of the documents referred to in Article 53 or Article 55(2), or in respect of a document appointing a representative ad litem.

CHAPTER IV
AUTHENTIC INSTRUMENTS AND COURT SETTLEMENTS

Article 57
   1. A document which has been formally drawn up or registered as an authentic instrument and is enforceable in one Member State shall, in another Member State, be declared enforceable there, on application made in accordance with the procedures provided for in Articles 38, et seq. The court with which an appeal is lodged under Article 43 or Article 44 shall refuse or revoke a declaration of enforceability only if enforcement of the instrument is manifestly contrary to public policy in the Member State addressed.
   2. Arrangements relating to maintenance obligations concluded with administrative authorities or authenticated by them shall also be regarded as authentic instruments within the meaning of paragraph 1.
   3. The instrument produced must satisfy the conditions necessary to establish its authenticity in the Member State of origin.
   4. Section 3 of Chapter III shall apply as appropriate. The competent authority of a Member State where an authentic instrument was drawn up or registered

shall issue, at the request of any interested party, a certificate using the standard form in Annex VI to this Regulation.

Article 58
A settlement which has been approved by a court in the course of proceedings and is enforceable in the Member State in which it was concluded shall be enforceable in the State addressed under the same conditions as authentic instruments. The court or competent authority of a Member State where a court settlement was approved shall issue, at the request of any interested party, a certificate using the standard form in Annex V to this Regulation.

CHAPTER V
GENERAL PROVISIONS

Article 59
1. In order to determine whether a party is domiciled in the Member State whose courts are seised of a matter, the court shall apply its internal law.
2. If a party is not domiciled in the Member State whose courts are seised of the matter, then, in order to determine whether the party is domiciled in another Member State, the court shall apply the law of that Member State.

Article 60
1. For the purposes of this Regulation, a company or other legal person or association of natural or legal persons is domiciled at the place where it has its:
    (a)   statutory seat, or
    (b)   central administration, or
    (c)   principal place of business.
2. For the purposes of the United Kingdom and Ireland 'statutory seat' means the registered office or, where there is no such office anywhere, the place of incorporation or, where there is no such place anywhere, the place under the law of which the formation took place.
3. In order to determine whether a trust is domiciled in the Member State whose courts are seised of the matter, the court shall apply its rules of private international law.

Article 61
Without prejudice to any more favourable provisions of national laws, persons domiciled in a Member State who are being prosecuted in the criminal courts of another Member State of which they are not nationals for an offence which was not intentionally committed may be defended by persons qualified to do so, even if they do not appear in person. However, the court seised of the matter may order appearance in person; in the case of failure to appear, a judgment given in the civil action without the person concerned having had the opportunity to arrange for his defence need not be recognised or enforced in the other Member States.

...

CHAPTER VI
TRANSITIONAL PROVISIONS

Article 66
1. This Regulation shall apply only to legal proceedings instituted and to documents formally drawn up or registered as authentic instruments after the entry into force thereof.
2. However, if the proceedings in the Member State of origin were instituted before the entry into force of this Regulation, judgments given after that date shall be recognised and enforced in accordance with Chapter III,
    (a)   if the proceedings in the Member State of origin were instituted after the

entry into force of the Brussels or the Lugano Convention both in the Member State or origin and in the Member State addressed;

(b)   in all other cases, if jurisdiction was founded upon rules which accorded with those provided for either in Chapter II or in a convention concluded between the Member State of origin and the Member State addressed which was in force when the proceedings were instituted.

CHAPTER VII
RELATIONS WITH OTHER INSTRUMENTS

Article 67
This Regulation shall not prejudice the application of provisions governing jurisdiction and the recognition and enforcement of judgments in specific matters which are contained in Community instruments or in national legislation harmonised pursuant to such instruments.

Article 68
1.   This Regulation shall, as between the Member States, supersede the Brussels Convention, except as regards the territories of the Member States which fall within the territorial scope of that Convention and which are excluded from this Regulation pursuant to Article 299 of the Treaty.
2.   In so far as this Regulation replaces the provisions of the Brussels Convention between Member States, any reference to the Convention shall be understood as a reference to this Regulation.

...

Article 71
1.   This Regulation shall not affect any conventions to which the Member States are parties and which in relation to particular matters, govern jurisdiction or the recognition or enforcement of judgments.
2.   With a view to its uniform interpretation, paragraph 1 shall be applied in the following manner:
(a)   this Regulation shall not prevent a court of a Member State, which is a party to a convention on a particular matter, from assuming jurisdiction in accordance with that convention, even where the defendant is domiciled in another Member State which is not a party to that convention. The court hearing the action shall, in any event, apply Article 26 of this Regulation;
(b)   judgments given in a Member State by a court in the exercise of jurisdiction provided for in a convention on a particular matter shall be recognised and enforced in the other Member States in accordance with this Regulation.
Where a convention on a particular matter to which both the Member State of origin and the Member State addressed are parties lays down conditions for the recognition or enforcement of judgments, those conditions shall apply. In any event, the provisions of this Regulation which concern the procedure for recognition and enforcement of judgments may be applied.

Article 72
This Regulation shall not affect agreements by which Member States undertook, prior to the entry into force of this Regulation pursuant to Article 59 of the Brussels Convention, not to recognise judgments given, in particular in other Contracting States to that Convention, against defendants domiciled or habitually resident in a third country where, in cases provided for in Article 4 of that Convention, the judgment could only be founded on a ground of jurisdiction specified in the second paragraph of Article 3 of that Convention.

CHAPTER VIII
FINAL PROVISIONS

Article 76
This Regulation shall enter into force on 1 March 2002.

This Regulation is binding in its entirety and directly applicable in the Member States in accordance with the Treaty establishing the European Community.

Done at Brussels, 22 December 2000.

COUNCIL REGULATION (EC) NO 1206/2001 OF 28 MAY 2001 ON COOPERATION BETWEEN THE COURTS OF THE MEMBER STATES IN THE TAKING OF EVIDENCE IN CIVIL OR COMMERCIAL MATTERS

Official Journal L 174, 27/06/2001 p 1

THE COUNCIL OF THE EUROPEAN UNION,

Having regard to the Treaty establishing the European Community, and in particular Article 61(c) and Article 67(1) thereof,
     Having regard to the initiative of the Federal Republic of Germany,
     Having regard to the opinion of the European Parliament,
     Having regard to the opinion of the Economic and Social Committee,

Whereas:
     (1)   The European Union has set itself the objective of maintaining and developing the European Union as an area of freedom, security and justice in which the free movement of persons is ensured. For the gradual establishment of such an area, the Community is to adopt, among others, the measures relating to judicial cooperation in civil matters needed for the proper functioning of the internal market.
     (2)   For the purpose of the proper functioning of the internal market, cooperation between courts in the taking of evidence should be improved, and in particular simplified and accelerated.
     (3)   At its meeting in Tampere on 15 and 16 October 1999, the European Council recalled that new procedural legislation in cross-border cases, in particular on the taking of evidence, should be prepared.
     (4)   This area falls within the scope of Article 65 of the Treaty.
     (5)   The objectives of the proposed action, namely the improvement of cooperation between the courts on the taking of evidence in civil or commercial matters, cannot be sufficiently achieved by the Member States and can therefore be better achieved at Community level. The Community may adopt measures in accordance with the principle of subsidiarity as set out in Article 5 of the Treaty. In accordance with the principle of proportionality, as set out in that Article, this Regulation does not go beyond what is necessary to achieve those objectives.
     (6)   To date, there is no binding instrument between all the Member States concerning the taking of evidence. The Hague Convention of 18 March 1970 on the taking of evidence abroad in civil or commercial matters applies between only 11 Member States of the European Union.
     (7)   As it is often essential for a decision in a civil or commercial matter pending before a court in a Member State to take evidence in another Member State, the Community's activity cannot be limited to the field of transmission of judicial and extrajudicial documents in civil or commercial matters which falls within the scope of Council Regulation (EC) No 1348/2000 of 29 May 2000 on the serving in the Member States of judicial and extrajudicial documents in civil or commercial matters. It is therefore necessary to continue the improvement of cooperation between courts of Member States in the field of taking of evidence.

(8) The efficiency of judicial procedures in civil or commercial matters requires that the transmission and execution of requests for the performance of taking of evidence is to be made directly and by the most rapid means possible between Member States' courts.

(9) Speed in transmission of requests for the performance of taking of evidence warrants the use of all appropriate means, provided that certain conditions as to the legibility and reliability of the document received are observed. So as to ensure the utmost clarity and legal certainty the request for the performance of taking of evidence must be transmitted on a form to be completed in the language of the Member State of the requested court or in another language accepted by that State. For the same reasons, forms should also be used as far as possible for further communication between the relevant courts.

(10) A request for the performance of the taking of evidence should be executed expeditiously. If it is not possible for the request to be executed within 90 days of receipt by the requested court, the latter should inform the requesting court accordingly, stating the reasons which prevent the request from being executed swiftly.

(11) To secure the effectiveness of this Regulation, the possibility of refusing to execute the request for the performance of taking of evidence should be confined to strictly limited exceptional situations.

(12) The requested court should execute the request in accordance with the law of its Member State.

(13) The parties and, if any, their representatives, should be able to be present at the performance of the taking of evidence, if that is provided for by the law of the Member State of the requesting court, in order to be able to follow the proceedings in a comparable way as if evidence were taken in the Member State of the requesting court. They should also have the right to request to participate in order to have a more active role in the performance of the taking of evidence. However, the conditions under which they may participate should be determined by the requested court in accordance with the law of its Member State.

(14) The representatives of the requesting court should be able to be present at the performance of the taking of evidence, if that is compatible with the law of the Member State of the requesting court, in order to have an improved possibility of evaluation of evidence. They should also have the right to request to participate, under the conditions laid down by the requested court in accordance with the law of its Member State, in order to have a more active role in the performance of the taking of evidence.

(15) In order to facilitate the taking of evidence it should be possible for a court in a Member State, in accordance with the law of its Member State, to take evidence directly in another Member State, if accepted by the latter, and under the conditions determined by the central body or competent authority of the requested Member State.

(16) The execution of the request, according to Article 10, should not give rise to a claim for any reimbursement of taxes or costs. Nevertheless, if the requested court requires reimbursement, the fees paid to experts and interpreters, as well as the costs occasioned by the application of Article 10(3) and (4), should not be borne by that court. In such a case, the requesting court is to take the necessary measures to ensure reimbursement without delay. Where the opinion of an expert is required, the requested court may, before executing the request, ask the requesting court for an adequate deposit or advance towards the costs.

(17) This Regulation should prevail over the provisions applying to its field of application, contained in international conventions concluded by the Member States. Member States should be free to adopt agreements or arrangements to further facilitate cooperation in the taking of evidence.

(18) The information transmitted pursuant to this Regulation should enjoy protection. Since Directive 95/46/EC of the European Parliament and of the Council

of 24 October 1995 on the protection of individuals with regard to the processing of personal data and on the free movement of such data, and Directive 97/66/EC of the European Parliament and of the Council of 15 December 1997 concerning the processing of personal data and the protection of privacy in the tele-communications sector, are applicable, there is no need for specific provisions on data protection in this Regulation.

(19) The measures necessary for the implementation of this Regulation should be adopted in accordance with Council Decision 1999/468/EC of 28 June 1999 laying down the procedures for the exercise of implementing powers conferred on the Commission.

(20) For the proper functioning of this Regulation, the Commission should review its application and propose such amendments as may appear necessary.

(21) The United Kingdom and Ireland, in accordance with Article 3 of the Protocol on the position of the United Kingdom and Ireland annexed to the Treaty on the European Union and to the Treaty establishing the European Community, have given notice of their wish to take part in the adoption and application of this Regulation.

(22) Denmark, in accordance with Articles 1 and 2 of the Protocol on the position of Denmark annexed to the Treaty on European Union and to the Treaty establishing the European Community, is not participating in the adoption of this Regulation, and is therefore not bound by it nor subject to its application,

HAS ADOPTED THIS REGULATION:

CHAPTER I
GENERAL PROVISIONS

Article 1. Scope

1. This Regulation shall apply in civil or commercial matters where the court of a Member State, in accordance with the provisions of the law of that State, requests:
(a) the competent court of another Member State to take evidence; or
(b) to take evidence directly in another Member State.

2. A request shall not be made to obtain evidence which is not intended for use in judicial proceedings, commenced or contemplated.

3. In this Regulation, the term 'Member State' shall mean Member States with the exception of Denmark.

Article 2. Direct transmission between the courts

1. Requests pursuant to Article 1(1)(a), hereinafter referred to as 'requests', shall be transmitted by the court before which the proceedings are commenced or contemplated, hereinafter referred to as the 'requesting court', directly to the competent court of another Member State, hereinafter referred to as the 'requested court', for the performance of the taking of evidence.

2. Each Member State shall draw up a list of the courts competent for the performance of taking of evidence according to this Regulation. The list shall also indicate the territorial and, where appropriate, the special jurisdiction of those courts.

Article 3. Central body

1. Each Member State shall designate a central body responsible for:
(a) supplying information to the courts;
(b) seeking solutions to any difficulties which may arise in respect of a request;
(c) forwarding, in exceptional cases, at the request of a requesting court, a request to the competent court.

2. A federal State, a State in which several legal systems apply or a State with

autonomous territorial entities shall be free to designate more than one central body.

3. Each Member State shall also designate the central body referred to in paragraph 1 or one or several competent authority(ies) to be responsible for taking decisions on requests pursuant to Article 17.

CHAPTER II
TRANSMISSION AND EXECUTION OF REQUESTS

Section 1
Transmission of the request

Article 4. Form and content of the request

1. The request shall be made using form A or, where appropriate, form I in the Annex. It shall contain the following details:

(a) the requesting and, where appropriate, the requested court;

(b) the names and addresses of the parties to the proceedings and their representatives, if any;

(c) the nature and subject matter of the case and a brief statement of the facts;

(d) a description of the taking of evidence to be performed;

(e) where the request is for the examination of a person:

– the name(s) and address(es) of the person(s) to be examined,

– the questions to be put to the person(s) to be examined or a statement of the facts about which he is (they are) to be examined,

– where appropriate, a reference to a right to refuse to testify under the law of the Member State of the requesting court,

– any requirement that the examination is to be carried out under oath or affirmation in lieu thereof, and any special form to be used,

– where appropriate, any other information that the requesting court deems necessary;

(f) where the request is for any other form of taking of evidence, the documents or other objects to be inspected;

(g) where appropriate, any request pursuant to Article 10(3) and (4), and Articles 11 and 12 and any information necessary for the application thereof.

2. The request and all documents accompanying the request shall be exempted from authentication or any equivalent formality.

3. Documents which the requesting court deems it necessary to enclose for the execution of the request shall be accompanied by a translation into the language in which the request was written.

Article 5. Language

The request and communications pursuant to this Regulation shall be drawn up in the official language of the requested Member State or, if there are several official languages in that Member State, in the official language or one of the official languages of the place where the requested taking of evidence is to be performed, or in another language which the requested Member State has indicated it can accept. Each Member State shall indicate the official language or languages of the institutions of the European Community other than its own which is or are acceptable to it for completion of the forms.

Article 6. Transmission of requests and other communications

Requests and communications pursuant to this Regulation shall be transmitted by the swiftest possible means, which the requested Member State has indicated it can accept. The transmission may be carried out by any appropriate means, provided that the document received accurately reflects the content of the document forwarded and that all information in it is legible.

Section 2
Receipt of request

Article 7. Receipt of request

1. Within seven days of receipt of the request, the requested competent court shall send an acknowledgement of receipt to the requesting court using form B in the Annex. Where the request does not comply with the conditions laid down in Articles 5 and 6, the requested court shall enter a note to that effect in the acknowledgement of receipt.

2. Where the execution of a request made using form A in the Annex, which complies with the conditions laid down in Article 5, does not fall within the jurisdiction of the court to which it was transmitted, the latter shall forward the request to the competent court of its Member State and shall inform the requesting court thereof using form A in the Annex.

Article 8. Incomplete request

1. If a request cannot be executed because it does not contain all of the necessary information pursuant to Article 4, the requested court shall inform the requesting court thereof without delay and, at the latest, within 30 days of receipt of the request using form C in the Annex, and shall request it to send the missing information, which should be indicated as precisely as possible.

2. If a request cannot be executed because a deposit or advance is necessary in accordance with Article 18(3), the requested court shall inform the requesting court thereof without delay and, at the latest, within 30 days of receipt of the request using form C in the Annex and inform the requesting court how the deposit or advance should be made. The requested Court shall acknowledge receipt of the deposit or advance without delay, at the latest within 10 days of receipt of the deposit or the advance using form D.

Article 9. Completion of the request

1. If the requested court has noted on the acknowledgement of receipt pursuant to Article 7(1) that the request does not comply with the conditions laid down in Articles 5 and 6 or has informed the requesting court pursuant to Article 8 that the request cannot be executed because it does not contain all of the necessary information pursuant to Article 4, the time limit pursuant to Article 10 shall begin to run when the requested court received the request duly completed.

2. Where the requested court has asked for a deposit or advance in accordance with Article 18(3), this time limit shall begin to run when the deposit or the advance is made.

Section 3
Taking of evidence by the requested court

Article 10. General provisions on the execution of the request

1. The requested court shall execute the request without delay and, at the latest, within 90 days of receipt of the request.

2. The requested court shall execute the request in accordance with the law of its Member State.

3. The requesting court may call for the request to be executed in accordance with a special procedure provided for by the law of its Member State, using form A in the Annex. The requested court shall comply with such a requirement unless this procedure is incompatible with the law of the Member State of the requested court or by reason of major practical difficulties. If the requested court does not comply with the requirement for one of these reasons it shall inform the requesting court using form E in the Annex.

4. The requesting court may ask the requested court to use communications technology at the performance of the taking of evidence, in particular by using videoconference and teleconference.

The requested court shall comply with such a requirement unless this is incompatible with the law of the Member State of the requested court or by reason of major practical difficulties.

If the requested court does not comply with the requirement for one of these reasons, it shall inform the requesting court, using form E in the Annex.

If there is no access to the technical means referred to above in the requesting or in the requested court, such means may be made available by the courts by mutual agreement.

Article 11. Performance with the presence and participation of the parties

1. If it is provided for by the law of the Member State of the requesting court, the parties and, if any, their representatives, have the right to be present at the performance of the taking of evidence by the requested court.

2. The requesting court shall, in its request, inform the requested court that the parties and, if any, their representatives, will be present and, where appropriate, that their participation is requested, using form A in the Annex. This information may also be given at any other appropriate time.

3. If the participation of the parties and, if any, their representatives, is requested at the performance of the taking of evidence, the requested court shall determine, in accordance with Article 10, the conditions under which they may participate.

4. The requested court shall notify the parties and, if any, their representatives, of the time when, the place where, the proceedings will take place, and, where appropriate, the conditions under which they may participate, using form F in the Annex.

5. Paragraphs 1 to 4 shall not affect the possibility for the requested court of asking the parties and, if any their representatives, to be present at or to participate in the performance of the taking of evidence if that possibility is provided for by the law of its Member State.

Article 12. Performance with the presence and participation of representatives of the requesting court

1. If it is compatible with the law of the Member State of the requesting court, representatives of the requesting court have the right to be present in the performance of the taking of evidence by the requested court.

2. For the purpose of this Article, the term 'representative' shall include members of the judicial personnel designated by the requesting court, in accordance with the law of its Member State. The requesting court may also designate, in accordance with the law of its Member State, any other person, such as an expert.

3. The requesting court shall, in its request, inform the requested court that its representatives will be present and, where appropriate, that their participation is requested, using form A in the Annex. This information may also be given at any other appropriate time.

4. If the participation of the representatives of the requesting court is requested in the performance of the taking of evidence, the requested court shall determine, in accordance with Article 10, the conditions under which they may participate.

5. The requested court shall notify the requesting court, of the time when, and the place where, the proceedings will take place, and, where appropriate, the conditions under which the representatives may participate, using form F in the Annex.

Article 13. Coercive measures

Where necessary, in executing a request the requested court shall apply the appropriate coercive measures in the instances and to the extent as are provided for by the law of the Member State of the requested court for the execution of a request made for the same purpose by its national authorities or one of the parties concerned.

Article 14. Refusal to execute

1.   A request for the hearing of a person shall not be executed when the person concerned claims the right to refuse to give evidence or to be prohibited from giving evidence,

(a)   under the law of the Member State of the requested court; or

(b)   under the law of the Member State of the requesting court, and such right has been specified in the request, or, if need be, at the instance of the requested court, has been confirmed by the requesting court.

2.   In addition to the grounds referred to in paragraph 1, the execution of a request may be refused only if:

(a)   the request does not fall within the scope of this Regulation as set out in Article 1; or

(b)   the execution of the request under the law of the Member State of the requested court does not fall within the functions of the judiciary; or

(c)   the requesting court does not comply with the request of the requested court to complete the request pursuant to Article 8 within 30 days after the requested court asked it to do so; or

(d)   a deposit or advance asked for in accordance with Article 18(3) is not made within 60 days after the requested court asked for such a deposit or advance.

3.   Execution may not be refused by the requested court solely on the ground that under the law of its Member State a court of that Member State has exclusive jurisdiction over the subject matter of the action or that the law of that Member State would not admit the right of action on it.

4.   If execution of the request is refused on one of the grounds referred to in paragraph 2, the requested court shall notify the requesting court thereof within 60 days of receipt of the request by the requested court using form H in the Annex.

Article 15. Notification of delay

If the requested court is not in a position to execute the request within 90 days of receipt, it shall inform the requesting court thereof, using form G in the Annex. When it does so, the grounds for the delay shall be given as well as the estimated time that the requested court expects it will need to execute the request.

Article 16. Procedure after execution of the request

The requested court shall send without delay to the requesting court the documents establishing the execution of the request and, where appropriate, return the documents received from the requesting court. The documents shall be accompanied by a confirmation of execution using form H in the Annex.

Section 4
Direct taking of evidence by the requesting court

Article 17

1.   Where a court requests to take evidence directly in another Member State, it shall submit a request to the central body or the competent authority referred to in Article 3(3) in that State, using form I in the Annex.

2.   Direct taking of evidence may only take place if it can be performed on a voluntary basis without the need for coercive measures.

Where the direct taking of evidence implies that a person shall be heard, the requesting court shall inform that person that the performance shall take place on a voluntary basis.

3.   The taking of evidence shall be performed by a member of the judicial per-

sonnel or by any other person such as an expert, who will be designated, in accordance with the law of the Member State of the requesting court.

4. Within 30 days of receiving the request, the central body or the competent authority of the requested Member State shall inform the requesting court if the request is accepted and, if necessary, under what conditions according to the law of its Member State such performance is to be carried out, using form J.

In particular, the central body or the competent authority may assign a court of its Member State to take part in the performance of the taking of evidence in order to ensure the proper application of this Article and the conditions that have been set out.

The central body or the competent authority shall encourage the use of communications technology, such as videoconferences and teleconferences.

5. The central body or the competent authority may refuse direct taking of evidence only if:

(a) the request does not fall within the scope of this Regulation as set out in Article 1;

(b) the request does not contain all of the necessary information pursuant to Article 4; or

(c) the direct taking of evidence requested is contrary to fundamental principles of law in its Member State.

6. Without prejudice to the conditions laid down in accordance with paragraph 4, the requesting court shall execute the request in accordance with the law of its Member State.

Section 5

Costs

Article 18

1. The execution of the request, in accordance with Article 10, shall not give rise to a claim for any reimbursement of taxes or costs.

2. Nevertheless, if the requested court so requires, the requesting court shall ensure the reimbursement, without delay, of:

– the fees paid to experts and interpreters, and

– the costs occasioned by the application of Article 10(3) and (4).

The duty for the parties to bear these fees or costs shall be governed by the law of the Member State of the requesting court.

3. Where the opinion of an expert is required, the requested court may, before executing the request, ask the requesting court for an adequate deposit or advance towards the requested costs. In all other cases, a deposit or advance shall not be a condition for the execution of a request.

The deposit or advance shall be made by the parties if that is provided for by the law of the Member State of the requesting court.

...

CHAPTER III

FINAL PROVISIONS

Article 22. Communication

By 1 July 2003 each Member State shall communicate to the Commission the following:

(a) the list pursuant to Article 2(2) indicating the territorial and, where appropriate, the special jurisdiction of the courts;

(b) the names and addresses of the central bodies and competent authorities pursuant to Article 3, indicating their territorial jurisdiction;

(c) the technical means for the receipt of requests available to the courts on the list pursuant to Article 2(2);

(d) the languages accepted for the requests as referred to in Article 5.

Member States shall inform the Commission of any subsequent changes to this information.

Article 23. Review

No later than 1 January 2007, and every five years thereafter, the Commission shall present to the European Parliament, the Council and the Economic and Social Committee a report on the application of this Regulation, paying special attention to the practical application of Article 3(1)(c) and 3, and Articles 17 and 18.

Article 24. Entry into force

1. This Regulation shall enter into force on 1 July 2001.

2. This Regulation shall apply from 1 January 2004, except for Articles 19, 21 and 22, which shall apply from 1 July 2001.

This Regulation shall be binding in its entirety and directly applicable in the Member States in accordance with the Treaty establishing the European Community.

Done at Brussels, 28 May 2001.

COUNCIL REGULATION (EC) NO 2201/2003 OF 27 NOVEMBER 2003 CONCERNING JURISDICTION AND THE RECOGNITION AND ENFORCEMENT OF JUDGMENTS IN MATRIMONIAL MATTERS AND THE MATTERS OF PARENTAL RESPONSIBILITY, REPEALING REGULATION (EC) NO 1347/2000 ('BRUSSELS II *BIS*')

Official Journal L 338, 23/12/2003 p 1

THE COUNCIL OF THE EUROPEAN UNION,

Having regard to the Treaty establishing the European Community, and in particular Article 61(c) and Article 67(1) thereof,

Having regard to the proposal from the Commission,

Having regard to the opinion of the European Parliament,

Having regard to the opinion of the European Economic and Social Committee,

Whereas:

(1) The European Community has set the objective of creating an area of freedom, security and justice, in which the free movement of persons is ensured. To this end, the Community is to adopt, among others, measures in the field of judicial cooperation in civil matters that are necessary for the proper functioning of the internal market.

(2) The Tampere European Council endorsed the principle of mutual recognition of judicial decisions as the cornerstone for the creation of a genuine judicial area, and identified visiting rights as a priority.

(3) Council Regulation (EC) No 1347/2000 sets out rules on jurisdiction, recognition and enforcement of judgments in matrimonial matters and matters of parental responsibility for the children of both spouses rendered on the occasion of the matrimonial proceedings. The content of this Regulation was substantially taken over from the Convention of 28 May 1998 on the same subject matter.

(4) On 3 July 2000 France presented an initiative for a Council Regulation on the mutual enforcement of judgments on rights of access to children.

(5) In order to ensure equality for all children, this Regulation covers all decisions on parental responsibility, including measures for the protection of the child, independently of any link with a matrimonial proceeding.

(6) Since the application of the rules on parental responsibility often arises in the context of matrimonial proceedings, it is more appropriate to have a single instrument for matters of divorce and parental responsibility.

(7)   The scope of this Regulation covers civil matters, whatever the nature of the court or tribunal.

(8)   As regards judgments on divorce, legal separation or marriage annulment, this Regulation should apply only to the dissolution of matrimonial ties and should not deal with issues such as the grounds for divorce, property consequences of the marriage or any other ancillary measures.

(9)   As regards the property of the child, this Regulation should apply only to measures for the protection of the child, i.e. (i) the designation and functions of a person or body having charge of the child's property, representing or assisting the child, and (ii) the administration, conservation or disposal of the child's property. In this context, this Regulation should, for instance, apply in cases where the parents are in dispute as regards the administration of the child's property. Measures relating to the child's property which do not concern the protection of the child should continue to be governed by Council Regulation (EC) No 44/2001 of 22 December 2000 on jurisdiction and the recognition and enforcement of judgments in civil and commercial matters.

(10)   This Regulation is not intended to apply to matters relating to social security, public measures of a general nature in matters of education or health or to decisions on the right of asylum and on immigration. In addition it does not apply to the establishment of parenthood, since this is a different matter from the attribution of parental responsibility, nor to other questions linked to the status of persons. Moreover, it does not apply to measures taken as a result of criminal offences committed by children.

(11)   Maintenance obligations are excluded from the scope of this Regulation as these are already covered by Council Regulation No 44/2001. The courts having jurisdiction under this Regulation will generally have jurisdiction to rule on maintenance obligations by application of Article 5(2) of Council Regulation No 44/ 2001.

(12)   The grounds of jurisdiction in matters of parental responsibility established in the present Regulation are shaped in the light of the best interests of the child, in particular on the criterion of proximity. This means that jurisdiction should lie in the first place with the Member State of the child's habitual residence, except for certain cases of a change in the child's residence or pursuant to an agreement between the holders of parental responsibility.

(13)   In the interest of the child, this Regulation allows, by way of exception and under certain conditions, that the court having jurisdiction may transfer a case to a court of another Member State if this court is better placed to hear the case. However, in this case the second court should not be allowed to transfer the case to a third court.

(14)   This Regulation should have effect without prejudice to the application of public international law concerning diplomatic immunities. Where jurisdiction under this Regulation cannot be exercised by reason of the existence of diplomatic immunity in accordance with international law, jurisdiction should be exercised in accordance with national law in a Member State in which the person concerned does not enjoy such immunity.

(15)   Council Regulation (EC) No 1348/2000 of 29 May 2000 on the service in the Member States of judicial and extrajudicial documents in civil or commercial matters should apply to the service of documents in proceedings instituted pursuant to this Regulation.

(16)   This Regulation should not prevent the courts of a Member State from taking provisional, including protective measures, in urgent cases, with regard to persons or property situated in that State.

(17)   In cases of wrongful removal or retention of a child, the return of the child should be obtained without delay, and to this end the Hague Convention of 25 October 1980 would continue to apply as complemented by the provisions of this Regulation, in particular Article 11. The courts of the Member State to or in which

the child has been wrongfully removed or retained should be able to oppose his or her return in specific, duly justified cases. However, such a decision could be replaced by a subsequent decision by the court of the Member State of habitual residence of the child prior to the wrongful removal or retention. Should that judgment entail the return of the child, the return should take place without any special procedure being required for recognition and enforcement of that judgment in the Member State to or in which the child has been removed or retained.

(18) Where a court has decided not to return a child on the basis of Article 13 of the 1980 Hague Convention, it should inform the court having jurisdiction or central authority in the Member State where the child was habitually resident prior to the wrongful removal or retention. Unless the court in the latter Member State has been seised, this court or the central authority should notify the parties. This obligation should not prevent the central authority from also notifying the relevant public authorities in accordance with national law.

(19) The hearing of the child plays an important role in the application of this Regulation, although this instrument is not intended to modify national procedures applicable.

(20) The hearing of a child in another Member State may take place under the arrangements laid down in Council Regulation (EC) No 1206/2001 of 28 May 2001 on cooperation between the courts of the Member States in the taking of evidence in civil or commercial matters.

(21) The recognition and enforcement of judgments given in a Member State should be based on the principle of mutual trust and the grounds for non-recognition should be kept to the minimum required.

(22) Authentic instruments and agreements between parties that are enforceable in one Member State should be treated as equivalent to 'judgments' for the purpose of the application of the rules on recognition and enforcement.

(23) The Tampere European Council considered in its conclusions (point 34) that judgments in the field of family litigation should be 'automatically recognised throughout the Union without any intermediate proceedings or grounds for refusal of enforcement'. This is why judgments on rights of access and judgments on return that have been certified in the Member State of origin in accordance with the provisions of this Regulation should be recognised and enforceable in all other Member States without any further procedure being required. Arrangements for the enforcement of such judgments continue to be governed by national law.

(24) The certificate issued to facilitate enforcement of the judgment should not be subject to appeal. It should be rectified only where there is a material error, i.e. where it does not correctly reflect the judgment.

(25) Central authorities should cooperate both in general matter and in specific cases, including for purposes of promoting the amicable resolution of family disputes, in matters of parental responsibility. To this end central authorities shall participate in the European Judicial Network in civil and commercial matters created by Council Decision 2001/470/EC of 28 May 2001 establishing a European Judicial Network in civil and commercial matters.

(26) The Commission should make publicly available and update the lists of courts and redress procedures communicated by the Member States.

(27) The measures necessary for the implementation of this Regulation should be adopted in accordance with Council Decision 1999/468/EC of 28 June 1999 laying down the procedures for the exercise of implementing powers conferred on the Commission.

(28) This Regulation replaces Regulation (EC) No 1347/2000 which is consequently repealed.

(29) For the proper functioning of this Regulation, the Commission should review its application and propose such amendments as may appear necessary.

(30) The United Kingdom and Ireland, in accordance with Article 3 of the Protocol on the position of the United Kingdom and Ireland annexed to the Treaty

on European Union and the Treaty establishing the European Community, have given notice of their wish to take part in the adoption and application of this Regulation.

(31) Denmark, in accordance with Articles 1 and 2 of the Protocol on the position of Denmark annexed to the Treaty on European Union and the Treaty establishing the European Community, is not participating in the adoption of this Regulation and is therefore not bound by it nor subject to its application.

(32) Since the objectives of this Regulation cannot be sufficiently achieved by the Member States and can therefore be better achieved at Community level, the Community may adopt measures, in accordance with the principle of subsidiarity as set out in Article 5 of the Treaty. In accordance with the principle of proportionality, as set out in that Article, this Regulation does not go beyond what is necessary in order to achieve those objectives.

(33) This Regulation recognises the fundamental rights and observes the principles of the Charter of Fundamental Rights of the European Union. In particular, it seeks to ensure respect for the fundamental rights of the child as set out in Article 24 of the Charter of Fundamental Rights of the European Union,

HAS ADOPTED THE PRESENT REGULATION:

CHAPTER I
SCOPE AND DEFINITIONS

Article 1. Scope
1. This Regulation shall apply, whatever the nature of the court or tribunal, in civil matters relating to:
  (a)   divorce, legal separation or marriage annulment;
  (b)   the attribution, exercise, delegation, restriction or termination of parental responsibility.
2. The matters referred to in paragraph 1(b) may, in particular, deal with:
  (a)   rights of custody and rights of access;
  (b)   guardianship, curatorship and similar institutions;
  (c)   the designation and functions of any person or body having charge of the child's person or property, representing or assisting the child;
  (d)   the placement of the child in a foster family or in institutional care;
  (e)   measures for the protection of the child relating to the administration, conservation or disposal of the child's property.
3. This Regulation shall not apply to:
  (a)   the establishment or contesting of a parent-child relationship;
  (b)   decisions on adoption, measures preparatory to adoption, or the annulment or revocation of adoption;
  (c)   the name and forenames of the child;
  (d)   emancipation;
  (e)   maintenance obligations;
  (f)   trusts or succession;
  (g)   measures taken as a result of criminal offences committed by children.

Article 2. Definitions
For the purposes of this Regulation:
1. the term 'court' shall cover all the authorities in the Member States with jurisdiction in the matters falling within the scope of this Regulation pursuant to Article 1;
2. the term 'judge' shall mean the judge or an official having powers equivalent to those of a judge in the matters falling within the scope of the Regulation;
3. the term 'Member State' shall mean all Member States with the exception of Denmark;
4. the term 'judgment' shall mean a divorce, legal separation or marriage

annulment, as well as a judgment relating to parental responsibility, pronounced by a court of a Member State, whatever the judgment may be called, including a decree, order or decision;

5. the term 'Member State of origin' shall mean the Member State where the judgment to be enforced was issued;

6. the term 'Member State of enforcement' shall mean the Member State where enforcement of the judgment is sought;

7. the term 'parental responsibility' shall mean all rights and duties relating to the person or the property of a child which are given to a natural or legal person by judgment, by operation of law or by an agreement having legal effect. The term shall include rights of custody and rights of access;

8. the term 'holder of parental responsibility' shall mean any person having parental responsibility over a child;

9. the term 'rights of custody' shall include rights and duties relating to the care of the person of a child, and in particular the right to determine the child's place of residence;

10. the term 'rights of access' shall include in particular the right to take a child to a place other than his or her habitual residence for a limited period of time;

11. the term 'wrongful removal or retention' shall mean a child's removal or retention where:

(a) it is in breach of rights of custody acquired by judgment or by operation of law or by an agreement having legal effect under the law of the Member State where the child was habitually resident immediately before the removal or retention; and

(b) provided that, at the time of removal or retention, the rights of custody were actually exercised, either jointly or alone, or would have been so exercised but for the removal or retention. Custody shall be considered to be exercised jointly when, pursuant to a judgment or by operation of law, one holder of parental responsibility cannot decide on the child's place of residence without the consent of another holder of parental responsibility.

CHAPTER II
JURISDICTION

Section 1
Divorce, legal separation and marriage annulment

Article 3. General jurisdiction

1. In matters relating to divorce, legal separation or marriage annulment, jurisdiction shall lie with the courts of the Member State

(a) in whose territory:
– the spouses are habitually resident, or
– the spouses were last habitually resident, insofar as one of them still resides there, or
– the respondent is habitually resident, or
– in the event of a joint application, either of the spouses is habitually resident, or
– the applicant is habitually resident if he or she resided there for at least a year immediately before the application was made, or
– the applicant is habitually resident if he or she resided there for at least six months immediately before the application was made and is either a national of the Member State in question or, in the case of the United Kingdom and Ireland, has his or her 'domicile' there;

(b) of the nationality of both spouses or, in the case of the United Kingdom and Ireland, of the 'domicile' of both spouses.

2. For the purpose of this Regulation, 'domicile' shall have the same meaning as it has under the legal systems of the United Kingdom and Ireland.

Article 4. Counterclaim
The court in which proceedings are pending on the basis of Article 3 shall also have jurisdiction to examine a counterclaim, insofar as the latter comes within the scope of this Regulation.

Article 5. Conversion of legal separation into divorce
Without prejudice to Article 3, a court of a Member State that has given a judgment on a legal separation shall also have jurisdiction for converting that judgment into a divorce, if the law of that Member State so provides.

Article 6. Exclusive nature of jurisdiction under Articles 3, 4 and 5
A spouse who:
>   (a)   is habitually resident in the territory of a Member State; or
>   (b)   is a national of a Member State, or, in the case of the United Kingdom and Ireland, has his or her 'domicile' in the territory of one of the latter Member States,

may be sued in another Member State only in accordance with Articles 3, 4 and 5.

Article 7. Residual jurisdiction
1. Where no court of a Member State has jurisdiction pursuant to Articles 3, 4 and 5, jurisdiction shall be determined, in each Member State, by the laws of that State.
2. As against a respondent who is not habitually resident and is not either a national of a Member State or, in the case of the United Kingdom and Ireland, does not have his 'domicile' within the territory of one of the latter Member States, any national of a Member State who is habitually resident within the territory of another Member State may, like the nationals of that State, avail himself of the rules of jurisdiction applicable in that State.

Section 2
Parental responsibility

Article 8. General jurisdiction
1. The courts of a Member State shall have jurisdiction in matters of parental responsibility over a child who is habitually resident in that Member State at the time the court is seised.
2. Paragraph 1 shall be subject to the provisions of Articles 9, 10 and 12.

Article 9. Continuing jurisdiction of the child's former habitual residence
1. Where a child moves lawfully from one Member State to another and acquires a new habitual residence there, the courts of the Member State of the child's former habitual residence shall, by way of exception to Article 8, retain jurisdiction during a three-month period following the move for the purpose of modifying a judgment on access rights issued in that Member State before the child moved, where the holder of access rights pursuant to the judgment on access rights continues to have his or her habitual residence in the Member State of the child's former habitual residence.
2. Paragraph 1 shall not apply if the holder of access rights referred to in paragraph 1 has accepted the jurisdiction of the courts of the Member State of the child's new habitual residence by participating in proceedings before those courts without contesting their jurisdiction.

Article 10. Jurisdiction in cases of child abduction
In case of wrongful removal or retention of the child, the courts of the Member State where the child was habitually resident immediately before the wrongful

removal or retention shall retain their jurisdiction until the child has acquired a habitual residence in another Member State and:

(a)   each person, institution or other body having rights of custody has acquiesced in the removal or retention; or

(b)   the child has resided in that other Member State for a period of at least one year after the person, institution or other body having rights of custody has had or should have had knowledge of the whereabouts of the child and the child is settled in his or her new environment and at least one of the following conditions is met:

(i)   within one year after the holder of rights of custody has had or should have had knowledge of the whereabouts of the child, no request for return has been lodged before the competent authorities of the Member State where the child has been removed or is being retained;

(ii)   a request for return lodged by the holder of rights of custody has been withdrawn and no new request has been lodged within the time limit set in paragraph (i);

(iii)   a case before the court in the Member State where the child was habitually resident immediately before the wrongful removal or retention has been closed pursuant to Article 11(7);

(iv)   a judgment on custody that does not entail the return of the child has been issued by the courts of the Member State where the child was habitually resident immediately before the wrongful removal or retention.

Article 11. Return of the child

1.   Where a person, institution or other body having rights of custody applies to the competent authorities in a Member State to deliver a judgment on the basis of the Hague Convention of 25 October 1980 on the Civil Aspects of International Child Abduction (hereinafter 'the 1980 Hague Convention'), in order to obtain the return of a child that has been wrongfully removed or retained in a Member State other than the Member State where the child was habitually resident immediately before the wrongful removal or retention, paragraphs 2 to 8 shall apply.

2.   When applying Articles 12 and 13 of the 1980 Hague Convention, it shall be ensured that the child is given the opportunity to be heard during the proceedings unless this appears inappropriate having regard to his or her age or degree of maturity.

3.   A court to which an application for return of a child is made as mentioned in paragraph 1 shall act expeditiously in proceedings on the application, using the most expeditious procedures available in national law.

Without prejudice to the first subparagraph, the court shall, except where exceptional circumstances make this impossible, issue its judgment no later than six weeks after the application is lodged.

4.   A court cannot refuse to return a child on the basis of Article 13b of the 1980 Hague Convention if it is established that adequate arrangements have been made to secure the protection of the child after his or her return.

5.   A court cannot refuse to return a child unless the person who requested the return of the child has been given an opportunity to be heard.

6.   If a court has issued an order on non-return pursuant to Article 13 of the 1980 Hague Convention, the court must immediately either directly or through its central authority, transmit a copy of the court order on non-return and of the relevant documents, in particular a transcript of the hearings before the court, to the court with jurisdiction or central authority in the Member State where the child was habitually resident immediately before the wrongful removal or retention, as determined by national law. The court shall receive all the mentioned documents within one month of the date of the non-return order.

7.   Unless the courts in the Member State where the child was habitually resident immediately before the wrongful removal or retention have already been

seised by one of the parties, the court or central authority that receives the information mentioned in paragraph 6 must notify it to the parties and invite them to
make submissions to the court, in accordance with national law, within three
months of the date of notification so that the court can examine the question of
custody of the child.

Without prejudice to the rules on jurisdiction contained in this Regulation, the
court shall close the case if no submissions have been received by the court within
the time limit.

8.   Notwithstanding a judgment of non-return pursuant to Article 13 of the 1980
Hague Convention, any subsequent judgment which requires the return of the
child issued by a court having jurisdiction under this Regulation shall be enforceable in accordance with Section 4 of Chapter III below in order to secure the return
of the child.

Article 12. Prorogation of jurisdiction

1.   The courts of a Member State exercising jurisdiction by virtue of Article 3 on
an application for divorce, legal separation or marriage annulment shall have jurisdiction in any matter relating to parental responsibility connected with that application where:

(a)   at least one of the spouses has parental responsibility in relation to the
child; and

(b)   the jurisdiction of the courts has been accepted expressly or otherwise in
an unequivocal manner by the spouses and by the holders of parental responsibility, at the time the court is seised, and is in the superior interests of the child.

2.   The jurisdiction conferred in paragraph 1 shall cease as soon as:

(a)   the judgment allowing or refusing the application for divorce, legal
separation or marriage annulment has become final;

(b)   in those cases where proceedings in relation to parental responsibility are
still pending on the date referred to in (a), a judgment in these proceedings has
become final;

(c)   the proceedings referred to in (a) and (b) have come to an end for
another reason.

3.   The courts of a Member State shall also have jurisdiction in relation to
parental responsibility in proceedings other than those referred to in paragraph 1
where:

(a)   the child has a substantial connection with that Member State, in particular by virtue of the fact that one of the holders of parental responsibility is
habitually resident in that Member State or that the child is a national of that
Member State; and

(b)   the jurisdiction of the courts has been accepted expressly or otherwise in
an unequivocal manner by all the parties to the proceedings at the time the court
is seised and is in the best interests of the child.

4.   Where the child has his or her habitual residence in the territory of a third
State which is not a contracting party to the Hague Convention of 19 October 1996
on jurisdiction, applicable law, recognition, enforcement and cooperation in
respect of parental responsibility and measures for the protection of children, jurisdiction under this Article shall be deemed to be in the child's interest, in particular
if it is found impossible to hold proceedings in the third State in question.

Article 13. Jurisdiction based on the child's presence

1.   Where a child's habitual residence cannot be established and jurisdiction
cannot be determined on the basis of Article 12, the courts of the Member State
where the child is present shall have jurisdiction.

2.   Paragraph 1 shall also apply to refugee children or children internationally
displaced because of disturbances occurring in their country.

Article 14. Residual jurisdiction
Where no court of a Member State has jurisdiction pursuant to Articles 8 to 13, jurisdiction shall be determined, in each Member State, by the laws of that State.

Article 15. Transfer to a court better placed to hear the case
   1.   By way of exception, the courts of a Member State having jurisdiction as to the substance of the matter may, if they consider that a court of another Member State, with which the child has a particular connection, would be better placed to hear the case, or a specific part thereof, and where this is in the best interests of the child:
   (a)   stay the case or the part thereof in question and invite the parties to introduce a request before the court of that other Member State in accordance with paragraph 4; or
   (b)   request a court of another Member State to assume jurisdiction in accordance with paragraph 5.
   2.   Paragraph 1 shall apply:
   (a)   upon application from a party; or
   (b)   of the court's own motion; or
   (c)   upon application from a court of another Member State with which the child has a particular connection, in accordance with paragraph 3.
A transfer made of the court's own motion or by application of a court of another Member State must be accepted by at least one of the parties.
   3.   The child shall be considered to have a particular connection to a Member State as mentioned in paragraph 1, if that Member State:
   (a)   has become the habitual residence of the child after the court referred to in paragraph 1 was seised; or
   (b)   is the former habitual residence of the child; or
   (c)   is the place of the child's nationality; or
   (d)   is the habitual residence of a holder of parental responsibility; or
   (e)   is the place where property of the child is located and the case concerns measures for the protection of the child relating to the administration, conservation or disposal of this property.
   4.   The court of the Member State having jurisdiction as to the substance of the matter shall set a time limit by which the courts of that other Member State shall be seised in accordance with paragraph 1.
If the courts are not seised by that time, the court which has been seised shall continue to exercise jurisdiction in accordance with Articles 8 to 14.
   5.   The courts of that other Member State may, where due to the specific circumstances of the case, this is in the best interests of the child, accept jurisdiction within six weeks of their seisure in accordance with paragraph 1(a) or 1(b). In this case, the court first seised shall decline jurisdiction. Otherwise, the court first seised shall continue to exercise jurisdiction in accordance with Articles 8 to 14.
   6.   The courts shall cooperate for the purposes of this Article, either directly or through the central authorities designated pursuant to Article 53.

Section 3
Common provisions

Article 16. Seising of a Court
   1.   A court shall be deemed to be seised:
   (a)   at the time when the document instituting the proceedings or an equivalent document is lodged with the court, provided that the applicant has not subsequently failed to take the steps he was required to take to have service effected on the respondent; or
   (b)   if the document has to be served before being lodged with the court, at the time when it is received by the authority responsible for service, provided

that the applicant has not subsequently failed to take the steps he was required to take to have the document lodged with the court.

Article 17. Examination as to jurisdiction
Where a court of a Member State is seised of a case over which it has no jurisdiction under this Regulation and over which a court of another Member State has jurisdiction by virtue of this Regulation, it shall declare of its own motion that it has no jurisdiction.

Article 18. Examination as to admissibility
1. Where a respondent habitually resident in a State other than the Member State where the action was brought does not enter an appearance, the court with jurisdiction shall stay the proceedings so long as it is not shown that the respondent has been able to receive the document instituting the proceedings or an equivalent document in sufficient time to enable him to arrange for his defence, or that all necessary steps have been taken to this end.

2. Article 19 of Regulation (EC) No 1348/2000 shall apply instead of the provisions of paragraph 1 of this Article if the document instituting the proceedings or an equivalent document had to be transmitted from one Member State to another pursuant to that Regulation.

3. Where the provisions of Regulation (EC) No 1348/2000 are not applicable, Article 15 of the Hague Convention of 15 November 1965 on the service abroad of judicial and extrajudicial documents in civil or commercial matters shall apply if the document instituting the proceedings or an equivalent document had to be transmitted abroad pursuant to that Convention.

Article 19. Lis pendens and dependent actions
1. Where proceedings relating to divorce, legal separation or marriage annulment between the same parties are brought before courts of different Member States, the court second seised shall of its own motion stay its proceedings until such time as the jurisdiction of the court first seised is established.

2. Where proceedings relating to parental responsibility relating to the same child and involving the same cause of action are brought before courts of different Member States, the court second seised shall of its own motion stay its proceedings until such time as the jurisdiction of the court first seised is established.

3. Where the jurisdiction of the court first seised is established, the court second seised shall decline jurisdiction in favour of that court.

In that case, the party who brought the relevant action before the court second seised may bring that action before the court first seised.

Article 20. Provisional, including protective, measures
1. In urgent cases, the provisions of this Regulation shall not prevent the courts of a Member State from taking such provisional, including protective, measures in respect of persons or assets in that State as may be available under the law of that Member State, even if, under this Regulation, the court of another Member State has jurisdiction as to the substance of the matter.

2. The measures referred to in paragraph 1 shall cease to apply when the court of the Member State having jurisdiction under this Regulation as to the substance of the matter has taken the measures it considers appropriate.

CHAPTER III
RECOGNITION AND ENFORCEMENT

Section 1
Recognition

Article 21. Recognition of a judgment

1.   A judgment given in a Member State shall be recognised in the other Member States without any special procedure being required.

2.   In particular, and without prejudice to paragraph 3, no special procedure shall be required for updating the civil-status records of a Member State on the basis of a judgment relating to divorce, legal separation or marriage annulment given in another Member State, and against which no further appeal lies under the law of that Member State.

3.   Without prejudice to Section 4 of this Chapter, any interested party may, in accordance with the procedures provided for in Section 2 of this Chapter, apply for a decision that the judgment be or not be recognised.

The local jurisdiction of the court appearing in the list notified by each Member State to the Commission pursuant to Article 68 shall be determined by the internal law of the Member State in which proceedings for recognition or non-recognition are brought.

4.   Where the recognition of a judgment is raised as an incidental question in a court of a Member State, that court may determine that issue.

Article 22. Grounds of non-recognition for judgments relating to divorce, legal separation or marriage annulment

A judgment relating to a divorce, legal separation or marriage annulment shall not be recognised:

(a)   if such recognition is manifestly contrary to the public policy of the Member State in which recognition is sought;

(b)   where it was given in default of appearance, if the respondent was not served with the document which instituted the proceedings or with an equivalent document in sufficient time and in such a way as to enable the respondent to arrange for his or her defence unless it is determined that the respondent has accepted the judgment unequivocally;

(c)   if it is irreconcilable with a judgment given in proceedings between the same parties in the Member State in which recognition is sought; or

(d)   if it is irreconcilable with an earlier judgment given in another Member State or in a non-Member State between the same parties, provided that the earlier judgment fulfils the conditions necessary for its recognition in the Member State in which recognition is sought.

Article 23. Grounds of non-recognition for judgments relating to parental responsibility

A judgment relating to parental responsibility shall not be recognised:

(a)   if such recognition is manifestly contrary to the public policy of the Member State in which recognition is sought taking into account the best interests of the child;

(b)   if it was given, except in case of urgency, without the child having been given an opportunity to be heard, in violation of fundamental principles of procedure of the Member State in which recognition is sought;

(c)   where it was given in default of appearance if the person in default was not served with the document which instituted the proceedings or with an equivalent document in sufficient time and in such a way as to enable that person to arrange for his or her defence unless it is determined that such person has accepted the judgment unequivocally;

(d)   on the request of any person claiming that the judgment infringes his or her parental responsibility, if it was given without such person having been given an opportunity to be heard;

(e)   if it is irreconcilable with a later judgment relating to parental responsibility given in the Member State in which recognition is sought;

(f)   if it is irreconcilable with a later judgment relating to parental responsibility given in another Member State or in the non-Member State of the habitual residence of the child provided that the later judgment fulfils the conditions necessary for its recognition in the Member State in which recognition is sought. or

(g)   if the procedure laid down in Article 56 has not been complied with.

Article 24. Prohibition of review of jurisdiction of the court of origin

The jurisdiction of the court of the Member State of origin may not be reviewed. The test of public policy referred to in Articles 22(a) and 23(a) may not be applied to the rules relating to jurisdiction set out in Articles 3 to 14.

Article 25. Differences in applicable law

The recognition of a judgment may not be refused because the law of the Member State in which such recognition is sought would not allow divorce, legal separation or marriage annulment on the same facts.

Article 26. Non-review as to substance

Under no circumstances may a judgment be reviewed as to its substance.

Article 27. Stay of proceedings

1.   A court of a Member State in which recognition is sought of a judgment given in another Member State may stay the proceedings if an ordinary appeal against the judgment has been lodged.

2.   A court of a Member State in which recognition is sought of a judgment given in Ireland or the United Kingdom may stay the proceedings if enforcement is suspended in the Member State of origin by reason of an appeal.

Section 2
Application for a declaration of enforceability

Article 28. Enforceable judgments

1.   A judgment on the exercise of parental responsibility in respect of a child given in a Member State which is enforceable in that Member State and has been served shall be enforced in another Member State when, on the application of any interested party, it has been declared enforceable there.

2.   However, in the United Kingdom, such a judgment shall be enforced in England and Wales, in Scotland or in Northern Ireland only when, on the application of any interested party, it has been registered for enforcement in that part of the United Kingdom.

Article 29. Jurisdiction of local courts

1.   An application for a declaration of enforceability shall be submitted to the court appearing in the list notified by each Member State to the Commission pursuant to Article 68.

2.   The local jurisdiction shall be determined by reference to the place of habitual residence of the person against whom enforcement is sought or by reference to the habitual residence of any child to whom the application relates.

Where neither of the places referred to in the first subparagraph can be found in the Member State of enforcement, the local jurisdiction shall be determined by reference to the place of enforcement.

Article 30. Procedure

1.   The procedure for making the application shall be governed by the law of the Member State of enforcement.

2.   The applicant must give an address for service within the area of jurisdiction of the court applied to. However, if the law of the Member State of enforcement does not provide for the furnishing of such an address, the applicant shall appoint a representative ad litem.

3.   The documents referred to in Articles 37 and 39 shall be attached to the application.

Article 31. Decision of the court

1.   The court applied to shall give its decision without delay. Neither the person against whom enforcement is sought, nor the child shall, at this stage of the proceedings, be entitled to make any submissions on the application.

2.   The application may be refused only for one of the reasons specified in Articles 22, 23 and 24.

3.   Under no circumstances may a judgment be reviewed as to its substance.

Article 32. Notice of the decision

The appropriate officer of the court shall without delay bring to the notice of the applicant the decision given on the application in accordance with the procedure laid down by the law of the Member State of enforcement.

Article 33. Appeal against the decision

1.   The decision on the application for a declaration of enforceability may be appealed against by either party.

2.   The appeal shall be lodged with the court appearing in the list notified by each Member State to the Commission pursuant to Article 68.

3.   The appeal shall be dealt with in accordance with the rules governing procedure in contradictory matters.

4.   If the appeal is brought by the applicant for a declaration of enforceability, the party against whom enforcement is sought shall be summoned to appear before the appellate court. If such person fails to appear, the provisions of Article 18 shall apply.

5.   An appeal against a declaration of enforceability must be lodged within one month of service thereof. If the party against whom enforcement is sought is habitually resident in a Member State other than that in which the declaration of enforceability was given, the time for appealing shall be two months and shall run from the date of service, either on him or at his residence. No extension of time may be granted on account of distance.

Article 34. Courts of appeal and means of contest

The judgment given on appeal may be contested only by the proceedings referred to in the list notified by each Member State to the Commission pursuant to Article 68.

Article 35. Stay of proceedings

1.   The court with which the appeal is lodged under Articles 33 or 34 may, on the application of the party against whom enforcement is sought, stay the proceedings if an ordinary appeal has been lodged in the Member State of origin, or if the time for such appeal has not yet expired. In the latter case, the court may specify the time within which an appeal is to be lodged.

2.   Where the judgment was given in Ireland or the United Kingdom, any form of appeal available in the Member State of origin shall be treated as an ordinary appeal for the purposes of paragraph 1.

Article 36. Partial enforcement

1.   Where a judgment has been given in respect of several matters and enforcement cannot be authorised for all of them, the court shall authorise enforcement for one or more of them.

2.   An applicant may request partial enforcement of a judgment.

Section 3
Provisions common to Sections 1 and 2

Article 37. Documents
1. A party seeking or contesting recognition or applying for a declaration of enforceability shall produce:
(a)   a copy of the judgment which satisfies the conditions necessary to establish its authenticity; and
(b)   the certificate referred to in Article 39.
2. In addition, in the case of a judgment given in default, the party seeking recognition or applying for a declaration of enforceability shall produce:
(a)   the original or certified true copy of the document which establishes that the defaulting party was served with the document instituting the proceedings or with an equivalent document; or
(b)   any document indicating that the defendant has accepted the judgment unequivocally.

Article 38. Absence of documents
1. If the documents specified in Article 37(1)(b) or (2) are not produced, the court may specify a time for their production, accept equivalent documents or, if it considers that it has sufficient information before it, dispense with their production.
2. If the court so requires, a translation of such documents shall be furnished. The translation shall be certified by a person qualified to do so in one of the Member States.

Article 39. Certificate concerning judgments in matrimonial matters and certificate concerning judgments on parental responsibility
The competent court or authority of a Member State of origin shall, at the request of any interested party, issue a certificate using the standard form set out in Annex I (judgments in matrimonial matters) or in Annex II (judgments on parental responsibility).

Section 4
Enforceability of certain judgments concerning rights of access and of certain judgments which require the return of the child

Article 40. Scope
1. This Section shall apply to:
(a)   rights of access; and
(b)   the return of a child entailed by a judgment given pursuant to Article 11(8).
2. The provisions of this Section shall not prevent a holder of parental responsibility from seeking recognition and enforcement of a judgment in accordance with the provisions in Sections 1 and 2 of this Chapter.

Article 41. Rights of access
1. The rights of access referred to in Article 40(1)(a) granted in an enforceable judgment given in a Member State shall be recognised and enforceable in another Member State without the need for a declaration of enforceability and without any possibility of opposing its recognition if the judgment has been certified in the Member State of origin in accordance with paragraph 2.
Even if national law does not provide for enforceability by operation of law of a judgment granting access rights, the court of origin may declare that the judgment shall be enforceable, notwithstanding any appeal.
2. The judge of origin shall issue the certificate referred to in paragraph 1 using the standard form in Annex III (certificate concerning rights of access) only if:
(a)   where the judgment was given in default, the person defaulting was

served with the document which instituted the proceedings or with an equivalent document in sufficient time and in such a way as to enable that person to arrange for his or her defence, or, the person has been served with the document but not in compliance with these conditions, it is nevertheless established that he or she accepted the decision unequivocally;

(b)   all parties concerned were given an opportunity to be heard; and

(c)   the child was given an opportunity to be heard, unless a hearing was considered inappropriate having regard to his or her age or degree of maturity.

The certificate shall be completed in the language of the judgment.

3.   Where the rights of access involve a cross-border situation at the time of the delivery of the judgment, the certificate shall be issued ex officio when the judgment becomes enforceable, even if only provisionally. If the situation subsequently acquires a cross-border character, the certificate shall be issued at the request of one of the parties.

Article 42. Return of the child

1.   The return of a child referred to in Article 40(1)(b) entailed by an enforceable judgment given in a Member State shall be recognised and enforceable in another Member State without the need for a declaration of enforceability and without any possibility of opposing its recognition if the judgment has been certified in the Member State of origin in accordance with paragraph 2.

Even if national law does not provide for enforceability by operation of law, notwithstanding any appeal, of a judgment requiring the return of the child mentioned in Article 11(b)(8), the court of origin may declare the judgment enforceable.

2.   The judge of origin who delivered the judgment referred to in Article 40(1)(b) shall issue the certificate referred to in paragraph 1 only if:

(a)   the child was given an opportunity to be heard, unless a hearing was considered inappropriate having regard to his or her age or degree of maturity;

(b)   the parties were given an opportunity to be heard; and

(c)   the court has taken into account in issuing its judgment the reasons for and evidence underlying the order issued pursuant to Article 13 of the 1980 Hague Convention.

In the event that the court or any other authority takes measures to ensure the protection of the child after its return to the State of habitual residence, the certificate shall contain details of such measures.

The judge of origin shall of his or her own motion issue that certificate using the standard form in Annex IV (certificate concerning return of the child(ren)).

The certificate shall be completed in the language of the judgment.

Article 43. Rectification of the certificate

1.   The law of the Member State of origin shall be applicable to any rectification of the certificate.

2.   No appeal shall lie against the issuing of a certificate pursuant to Articles 41(1) or 42(1).

Article 44. Effects of the certificate

The certificate shall take effect only within the limits of the enforceability of the judgment.

Article 45. Documents

1.   A party seeking enforcement of a judgment shall produce:

(a)   a copy of the judgment which satisfies the conditions necessary to establish its authenticity; and

(b)   the certificate referred to in Article 41(1) or Article 42(1).

2.   For the purposes of this Article,

– the certificate referred to in Article 41(1) shall be accompanied by a translation of point 12 relating to the arrangements for exercising right of access,

– the certificate referred to in Article 42(1) shall be accompanied by a translation of its point 14 relating to the arrangements for implementing the measures taken to ensure the child's return.

The translation shall be into the official language or one of the official languages of the Member State of enforcement or any other language that the Member State of enforcement expressly accepts. The translation shall be certified by a person qualified to do so in one of the Member States.

Section 5
Authentic instruments and agreements

Article 46

Documents which have been formally drawn up or registered as authentic instruments and are enforceable in one Member State and also agreements between the parties that are enforceable in the Member State in which they were concluded shall be recognised and declared enforceable under the same conditions as judgments.

Section 6
Other provisions

Article 47. Enforcement procedure

1. The enforcement procedure is governed by the law of the Member State of enforcement.

2. Any judgment delivered by a court of another Member State and declared to be enforceable in accordance with Section 2 or certified in accordance with Article 41(1) or Article 42(1) shall be enforced in the Member State of enforcement in the same conditions as if it had been delivered in that Member State.

In particular, a judgment which has been certified according to Article 41(1) or Article 42(1) cannot be enforced if it is irreconcilable with a subsequent enforceable judgment.

Article 48. Practical arrangements for the exercise of rights of access

1. The courts of the Member State of enforcement may make practical arrangements for organising the exercise of rights of access, if the necessary arrangements have not or have not sufficiently been made in the judgment delivered by the courts of the Member State having jurisdiction as to the substance of the matter and provided the essential elements of this judgment are respected.

2. The practical arrangements made pursuant to paragraph 1 shall cease to apply pursuant to a later judgment by the courts of the Member State having jurisdiction as to the substance of the matter.

...

CHAPTER IV
COOPERATION BETWEEN CENTRAL AUTHORITIES IN MATTERS OF
PARENTAL RESPONSIBILITY

...

Article 55. Cooperation on cases specific to parental responsibility

The central authorities shall, upon request from a central authority of another Member State or from a holder of parental responsibility, cooperate on specific cases to achieve the purposes of this Regulation. To this end, they shall, acting directly or through public authorities or other bodies, take all appropriate steps in accordance with the law of that Member State in matters of personal data protection to:

    (a)   collect and exchange information:

      (i)   on the situation of the child;

      (ii)   on any procedures under way; or

      (iii)   on decisions taken concerning the child;

(b)   provide information and assistance to holders of parental responsibility seeking the recognition and enforcement of decisions on their territory, in particular concerning rights of access and the return of the child;

(c)   facilitate communications between courts, in particular for the application of Article 11(6) and (7) and Article 15;

(d)   provide such information and assistance as is needed by courts to apply Article 56; and

(e)   facilitate agreement between holders of parental responsibility through mediation or other means, and facilitate cross-border cooperation to this end.

Article 56. Placement of a child in another Member State

1.   Where a court having jurisdiction under Articles 8 to 15 contemplates the placement of a child in institutional care or with a foster family and where such placement is to take place in another Member State, it shall first consult the central authority or other authority having jurisdiction in the latter State where public authority intervention in that Member State is required for domestic cases of child placement.

2.   The judgment on placement referred to in paragraph 1 may be made in the requesting State only if the competent authority of the requested State has consented to the placement.

3.   The procedures for consultation or consent referred to in paragraphs 1 and 2 shall be governed by the national law of the requested State.

4.   Where the authority having jurisdiction under Articles 8 to 15 decides to place the child in a foster family, and where such placement is to take place in another Member State and where no public authority intervention is required in the latter Member State for domestic cases of child placement, it shall so inform the central authority or other authority having jurisdiction in the latter State.

Article 57. Working method

1.   Any holder of parental responsibility may submit, to the central authority of the Member State of his or her habitual residence or to the central authority of the Member State where the child is habitually resident or present, a request for assistance as mentioned in Article 55. In general, the request shall include all available information of relevance to its enforcement. Where the request for assistance concerns the recognition or enforcement of a judgment on parental responsibility that falls within the scope of this Regulation, the holder of parental responsibility shall attach the relevant certificates provided for in Articles 39, 41(1) or 42(1).

2.   Member States shall communicate to the Commission the official language or languages of the Community institutions other than their own in which communications to the central authorities can be accepted.

3.   The assistance provided by the central authorities pursuant to Article 55 shall be free of charge.

4.   Each central authority shall bear its own costs.

...

CHAPTER V
RELATIONS WITH OTHER INSTRUMENTS

Article 59. Relation with other instruments

1.   Subject to the provisions of Articles 60, 63, 64 and paragraph 2 of this Article, this Regulation shall, for the Member States, supersede conventions existing at the time of entry into force of this Regulation which have been concluded between two or more Member States and relate to matters governed by this Regulation.

2.   (a) Finland and Sweden shall have the option of declaring that the Convention of 6 February 1931 between Denmark, Finland, Iceland, Norway and Sweden comprising international private law provisions on marriage, adoption and guar-

dianship, together with the Final Protocol thereto, will apply, in whole or in part, in their mutual relations, in place of the rules of this Regulation. Such declarations shall be annexed to this Regulation and published in the Official Journal of the European Union. They may be withdrawn, in whole or in part, at any moment by the said Member States.

(b) The principle of non-discrimination on the grounds of nationality between citizens of the Union shall be respected.

(c) The rules of jurisdiction in any future agreement to be concluded between the Member States referred to in subparagraph (a) which relate to matters governed by this Regulation shall be in line with those laid down in this Regulation.

(d) Judgments handed down in any of the Nordic States which have made the declaration provided for in subparagraph (a) under a forum of jurisdiction corresponding to one of those laid down in Chapter II of this Regulation, shall be recognised and enforced in the other Member States under the rules laid down in Chapter III of this Regulation.

3. Member States shall send to the Commission:

(a) a copy of the agreements and uniform laws implementing these agreements referred to in paragraph 2(a) and (c);

(b) any denunciations of, or amendments to, those agreements or uniform laws.

Article 60. Relations with certain multilateral conventions
In relations between Member States, this Regulation shall take precedence over the following Conventions in so far as they concern matters governed by this Regulation:

(a) the Hague Convention of 5 October 1961 concerning the Powers of Authorities and the Law Applicable in respect of the Protection of Minors;

(b) the Luxembourg Convention of 8 September 1967 on the Recognition of Decisions Relating to the Validity of Marriages;

(c) the Hague Convention of 1 June 1970 on the Recognition of Divorces and Legal Separations;

(d) the European Convention of 20 May 1980 on Recognition and Enforcement of Decisions concerning Custody of Children and on Restoration of Custody of Children; and

(e) the Hague Convention of 25 October 1980 on the Civil Aspects of International Child Abduction.

Article 61. Relation with the Hague Convention of 19 October 1996 on Jurisdiction, Applicable law, Recognition, Enforcement and Cooperation in Respect of Parental Responsibility and Measures for the Protection of Children
As concerns the relation with the Hague Convention of 19 October 1996 on Jurisdiction, Applicable law, Recognition, Enforcement and Cooperation in Respect of Parental Responsibility and Measures for the Protection of Children, this Regulation shall apply:

(a) where the child concerned has his or her habitual residence on the territory of a Member State;

(b) as concerns the recognition and enforcement of a judgment given in a court of a Member State on the territory of another Member State, even if the child concerned has his or her habitual residence on the territory of a third State which is a contracting Party to the said Convention.

Article 62. Scope of effects
1. The agreements and conventions referred to in Articles 59(1), 60 and 61 shall continue to have effect in relation to matters not governed by this Regulation.

2. The conventions mentioned in Article 60, in particular the 1980 Hague Con-

vention, continue to produce effects between the Member States which are party thereto, in compliance with Article 60.

...

CHAPTER VI
TRANSITIONAL PROVISIONS

Article 64

1.   The provisions of this Regulation shall apply only to legal proceedings instituted, to documents formally drawn up or registered as authentic instruments and to agreements concluded between the parties after its date of application in accordance with Article 72.

2.   Judgments given after the date of application of this Regulation in proceedings instituted before that date but after the date of entry into force of Regulation (EC) No 1347/2000 shall be recognised and enforced in accordance with the provisions of Chapter III of this Regulation if jurisdiction was founded on rules which accorded with those provided for either in Chapter II or in Regulation (EC) No 1347/2000 or in a convention concluded between the Member State of origin and the Member State addressed which was in force when the proceedings were instituted.

3.   Judgments given before the date of application of this Regulation in proceedings instituted after the entry into force of Regulation (EC) No 1347/2000 shall be recognised and enforced in accordance with the provisions of Chapter III of this Regulation provided they relate to divorce, legal separation or marriage annulment or parental responsibility for the children of both spouses on the occasion of these matrimonial proceedings.

4.   Judgments given before the date of application of this Regulation but after the date of entry into force of Regulation (EC) No 1347/2000 in proceedings instituted before the date of entry into force of Regulation (EC) No 1347/2000 shall be recognised and enforced in accordance with the provisions of Chapter III of this Regulation provided they relate to divorce, legal separation or marriage annulment or parental responsibility for the children of both spouses on the occasion of these matrimonial proceedings and that jurisdiction was founded on rules which accorded with those provided for either in Chapter II of this Regulation or in Regulation (EC) No 1347/2000 or in a convention concluded between the Member State of origin and the Member State addressed which was in force when the proceedings were instituted.

CHAPTER VII
FINAL PROVISIONS

Article 65. Review

No later than 1 January 2012, and every five years thereafter, the Commission shall present to the European Parliament, to the Council and to the European Economic and Social Committee a report on the application of this Regulation on the basis of information supplied by the Member States. The report shall be accompanied if need be by proposals for adaptations.

Article 66. Member States with two or more legal systems

With regard to a Member State in which two or more systems of law or sets of rules concerning matters governed by this Regulation apply in different territorial units:

(a)   any reference to habitual residence in that Member State shall refer to habitual residence in a territorial unit;

(b)   any reference to nationality, or in the case of the United Kingdom 'domicile', shall refer to the territorial unit designated by the law of that State;

(c)   any reference to the authority of a Member State shall refer to the authority of a territorial unit within that State which is concerned;
(d)   any reference to the rules of the requested Member State shall refer to the rules of the territorial unit in which jurisdiction, recognition or enforcement is invoked.

...

Article 71. Repeal of Regulation (EC) No 1347/2000
1.   Regulation (EC) No 1347/2000 shall be repealed as from the date of application of this Regulation.
2.   Any reference to Regulation (EC) No 1347/2000 shall be construed as a reference to this Regulation according to the comparative table in Annex V.

Article 72. Entry into force
This Regulation shall enter into force on 1 August 2004.
The Regulation shall apply from 1 March 2005, with the exception of Articles 67, 68, 69 and 70, which shall apply from 1 August 2004.
This Regulation shall be binding in its entirety and directly applicable in the Member States in accordance with the Treaty establishing the European Community.

Done at Brussels, 27 November 2003.

REGULATION (EC) NO 805/2004 OF THE EUROPEAN PARLIAMENT AND OF THE COUNCIL OF 21 APRIL 2004 CREATING A EUROPEAN ENFORCEMENT ORDER FOR UNCONTESTED CLAIMS

Official Journal L 143, 30/04/2004 p 15

THE EUROPEAN PARLIAMENT AND THE COUNCIL OF THE EUROPEAN UNION,
Having regard to the Treaty establishing the European Community, and in particular Articles 61(c) and the second indent of Article 67(5) thereof,
Having regard to the proposal from the Commission,
Having regard to the Opinion of the European Economic and Social Committee,
Acting in accordance with the procedure laid down in Article 251 of the Treaty,

Whereas:
(1)   The Community has set itself the objective of maintaining and developing an area of freedom, security and justice, in which the free movement of persons is ensured. To this end, the Community is to adopt, inter alia, measures in the field of judicial cooperation in civil matters that are necessary for the proper functioning of the internal market.
(2)   On 3 December 1998, the Council adopted an Action Plan of the Council and the Commission on how best to implement the provisions of the Treaty of Amsterdam on an area of freedom, security and justice (the Vienna Action Plan).
(3)   The European Council meeting in Tampere on 15 and 16 October 1999 endorsed the principle of mutual recognition of judicial decisions as the cornerstone for the creation of a genuine judicial area.
(4)   On 30 November 2000, the Council adopted a programme of measures for implementation of the principle of mutual recognition of decisions in civil and commercial matters. This programme includes in its first stage the abolition of exequatur, that is to say, the creation of a European Enforcement Order for uncontested claims.
(5)   The concept of 'uncontested claims' should cover all situations in which a creditor, given the verified absence of any dispute by the debtor as to the nature or extent of a pecuniary claim, has obtained either a court decision against that

debtor or an enforceable document that requires the debtor's express consent, be it a court settlement or an authentic instrument.

(6)   The absence of objections from the debtor as stipulated in Article 3(1)(b) can take the shape of default of appearance at a court hearing or of failure to comply with an invitation by the court to give written notice of an intention to defend the case.

(7)   This Regulation should apply to judgments, court settlements and authentic instruments on uncontested claims and to decisions delivered following challenges to judgments, court settlements and authentic instruments certified as European Enforcement Orders.

(8)   In its Tampere conclusions, the European Council considered that access to enforcement in a Member State other than that in which the judgment has been given should be accelerated and simplified by dispensing with any intermediate measures to be taken prior to enforcement in the Member State in which enforcement is sought. A judgment that has been certified as a European Enforcement Order by the court of origin should, for enforcement purposes, be treated as if it had been delivered in the Member State in which enforcement is sought. In the United Kingdom, for example, the registration of a certified foreign judgment will therefore follow the same rules as the registration of a judgment from another part of the United Kingdom and is not to imply a review as to the substance of the foreign judgment. Arrangements for the enforcement of judgments should continue to be governed by national law.

(9)   Such a procedure should offer significant advantages as compared with the exequatur procedure provided for in Council Regulation (EC) No 44/2001 of 22 December 2000 on jurisdiction and the recognition and enforcement of judgments in civil and commercial matters, in that there is no need for approval by the judiciary in a second Member State with the delays and expenses that this entails.

(10)   Where a court in a Member State has given judgment on an uncontested claim in the absence of participation of the debtor in the proceedings, the abolition of any checks in the Member State of enforcement is inextricably linked to and dependent upon the existence of a sufficient guarantee of observance of the rights of the defence.

(11)   This Regulation seeks to promote the fundamental rights and takes into account the principles recognised in particular by the Charter of Fundamental Rights of the European Union. In particular, it seeks to ensure full respect for the right to a fair trial as recognised in Article 47 of the Charter.

(12)   Minimum standards should be established for the proceedings leading to the judgment in order to ensure that the debtor is informed about the court action against him, the requirements for his active participation in the proceedings to contest the claim and the consequences of his non-participation in sufficient time and in such a way as to enable him to arrange for his defence.

(13)   Due to differences between the Member States as regards the rules of civil procedure and especially those governing the service of documents, it is necessary to lay down a specific and detailed definition of those minimum standards. In particular, any method of service that is based on a legal fiction as regards the fulfilment of those minimum standards cannot be considered sufficient for the certification of a judgment as a European Enforcement Order.

(14)   All the methods of service listed in Articles 13 and 14 are characterised by either full certainty (Article 13) or a very high degree of likelihood (Article 14) that the document served has reached its addressee. In the second category, a judgment should only be certified as a European Enforcement Order if the Member State of origin has an appropriate mechanism in place enabling the debtor to apply for a full review of the judgment under the conditions set out in Article 19 in those exceptional cases where, in spite of compliance with Article 14, the document has not reached the addressee.

(15)   Personal service on certain persons other than the debtor himself pursuant

to Article 14(1)(a) and (b) should be understood to meet the requirements of those provisions only if those persons actually accepted/received the document in question.

(16)   Article 15 should apply to situations where the debtor cannot represent himself in court, as in the case of a legal person, and where a person to represent him is determined by law as well as situations where the debtor has authorised another person, in particular a lawyer, to represent him in the specific court proceedings at issue.

(17)   The courts competent for scrutinising full compliance with the minimum procedural standards should, if satisfied, issue a standardised European Enforcement Order certificate that makes that scrutiny and its result transparent.

(18)   Mutual trust in the administration of justice in the Member States justifies the assessment by the court of one Member State that all conditions for certification as a European Enforcement Order are fulfilled to enable a judgment to be enforced in all other Member States without judicial review of the proper application of the minimum procedural standards in the Member State where the judgment is to be enforced.

(19)   This Regulation does not imply an obligation for the Member States to adapt their national legislation to the minimum procedural standards set out herein. It provides an incentive to that end by making available a more efficient and rapid enforceability of judgments in other Member States only if those minimum standards are met.

(20)   Application for certification as a European Enforcement Order for uncontested claims should be optional for the creditor, who may instead choose the system of recognition and enforcement under Regulation (EC) No 44/2001 or other Community instruments.

(21)   When a document has to be sent from one Member State to another for service there, this Regulation and in particular the rules on service set out herein should apply together with Council Regulation (EC) No 1348/2000 of 29 May 2000 on the service in the Member States of judicial and extrajudicial documents in civil or commercial matters, and in particular Article 14 thereof in conjunction with Member States declarations made under Article 23 thereof.

(22)   Since the objectives of the proposed action cannot be sufficiently achieved by the Member States and can therefore, by reason of the scale or effects of the action, be better achieved at Community level, the Community may adopt measures, in accordance with the principle of subsidiarity as set out in Article 5 of the Treaty. In accordance with the principle of proportionality, as set out in that Article, this Regulation does not go beyond what is necessary in order to achieve those objectives.

(23)   The measures necessary for the implementation of this Regulation should be adopted in accordance with Council Decision 1999/468/EC of 28 June 1999 laying down the procedures for the exercise of implementing powers conferred on the Commission (8).

(24)   In accordance with Article 3 of the Protocol on the position of the United Kingdom and Ireland annexed to the Treaty on European Union and the Treaty establishing the European Community, the United Kingdom and Ireland have notified their wish to take part in the adoption and application of this Regulation.

(25)   In accordance with Articles 1 and 2 of the Protocol on the position of Denmark annexed to the Treaty on European Union and the Treaty establishing the European Community, Denmark does not take part in the adoption of this Regulation, and is therefore not bound by it or subject to its application.

(26)   Pursuant to the second indent of Article 67(5) of the Treaty, the codecision procedure is applicable from 1 February 2003 for the measures laid down in this Regulation,

HAVE ADOPTED THIS REGULATION:

CHAPTER I
SUBJECT MATTER, SCOPE AND DEFINITIONS

Article 1. Subject matter

The purpose of this Regulation is to create a European Enforcement Order for uncontested claims to permit, by laying down minimum standards, the free circulation of judgments, court settlements and authentic instruments throughout all Member States without any intermediate proceedings needing to be brought in the Member State of enforcement prior to recognition and enforcement.

Article 2. Scope

1.   This Regulation shall apply in civil and commercial matters, whatever the nature of the court or tribunal. It shall not extend, in particular, to revenue, customs or administrative matters or the liability of the State for acts and omissions in the exercise of State authority ('acta iure imperii').

2.   This Regulation shall not apply to:

(a)   the status or legal capacity of natural persons, rights in property arising out of a matrimonial relationship, wills and succession;

(b)   bankruptcy, proceedings relating to the winding-up of insolvent companies or other legal persons, judicial arrangements, compositions and analogous proceedings;

(c)   social security;

(d)   arbitration.

3.   In this Regulation, the term 'Member State' shall mean Member States with the exception of Denmark.

Article 3. Enforcement titles to be certified as a European Enforcement Order

1.   This Regulation shall apply to judgments, court settlements and authentic instruments on uncontested claims.

A claim shall be regarded as uncontested if:

(a)   the debtor has expressly agreed to it by admission or by means of a settlement which has been approved by a court or concluded before a court in the course of proceedings; or

(b)   the debtor has never objected to it, in compliance with the relevant procedural requirements under the law of the Member State of origin, in the course of the court proceedings; or

(c)   the debtor has not appeared or been represented at a court hearing regarding that claim after having initially objected to the claim in the course of the court proceedings, provided that such conduct amounts to a tacit admission of the claim or of the facts alleged by the creditor under the law of the Member State of origin; or

(d)   the debtor has expressly agreed to it in an authentic instrument.

2.   This Regulation shall also apply to decisions delivered following challenges to judgments, court settlements or authentic instruments certified as European Enforcement Orders.

Article 4. Definitions

For the purposes of this Regulation, the following definitions shall apply:

1.   'judgment': any judgment given by a court or tribunal of a Member State, whatever the judgment may be called, including a decree, order, decision or writ of execution, as well as the determination of costs or expenses by an officer of the court;

2.   'claim': a claim for payment of a specific sum of money that has fallen due or for which the due date is indicated in the judgment, court settlement or authentic instrument;

3.   'authentic instrument':

(a)   a document which has been formally drawn up or registered as an authentic instrument, and the authenticity of which:

(i) relates to the signature and the content of the instrument; and
(ii) has been established by a public authority or other authority empowered for that purpose by the Member State in which it originates; or

(b) an arrangement relating to maintenance obligations concluded with administrative authorities or authenticated by them;

4. 'Member State of origin': the Member State in which the judgment has been given, the court settlement has been approved or concluded or the authentic instrument has been drawn up or registered, and is to be certified as a European Enforcement Order;

5. 'Member State of enforcement': the Member State in which enforcement of the judgment, court settlement or authentic instrument certified as a European Enforcement Order is sought;

6. 'court of origin': the court or tribunal seised of the proceedings at the time of fulfilment of the conditions set out in Article 3(1)(a), (b) or (c);

7. in Sweden, in summary proceedings concerning orders to pay (betalnings-forelaggande), the expression 'court' includes the Swedish enforcement service (kronofogdemyndighet).

CHAPTER II
EUROPEAN ENFORCEMENT ORDER

Article 5. Abolition of exequatur
A judgment which has been certified as a European Enforcement Order in the Member State of origin shall be recognised and enforced in the other Member States without the need for a declaration of enforceability and without any possibility of opposing its recognition.

Article 6. Requirements for certification as a European Enforcement Order
1. A judgment on an uncontested claim delivered in a Member State shall, upon application at any time to the court of origin, be certified as a European Enforcement Order if:

(a) the judgment is enforceable in the Member State of origin; and
(b) the judgment does not conflict with the rules on jurisdiction as laid down in sections 3 and 6 of Chapter II of Regulation (EC) No 44/2001; and
(c) the court proceedings in the Member State of origin met the requirements as set out in Chapter III where a claim is uncontested within the meaning of Article 3(1)(b) or (c); and
(d) the judgment was given in the Member State of the debtor's domicile within the meaning of Article 59 of Regulation (EC) No 44/2001, in cases where
– a claim is uncontested within the meaning of Article 3(1)(b) or (c); and
– it relates to a contract concluded by a person, the consumer, for a purpose which can be regarded as being outside his trade or profession; and
– the debtor is the consumer.

2. Where a judgment certified as a European Enforcement Order has ceased to be enforceable or its enforceability has been suspended or limited, a certificate indicating the lack or limitation of enforceability shall, upon application at any time to the court of origin, be issued, using the standard form in Annex IV.

3. Without prejudice to Article 12(2), where a decision has been delivered following a challenge to a judgment certified as a European Enforcement Order in accordance with paragraph 1 of this Article, a replacement certificate shall, upon application at any time, be issued, using the standard form in Annex V, if that decision on the challenge is enforceable in the Member State of origin.

Article 7. Costs related to court proceedings
Where a judgment includes an enforceable decision on the amount of costs related to the court proceedings, including the interest rates, it shall be certified as a European Enforcement Order also with regard to the costs unless the debtor has

specifically objected to his obligation to bear such costs in the course of the court proceedings, in accordance with the law of the Member State of origin.

Article 8. Partial European Enforcement Order certificate
If only parts of the judgment meet the requirements of this Regulation, a partial European Enforcement Order certificate shall be issued for those parts.

Article 9. Issue of the European Enforcement Order certificate
1. The European Enforcement Order certificate shall be issued using the standard form in Annex I.
2. The European Enforcement Order certificate shall be issued in the language of the judgment.

Article 10. Rectification or withdrawal of the European Enforcement Order certificate
1. The European Enforcement Order certificate shall, upon application to the court of origin, be
    (a) rectified where, due to a material error, there is a discrepancy between the judgment and the certificate;
    (b) withdrawn where it was clearly wrongly granted, having regard to the requirements laid down in this Regulation.
2. The law of the Member State of origin shall apply to the rectification or withdrawal of the European Enforcement Order certificate.
3. An application for the rectification or withdrawal of a European Enforcement Order certificate may be made using the standard form in Annex VI.
4. No appeal shall lie against the issuing of a European Enforcement Order certificate.

Article 11. Effect of the European Enforcement Order certificate
The European Enforcement Order certificate shall take effect only within the limits of the enforceability of the judgment.

CHAPTER III
MINIMUM STANDARDS FOR UNCONTESTED CLAIMS PROCEDURES

Article 12. Scope of application of minimum standards
1. A judgment on a claim that is uncontested within the meaning of Article 3(1)(b) or (c) can be certified as a European Enforcement Order only if the court proceedings in the Member State of origin met the procedural requirements as set out in this Chapter.
2. The same requirements shall apply to the issuing of a European Enforcement Order certificate or a replacement certificate within the meaning of Article 6(3) for a decision following a challenge to a judgment where, at the time of that decision, the conditions of Article 3(1)(b) or (c) are fulfilled.

Article 13. Service with proof of receipt by the debtor
1. The document instituting the proceedings or an equivalent document may have been served on the debtor by one of the following methods:
    (a) personal service attested by an acknowledgement of receipt, including the date of receipt, which is signed by the debtor;
    (b) personal service attested by a document signed by the competent person who effected the service stating that the debtor has received the document or refused to receive it without any legal justification, and the date of the service;
    (c) postal service attested by an acknowledgement of receipt including the date of receipt, which is signed and returned by the debtor;
    (d) service by electronic means such as fax or e-mail, attested by an acknowledgement of receipt including the date of receipt, which is signed and returned by the debtor.
2. Any summons to a court hearing may have been served on the debtor in

compliance with paragraph 1 or orally in a previous court hearing on the same claim and stated in the minutes of that previous court hearing.

Article 14. Service without proof of receipt by the debtor

1. Service of the document instituting the proceedings or an equivalent document and any summons to a court hearing on the debtor may also have been effected by one of the following methods:

(a)   personal service at the debtor's personal address on persons who are living in the same household as the debtor or are employed there;

(b)   in the case of a self-employed debtor or a legal person, personal service at the debtor's business premises on persons who are employed by the debtor;

(c)   deposit of the document in the debtor's mailbox;

(d)   deposit of the document at a post office or with competent public authorities and the placing in the debtor's mailbox of written notification of that deposit, provided that the written notification clearly states the character of the document as a court document or the legal effect of the notification as effecting service and setting in motion the running of time for the purposes of time limits;

(e)   postal service without proof pursuant to paragraph 3 where the debtor has his address in the Member State of origin;

(f)   electronic means attested by an automatic confirmation of delivery, provided that the debtor has expressly accepted this method of service in advance.

2. For the purposes of this Regulation, service under paragraph 1 is not admissible if the debtor's address is not known with certainty.

3. Service pursuant to paragraph 1, (a) to (d), shall be attested by:

(a)   a document signed by the competent person who effected the service, indicating:

   (i)   the method of service used; and

   (ii)   the date of service; and

   (iii)   where the document has been served on a person other than the debtor, the name of that person and his relation to the debtor, or

(b)   an acknowledgement of receipt by the person served, for the purposes of paragraphs 1(a) and (b).

Article 15. Service on the debtor's representatives

Service pursuant to Articles 13 or 14 may also have been effected on a debtor's representative.

Article 16. Provision to the debtor of due information about the claim

In order to ensure that the debtor was provided with due information about the claim, the document instituting the proceedings or the equivalent document must have contained the following:

(a)   the names and the addresses of the parties;

(b)   the amount of the claim;

(c)   if interest on the claim is sought, the interest rate and the period for which interest is sought unless statutory interest is automatically added to the principal under the law of the Member State of origin;

(d)   a statement of the reason for the claim.

Article 17. Provision to the debtor of due information about the procedural steps necessary to contest the claim

The following must have been clearly stated in or together with the document instituting the proceedings, the equivalent document or any summons to a court hearing:

(a)   the procedural requirements for contesting the claim, including the time limit for contesting the claim in writing or the time for the court hearing, as applicable, the name and the address of the institution to which to respond or before which to appear, as applicable, and whether it is mandatory to be represented by a lawyer;

(b)   the consequences of an absence of objection or default of appearance, in particular, where applicable, the possibility that a judgment may be given or enforced against the debtor and the liability for costs related to the court proceedings.

Article 18. Cure of non-compliance with minimum standards

1.   If the proceedings in the Member State of origin did not meet the procedural requirements as set out in Articles 13 to 17, such non-compliance shall be cured and a judgment may be certified as a European Enforcement Order if:
(a)   the judgment has been served on the debtor in compliance with the requirements pursuant to Article 13 or Article 14; and
(b)   it was possible for the debtor to challenge the judgment by means of a full review and the debtor has been duly informed in or together with the judgment about the procedural requirements for such a challenge, including the name and address of the institution with which it must be lodged and, where applicable, the time limit for so doing; and
(c)   the debtor has failed to challenge the judgment in compliance with the relevant procedural requirements.
2.   If the proceedings in the Member State of origin did not comply with the procedural requirements as set out in Article 13 or Article 14, such non-compliance shall be cured if it is proved by the conduct of the debtor in the court proceedings that he has personally received the document to be served in sufficient time to arrange for his defence.

Article 19. Minimum standards for review in exceptional cases

1.   Further to Articles 13 to 18, a judgment can only be certified as a European Enforcement Order if the debtor is entitled, under the law of the Member State of origin, to apply for a review of the judgment where:
(a)   (i) the document instituting the proceedings or an equivalent document or, where applicable, the summons to a court hearing, was served by one of the methods provided for in Article 14; and
(ii)   service was not effected in sufficient time to enable him to arrange for his defence, without any fault on his part; or
(b)   the debtor was prevented from objecting to the claim by reason of force majeure, or due to extraordinary circumstances without any fault on his part, provided in either case that he acts promptly.
2.   This Article is without prejudice to the possibility for Member States to grant access to a review of the judgment under more generous conditions than those mentioned in paragraph 1.

CHAPTER IV
ENFORCEMENT

Article 20. Enforcement procedure

1.   Without prejudice to the provisions of this Chapter, the enforcement procedures shall be governed by the law of the Member State of enforcement.
A judgment certified as a European Enforcement Order shall be enforced under the same conditions as a judgment handed down in the Member State of enforcement.
2.   The creditor shall be required to provide the competent enforcement authorities of the Member State of enforcement with:
(a)   a copy of the judgment which satisfies the conditions necessary to establish its authenticity; and
(b)   a copy of the European Enforcement Order certificate which satisfies the conditions necessary to establish its authenticity; and
(c)   where necessary, a transcription of the European Enforcement Order certificate or a translation thereof into the official language of the Member State of

enforcement or, if there are several official languages in that Member State, the official language or one of the official languages of court proceedings of the place where enforcement is sought, in conformity with the law of that Member State, or into another language that the Member State of enforcement has indicated it can accept. Each Member State may indicate the official language or languages of the institutions of the European Community other than its own which it can accept for the completion of the certificate. The translation shall be certified by a person qualified to do so in one of the Member States.

3. No security, bond or deposit, however described, shall be required of a party who in one Member State applies for enforcement of a judgment certified as a European Enforcement Order in another Member State on the ground that he is a foreign national or that he is not domiciled or resident in the Member State of enforcement.

Article 21. Refusal of enforcement

1. Enforcement shall, upon application by the debtor, be refused by the competent court in the Member State of enforcement if the judgment certified as a European Enforcement Order is irreconcilable with an earlier judgment given in any Member State or in a third country, provided that:

    (a) the earlier judgment involved the same cause of action and was between the same parties; and

    (b) the earlier judgment was given in the Member State of enforcement or fulfils the conditions necessary for its recognition in the Member State of enforcement; and

    (c) the irreconcilability was not and could not have been raised as an objection in the court proceedings in the Member State of origin.

2. Under no circumstances may the judgment or its certification as a European Enforcement Order be reviewed as to their substance in the Member State of enforcement.

Article 22. Agreements with third countries

This Regulation shall not affect agreements by which Member States undertook, prior to the entry into force of Regulation (EC) No 44/2001, pursuant to Article 59 of the Brussels Convention on jurisdiction and the enforcement of judgments in civil and commercial matters, not to recognise judgments given, in particular in other Contracting States to that Convention, against defendants domiciled or habitually resident in a third country where, in cases provided for in Article 4 of that Convention, the judgment could only be founded on a ground of jurisdiction specified in the second paragraph of Article 3 of that Convention.

Article 23. Stay or limitation of enforcement

Where the debtor has

– challenged a judgment certified as a European Enforcement Order, including an application for review within the meaning of Article 19, or

– applied for the rectification or withdrawal of a European Enforcement Order certificate in accordance with Article 10,

the competent court or authority in the Member State of enforcement may, upon application by the debtor:

    (a) limit the enforcement proceedings to protective measures; or

    (b) make enforcement conditional on the provision of such security as it shall determine; or

    (c) under exceptional circumstances, stay the enforcement proceedings.

CHAPTER V
COURT SETTLEMENTS AND AUTHENTIC INSTRUMENTS

Article 24. Court settlements

1. A settlement concerning a claim within the meaning of Article 4(2) which

has been approved by a court or concluded before a court in the course of proceedings and is enforceable in the Member State in which it was approved or concluded shall, upon application to the court that approved it or before which it was
concluded, be certified as a European Enforcement Order using the standard form
in Annex II.

2.   A settlement which has been certified as a European Enforcement Order in
the Member State of origin shall be enforced in the other Member States without
the need for a declaration of enforceability and without any possibility of opposing
its enforceability.

3.   The provisions of Chapter II, with the exception of Articles 5, 6(1) and 9(1),
and of Chapter IV, with the exception of Articles 21(1) and 22, shall apply as
appropriate.

Article 25. Authentic instruments

1.   An authentic instrument concerning a claim within the meaning of Article
4(2) which is enforceable in one Member State shall, upon application to the
authority designated by the Member State of origin, be certified as a European
Enforcement Order, using the standard form in Annex III.

2.   An authentic instrument which has been certified as a European Enforcement Order in the Member State of origin shall be enforced in the other Member
States without the need for a declaration of enforceability and without any possibility of opposing its enforceability.

3.   The provisions of Chapter II, with the exception of Articles 5, 6(1) and 9(1),
and of Chapter IV, with the exception of Articles 21(1) and 22, shall apply as
appropriate.

CHAPTER VI
TRANSITIONAL PROVISION

Article 26. Transitional provision
This Regulation shall apply only to judgments given, to court settlements
approved or concluded and to documents formally drawn up or registered as
authentic instruments after the entry into force of this Regulation.

CHAPTER VII
RELATIONSHIP WITH OTHER COMMUNITY INSTRUMENTS

Article 27. Relationship with Regulation (EC) No 44/2001
This Regulation shall not affect the possibility of seeking recognition and enforcement, in accordance with Regulation (EC) No 44/2001, of a judgment, a court
settlement or an authentic instrument on an uncontested claim.

Article 28. Relationship with Regulation (EC) No 1348/2000
This Regulation shall not affect the application of Regulation (EC) No 1348/2000.

CHAPTER VIII
GENERAL AND FINAL PROVISIONS

Article 33. Entry into force
This Regulation shall enter into force on 21 January 2004.

It shall apply from 21 October 2005, with the exception of Articles 30, 31 and 32,
which shall apply from 21 January 2005.

This Regulation shall be binding in its entirety and directly applicable in the
Member States in accordance with the Treaty establishing the European Community.

Done at Strasbourg, 21 April 2004.

AGREEMENT MADE 19TH OCTOBER 2005 BETWEEN THE EUROPEAN COMMUNITY AND THE KINGDOM OF DENMARK ON JURISDICTION AND THE RECOGNITION AND ENFORCEMENT OF JUDGMENTS IN CIVIL AND COMMERCIAL MATTERS

Official Journal L 299, 16/11/2005 p 62

THE EUROPEAN COMMUNITY, hereinafter referred to as 'the Community', of the one part, and

THE KINGDOM OF DENMARK, hereinafter referred to as 'Denmark', of the other part,

DESIRING to unify the rules of conflict of jurisdiction in civil and commercial matters and to simplify the formalities with a view to rapid and simple recognition and enforcement of judgments within the Community,

WHEREAS on 27 September 1968 the Member States, acting under Article 293, fourth indent, of the Treaty establishing the European Community, concluded the Brussels Convention on Jurisdiction and the Enforcement of Judgments in Civil and Commercial Matters (the Brussels Convention), as amended by Conventions on the Accession of the new Member States to that Convention. On 16 September 1988 the Member States and the EFTA States concluded the Convention on Jurisdiction and the Enforcement of Judgments in Civil and Commercial Matters (the Lugano Convention), which is a parallel Convention to the Brussels Convention,

WHEREAS the main content of the Brussels Convention has been taken over in Council Regulation (EC) No 44/2001 of 22 December 2000 on jurisdiction and the recognition and enforcement of judgments in civil and commercial matters (the Brussels I Regulation),

REFERRING to the Protocol on the position of Denmark annexed to the Treaty on European Union and to the Treaty establishing the European Community (the Protocol on the position of Denmark) pursuant to which the Brussels I Regulation shall not be binding upon or applicable in Denmark,

STRESSING that a solution to the unsatisfactory legal situation arising from differences in applicable rules on jurisdiction, recognition and enforcement of judgments within the Community must be found,

DESIRING that the provisions of the Brussels I Regulation, future amendments thereto and the implementing measures relating to it should under international law apply to the relations between the Community and Denmark being a Member State with a special position with respect to Title IV of the Treaty establishing the European Community,

STRESSING that continuity between the Brussels Convention and this Agreement should be ensured, and that transitional provisions as in the Brussels I Regulation should be applied to this Agreement as well. The same need for continuity applies as regards the interpretation of the Brussels Convention by the Court of Justice of the European Communities and the 1971 Protocol should remain applicable also to cases already pending when this Agreement enters into force,

STRESSING that the Brussels Convention also continues to apply to the territories of the Member States which fall within the territorial scope of that Convention and which are excluded from this Agreement,

STRESSING the importance of proper coordination between the Community and Denmark with regard to the negotiation and conclusion of international agreements that may affect or alter the scope of the Brussels I Regulation,

STRESSING that Denmark should seek to join international agreements entered into by the Community where Danish participation in such agreements is relevant for the coherent application of the Brussels I Regulation and this Agreement,

STATING that the Court of Justice of the European Communities should have jurisdiction in order to secure the uniform application and interpretation of this

Agreement including the provisions of the Brussels I Regulation and any implementing Community measures forming part of this Agreement,

REFERRING to the jurisdiction conferred to the Court of Justice of the European Communities pursuant to Article 68(1) of the Treaty establishing the European Community to give rulings on preliminary questions relating to the validity and interpretation of acts of the institutions of the Community based on Title IV of the Treaty, including the validity and interpretation of this Agreement, and to the circumstance that this provision shall not be binding upon or applicable in Denmark, as results from the Protocol on the position of Denmark,

CONSIDERING that the Court of Justice of the European Communities should have jurisdiction under the same conditions to give preliminary rulings on questions concerning the validity and interpretation of this Agreement which are raised by a Danish court or tribunal, and that Danish courts and tribunals should therefore request preliminary rulings under the same conditions as courts and tribunals of other Member States in respect of the interpretation of the Brussels I Regulation and its implementing measures,

REFERRING to the provision that, pursuant to Article 68(3) of the Treaty establishing the European Community, the Council of the European Union, the European Commission and the Member States may request the Court of Justice of the European Communities to give a ruling on the interpretation of acts of the institutions of the Community based on Title IV of the Treaty, including the interpretation of this Agreement, and the circumstance that this provision shall not be binding upon or applicable in Denmark, as results from the Protocol on the position of Denmark,

CONSIDERING that Denmark should, under the same conditions as other Member States in respect of the Brussels I Regulation and its implementing measures, be accorded the possibility to request the Court of Justice of the European Communities to give rulings on questions relating to the interpretation of this Agreement,

STRESSING that under Danish law the courts in Denmark should, when interpreting this Agreement including the provisions of the Brussels I Regulation and any implementing Community measures forming part of this Agreement, take due account of the rulings contained in the case law of the Court of Justice of the European Communities and of the courts of the Member States of the European Communities in respect of provisions of the Brussels Convention, the Brussels I Regulation and any implementing Community measures,

CONSIDERING that it should be possible to request the Court of Justice of the European Communities to rule on questions relating to compliance with obligations under this Agreement pursuant to the provisions of the Treaty establishing the European Community governing proceedings before the Court,

WHEREAS, by virtue of Article 300(7) of the Treaty establishing the European Community, this Agreement binds Member States; it is therefore appropriate that Denmark, in the case of non-compliance by a Member State, should be able to seize the Commission as guardian of the Treaty,

HAVE AGREED AS FOLLOWS:

Article 1. Aim

1. The aim of this Agreement is to apply the provisions of the Brussels I Regulation and its implementing measures to the relations between the Community and Denmark, in accordance with Article 2(1) of this Agreement.

2. It is the objective of the Contracting Parties to arrive at a uniform application and interpretation of the provisions of the Brussels I Regulation and its implementing measures in all Member States.

3. The provisions of Articles 3(1), 4(1) and 5(1) of this Agreement result from the Protocol on the position of Denmark.

Article 2. Jurisdiction and the recognition and enforcement of judgments in civil and commercial matters

1. The provisions of the Brussels I Regulation, which is annexed to this Agreement and forms part thereof, together with its implementing measures adopted pursuant to Article 74(2) of the Regulation and, in respect of implementing measures adopted after the entry into force of this Agreement, implemented by Denmark as referred to in Article 4 of this Agreement, and the measures adopted pursuant to Article 74(1) of the Regulation, shall under international law apply to the relations between the Community and Denmark.

2. However, for the purposes of this Agreement, the application of the provisions of that Regulation shall be modified as follows:

   (a)   Article 1(3) shall not apply.

   (b)   Article 50 shall be supplemented by the following paragraph (as paragraph 2):

   '2.   However, an applicant who requests the enforcement of a decision given by an administrative authority in Denmark in respect of a maintenance order may, in the Member State addressed, claim the benefits referred to in the first paragraph if he presents a statement from the Danish Ministry of Justice to the effect that he fulfils the financial requirements to qualify for the grant of complete or partial legal aid or exemption from costs or expenses.'

   (c)   Article 62 shall be supplemented by the following paragraph (as paragraph 2):

   '2.   In matters relating to maintenance, the expression "court" includes the Danish administrative authorities.'

   (d)   Article 64 shall apply to seagoing ships registered in Denmark as well as in Greece and Portugal.

   (e)   The date of entry into force of this Agreement shall apply instead of the date of entry into force of the Regulation as referred to in Articles 70(2), 72 and 76 thereof.

   (f)   The transitional provisions of this Agreement shall apply instead of Article 66 of the Regulation.

Article 3. Amendments to the Brussels I Regulation

1. Denmark shall not take part in the adoption of amendments to the Brussels I Regulation and no such amendments shall be binding upon or applicable in Denmark.

2. Whenever amendments to the Regulation are adopted Denmark shall notify the Commission of its decision whether or not to implement the content of such amendments. Notification shall be given at the time of the adoption of the amendments or within 30 days thereafter.

3. If Denmark decides that it will implement the content of the amendments the notification shall indicate whether implementation can take place administratively or requires parliamentary approval.

4. If the notification indicates that implementation can take place administratively the notification shall, moreover, state that all necessary administrative measures enter into force on the date of entry into force of the amendments to the Regulation or have entered into force on the date of the notification, whichever date is the latest.

5. If the notification indicates that implementation requires parliamentary approval in Denmark, the following rules shall apply:

   (a)   Legislative measures in Denmark shall enter into force on the date of entry into force of the amendments to the Regulation or within 6 months after the notification, whichever date is the latest;

   (b)   Denmark shall notify the Commission of the date upon which the implementing legislative measures enter into force.

6. A Danish notification that the content of the amendments has been imple-

mented in Denmark, in accordance with paragraphs 4 and 5, creates mutual obligations under international law between Denmark and the Community. The amendments to the Regulation shall then constitute amendments to this Agreement and shall be considered annexed hereto.

7.   In cases where:

(a)   Denmark notifies its decision not to implement the content of the amendments; or

(b)   Denmark does not make a notification within the 30-day time-limit set out in paragraph 2; or

(c)   Legislative measures in Denmark do not enter into force within the time-limits set out in paragraph 5,

this Agreement shall be considered terminated unless the parties decide otherwise within 90 days or, in the situation referred to under (c), legislative measures in Denmark enter into force within the same period. Termination shall take effect three months after the expiry of the 90-day period.

8.   Legal proceedings instituted and documents formally drawn up or registered as authentic instruments before the date of termination of the Agreement as set out in paragraph 7 are not affected hereby.

Article 4. Implementing measures

1.   Denmark shall not take part in the adoption of opinions by the Committee referred to in Article 75 of the Brussels I Regulation. Implementing measures adopted pursuant to Article 74(2) of that Regulation shall not be binding upon and shall not be applicable in Denmark.

2.   Whenever implementing measures are adopted pursuant to Article 74(2) of the Regulation, the implementing measures shall be communicated to Denmark. Denmark shall notify the Commission of its decision whether or not to implement the content of the implementing measures. Notification shall be given upon receipt of the implementing measures or within 30 days thereafter.

3.   The notification shall state that all necessary administrative measures in Denmark enter into force on the date of entry into force of the implementing measures or have entered into force on the date of the notification, whichever date is the latest.

4.   A Danish notification that the content of the implementing measures has been implemented in Denmark creates mutual obligations under international law between Denmark and the Community. The implementing measures will then form part of this Agreement.

5.   In cases where:

(a)   Denmark notifies its decision not to implement the content of the implementing measures; or

(b)   Denmark does not make a notification within the 30-day time-limit set out in paragraph 2,

this Agreement shall be considered terminated unless the parties decide otherwise within 90 days. Termination shall take effect three months after the expiry of the 90-day period.

6.   Legal proceedings instituted and documents formally drawn up or registered as authentic instruments before the date of termination of the Agreement as set out in paragraph 5 are not affected hereby.

7.   If in exceptional cases the implementation requires parliamentary approval in Denmark, the Danish notification under paragraph 2 shall indicate this and the provisions of Article 3(5) to (8) shall apply.

8.   Denmark shall notify the Commission of texts amending the items set out in Article 2(2)(g) to (j) of this Agreement. The Commission shall adapt Article 2(2)(g) to (j) accordingly.

Article 5. International agreements which affect the Brussels I Regulation

1.   International agreements entered into by the Community based on the rules

of the Brussels I Regulation shall not be binding upon and shall not be applicable in Denmark.

2.   Denmark will abstain from entering into international agreements which may affect or alter the scope of the Brussels I Regulation as annexed to this Agreement unless it is done in agreement with the Community and satisfactory arrangements have been made with regard to the relationship between this Agreement and the international agreement in question.

3.   When negotiating international agreements that may affect or alter the scope of the Brussels I Regulation as annexed to this Agreement, Denmark will coordinate its position with the Community and will abstain from any actions that would jeopardise the objectives of a Community position within its sphere of competence in such negotiations.

Article 6. Jurisdiction of the Court of Justice of the European Communities in relation to the interpretation of the Agreement

1.   Where a question on the validity or interpretation of this Agreement is raised in a case pending before a Danish court or tribunal, that court or tribunal shall request the Court of Justice to give a ruling thereon whenever under the same circumstances a court or tribunal of another Member State of the European Union would be required to do so in respect of the Brussels I Regulation and its implementing measures referred to in Article 2(1) of this Agreement.

2.   Under Danish law, the courts in Denmark shall, when interpreting this Agreement, take due account of the rulings contained in the case law of the Court of Justice in respect of provisions of the Brussels Convention, the Brussels I Regulation and any implementing Community measures.

3.   Denmark may, like the Council, the Commission and any Member State, request the Court of Justice to give a ruling on a question of interpretation of this Agreement. The ruling given by the Court of Justice in response to such a request shall not apply to judgments of courts or tribunals of the Member States which have become res judicata.

4.   Denmark shall be entitled to submit observations to the Court of Justice in cases where a question has been referred to it by a court or tribunal of a Member State for a preliminary ruling concerning the interpretation of any provision referred to in Article 2(1).

5.   The Protocol on the Statute of the Court of Justice of the European Communities and its Rules of Procedure shall apply.

6.   If the provisions of the Treaty establishing the European Community regarding rulings by the Court of Justice are amended with consequences for rulings in respect of the Brussels I Regulation, Denmark may notify the Commission of its decision not to apply the amendments in respect of this Agreement. Notification shall be given at the time of the entry into force of the amendments or within 60 days thereafter.

In such a case this Agreement shall be considered terminated. Termination shall take effect three months after the notification.

7.   Legal proceedings instituted and documents formally drawn up or registered as authentic instruments before the date of termination of the Agreement as set out in paragraph 6 are not affected hereby.

Article 7. Jurisdiction of the Court of Justice of the European Communities in relation to compliance with the Agreement

1.   The Commission may bring before the Court of Justice cases against Denmark concerning non-compliance with any obligation under this Agreement.

2.   Denmark may bring a complaint before the Commission as to the non-compliance by a Member State of its obligations under this Agreement.

3.   The relevant provisions of the Treaty establishing the European Community governing proceedings before the Court of Justice as well as the Protocol on the

Statute of the Court of Justice of the European Communities and its Rules of Procedure shall apply.

Article 8. Territorial application
1.   This Agreement shall apply to the territories referred to in Article 299 of the Treaty establishing the European Community.

2.   If the Community decides to extend the application of the Brussels I Regulation to territories currently governed by the Brussels Convention, the Community and Denmark shall cooperate in order to ensure that such an application also extends to Denmark.

Article 9. Transitional provisions
1.   This Agreement shall apply only to legal proceedings instituted and to documents formally drawn up or registered as authentic instruments after the entry into force thereof.

2.   However, if the proceedings in the Member State of origin were instituted before the entry into force of this Agreement, judgments given after that date shall be recognised and enforced in accordance with this Agreement,
    (a)   if the proceedings in the Member State of origin were instituted after the entry into force of the Brussels or the Lugano Convention both in the Member State of origin and in the Member State addressed;
    (b)   in all other cases, if jurisdiction was founded upon rules which accorded with those provided for either in this Agreement or in a convention concluded between the Member State of origin and the Member State addressed which was in force when the proceedings were instituted.

Article 10. Relationship to the Brussels I Regulation
1.   This Agreement shall not prejudice the application by the Member States of the Community other than Denmark of the Brussels I Regulation.

2.   However, this Agreement shall in any event be applied:
    (a)   in matters of jurisdiction, where the defendant is domiciled in Denmark, or where Article 22 or 23 of the Regulation, applicable to the relations between the Community and Denmark by virtue of Article 2 of this Agreement, confer jurisdiction on the courts of Denmark;
    (b)   in relation to a lis pendens or to related actions as provided for in Articles 27 and 28 of the Brussels I Regulation, applicable to the relations between the Community and Denmark by virtue of Article 2 of this Agreement, when proceedings are instituted in a Member State other than Denmark and in Denmark;
    (c)   in matters of recognition and enforcement, where Denmark is either the State of origin or the State addressed.

Article 11. Termination of the agreement
1.   This Agreement shall terminate if Denmark informs the other Member States that it no longer wishes to avail itself of the provisions of Part I of the Protocol on the position of Denmark, in accordance with Article 7 of that Protocol.

2.   This Agreement may be terminated by either Contracting Party giving notice to the other Contracting Party. Termination shall be effective six months after the date of such notice.

3.   Legal proceedings instituted and documents formally drawn up or registered as authentic instruments before the date of termination of the Agreement as set out in paragraph 1 or 2 are not affected hereby.

Article 12. Entry into force
1.   The Agreement shall be adopted by the Contracting Parties in accordance with their respective procedures.

2.   The Agreement shall enter into force on the first day of the sixth month following the notification by the Contracting Parties of the completion of their respective procedures required for this purpose.

COUNCIL DECISION OF 27 APRIL 2006 CONCERNING THE CONCLUSION OF THE AGREEMENT BETWEEN THE EUROPEAN COMMUNITY AND THE KINGDOM OF DENMARK ON JURISDICTION AND THE RECOGNITION AND ENFORCEMENT OF JUDGMENTS IN CIVIL AND COMMERCIAL MATTERS (2006/325/EC)

Official Journal L 120, 05/05/2006 p 22

THE COUNCIL OF THE EUROPEAN UNION,

Having regard to the Treaty establishing the European Community, and in particular Article 61(c) thereof, in conjunction with the first sentence of the first subparagraph of Article 300(2) and the first subparagraph of Article 300(3) thereof,

Having regard to the proposal from the Commission,

Having regard to the opinion of the European Parliament,

Whereas:

(1) In accordance with Articles 1 and 2 of the Protocol on the position of Denmark annexed to the Treaty on European Union and the Treaty establishing the European Community, Denmark is not bound by the provisions of Council Regulation (EC) No 44/2001 of 22 December 2000 on jurisdiction and the recognition and enforcement of judgments in civil and commercial matters, nor subject to their application.

(2) The Commission has negotiated an Agreement between the European Community and the Kingdom of Denmark extending to Denmark the provisions of Regulation (EC) No 44/2001.

(3) The Agreement was signed, on behalf of the European Community, on 19 October 2005, subject to its possible conclusion at a later date, in accordance with Council Decision 2005/790/EC of 20 September 2005.

(4) In accordance with Article 3 of the Protocol on the position of the United Kingdom and Ireland annexed to the Treaty on European Union and the Treaty establishing the European Community, the United Kingdom and Ireland are taking part in the adoption and application of this Decision.

(5) In accordance with Articles 1 and 2 of the Protocol on the position of Denmark, Denmark is not taking part in the adoption of this Decision and is not bound by it or subject to its application.

(6) The Agreement should be approved,

HAS DECIDED AS FOLLOWS:

Article 1

The Agreement between the European Community and the Kingdom of Denmark on jurisdiction and the recognition and enforcement of judgments in civil and commercial matters is hereby approved on behalf of the Community.

Article 2

The President of the Council is hereby authorised to designate the person empowered to make the notification provided for in Article 12(2) of the Agreement.

Done at Luxembourg, 27 April 2006.

REGULATION (EC) NO 1896/2006 OF THE EUROPEAN PARLIAMENT AND OF THE COUNCIL OF 12 DECEMBER 2006 CREATING A EUROPEAN ORDER FOR PAYMENT PROCEDURE

Official Journal L 399, 30/12/2006 p 1

THE EUROPEAN PARLIAMENT AND THE COUNCIL OF THE EUROPEAN UNION,

Having regard to the Treaty establishing the European Community, and in particular Article 61(c) thereof,

Having regard to the proposal from the Commission,

Having regard to the Opinion of the European Economic and Social Committee,

Acting in accordance with the procedure laid down in Article 251 of the Treaty,

Whereas:

(1) The Community has set itself the objective of maintaining and developing an area of freedom, security and justice in which the free movement of persons is ensured. For the gradual establishment of such an area, the Community is to adopt, inter alia, measures in the field of judicial cooperation in civil matters having cross-border implications and needed for the proper functioning of the internal market.

(2) According to Article 65(c) of the Treaty, these measures are to include measures eliminating obstacles to the good functioning of civil proceedings, if necessary by promoting the compatibility of the rules on civil procedure applicable in the Member States.

(3) The European Council meeting in Tampere on 15 and 16 October 1999 invited the Council and the Commission to prepare new legislation on issues that are instrumental to smooth judicial cooperation and to enhanced access to law and specifically made reference, in that context, to orders for money payment.

(4) On 30 November 2000, the Council adopted a joint Commission and Council programme of measures for implementation of the principle of mutual recognition of decisions in civil and commercial matters. The programme envisages the possibility of a specific, uniform or harmonised procedure laid down within the Community to obtain a judicial decision in specific areas including that of uncontested claims. This was taken forward by the Hague Programme, adopted by the European Council on 5 November 2004, which called for work to be actively pursued on the European order for payment.

(5) The Commission adopted a Green Paper on a European order for payment procedure and on measures to simplify and speed up small claims litigation on 20 December 2002. The Green Paper launched consultations on the possible objectives and features of a uniform or harmonised European procedure for the recovery of uncontested claims.

(6) The swift and efficient recovery of outstanding debts over which no legal controversy exists is of paramount importance for economic operators in the European Union, as late payments constitute a major reason for insolvency threatening the survival of businesses, particularly small and medium-sized enterprises, and resulting in numerous job losses.

(7) All Member States are trying to tackle the issue of mass recovery of uncontested claims, in the majority of States by means of a simplified order for payment procedure, but both the content of national legislation and the performance of domestic procedures vary substantially. Furthermore, the procedures currently in existence are frequently either inadmissible or impracticable in cross-border cases.

(8) The resulting impediments to access to efficient justice in cross-border cases and the distortion of competition within the internal market due to imbalances in the functioning of procedural means afforded to creditors in different Member

States necessitate Community legislation guaranteeing a level playing field for creditors and debtors throughout the European Union.

(9)   The purpose of this Regulation is to simplify, speed up and reduce the costs of litigation in cross-border cases concerning uncontested pecuniary claims by creating a European order for payment procedure, and to permit the free circulation of European orders for payment throughout the Member States by laying down minimum standards, compliance with which renders unnecessary any intermediate proceedings in the Member State of enforcement prior to recognition and enforcement.

(10)   The procedure established by this Regulation should serve as an additional and optional means for the claimant, who remains free to resort to a procedure provided for by national law. Accordingly, this Regulation neither replaces nor harmonises the existing mechanisms for the recovery of uncontested claims under national law.

(11)   The procedure should be based, to the largest extent possible, on the use of standard forms in any communication between the court and the parties in order to facilitate its administration and enable the use of automatic data processing.

(12)   When deciding which courts are to have jurisdiction to issue a European order for payment, Member States should take due account of the need to ensure access to justice.

(13)   In the application for a European order for payment, the claimant should be obliged to provide information that is sufficient to clearly identify and support the claim in order to place the defendant in a position to make a well informed choice either to oppose the claim or to leave it uncontested.

(14)   In that context, it should be compulsory for the claimant to include a description of evidence supporting the claim. For that purpose the application form should include as exhaustive a list as possible of types of evidence that are usually produced in support of pecuniary claims.

(15)   The lodging of an application for a European order for payment should entail the payment of any applicable court fees.

(16)   The court should examine the application, including the issue of jurisdiction and the description of evidence, on the basis of the information provided in the application form. This would allow the court to examine prima facie the merits of the claim and inter alia to exclude clearly unfounded claims or inadmissible applications. The examination should not need to be carried out by a judge.

(17)   There is to be no right of appeal against the rejection of the application. This does not preclude, however, a possible review of the decision rejecting the application at the same level of jurisdiction in accordance with national law.

(18)   The European order for payment should apprise the defendant of his options to pay the amount awarded to the claimant or to send a statement of opposition within a time limit of 30 days if he wishes to contest the claim. In addition to being provided with full information concerning the claim as supplied by the claimant, the defendant should be advised of the legal significance of the European order for payment and in particular of the consequences of leaving the claim uncontested.

(19)   Due to differences between Member States' rules of civil procedure and especially those governing the service of documents, it is necessary to lay down a specific and detailed definition of minimum standards that should apply in the context of the European order for payment procedure. In particular, as regards the fulfilment of those standards, any method based on legal fiction should not be considered sufficient for the service of the European order for payment.

(20)   All the methods of service listed in Articles 13 and 14 are characterised by either complete certainty (Article 13) or a very high degree of likelihood (Article 14) that the document served has reached its addressee.

(21)   Personal service on certain persons other than the defendant himself pursuant to Article 14(1)(a) and (b) should be deemed to meet the requirements of those provisions only if those persons actually accepted/received the European order for payment.

(22)   Article 15 should apply to situations where the defendant cannot represent himself in court, as in the case of a legal person, and where a person authorised to represent him is determined by law, as well as to situations where the defendant has authorised another person, in particular a lawyer, to represent him in the specific court proceedings at issue.

(23)   The defendant may submit his statement of opposition using the standard form set out in this Regulation. However, the courts should take into account any other written form of opposition if it is expressed in a clear manner.

(24)   A statement of opposition filed within the time limit should terminate the European order for payment procedure and should lead to an automatic transfer of the case to ordinary civil proceedings unless the claimant has explicitly requested that the proceedings be terminated in that event. For the purposes of this Regulation the concept of ordinary civil proceedings should not necessarily be interpreted within the meaning of national law.

(25)   After the expiry of the time limit for submitting the statement of opposition, in certain exceptional cases the defendant should be entitled to apply for a review of the European order for payment. Review in exceptional cases should not mean that the defendant is given a second opportunity to oppose the claim. During the review procedure the merits of the claim should not be evaluated beyond the grounds resulting from the exceptional circumstances invoked by the defendant. The other exceptional circumstances could include a situation where the European order for payment was based on false information provided in the application form.

(26)   Court fees covered by Article 25 should not include for example lawyers' fees or costs of service of documents by an entity other than a court.

(27)   A European order for payment issued in one Member State which has become enforceable should be regarded for the purposes of enforcement as if it had been issued in the Member State in which enforcement is sought. Mutual trust in the administration of justice in the Member States justifies the assessment by the court of one Member State that all conditions for issuing a European order for payment are fulfilled to enable the order to be enforced in all other Member States without judicial review of the proper application of minimum procedural standards in the Member State where the order is to be enforced. Without prejudice to the provisions of this Regulation, in particular the minimum standards laid down in Article 22(1) and (2) and Article 23, the procedures for the enforcement of the European order for payment should continue to be governed by national law.

(28)   For the purposes of calculating time limits, Regulation (EEC, Euratom) No 1182/71 of the Council of 3 June 1971 determining the rules applicable to periods, dates and time limits should apply. The defendant should be advised of this and should be informed that account will be taken of the public holidays of the Member State in which the court issuing the European order for payment is situated.

(29)   Since the objective of this Regulation, namely to establish a uniform rapid and efficient mechanism for the recovery of uncontested pecuniary claims throughout the European Union, cannot be sufficiently achieved by the Member States and can therefore, by reason of the scale and effects of the Regulation, be better achieved at Community level, the Community may adopt measures in accordance with the principle of subsidiarity as set out in Article 5 of the Treaty. In accordance with the principle of proportionality as set out in that Article, this Regulation does not go beyond what is necessary in order to achieve that objective.

(30)   The measures necessary for the implementation of this Regulation should be adopted in accordance with Council Decision 1999/468/EC of 28 June 1999 lay-

ing down the procedures for the exercise of implementing powers conferred on the Commission.

(31)   The United Kingdom and Ireland, in accordance with Article 3 of the Protocol on the position of the United Kingdom and Ireland annexed to the Treaty on European Union and the Treaty establishing the European Community, have given notice of their wish to take part in the adoption and application of this Regulation.

(32)   In accordance with Articles 1 and 2 of the Protocol on the position of Denmark annexed to the Treaty on European Union and the Treaty establishing the European Community, Denmark does not take part in the adoption of this Regulation, and is not bound by it or subject to its application,

HAVE ADOPTED THIS REGULATION:

Article 1. Subject matter
1.   The purpose of this Regulation is:
(a)   to simplify, speed up and reduce the costs of litigation in cross-border cases concerning uncontested pecuniary claims by creating a European order for payment procedure; and
(b)   to permit the free circulation of European orders for payment throughout the Member States by laying down minimum standards, compliance with which renders unnecessary any intermediate proceedings in the Member State of enforcement prior to recognition and enforcement.
2.   This Regulation shall not prevent a claimant from pursuing a claim within the meaning of Article 4 by making use of another procedure available under the law of a Member State or under Community law.

Article 2. Scope
1.   This Regulation shall apply to civil and commercial matters in cross-border cases, whatever the nature of the court or tribunal. It shall not extend, in particular, to revenue, customs or administrative matters or the liability of the State for acts and omissions in the exercise of State authority ('acta iure imperii').
2.   This Regulation shall not apply to:
(a)   rights in property arising out of a matrimonial relationship, wills and succession;
(b)   bankruptcy, proceedings relating to the winding-up of insolvent companies or other legal persons, judicial arrangements, compositions and analogous proceedings;
(c)   social security;
(d)   claims arising from non-contractual obligations, unless:
(i)   they have been the subject of an agreement between the parties or there has been an admission of debt, or
(ii)   they relate to liquidated debts arising from joint ownership of property.
3.   In this Regulation, the term 'Member State' shall mean Member States with the exception of Denmark.

Article 3. Cross-border cases
1.   For the purposes of this Regulation, a cross-border case is one in which at least one of the parties is domiciled or habitually resident in a Member State other than the Member State of the court seised.
2.   Domicile shall be determined in accordance with Articles 59 and 60 of Council Regulation (EC) No 44/2001 of 22 December 2000 on jurisdiction and the recognition and enforcement of judgments in civil and commercial matters.
3.   The relevant moment for determining whether there is a cross-border case shall be the time when the application for a European order for payment is submitted in accordance with this Regulation.

Article 4. European order for payment procedure
The European order for payment procedure shall be established for the collection of pecuniary claims for a specific amount that have fallen due at the time when the application for a European order for payment is submitted.

Article 5. Definitions
For the purposes of this Regulation, the following definitions shall apply:

(1) 'Member State of origin' means the Member State in which a European order for payment is issued;

(2) 'Member State of enforcement' means the Member State in which enforcement of a European order for payment is sought;

(3) 'court' means any authority in a Member State with competence regarding European orders for payment or any other related matters;

(4) 'court of origin' means the court which issues a European order for payment.

Article 6. Jurisdiction
1. For the purposes of applying this Regulation, jurisdiction shall be determined in accordance with the relevant rules of Community law, in particular Regulation (EC) No 44/2001.

2. However, if the claim relates to a contract concluded by a person, the consumer, for a purpose which can be regarded as being outside his trade or profession, and if the defendant is the consumer, only the courts in the Member State in which the defendant is domiciled, within the meaning of Article 59 of Regulation (EC) No 44/2001, shall have jurisdiction.

Article 7. Application for a European order for payment
1. An application for a European order for payment shall be made using standard form A as set out in Annex I.

2. The application shall state:

(a) the names and addresses of the parties, and, where applicable, their representatives, and of the court to which the application is made;

(b) the amount of the claim, including the principal and, where applicable, interest, contractual penalties and costs;

(c) if interest on the claim is demanded, the interest rate and the period of time for which that interest is demanded unless statutory interest is automatically added to the principal under the law of the Member State of origin;

(d) the cause of the action, including a description of the circumstances invoked as the basis of the claim and, where applicable, of the interest demanded;

(e) a description of evidence supporting the claim;

(f) the grounds for jurisdiction; and

(g) the cross-border nature of the case within the meaning of Article 3.

3. In the application, the claimant shall declare that the information provided is true to the best of his knowledge and belief and shall acknowledge that any deliberate false statement could lead to appropriate penalties under the law of the Member State of origin.

4. In an Appendix to the application the claimant may indicate to the court that he opposes a transfer to ordinary civil proceedings within the meaning of Article 17 in the event of opposition by the defendant. This does not prevent the claimant from informing the court thereof subsequently, but in any event before the order is issued.

5. The application shall be submitted in paper form or by any other means of communication, including electronic, accepted by the Member State of origin and available to the court of origin.

6. The application shall be signed by the claimant or, where applicable, by his representative. Where the application is submitted in electronic form in accordance

with paragraph 5, it shall be signed in accordance with Article 2(2) of Directive 1999/93/EC of the European Parliament and of the Council of 13 December 1999 on a Community framework for electronic signatures. The signature shall be recognised in the Member State of origin and may not be made subject to additional requirements.

However, such electronic signature shall not be required if and to the extent that an alternative electronic communications system exists in the courts of the Member State of origin which is available to a certain group of pre-registered authenticated users and which permits the identification of those users in a secure manner. Member States shall inform the Commission of such communications systems.

Article 8. Examination of the application
The court seised of an application for a European order for payment shall examine, as soon as possible and on the basis of the application form, whether the requirements set out in Articles 2, 3, 4, 6 and 7 are met and whether the claim appears to be founded. This examination may take the form of an automated procedure.

Article 9. Completion and rectification
1.   If the requirements set out in Article 7 are not met and unless the claim is clearly unfounded or the application is inadmissible, the court shall give the claimant the opportunity to complete or rectify the application. The court shall use standard form B as set out in Annex II.

2.   Where the court requests the claimant to complete or rectify the application, it shall specify a time limit it deems appropriate in the circumstances. The court may at its discretion extend that time limit.

Article 10. Modification of the application
1.   If the requirements referred to in Article 8 are met for only part of the claim, the court shall inform the claimant to that effect, using standard form C as set out in Annex III.

The claimant shall be invited to accept or refuse a proposal for a European order for payment for the amount specified by the court and shall be informed of the consequences of his decision. The claimant shall reply by returning standard form C sent by the court within a time limit specified by the court in accordance with Article 9(2).

2.   If the claimant accepts the court's proposal, the court shall issue a European order for payment, in accordance with Article 12, for that part of the claim accepted by the claimant. The consequences with respect to the remaining part of the initial claim shall be governed by national law.

3.   If the claimant fails to send his reply within the time limit specified by the court or refuses the court's proposal, the court shall reject the application for a European order for payment in its entirety.

Article 11. Rejection of the application
1.   The court shall reject the application if:
   (a)   the requirements set out in Articles 2, 3, 4, 6 and 7 are not met; or
   (b)   the claim is clearly unfounded; or
   (c)   the claimant fails to send his reply within the time limit specified by the court under Article 9(2); or
   (d)   the claimant fails to send his reply within the time limit specified by the court or refuses the court's proposal, in accordance with Article 10.

The claimant shall be informed of the grounds for the rejection by means of standard form D as set out in Annex IV.

2.   There shall be no right of appeal against the rejection of the application.

3.   The rejection of the application shall not prevent the claimant from pursuing the claim by means of a new application for a European order for payment or of any other procedure available under the law of a Member State.

Article 12. Issue of a European order for payment
1. If the requirements referred to in Article 8 are met, the court shall issue, as soon as possible and normally within 30 days of the lodging of the application, a European order for payment using standard form E as set out in Annex V.
The 30-day period shall not include the time taken by the claimant to complete, rectify or modify the application.
2. The European order for payment shall be issued together with a copy of the application form. It shall not comprise the information provided by the claimant in Appendices 1 and 2 to form A.
3. In the European order for payment, the defendant shall be advised of his options to:
   (a)   pay the amount indicated in the order to the claimant; or
   (b)   oppose the order by lodging with the court of origin a statement of opposition, to be sent within 30 days of service of the order on him.
4. In the European order for payment, the defendant shall be informed that:
   (a)   the order was issued solely on the basis of the information which was provided by the claimant and was not verified by the court;
   (b)   the order will become enforceable unless a statement of opposition has been lodged with the court in accordance with Article 16;
   (c)   where a statement of opposition is lodged, the proceedings shall continue before the competent courts of the Member State of origin in accordance with the rules of ordinary civil procedure unless the claimant has explicitly requested that the proceedings be terminated in that event.
5. The court shall ensure that the order is served on the defendant in accordance with national law by a method that shall meet the minimum standards laid down in Articles 13, 14 and 15.

Article 13. Service with proof of receipt by the defendant
The European order for payment may be served on the defendant in accordance with the national law of the State in which the service is to be effected, by one of the following methods:
   (a)   personal service attested by an acknowledgement of receipt, including the date of receipt, which is signed by the defendant;
   (b)   personal service attested by a document signed by the competent person who effected the service stating that the defendant has received the document or refused to receive it without any legal justification, and the date of service;
   (c)   postal service attested by an acknowledgement of receipt, including the date of receipt, which is signed and returned by the defendant;
   (d)   service by electronic means such as fax or e-mail, attested by an acknowledgement of receipt, including the date of receipt, which is signed and returned by the defendant.

Article 14. Service without proof of receipt by the defendant
1. The European order for payment may also be served on the defendant in accordance with the national law of the State in which service is to be effected, by one of the following methods:
   (a)   personal service at the defendant's personal address on persons who are living in the same household as the defendant or are employed there;
   (b)   in the case of a self-employed defendant or a legal person, personal service at the defendant's business premises on persons who are employed by the defendant;
   (c)   deposit of the order in the defendant's mailbox;
   (d)   deposit of the order at a post office or with competent public authorities and the placing in the defendant's mailbox of written notification of that deposit, provided that the written notification clearly states the character of the document as a court document or the legal effect of the notification as effecting service and setting in motion the running of time for the purposes of time limits;

(e)   postal service without proof pursuant to paragraph 3 where the defendant has his address in the Member State of origin;

(f)   electronic means attested by an automatic confirmation of delivery, provided that the defendant has expressly accepted this method of service in advance.

2.   For the purposes of this Regulation, service under paragraph 1 is not admissible if the defendant's address is not known with certainty.

3.   Service pursuant to paragraph 1(a), (b), (c) and (d) shall be attested by:

(a)   a document signed by the competent person who effected the service, indicating:

(i)   the method of service used; and

(ii)   the date of service; and

(iii)   where the order has been served on a person other than the defendant, the name of that person and his relation to the defendant; or

(b)   an acknowledgement of receipt by the person served, for the purposes of paragraphs (1)(a) and (b).

Article 15. Service on a representative

Service pursuant to Articles 13 or 14 may also be effected on a defendant's representative.

Article 16. Opposition to the European order for payment

1.   The defendant may lodge a statement of opposition to the European order for payment with the court of origin using standard form F as set out in Annex VI, which shall be supplied to him together with the European order for payment.

2.   The statement of opposition shall be sent within 30 days of service of the order on the defendant.

3.   The defendant shall indicate in the statement of opposition that he contests the claim, without having to specify the reasons for this.

4.   The statement of opposition shall be submitted in paper form or by any other means of communication, including electronic, accepted by the Member State of origin and available to the court of origin.

5.   The statement of opposition shall be signed by the defendant or, where applicable, by his representative. Where the statement of opposition is submitted in electronic form in accordance with paragraph 4, it shall be signed in accordance with Article 2(2) of Directive 1999/93/EC. The signature shall be recognised in the Member State of origin and may not be made subject to additional requirements.

However, such electronic signature shall not be required if and to the extent that an alternative electronic communications system exists in the courts of the Member State of origin which is available to a certain group of pre-registered authenticated users and which permits the identification of those users in a secure manner. Member States shall inform the Commission of such communications systems.

Article 17. Effects of the lodging of a statement of opposition

1.   If a statement of opposition is entered within the time limit laid down in Article 16(2), the proceedings shall continue before the competent courts of the Member State of origin in accordance with the rules of ordinary civil procedure unless the claimant has explicitly requested that the proceedings be terminated in that event.

Where the claimant has pursued his claim through the European order for payment procedure, nothing under national law shall prejudice his position in subsequent ordinary civil proceedings.

2.   The transfer to ordinary civil proceedings within the meaning of paragraph 1 shall be governed by the law of the Member State of origin.

3.   The claimant shall be informed whether the defendant has lodged a statement of opposition and of any transfer to ordinary civil proceedings.

Article 18. Enforceability

1.   If within the time limit laid down in Article 16(2), taking into account an appropriate period of time to allow a statement to arrive, no statement of opposition has been lodged with the court of origin, the court of origin shall without delay declare the European order for payment enforceable using standard form G as set out in Annex VII. The court shall verify the date of service.

2.   Without prejudice to paragraph 1, the formal requirements for enforceability shall be governed by the law of the Member State of origin.

3.   The court shall send the enforceable European order for payment to the claimant.

Article 19. Abolition of exequatur

A European order for payment which has become enforceable in the Member State of origin shall be recognised and enforced in the other Member States without the need for a declaration of enforceability and without any possibility of opposing its recognition.

Article 20. Review in exceptional cases

1.   After the expiry of the time limit laid down in Article 16(2) the defendant shall be entitled to apply for a review of the European order for payment before the competent court in the Member State of origin where:

(a)   (i)   the order for payment was served by one of the methods provided for in Article 14, and

(ii)   service was not effected in sufficient time to enable him to arrange for his defence, without any fault on his part, or

(b)   the defendant was prevented from objecting to the claim by reason of force majeure or due to extraordinary circumstances without any fault on his part,

provided in either case that he acts promptly.

2.   After expiry of the time limit laid down in Article 16(2) the defendant shall also be entitled to apply for a review of the European order for payment before the competent court in the Member State of origin where the order for payment was clearly wrongly issued, having regard to the requirements laid down in this Regulation, or due to other exceptional circumstances.

3.   If the court rejects the defendant's application on the basis that none of the grounds for review referred to in paragraphs 1 and 2 apply, the European order for payment shall remain in force.

If the court decides that the review is justified for one of the reasons laid down in paragraphs 1 and 2, the European order for payment shall be null and void.

Article 21. Enforcement

1.   Without prejudice to the provisions of this Regulation, enforcement procedures shall be governed by the law of the Member State of enforcement.

A European order for payment which has become enforceable shall be enforced under the same conditions as an enforceable decision issued in the Member State of enforcement.

2.   For enforcement in another Member State, the claimant shall provide the competent enforcement authorities of that Member State with:

(a)   a copy of the European order for payment, as declared enforceable by the court of origin, which satisfies the conditions necessary to establish its authenticity; and

(b)   where necessary, a translation of the European order for payment into the official language of the Member State of enforcement or, if there are several official languages in that Member State, the official language or one of the official languages of court proceedings of the place where enforcement is sought, in conformity with the law of that Member State, or into another language that the Member State of enforcement has indicated it can accept. Each Member State may indicate the official language or languages of the institutions of the European Union other than its own which it can accept for the European order for payment. The translation shall be certified by a person qualified to do so in one of the Member States.

3.   No security, bond or deposit, however described, shall be required of a claimant who in one Member State applies for enforcement of a European order for payment issued in another Member State on the ground that he is a foreign national or that he is not domiciled or resident in the Member State of enforcement.

Article 22. Refusal of enforcement

1.   Enforcement shall, upon application by the defendant, be refused by the competent court in the Member State of enforcement if the European order for payment is irreconcilable with an earlier decision or order previously given in any Member State or in a third country, provided that:

   (a)   the earlier decision or order involved the same cause of action between the same parties; and

   (b)   the earlier decision or order fulfils the conditions necessary for its recognition in the Member State of enforcement; and

   (c)   the irreconcilability could not have been raised as an objection in the court proceedings in the Member State of origin.

2.   Enforcement shall, upon application, also be refused if and to the extent that the defendant has paid the claimant the amount awarded in the European order for payment.

3.   Under no circumstances may the European order for payment be reviewed as to its substance in the Member State of enforcement.

Article 23. Stay or limitation of enforcement

Where the defendant has applied for a review in accordance with Article 20, the competent court in the Member State of enforcement may, upon application by the defendant:

   (a)   limit the enforcement proceedings to protective measures; or

   (b)   make enforcement conditional on the provision of such security as it shall determine; or

   (c)   under exceptional circumstances, stay the enforcement proceedings.

Article 24. Legal representation

Representation by a lawyer or another legal professional shall not be mandatory:

   (a)   for the claimant in respect of the application for a European order for payment;

   (b)   for the defendant in respect of the statement of opposition to a European order for payment.

Article 25. Court fees

1.   The combined court fees of a European order for payment procedure and of the ordinary civil proceedings that ensue in the event of a statement of opposition to a European order for payment in a Member State shall not exceed the court fees of ordinary civil proceedings without a preceding European order for payment procedure in that Member State.

2.   For the purposes of this Regulation, court fees shall comprise fees and charges to be paid to the court, the amount of which is fixed in accordance with national law.

Article 26. Relationship with national procedural law

All procedural issues not specifically dealt with in this Regulation shall be governed by national law.

Article 27. Relationship with Regulation (EC) No 1348/2000

This Regulation shall not affect the application of Council Regulation (EC) No

1348/2000 of 29 May 2000 on the service in the Member States of judicial and extrajudicial documents in civil and commercial matters.

...

Article 29. Information relating to jurisdiction, review procedures, means of communication and languages
1.   By 12 June 2008, Member States shall communicate to the Commission:
(a)   which courts have jurisdiction to issue a European order for payment;
(b)   the review procedure and the competent courts for the purposes of the application of Article 20;
(c)   the means of communication accepted for the purposes of the European order for payment procedure and available to the courts;
(d)   languages accepted pursuant to Article 21(2)(b).
Member States shall apprise the Commission of any subsequent changes to this information.
2.   The Commission shall make the information notified in accordance with paragraph 1 publicly available through publication in the Official Journal of the European Union and through any other appropriate means.

...

Article 32. Review
By 12 December 2013, the Commission shall present to the European Parliament, the Council and the European Economic and Social Committee a detailed report reviewing the operation of the European order for payment procedure. That report shall contain an assessment of the procedure as it has operated and an extended impact assessment for each Member State.
To that end, and in order to ensure that best practice in the European Union is duly taken into account and reflects the principles of better legislation, Member States shall provide the Commission with information relating to the cross-border operation of the European order for payment. This information shall cover court fees, speed of the procedure, efficiency, ease of use and the internal payment order procedures of the Member States.
The Commission's report shall be accompanied, if appropriate, by proposals for adaptation.

Article 33. Entry into force
This Regulation shall enter into force on the day following the date of its publication in the Official Journal of the European Union.
It shall apply from 12 December 2008, with the exception of Articles 28, 29, 30 and 31 which shall apply from 12 June 2008.
This Regulation shall be binding in its entirety and directly applicable in the Member States in accordance with the Treaty establishing the European Community.

Done at Strasbourg, 12 December 2006.

REGULATION (EC) NO 864/2007 OF THE EUROPEAN PARLIAMENT AND OF THE COUNCIL OF 11 JULY 2007 ON THE LAW APPLICABLE TO NON-CONTRACTUAL OBLIGATIONS ('ROME II')

THE EUROPEAN PARLIAMENT AND THE COUNCIL OF THE EUROPEAN UNION,
Having regard to the Treaty establishing the European Community, and in particular Articles 61(c) and 67 thereof,
Having regard to the proposal from the Commission,
Having regard to the opinion of the European Economic and Social Committee,

Acting in accordance with the procedure laid down in Article 251 of the Treaty in the light of the joint text approved by the Conciliation Committee on 25 June 2007.

Whereas:

(1)   The Community has set itself the objective of maintaining and developing an area of freedom, security and justice. For the progressive establishment of such an area, the Community is to adopt measures relating to judicial cooperation in civil matters with a cross-border impact to the extent necessary for the proper functioning of the internal market.

(2)   According to Article 65(b) of the Treaty, these measures are to include those promoting the compatibility of the rules applicable in the Member States concerning the conflict of laws and of jurisdiction.

(3)   The European Council meeting in Tampere on 15 and 16 October 1999 endorsed the principle of mutual recognition of judgments and other decisions of judicial authorities as the cornerstone of judicial cooperation in civil matters and invited the Council and the Commission to adopt a programme of measures to implement the principle of mutual recognition.

(4)   On 30 November 2000, the Council adopted a joint Commission and Council programme of measures for implementation of the principle of mutual recognition of decisions in civil and commercial matters. The programme identifies measures relating to the harmonisation of conflict-of-law rules as those facilitating the mutual recognition of judgments.

(5)   The Hague Programme, adopted by the European Council on 5 November 2004, called for work to be pursued actively on the rules of conflict of laws regarding non-contractual obligations ('Rome II').

(6)   The proper functioning of the internal market creates a need, in order to improve the predictability of the outcome of litigation, certainty as to the law applicable and the free movement of judgments, for the conflict-of-law rules in the Member States to designate the same national law irrespective of the country of the court in which an action is brought.

(7)   The substantive scope and the provisions of this Regulation should be consistent with Council Regulation (EC) No 44/2001 of 22 December 2000 on jurisdiction and the recognition and enforcement of judgments in civil and commercial matters ('Brussels I') and the instruments dealing with the law applicable to contractual obligations.

(8)   This Regulation should apply irrespective of the nature of the court or tribunal seised.

(9)   Claims arising out of 'acta iure imperii' should include claims against officials who act on behalf of the State and liability for acts of public authorities, including liability of publicly appointed office-holders. Therefore, these matters should be excluded from the scope of this Regulation.

(10)   Family relationships should cover parentage, marriage, affinity and collateral relatives. The reference in Article 1(2) to relationships having comparable effects to marriage and other family relationships should be interpreted in accordance with the law of the Member State in which the court is seised.

(11)   The concept of a non-contractual obligation varies from one Member State to another. Therefore for the purposes of this Regulation non-contractual obligation should be understood as an autonomous concept. The conflict-of-law rules set out in this Regulation should also cover non-contractual obligations arising out of strict liability.

(12)   The law applicable should also govern the question of the capacity to incur liability in tort/delict.

(13)   Uniform rules applied irrespective of the law they designate may avert the risk of distortions of competition between Community litigants.

(14)   The requirement of legal certainty and the need to do justice in individual cases are essential elements of an area of justice. This Regulation provides for the

connecting factors which are the most appropriate to achieve these objectives. Therefore, this Regulation provides for a general rule but also for specific rules and, in certain provisions, for an 'escape clause' which allows a departure from these rules where it is clear from all the circumstances of the case that the tort/ delict is manifestly more closely connected with another country. This set of rules thus creates a flexible framework of conflict-of-law rules. Equally, it enables the court seised to treat individual cases in an appropriate manner.

(15)   The principle of the *lex loci delicti commissi* is the basic solution for non-contractual obligations in virtually all the Member States, but the practical application of the principle where the component factors of the case are spread over several countries varies. This situation engenders uncertainty as to the law applicable.

(16)   Uniform rules should enhance the foreseeability of court decisions and ensure a reasonable balance between the interests of the person claimed to be liable and the person who has sustained damage. A connection with the country where the direct damage occurred (*lex loci damni*) strikes a fair balance between the interests of the person claimed to be liable and the person sustaining the damage, and also reflects the modern approach to civil liability and the development of systems of strict liability.

(17)   The law applicable should be determined on the basis of where the damage occurs, regardless of the country or countries in which the indirect consequences could occur. Accordingly, in cases of personal injury or damage to property, the country in which the damage occurs should be the country where the injury was sustained or the property was damaged respectively.

(18)   The general rule in this Regulation should be the '*lex loci damni*' provided for in Article 4(1). Article 4(2) should be seen as an exception to this general principle, creating a special connection where the parties have their habitual residence in the same country. Article 4(3) should be understood as an 'escape clause' from Article 4(1) and (2), where it is clear from all the circumstances of the case that the tort/delict is manifestly more closely connected with another country.

(19)   Specific rules should be laid down for special torts/delicts where the general rule does not allow a reasonable balance to be struck between the interests at stake.

(20)   The conflict-of-law rule in matters of product liability should meet the objectives of fairly spreading the risks inherent in a modern high-technology society, protecting consumers' health, stimulating innovation, securing undistorted competition and facilitating trade. Creation of a cascade system of connecting factors, together with a foreseeability clause, is a balanced solution in regard to these objectives. The first element to be taken into account is the law of the country in which the person sustaining the damage had his or her habitual residence when the damage occurred, if the product was marketed in that country. The other elements of the cascade are triggered if the product was not marketed in that country, without prejudice to Article 4(2) and to the possibility of a manifestly closer connection to another country.

(21)   The special rule in Article 6 is not an exception to the general rule in Article 4(1) but rather a clarification of it. In matters of unfair competition, the conflict-of-law rule should protect competitors, consumers and the general public and ensure that the market economy functions properly. The connection to the law of the country where competitive relations or the collective interests of consumers are, or are likely to be, affected generally satisfies these objectives.

(22)   The non-contractual obligations arising out of restrictions of competition in Article 6(3) should cover infringements of both national and Community competition law. The law applicable to such non-contractual obligations should be the law of the country where the market is, or is likely to be, affected. In cases where the market is, or is likely to be, affected in more than one country, the claimant should

be able in certain circumstances to choose to base his or her claim on the law of the court seised.

(23)   For the purposes of this Regulation, the concept of restriction of competition should cover prohibitions on agreements between undertakings, decisions by associations of undertakings and concerted practices which have as their object or effect the prevention, restriction or distortion of competition within a Member State or within the internal market, as well as prohibitions on the abuse of a dominant position within a Member State or within the internal market, where such agreements, decisions, concerted practices or abuses are prohibited by Articles 81 and 82 of the Treaty or by the law of a Member State.

(24)   'Environmental damage' should be understood as meaning adverse change in a natural resource, such as water, land or air, impairment of a function performed by that resource for the benefit of another natural resource or the public, or impairment of the variability among living organisms.

(25)   Regarding environmental damage, Article 174 of the Treaty, which provides that there should be a high level of protection based on the precautionary principle and the principle that preventive action should be taken, the principle of priority for corrective action at source and the principle that the polluter pays, fully justifies the use of the principle of discriminating in favour of the person sustaining the damage. The question of when the person seeking compensation can make the choice of the law applicable should be determined in accordance with the law of the Member State in which the court is seised.

(26)   Regarding infringements of intellectual property rights, the universally acknowledged principle of the *lex loci protectionis* should be preserved. For the purposes of this Regulation, the term 'intellectual property rights' should be interpreted as meaning, for instance, copyright, related rights, the *sui generis* right for the protection of databases and industrial property rights.

(27)   The exact concept of industrial action, such as strike action or lock-out, varies from one Member State to another and is governed by each Member State's internal rules. Therefore, this Regulation assumes as a general principle that the law of the country where the industrial action was taken should apply, with the aim of protecting the rights and obligations of workers and employers.

(28)   The special rule on industrial action in Article 9 is without prejudice to the conditions relating to the exercise of such action in accordance with national law and without prejudice to the legal status of trade unions or of the representative organisations of workers as provided for in the law of the Member States.

(29)   Provision should be made for special rules where damage is caused by an act other than a tort/delict, such as unjust enrichment, *negotiorum gestio* and *culpa in contrahendo*.

(30)   Culpa in contrahendo for the purposes of this Regulation is an autonomous concept and should not necessarily be interpreted within the meaning of national law. It should include the violation of the duty of disclosure and the breakdown of contractual negotiations. Article 12 covers only non-contractual obligations presenting a direct link with the dealings prior to the conclusion of a contract. This means that if, while a contract is being negotiated, a person suffers personal injury, Article 4 or other relevant provisions of this Regulation should apply.

(31)   To respect the principle of party autonomy and to enhance legal certainty, the parties should be allowed to make a choice as to the law applicable to a non-contractual obligation. This choice should be expressed or demonstrated with reasonable certainty by the circumstances of the case. Where establishing the existence of the agreement, the court has to respect the intentions of the parties. Protection should be given to weaker parties by imposing certain conditions on the choice.

(32)   Considerations of public interest justify giving the courts of the Member States the possibility, in exceptional circumstances, of applying exceptions based

on public policy and overriding mandatory provisions. In particular, the application of a provision of the law designated by this Regulation which would have the effect of causing non-compensatory exemplary or punitive damages of an excessive nature to be awarded may, depending on the circumstances of the case and the legal order of the Member State of the court seised, be regarded as being contrary to the public policy (*ordre public*) of the forum.

(33) According to the current national rules on compensation awarded to victims of road traffic accidents, when quantifying damages for personal injury in cases in which the accident takes place in a State other than that of the habitual residence of the victim, the court seised should take into account all the relevant actual circumstances of the specific victim, including in particular the actual losses and costs of after-care and medical attention.

(34) In order to strike a reasonable balance between the parties, account must be taken, in so far as appropriate, of the rules of safety and conduct in operation in the country in which the harmful act was committed, even where the non-contractual obligation is governed by the law of another country. The term 'rules of safety and conduct' should be interpreted as referring to all regulations having any relation to safety and conduct, including, for example, road safety rules in the case of an accident.

(35) A situation where conflict-of-law rules are dispersed among several instruments and where there are differences between those rules should be avoided. This Regulation, however, does not exclude the possibility of inclusion of conflict-of-law rules relating to non-contractual obligations in provisions of Community law with regard to particular matters.

This Regulation should not prejudice the application of other instruments laying down provisions designed to contribute to the proper functioning of the internal market in so far as they cannot be applied in conjunction with the law designated by the rules of this Regulation. The application of provisions of the applicable law designated by the rules of this Regulation should not restrict the free movement of goods and services as regulated by Community instruments, such as Directive 2000/31/EC of the European Parliament and of the Council of 8 June 2000 on certain legal aspects of information society services, in particular electronic commerce, in the Internal Market ('Directive on electronic commerce').

(36) Respect for international commitments entered into by the Member States means that this Regulation should not affect international conventions to which one or more Member States are parties at the time this Regulation is adopted. To make the rules more accessible, the Commission should publish the list of the relevant conventions in the *Official Journal of the European Union* on the basis of information supplied by the Member States.

(37) The Commission will make a proposal to the European Parliament and the Council concerning the procedures and conditions according to which Member States would be entitled to negotiate and conclude on their own behalf agreements with third countries in individual and exceptional cases, concerning sectoral matters, containing provisions on the law applicable to non-contractual obligations.

(38) Since the objective of this Regulation cannot be sufficiently achieved by the Member States, and can therefore, by reason of the scale and effects of this Regulation, be better achieved at Community level, the Community may adopt measures, in accordance with the principle of subsidiarity set out in Article 5 of the Treaty. In accordance with the principle of proportionality set out in that Article, this Regulation does not go beyond what is necessary to attain that objective.

(39) In accordance with Article 3 of the Protocol on the position of the United Kingdom and Ireland annexed to the Treaty on European Union and to the Treaty establishing the European Community, the United Kingdom and Ireland are taking part in the adoption and application of this Regulation.

(40)   In accordance with Articles 1 and 2 of the Protocol on the position of
Denmark, annexed to the Treaty on European Union and to the Treaty establishing
the European Community, Denmark does not take part in the adoption of this
Regulation, and is not bound by it or subject to its application,

HAVE ADOPTED THIS REGULATION:

CHAPTER I
SCOPE

Article 1. Scope

1.   This Regulation shall apply, in situations involving a conflict of laws, to non-
contractual obligations in civil and commercial matters. It shall not apply, in particular, to revenue, customs or administrative matters or to the liability of the State
for acts and omissions in the exercise of State authority (*acta iure imperii*).

2.   The following shall be excluded from the scope of this Regulation:

(a)   non-contractual obligations arising out of family relationships and relationships deemed by the law applicable to such relationships to have comparable effects including maintenance obligations;

(b)   non-contractual obligations arising out of matrimonial property regimes,
property regimes of relationships deemed by the law applicable to such relationships to have comparable effects to marriage, and wills and succession;

(c)   non-contractual obligations arising under bills of exchange, cheques and
promissory notes and other negotiable instruments to the extent that the obligations under such other negotiable instruments arise out of their negotiable
character;

(d)   non-contractual obligations arising out of the law of companies and other
bodies corporate or unincorporated regarding matters such as the creation, by
registration or otherwise, legal capacity, internal organisation or winding up of
companies and other bodies corporate or unincorporated, the personal liability
of officers and members as such for the obligations of the company or body and
the personal liability of auditors to a company or to its members in the statutory
audits of accounting documents;

(e)   non-contractual obligations arising out of the relations between the
settlors, trustees and beneficiaries of a trust created voluntarily;

(f)   non-contractual obligations arising out of nuclear damage;

(g)   non-contractual obligations arising out of violations of privacy and rights
relating to personality, including defamation.

3.   This Regulation shall not apply to evidence and procedure, without prejudice to Articles 21 and 22.

4.   For the purposes of this Regulation, 'Member State' shall mean any Member
State other than Denmark.

Article 2. Non-contractual obligations

1.   For the purposes of this Regulation, damage shall cover any consequence
arising out of tort/delict, unjust enrichment, *negotiorum gestio* or *culpa in contrahendo*.

2.   This Regulation shall apply also to non-contractual obligations that are likely
to arise.

3.   Any reference in this Regulation to:

(a)   an event giving rise to damage shall include events giving rise to
damage that are likely to occur; and

(b)   damage shall include damage that is likely to occur.

Article 3. Universal application

Any law specified by this Regulation shall be applied whether or not it is the law
of a Member State.

CHAPTER II
TORTS/DELICTS

Article 4. General rule
1.   Unless otherwise provided for in this Regulation, the law applicable to a non-contractual obligation arising out of a tort/delict shall be the law of the country in which the damage occurs irrespective of the country in which the event giving rise to the damage occurred and irrespective of the country or countries in which the indirect consequences of that event occur.
2.   However, where the person claimed to be liable and the person sustaining damage both have their habitual residence in the same country at the time when the damage occurs, the law of that country shall apply.
3.   Where it is clear from all the circumstances of the case that the tort/delict is manifestly more closely connected with a country other than that indicated in paragraphs 1 or 2, the law of that other country shall apply. A manifestly closer connection with another country might be based in particular on a pre-existing relationship between the parties, such as a contract, that is closely connected with the tort/delict in question.

Article 5. Product liability
1.   Without prejudice to Article 4(2), the law applicable to a non-contractual obligation arising out of damage caused by a product shall be:
    (a)   the law of the country in which the person sustaining the damage had his or her habitual residence when the damage occurred, if the product was marketed in that country; or, failing that,
    (b)   the law of the country in which the product was acquired, if the product was marketed in that country; or, failing that,
    (c)   the law of the country in which the damage occurred, if the product was marketed in that country.
However, the law applicable shall be the law of the country in which the person claimed to be liable is habitually resident if he or she could not reasonably foresee the marketing of the product, or a product of the same type, in the country the law of which is applicable under (a), (b) or (c).
2.   Where it is clear from all the circumstances of the case that the tort/delict is manifestly more closely connected with a country other than that indicated in paragraph 1, the law of that other country shall apply. A manifestly closer connection with another country might be based in particular on a pre-existing relationship between the parties, such as a contract, that is closely connected with the tort/delict in question.

Article 6. Unfair competition and acts restricting free competition
1.   The law applicable to a non-contractual obligation arising out of an act of unfair competition shall be the law of the country where competitive relations or the collective interests of consumers are, or are likely to be, affected.
2.   Where an act of unfair competition affects exclusively the interests of a specific competitor, Article 4 shall apply.
3.   (a) The law applicable to a non-contractual obligation arising out of a restriction of competition shall be the law of the country where the market is, or is likely to be, affected.
    (b)   When the market is, or is likely to be, affected in more than one country, the person seeking compensation for damage who sues in the court of the domicile of the defendant, may instead choose to base his or her claim on the law of the court seised, provided that the market in that Member State is amongst those directly and substantially affected by the restriction of competition out of which the non-contractual obligation on which the claim is based arises; where the claimant sues, in accordance with the applicable rules on jurisdiction, more than one defendant in that court, he or she can only choose to base

his or her claim on the law of that court if the restriction of competition on which the claim against each of these defendants relies directly and substantially affects also the market in the Member State of that court.

4. The law applicable under this Article may not be derogated from by an agreement pursuant to Article 14.

Article 7. Environmental damage

The law applicable to a non-contractual obligation arising out of environmental damage or damage sustained by persons or property as a result of such damage shall be the law determined pursuant to Article 4(1), unless the person seeking compensation for damage chooses to base his or her claim on the law of the country in which the event giving rise to the damage occurred.

Article 8. Infringement of intellectual property rights

1. The law applicable to a non-contractual obligation arising from an infringement of an intellectual property right shall be the law of the country for which protection is claimed.

2. In the case of a non-contractual obligation arising from an infringement of a unitary Community intellectual property right, the law applicable shall, for any question that is not governed by the relevant Community instrument, be the law of the country in which the act of infringement was committed.

3. The law applicable under this Article may not be derogated from by an agreement pursuant to Article 14.

Article 9. Industrial action

Without prejudice to Article 4(2), the law applicable to a non-contractual obligation in respect of the liability of a person in the capacity of a worker or an employer or the organisations representing their professional interests for damages caused by an industrial action, pending or carried out, shall be the law of the country where the action is to be, or has been, taken.

CHAPTER III

UNJUST ENRICHMENT, NEGOTIORUM GESTIO AND CULPA IN CONTRAHENDO

Article 10. Unjust enrichment

1. If a non-contractual obligation arising out of unjust enrichment, including payment of amounts wrongly received, concerns a relationship existing between the parties, such as one arising out of a contract or a tort/delict, that is closely connected with that unjust enrichment, it shall be governed by the law that governs that relationship.

2. Where the law applicable cannot be determined on the basis of paragraph 1 and the parties have their habitual residence in the same country when the event giving rise to unjust enrichment occurs, the law of that country shall apply.

3. Where the law applicable cannot be determined on the basis of paragraphs 1 or 2, it shall be the law of the country in which the unjust enrichment took place.

4. Where it is clear from all the circumstances of the case that the non-contractual obligation arising out of unjust enrichment is manifestly more closely connected with a country other than that indicated in paragraphs 1, 2 and 3, the law of that other country shall apply.

Article 11. Negotiorum gestio

1. If a non-contractual obligation arising out of an act performed without due authority in connection with the affairs of another person concerns a relationship existing between the parties, such as one arising out of a contract or a tort/delict, that is closely connected with that non-contractual obligation, it shall be governed by the law that governs that relationship.

2. Where the law applicable cannot be determined on the basis of paragraph 1,

and the parties have their habitual residence in the same country when the event giving rise to the damage occurs, the law of that country shall apply.

3.   Where the law applicable cannot be determined on the basis of paragraphs 1 or 2, it shall be the law of the country in which the act was performed.

4.   Where it is clear from all the circumstances of the case that the non-contractual obligation arising out of an act performed without due authority in connection with the affairs of another person is manifestly more closely connected with a country other than that indicated in paragraphs 1, 2 and 3, the law of that other country shall apply.

Article 12. Culpa in contrahendo

1.   The law applicable to a non-contractual obligation arising out of dealings prior to the conclusion of a contract, regardless of whether the contract was actually concluded or not, shall be the law that applies to the contract or that would have been applicable to it had it been entered into.

2.   Where the law applicable cannot be determined on the basis of paragraph 1, it shall be:

(a)   the law of the country in which the damage occurs, irrespective of the country in which the event giving rise to the damage occurred and irrespective of the country or countries in which the indirect consequences of that event occurred; or

(b)   where the parties have their habitual residence in the same country at the time when the event giving rise to the damage occurs, the law of that country; or

(c)   where it is clear from all the circumstances of the case that the non-contractual obligation arising out of dealings prior to the conclusion of a contract is manifestly more closely connected with a country other than that indicated in points (a) and (b),the law of that other country.

Article 13. Applicability of Article 8

For the purposes of this Chapter, Article 8 shall apply to non-contractual obligations arising from an infringement of an intellectual property right.

CHAPTER IV
FREEDOM OF CHOICE

Article 14. Freedom of choice

1.   The parties may agree to submit non-contractual obligations to the law of their choice:

(a)   by an agreement entered into after the event giving rise to the damage occurred; or

(b)   where all the parties are pursuing a commercial activity, also by an agreement freely negotiated before the event giving rise to the damage occurred.

The choice shall be expressed or demonstrated with reasonable certainty by the circumstances of the case and shall not prejudice the rights of third parties.

2.   Where all the elements relevant to the situation at the time when the event giving rise to the damage occurs are located in a country other than the country whose law has been chosen, the choice of the parties shall not prejudice the application of provisions of the law of that other country which cannot be derogated from by agreement.

3.   Where all the elements relevant to the situation at the time when the event giving rise to the damage occurs are located in one or more of the Member States, the parties' choice of the law applicable other than that of a Member State shall not prejudice the application of provisions of Community law, where appropriate as implemented in the Member State of the forum, which cannot be derogated from by agreement.

CHAPTER V
COMMON RULES

Article 15. Scope of the law applicable

The law applicable to non-contractual obligations under this Regulation shall govern in particular:

(a)   the basis and extent of liability, including the determination of persons who may be held liable for acts performed by them;

(b)   the grounds for exemption from liability, any limitation of liability and any division of liability;

(c)   the existence, the nature and the assessment of damage or the remedy claimed;

(d)   within the limits of powers conferred on the court by its procedural law, the measures which a court may take to prevent or terminate injury or damage or to ensure the provision of compensation;

(e)   the question whether a right to claim damages or a remedy may be transferred, including by inheritance;

(f)   persons entitled to compensation for damage sustained personally;

(g)   liability for the acts of another person;

(h)   the manner in which an obligation may be extinguished and rules of prescription and limitation, including rules relating to the commencement, interruption and suspension of a period of prescription or limitation.

Article 16. Overriding mandatory provisions

Nothing in this Regulation shall restrict the application of the provisions of the law of the forum in a situation where they are mandatory irrespective of the law otherwise applicable to the non-contractual obligation.

Article 17. Rules of safety and conduct

In assessing the conduct of the person claimed to be liable, account shall be taken, as a matter of fact and in so far as is appropriate, of the rules of safety and conduct which were in force at the place and time of the event giving rise to the liability.

Article 18. Direct action against the insurer of the person liable

The person having suffered damage may bring his or her claim directly against the insurer of the person liable to provide compensation if the law applicable to the non-contractual obligation or the law applicable to the insurance contract so provides.

Article 19. Subrogation

Where a person ('the creditor') has a non-contractual claim upon another ('the debtor'), and a third person has a duty to satisfy the creditor, or has in fact satisfied the creditor in discharge of that duty, the law which governs the third person's duty to satisfy the creditor shall determine whether, and the extent to which, the third person is entitled to exercise against the debtor the rights which the creditor had against the debtor under the law governing their relationship.

Article 20. Multiple liability

If a creditor has a claim against several debtors who are liable for the same claim, and one of the debtors has already satisfied the claim in whole or in part, the question of that debtor's right to demand compensation from the other debtors shall be governed by the law applicable to that debtor's non-contractual obligation towards the creditor.

Article 21. Formal validity

A unilateral act intended to have legal effect and relating to a non-contractual obligation shall be formally valid if it satisfies the formal requirements of the law governing the non-contractual obligation in question or the law of the country in which the act is performed.

Article 22. Burden of proof

1.   The law governing a non-contractual obligation under this Regulation shall apply to the extent that, in matters of non-contractual obligations, it contains rules which raise presumptions of law or determine the burden of proof.

2.   Acts intended to have legal effect may be proved by any mode of proof recognised by the law of the forum or by any of the laws referred to in Article 21 under which that act is formally valid, provided that such mode of proof can be administered by the forum.

CHAPTER VI
OTHER PROVISIONS

Article 23. Habitual residence

1.   For the purposes of this Regulation, the habitual residence of companies and other bodies, corporate or unincorporated, shall be the place of central administration.

Where the event giving rise to the damage occurs, or the damage arises, in the course of operation of a branch, agency or any other establishment, the place where the branch, agency or any other establishment is located shall be treated as the place of habitual residence.

2.   For the purposes of this Regulation, the habitual residence of a natural person acting in the course of his or her business activity shall be his or her principal place of business.

Article 24. Exclusion of renvoi

The application of the law of any country specified by this Regulation means the application of the rules of law in force in that country other than its rules of private international law.

Article 25. States with more than one legal system

1.   Where a State comprises several territorial units, each of which has its own rules of law in respect of non-contractual obligations, each territorial unit shall be considered as a country for the purposes of identifying the law applicable under this Regulation.

2.   A Member State within which different territorial units have their own rules of law in respect of non-contractual obligations shall not be required to apply this Regulation to conflicts solely between the laws of such units.

Article 26. Public policy of the forum

The application of a provision of the law of any country specified by this Regulation may be refused only if such application is manifestly incompatible with the public policy (*ordre public*) of the forum.

Article 27. Relationship with other provisions of Community law

This Regulation shall not prejudice the application of provisions of Community law which, in relation to particular matters, lay down conflict-of-law rules relating to non-contractual obligations.

Article 28. Relationship with existing international conventions

1.   This Regulation shall not prejudice the application of international conventions to which one or more Member States are parties at the time when this Regulation is adopted and which lay down conflict-of-law rules relating to non-contractual obligations.

2.   However, this Regulation shall, as between Member States, take precedence over conventions concluded exclusively between two or more of them in so far as such conventions concern matters governed by this Regulation.

CHAPTER VII
FINAL PROVISIONS

Article 29. List of conventions
1. By 11 July 2008, Member States shall notify the Commission of the conventions referred to in Article 28(1). After that date, Member States shall notify the Commission of all denunciations of such conventions.
2. The Commission shall publish in the *Official Journal of the European Union* within six months of receipt:
>   (i)   a list of the conventions referred to in paragraph 1;
>   (ii) the denunciations referred to in paragraph 1.

Article 30. Review clause
1. Not later than 20 August 2011, the Commission shall submit to the European Parliament, the Council and the European Economic and Social Committee a report on the application of this Regulation. If necessary, the report shall be accompanied by proposals to adapt this Regulation. The report shall include:
>   (i)   a study on the effects of the way in which foreign law is treated in the different jurisdictions and on the extent to which courts in the Member States apply foreign law in practice pursuant to this Regulation;
>   (ii) a study on the effects of Article 28 of this Regulation with respect to the Hague Convention of 4 May 1971 on the law applicable to traffic accidents.
2. Not later than 31 December 2008, the Commission shall submit to the European Parliament, the Council and the European Economic and Social Committee a study on the situation in the field of the law applicable to non-contractual obligations arising out of violations of privacy and rights relating to personality, taking into account rules relating to freedom of the press and freedom of expression in the media, and conflict-of-law issues related to Directive 95/46/EC of the European Parliament and of the Council of 24 October 1995 on the protection of individuals with regard to the processing of personal data and on the free movement of such data.

Article 31. Application in time
This Regulation shall apply to events giving rise to damage which occur after its entry into force.

Article 32. Date of application
This Regulation shall apply from 11 January 2009, except for Article 29, which shall apply from 11 July 2007. This Regulation shall be binding in its entirety and directly applicable in the Member States in accordance with the Treaty establishing the European Community.

Done at Strasbourg, 11 July 2007

PART V

INTERNATIONAL CONVENTIONS

HAGUE CONVENTION ON THE CIVIL ASPECTS OF INTERNATIONAL CHILD ABDUCTION 1980

See Child Abduction and Custody Act 1985, Schedule 1, p 79 above.

HAGUE CONVENTION ON THE LAW APPLICABLE TO TRUSTS AND ON THEIR RECOGNITION 1986

See Recognition of Trusts Act 1987, Schedule, p 102 above.

ROME CONVENTION ON THE LAW APPLICABLE TO CONTRACTUAL OBLIGATIONS

See Contracts (Applicable Law) Act 1990, Schedule 1, p 106 above.

HAGUE CONVENTION ON CHOICE OF COURT AGREEMENTS*

(Concluded 30 June 2005)

CHAPTER I – SCOPE AND DEFINITIONS

Article 1. Scope

1. This Convention shall apply in international cases to exclusive choice of court agreements concluded in civil or commercial matters.

2. For the purposes of Chapter II, a case is international unless the parties are resident in the same Contracting State and the relationship of the parties and all other elements relevant to the dispute, regardless of the location of the chosen court, are connected only with that State.

3. For the purposes of Chapter III, a case is international where recognition or enforcement of a foreign judgment is sought.

Article 2. Exclusions from scope

1. This Convention shall not apply to exclusive choice of court agreements—
    (a)   to which a natural person acting primarily for personal, family or household purposes (a consumer) is a party;
    (b)   relating to contracts of employment, including collective agreements.

2. This Convention shall not apply to the following matters—
    (a)   the status and legal capacity of natural persons;
    (b)   maintenance obligations;
    (c)   other family law matters, including matrimonial property regimes and other rights or obligations arising out of marriage or similar relationships;
    (d)   wills and succession;
    (e)   insolvency, composition and analogous matters;
    (f)   the carriage of passengers and goods;
    (g)   marine pollution, limitation of liability for maritime claims, general average, and emergency towage and salvage;
    (h)   anti-trust (competition) matters;

* © Hague Conference on Private International Law.

291

(i)   liability for nuclear damage;
(j)   claims for personal injury brought by or on behalf of natural persons;
(k)   tort or delict claims for damage to tangible property that do not arise from a contractual relationship;
(l)   rights *in rem* in immovable property, and tenancies of immovable property;
(m)   the validity, nullity, or dissolution of legal persons, and the validity of decisions of their organs;
(n)   the validity of intellectual property rights other than copyright and related rights;
(o)   infringement of intellectual property rights other than copyright and related rights, except where infringement proceedings are brought for breach of a contract between the parties relating to such rights, or could have been brought for breach of that contract;
(p)   the validity of entries in public registers.

3.   Notwithstanding paragraph 2, proceedings are not excluded from the scope of this Convention where a matter excluded under that paragraph arises merely as a preliminary question and not as an object of the proceedings. In particular, the mere fact that a matter excluded under paragraph 2 arises by way of defence does not exclude proceedings from the Convention, if that matter is not an object of the proceedings.

4.   This Convention shall not apply to arbitration and related proceedings.

5.   Proceedings are not excluded from the scope of this Convention by the mere fact that a State, including a government, a governmental agency or any person acting for a State, is a party thereto.

6.   Nothing in this Convention shall affect privileges and immunities of States or of international organisations, in respect of themselves and of their property.

Article 3. Exclusive choice of court agreements
For the purposes of this Convention—
(a)   "exclusive choice of court agreement" means an agreement concluded by two or more parties that meets the requirements of paragraph *c)* and designates, for the purpose of deciding disputes which have arisen or may arise in connection with a particular legal relationship, the courts of one Contracting State or one or more specific courts of one Contracting State to the exclusion of the jurisdiction of any other courts;
(b)   a choice of court agreement which designates the courts of one Contracting State or one or more specific courts of one Contracting State shall be deemed to be exclusive unless the parties have expressly provided otherwise;
(c)   an exclusive choice of court agreement must be concluded or documented—
(i)   in writing; or
(ii)   by any other means of communication which renders information accessible so as to be usable for subsequent reference;
(d)   an exclusive choice of court agreement that forms part of a contract shall be treated as an agreement independent of the other terms of the contract. The validity of the exclusive choice of court agreement cannot be contested solely on the ground that the contract is not valid.

Article 4. Other definitions
1.   In this Convention, "judgment" means any decision on the merits given by a court, whatever it may be called, including a decree or order, and a determination of costs or expenses by the court (including an officer of the court), provided that the determination relates to a decision on the merits which may be recognised or enforced under this Convention. An interim measure of protection is not a judgment.

2.   For the purposes of this Convention, an entity or person other than a natural person shall be considered to be resident in the State—
    (a)   where it has its statutory seat;
    (b)   under whose law it was incorporated or formed;
    (c)   where it has its central administration; or
    (d)   where it has its principal place of business.

CHAPTER II – JURISDICTION

Article 5 Jurisdiction of the chosen court
1.   The court or courts of a Contracting State designated in an exclusive choice of court agreement shall have jurisdiction to decide a dispute to which the agreement applies, unless the agreement is null and void under the law of that State.
2.   A court that has jurisdiction under paragraph 1 shall not decline to exercise jurisdiction on the ground that the dispute should be decided in a court of another State.
3.   The preceding paragraphs shall not affect rules—
    (a)   on jurisdiction related to subject matter or to the value of the claim;
    (b)   on the internal allocation of jurisdiction among the courts of a Contracting State.
However, where the chosen court has discretion as to whether to transfer a case, due consideration should be given to the choice of the parties.

Article 6. Obligations of a court not chosen
A court of a Contracting State other than that of the chosen court shall suspend or dismiss proceedings to which an exclusive choice of court agreement applies unless—
    (a)   the agreement is null and void under the law of the State of the chosen court;
    (b)   a party lacked the capacity to conclude the agreement under the law of the State of the court seised;
    (c)   giving effect to the agreement would lead to a manifest injustice or would be manifestly contrary to the public policy of the State of the court seised;
    (d)   for exceptional reasons beyond the control of the parties, the agreement cannot reasonably be performed; or
    (e)   the chosen court has decided not to hear the case.

Article 7. Interim measures of protection
Interim measures of protection are not governed by this Convention. This Convention neither requires nor precludes the grant, refusal or termination of interim measures of protection by a court of a Contracting State and does not affect whether or not a party may request or a court should grant, refuse or terminate such measures.

CHAPTER III – RECOGNITION AND ENFORCEMENT

Article 8 Recognition and enforcement
1.   A judgment given by a court of a Contracting State designated in an exclusive choice of court agreement shall be recognised and enforced in other Contracting States in accordance with this Chapter. Recognition or enforcement may be refused only on the grounds specified in this Convention.
2.   Without prejudice to such review as is necessary for the application of the provisions of this Chapter, there shall be no review of the merits of the judgment given by the court of origin. The court addressed shall be bound by the findings of fact on which the court of origin based its jurisdiction, unless the judgment was given by default.
3.   A judgment shall be recognised only if it has effect in the State of origin, and shall be enforced only if it is enforceable in the State of origin.

4.   Recognition or enforcement may be postponed or refused if the judgment is the subject of review in the State of origin or if the time limit for seeking ordinary review has not expired. A refusal does not prevent a subsequent application for recognition or enforcement of the judgment.

5.   This Article shall also apply to a judgment given by a court of a Contracting State pursuant to a transfer of the case from the chosen court in that Contracting State as permitted by Article 5, paragraph 3. However, where the chosen court had discretion as to whether to transfer the case to another court, recognition or enforcement of the judgment may be refused against a party who objected to the transfer in a timely manner in the State of origin.

Article 9. Refusal of recognition or enforcement
Recognition or enforcement may be refused if—
(a)   the agreement was null and void under the law of the State of the chosen court, unless the chosen court has determined that the agreement is valid;
(b)   a party lacked the capacity to conclude the agreement under the law of the requested State;
(c)   the document which instituted the proceedings or an equivalent document, including the essential elements of the claim,
(i)   was not notified to the defendant in sufficient time and in such a way as to enable him to arrange for his defence, unless the defendant entered an appearance and presented his case without contesting notification in the court of origin, provided that the law of the State of origin permitted notification to be contested; or
(ii)   was notified to the defendant in the requested State in a manner that is incompatible with fundamental principles of the requested State concerning service of documents;
(d)   the judgment was obtained by fraud in connection with a matter of procedure;
(e)   recognition or enforcement would be manifestly incompatible with the public policy of the requested State, including situations where the specific proceedings leading to the judgment were incompatible with fundamental principles of procedural fairness of that State;
(f)   the judgment is inconsistent with a judgment given in the requested State in a dispute between the same parties; or
(g)   the judgment is inconsistent with an earlier judgment given in another State between the same parties on the same cause of action, provided that the earlier judgment fulfils the conditions necessary for its recognition in the requested State.

Article 10. Preliminary questions
1.   Where a matter excluded under Article 2, paragraph 2, or under Article 21, arose as a preliminary question, the ruling on that question shall not be recognised or enforced under this Convention.

2.   Recognition or enforcement of a judgment may be refused if, and to the extent that, the judgment was based on a ruling on a matter excluded under Article 2, paragraph 2.

3.   However, in the case of a ruling on the validity of an intellectual property right other than copyright or a related right, recognition or enforcement of a judgment may be refused or postponed under the preceding paragraph only where—
(a)   that ruling is inconsistent with a judgment or a decision of a competent authority on that matter given in the State under the law of which the intellectual property right arose; or
(b)   proceedings concerning the validity of the intellectual property right are pending in that State.

4.   Recognition or enforcement of a judgment may be refused if, and to the

extent that, the judgment was based on a ruling on a matter excluded pursuant to a declaration made by the requested State under Article 21.

Article 11. Damages
1.   Recognition or enforcement of a judgment may be refused if, and to the extent that, the judgment awards damages, including exemplary or punitive damages, that do not compensate a party for actual loss or harm suffered.
2.   The court addressed shall take into account whether and to what extent the damages awarded by the court of origin serve to cover costs and expenses relating to the proceedings.

Article 12. Judicial settlements (transactions judiciaires)
Judicial settlements (*transactions judiciaires*) which a court of a Contracting State designated in an exclusive choice of court agreement has approved, or which have been concluded before that court in the course of proceedings, and which are enforceable in the same manner as a judgment in the State of origin, shall be enforced under this Convention in the same manner as a judgment.

Article 13. Documents to be produced
1.   The party seeking recognition or applying for enforcement shall produce—
   (a)   a complete and certified copy of the judgment;
   (b)   the exclusive choice of court agreement, a certified copy thereof, or other evidence of its existence;
   (c)   if the judgment was given by default, the original or a certified copy of a document establishing that the document which instituted the proceedings or an equivalent document was notified to the defaulting party;
   (d)   any documents necessary to establish that the judgment has effect or, where applicable, is enforceable in the State of origin;
   (e)   in the case referred to in Article 12, a certificate of a court of the State of origin that the judicial settlement or a part of it is enforceable in the same manner as a judgment in the State of origin.
2.   If the terms of the judgment do not permit the court addressed to verify whether the conditions of this Chapter have been complied with, that court may require any necessary documents.
3.   An application for recognition or enforcement may be accompanied by a document, issued by a court (including an officer of the court) of the State of origin, in the form recommended and published by the Hague Conference on Private International Law.
4.   If the documents referred to in this Article are not in an official language of the requested State, they shall be accompanied by a certified translation into an official language, unless the law of the requested State provides otherwise.

Article 14. Procedure
The procedure for recognition, declaration of enforceability or registration for enforcement, and the enforcement of the judgment, are governed by the law of the requested State unless this Convention provides otherwise. The court addressed shall act expeditiously.

Article 15. Severability
Recognition or enforcement of a severable part of a judgment shall be granted where recognition or enforcement of that part is applied for, or only part of the judgment is capable of being recognised or enforced under this Convention.

CHAPTER IV – GENERAL CLAUSES

Article 16. Transitional provisions
1.   This Convention shall apply to exclusive choice of court agreements concluded after its entry into force for the State of the chosen court.

2.　This Convention shall not apply to proceedings instituted before its entry into force for the State of the court seised.

Article 17. Contracts of insurance and reinsurance
1.　Proceedings under a contract of insurance or reinsurance are not excluded from the scope of this Convention on the ground that the contract of insurance or reinsurance relates to a matter to which this Convention does not apply.

2.　Recognition and enforcement of a judgment in respect of liability under the terms of a contract of insurance or reinsurance may not be limited or refused on the ground that the liability under that contract includes liability to indemnify the insured or reinsured in respect of—
　　(a)　a matter to which this Convention does not apply; or
　　(b)　an award of damages to which Article 11 might apply.

...

Article 19. Declarations limiting jurisdiction
A State may declare that its courts may refuse to determine disputes to which an exclusive choice of court agreement applies if, except for the location of the chosen court, there is no connection between that State and the parties or the dispute.

Article 20. Declarations limiting recognition and enforcement
A State may declare that its courts may refuse to recognise or enforce a judgment given by a court of another Contracting State if the parties were resident in the requested State, and the relationship of the parties and all other elements relevant to the dispute, other than the location of the chosen court, were connected only with the requested State.

Article 21. Declarations with respect to specific matters
1.　Where a State has a strong interest in not applying this Convention to a specific matter, that State may declare that it will not apply the Convention to that matter. The State making such a declaration shall ensure that the declaration is no broader than necessary and that the specific matter excluded is clearly and precisely defined.

2.　With regard to that matter, the Convention shall not apply—
　　(a)　in the Contracting State that made the declaration;
　　(b)　in other Contracting States, where an exclusive choice of court agreement designates the courts, or one or more specific courts, of the State that made the declaration.

Article 22. Reciprocal declarations on non-exclusive choice of court agreements
1.　A Contracting State may declare that its courts will recognise and enforce judgments given by courts of other Contracting States designated in a choice of court agreement concluded by two or more parties that meets the requirements of Article 3, paragraph c), and designates, for the purpose of deciding disputes which have arisen or may arise in connection with a particular legal relationship, a court or courts of one or more Contracting States (a non-exclusive choice of court agreement).

2.　Where recognition or enforcement of a judgment given in a Contracting State that has made such a declaration is sought in another Contracting State that has made such a declaration, the judgment shall be recognised and enforced under this Convention, if—
　　(a)　the court of origin was designated in a non-exclusive choice of court agreement;
　　(b)　there exists neither a judgment given by any other court before which proceedings could be brought in accordance with the non-exclusive choice of court agreement, nor a proceeding pending between the same parties in any other such court on the same cause of action; and
　　(c)　the court of origin was the court first seised.

Article 23. Uniform interpretation
In the interpretation of this Convention, regard shall be had to its international character and to the need to promote uniformity in its application.

Article 24. Review of operation of the Convention
The Secretary General of the Hague Conference on Private International Law shall at regular intervals make arrangements for—
   (a)   review of the operation of this Convention, including any declarations; and
   (b)   consideration of whether any amendments to this Convention are desirable.

Article 25. Non-unified legal systems
   1.   In relation to a Contracting State in which two or more systems of law apply in different territorial units with regard to any matter dealt with in this Convention——
   (a)   any reference to the law or procedure of a State shall be construed as referring, where appropriate, to the law or procedure in force in the relevant territorial unit;
   (b)   any reference to residence in a State shall be construed as referring, where appropriate, to residence in the relevant territorial unit;
   (c)   any reference to the court or courts of a State shall be construed as referring, where appropriate, to the court or courts in the relevant territorial unit;
   (d)   any reference to a connection with a State shall be construed as referring, where appropriate, to a connection with the relevant territorial unit.
   2.   Notwithstanding the preceding paragraph, a Contracting State with two or more territorial units in which different systems of law apply shall not be bound to apply this Convention to situations which involve solely such different territorial units.
   3.   A court in a territorial unit of a Contracting State with two or more territorial units in which different systems of law apply shall not be bound to recognise or enforce a judgment from another Contracting State solely because the judgment has been recognised or enforced in another territorial unit of the same Contracting State under this Convention.
   4.   This Article shall not apply to a Regional Economic Integration Organisation.

Article 26. Relationship with other international instruments
   1.   This Convention shall be interpreted so far as possible to be compatible with other treaties in force for Contracting States, whether concluded before or after this Convention.
   2.   This Convention shall not affect the application by a Contracting State of a treaty, whether concluded before or after this Convention, in cases where none of the parties is resident in a Contracting State that is not a Party to the treaty.
   3.   This Convention shall not affect the application by a Contracting State of a treaty that was concluded before this Convention entered into force for that Contracting State, if applying this Convention would be inconsistent with the obligations of that Contracting State to any non-Contracting State. This paragraph shall also apply to treaties that revise or replace a treaty concluded before this Convention entered into force for that Contracting State, except to the extent that the revision or replacement creates new inconsistencies with this Convention.
   4.   This Convention shall not affect the application by a Contracting State of a treaty, whether concluded before or after this Convention, for the purposes of obtaining recognition or enforcement of a judgment given by a court of a Contracting State that is also a Party to that treaty. However, the judgment shall not be recognised or enforced to a lesser extent than under this Convention.
   5.   This Convention shall not affect the application by a Contracting State of a treaty which, in relation to a specific matter, governs jurisdiction or the recognition

or enforcement of judgments, even if concluded after this Convention and even if all States concerned are Parties to this Convention. This paragraph shall apply only if the Contracting State has made a declaration in respect of the treaty under this paragraph. In the case of such a declaration, other Contracting States shall not be obliged to apply this Convention to that specific matter to the extent of any inconsistency, where an exclusive choice of court agreement designates the courts, or one or more specific courts, of the Contracting State that made the declaration.

6.   This Convention shall not affect the application of the rules of a Regional Economic Integration Organisation that is a Party to this Convention, whether adopted before or after this Convention—

(a)   where none of the parties is resident in a Contracting State that is not a Member State of the Regional Economic Integration Organisation;

(b)   as concerns the recognition or enforcement of judgments as between Member States of the Regional Economic Integration Organisation.

CHAPTER V – FINAL CLAUSES

Article 28. Declarations with respect to non-unified legal systems

1.   If a State has two or more territorial units in which different systems of law apply in relation to matters dealt with in this Convention, it may at the time of signature, ratification, acceptance, approval or accession declare that the Convention shall extend to all its territorial units or only to one or more of them and may modify this declaration by submitting another declaration at any time.

2.   A declaration shall be notified to the depositary and shall state expressly the territorial units to which the Convention applies.

3.   If a State makes no declaration under this Article, the Convention shall extend to all territorial units of that State.

4.   This Article shall not apply to a Regional Economic Integration Organisation.

Article 29. Regional Economic Integration Organisations

1.   A Regional Economic Integration Organisation which is constituted solely by sovereign States and has competence over some or all of the matters governed by this Convention may similarly sign, accept, approve or accede to this Convention. The Regional Economic Integration Organisation shall in that case have the rights and obligations of a Contracting State, to the extent that the Organisation has competence over matters governed by this Convention.

2.   The Regional Economic Integration Organisation shall, at the time of signature, acceptance, approval or accession, notify the depositary in writing of the matters governed by this Convention in respect of which competence has been transferred to that Organisation by its Member States. The Organisation shall promptly notify the depositary in writing of any changes to its competence as specified in the most recent notice given under this paragraph.

3.   For the purposes of the entry into force of this Convention, any instrument deposited by a Regional Economic Integration Organisation shall not be counted unless the Regional Economic Integration Organisation declares in accordance with Article 30 that its Member States will not be Parties to this Convention.

4.   Any reference to a "Contracting State" or "State" in this Convention shall apply equally, where appropriate, to a Regional Economic Integration Organisation that is a Party to it.

Article 30. Accession by a Regional Economic Integration Organisation without its Member States

1.   At the time of signature, acceptance, approval or accession, a Regional Economic Integration Organisation may declare that it exercises competence over all the matters governed by this Convention and that its Member States will not be Parties to this Convention but shall be bound by virtue of the signature, acceptance, approval or accession of the Organisation.

2. In the event that a declaration is made by a Regional Economic Integration Organisation in accordance with paragraph 1, any reference to a "Contracting State" or "State" in this Convention shall apply equally, where appropriate, to the Member States of the Organisation.

Article 31. Entry into force

1. This Convention shall enter into force on the first day of the month following the expiration of three months after the deposit of the second instrument of ratification, acceptance, approval or accession referred to in Article 27.

2. Thereafter this Convention shall enter into force—

(a) for each State or Regional Economic Integration Organisation subsequently ratifying, accepting, approving or acceding to it, on the first day of the month following the expiration of three months after the deposit of its instrument of ratification, acceptance, approval or accession;

(b) for a territorial unit to which this Convention has been extended in accordance with Article 28, paragraph 1, on the first day of the month following the expiration of three months after the notification of the declaration referred to in that Article.

Article 32. Declarations

1. Declarations referred to in Articles 19, 20, 21, 22 and 26 may be made upon signature, ratification, acceptance, approval or accession or at any time thereafter, and may be modified or withdrawn at any time.

2. Declarations, modifications and withdrawals shall be notified to the depositary.

3. A declaration made at the time of signature, ratification, acceptance, approval or accession shall take effect simultaneously with the entry into force of this Convention for the State concerned.

4. A declaration made at a subsequent time, and any modification or withdrawal of a declaration, shall take effect on the first day of the month following the expiration of three months after the date on which the notification is received by the depositary.

5. A declaration under Articles 19, 20, 21 and 26 shall not apply to exclusive choice of court agreements concluded before it takes effect.

Article 33. Denunciation

1. This Convention may be denounced by notification in writing to the depositary. The denunciation may be limited to certain territorial units of a non-unified legal system to which this Convention applies.

2. The denunciation shall take effect on the first day of the month following the expiration of twelve months after the date on which the notification is received by the depositary. Where a longer period for the denunciation to take effect is specified in the notification, the denunciation shall take effect upon the expiration of such longer period after the date on which the notification is received by the depositary.

PART VI

DRAFT MATERIAL

THE LUGANO CONVENTION

At the date of going to press the Lugano Convention, which forms Schedule 3C to the Civil Jurisdiction and Judgments Act 1982, was undergoing revision. The version given below, dated 28 March 2007, was the most up-to-date available for inclusion in this volume.

CONVENTION ON JURISDICTION AND THE ENFORCEMENT OF JUDGMENTS IN CIVIL AND COMMERCIAL MATTERS

Done at Lugano on ...

PREAMBLE

THE HIGH CONTRACTING PARTIES TO THIS CONVENTION

DETERMINED to strengthen in their territories the legal protection of persons therein established,

CONSIDERING that it is necessary for this purpose to determine the international jurisdiction of the courts, to facilitate recognition, and to introduce an expeditious procedure for securing the enforcement of judgments, authentic instruments and court settlements,

AWARE OF the links between them, which have been sanctioned in the economic field by the free trade agreements concluded between the European Community and certain States members of the European Free Trade Association,

TAKING INTO ACCOUNT:
 – the Brussels Convention of 27 September 1968 on jurisdiction and the enforcement of judgments in civil and commercial matters, as amended by the Accession Conventions under the successive enlargements of the European Union;
 – the Lugano Convention of 16 September 1988 on jurisdiction and the enforcement of judgments in civil and commercial matters, which extends the application of the rules of the 1968 Brussels Convention to certain States members of the European Free Trade Association;
 – Council Regulation (EC) No 44/2001 of 22 December 2000 on jurisdiction and the recognition and enforcement of judgments in civil and commercial matters, which has replaced the above-mentioned Brussels Convention;
 – the Agreement between the European Community and the Kingdom of Denmark on jurisdiction and the recognition and enforcement of judgments in civil and commercial matters, signed at Brussels on 19 October 2005;

PERSUADED that the extension of the principles laid down in Regulation (EC) No 44/2001 to the Contracting Parties to this instrument will strengthen legal and economic cooperation,

DESIRING to ensure as uniform an interpretation as possible of this instrument,

HAVE in this spirit DECIDED to conclude this Convention, and

HAVE AGREED AS FOLLOWS:

TITLE I
SCOPE

Article 1

1. This Convention shall apply in civil and commercial matters whatever the nature of the court or tribunal. It shall not extend, in particular, to revenue, customs or administrative matters.

2. The Convention shall not apply to:

(a)   the status or legal capacity of natural persons, rights in property arising out of a matrimonial relationship, wills and succession;

(b)   bankruptcy, proceedings relating to the winding-up of insolvent companies or other legal persons, judicial arrangements, compositions and analogous proceedings;

(c)   social security;

(d)   arbitration.

3. In this Convention, the term 'State bound by this Convention' shall mean any State that is a Contracting Party to this Convention or a Member State of the European Community. It may also mean the European Community.

TITLE II
JURISDICTION

Section 1
General provisions

Article 2

1. Subject to the provisions of this Convention, persons domiciled in a State bound by this Convention shall, whatever their nationality, be sued in the courts of that State.

2. Persons who are not nationals of the State bound by this Convention in which they are domiciled shall be governed by the rules of jurisdiction applicable to nationals of that State.

Article 3

1. Persons domiciled in a State bound by this Convention may be sued in the courts of another State bound by this Convention only by virtue of the rules set out in Sections 2 to 7 of this Title.

2. In particular the rules of national jurisdiction set out in Annex I shall not be applicable as against them.

Article 4

1. If the defendant is not domiciled in a State bound by this Convention, the jurisdiction of the courts of each State bound by this Convention shall, subject to the provisions of Articles 22 and 23, be determined by the law of that State.

2. As against such a defendant, any person domiciled in a State bound by this Convention may, whatever his nationality, avail himself in that State of the rules of jurisdiction there in force, and in particular those specified in Annex I, in the same way as the nationals of that State.

Section 2
Special jurisdiction

Article 5

A person domiciled in a State bound by this Convention may, in another State bound by this Convention, be sued:

1.   (a)   in matters relating to a contract, in the courts for the place of performance of the obligation in question;

    (b)   for the purpose of this provision and unless otherwise agreed, the place of performance of the obligation in question shall be:

        – in the case of the sale of goods, the place in a State bound by this Convention where, under the contract, the goods were delivered or should have been delivered,

        – in the case of the provision of services, the place in a State bound by this Convention where, under the contract, the services were provided or should have been provided;

    (c)   if subparagraph (b) does not apply then subparagraph (a) applies;

2.   in matters relating to maintenance,

    (a)   in the courts for the place where the maintenance creditor is domiciled or habitually resident, or

    (b)   in the court which, according to its own law, has jurisdiction to entertain proceedings concerning the status of a person if the matter relating to maintenance is ancillary to those proceedings, unless that jurisdiction is based solely on the nationality of one of the parties, or

    (c)   in the court which, according to its own law, has jurisdiction to entertain proceedings concerning parental responsibility, if the matter relating to maintenance is ancillary to those proceedings, unless that jurisdiction is based solely on the nationality of one of the parties;

3.   in matters relating to tort, *delict* or *quasi-delict*, in the courts for the place where the harmful event occurred or may occur;

4.   as regards a civil claim for damages or restitution which is based on an act giving rise to criminal proceedings, in the court seised of those proceedings, to the extent that that court has jurisdiction under its own law to entertain civil proceedings;

5.   as regards a dispute arising out of the operations of a branch, agency or other establishment, in the courts for the place in which the branch, agency or other establishment is situated;

6.   as settlor, trustee or beneficiary of a trust created by the operation of a statute, or by a written instrument, or created orally and evidenced in writing, in the courts of the State bound by this Convention in which the trust is domiciled;

7.   as regards a dispute concerning the payment of remuneration claimed in respect of the salvage of a cargo or freight, in the court under the authority of which the cargo or freight in question:

    (a)   has been arrested to secure such payment, or

    (b)   could have been so arrested, but bail or other security has been given,

provided that this provision shall apply only if it is claimed that the defendant has an interest in the cargo or freight or had such an interest at the time of salvage.

Article 6

A person domiciled in a State bound by this Convention may also be sued:

1.   where he is one of a number of defendants, in the courts for the place where any one of them is domiciled, provided the claims are so closely connected that it is expedient to hear and determine them together to avoid the risk of irreconcilable judgments resulting from separate proceedings;

2.   as a third party in an action on a warranty or guarantee or in any other third party proceedings, in the court seised of the original proceedings, unless these were instituted solely with the object of removing him from the jurisdiction of the court which would be competent in his case;

3.   on a counter-claim arising from the same contract or facts on which the original claim was based, in the court in which the original claim is pending;

4.   in matters relating to a contract, if the action may be combined with an action against the same defendant in matters relating to rights *in rem* in immovable

property, in the court of the State bound by this Convention in which the property is situated.

Article 7
Where by virtue of this Convention a court of a State bound by this Convention has jurisdiction in actions relating to liability from the use or operation of a ship, that court, or any other court substituted for this purpose by the internal law of that State, shall also have jurisdiction over claims for limitation of such liability.

Section 3
Jurisdiction in matters relating to insurance

Article 8
In matters relating to insurance, jurisdiction shall be determined by this Section, without prejudice to Articles 4 and 5(5).

Article 9
1. An insurer domiciled in a State bound by this Convention may be sued:
   (a) in the courts of the State where he is domiciled, or
   (b) in another State bound by this Convention, in the case of actions brought by the policyholder, the insured or a beneficiary, in the courts for the place where the plaintiff is domiciled, or
   (c) if he is a co-insurer, in the courts of a State bound by this Convention in which proceedings are brought against the leading insurer.
2. An insurer who is not domiciled in a State bound by this Convention but has a branch, agency or other establishment in one of the States bound by this Convention shall, in disputes arising out of the operations of the branch, agency or establishment, be deemed to be domiciled in that State.

Article 10
In respect of liability insurance or insurance of immovable property, the insurer may in addition be sued in the courts for the place where the harmful event occurred. The same applies if movable and immovable property are covered by the same insurance policy and both are adversely affected by the same contingency.

Article 11
1. In respect of liability insurance, the insurer may also, if the law of the court permits it, be joined in proceedings which the injured party has brought against the insured.
2. Articles 8, 9 and 10 shall apply to actions brought by the injured party directly against the insurer, where such direct actions are permitted.
3. If the law governing such direct actions provides that the policyholder or the insured may be joined as a party to the action, the same court shall have jurisdiction over them.

Article 12
1. Without prejudice to Article 11(3), an insurer may bring proceedings only in the courts of the State bound by this Convention in which the defendant is domiciled, irrespective of whether he is the policyholder, the insured or a beneficiary.
2. The provisions of this Section shall not affect the right to bring a counterclaim in the court in which, in accordance with this Section, the original claim is pending.

Article 13
The provisions of this Section may be departed from only by an agreement:
1. which is entered into after the dispute has arisen, or
2. which allows the policyholder, the insured or a beneficiary to bring proceedings in courts other than those indicated in this Section, or
3. which is concluded between a policyholder and an insurer, both of whom

are at the time of conclusion of the contract domiciled or habitually resident in the same State bound by this Convention, and which has the effect of conferring jurisdiction on the courts of that State even if the harmful event were to occur abroad, provided that such an agreement is not contrary to the law of that State, or

4.   which is concluded with a policyholder who is not domiciled in a State bound by this Convention, except in so far as the insurance is compulsory or relates to immovable property in a State bound by this Convention, or

5.   which relates to a contract of insurance in so far as it covers one or more of the risks set out in Article 14.

Article 14
The following are the risks referred to in Article 13(5):

1.   any loss of or damage to:
   (a)   seagoing ships, installations situated offshore or on the high seas, or aircraft, arising from perils which relate to their use for commercial purposes;
   (b)   goods in transit other than passengers' baggage where the transit consists of or includes carriage by such ships or aircraft;

2.   any liability, other than for bodily injury to passengers or loss of or damage to their baggage:
   (a)   arising out of the use or operation of ships, installations or aircraft as referred to in point 1(a) in so far as, in respect of the latter, the law of the State bound by this Convention in which such aircraft are registered does not prohibit agreements on jurisdiction regarding insurance of such risks;
   (b)   for loss or damage caused by goods in transit as described in point 1(b);

3.   any financial loss connected with the use or operation of ships, installations or aircraft as referred to in point 1(a), in particular loss of freight or charter-hire;

4.   any risk or interest connected with any of those referred to in points 1 to 3;

5.   notwithstanding points 1 to 4, all large risks.

Section 4
Jurisdiction over consumer contracts

Article 15
1.   In matters relating to a contract concluded by a person, the consumer, for a purpose which can be regarded as being outside his trade or profession, jurisdiction shall be determined by this Section, without prejudice to Articles 4 and 5(5), if:
   (a)   it is a contract for the sale of goods on instalment credit terms, or
   (b)   it is a contract for a loan repayable by instalments, or for any other form of credit, made to finance the sale of goods, or
   (c)   in all other cases, the contract has been concluded with a person who pursues commercial or professional activities in the State bound by this Convention of the consumer's domicile or, by any means, directs such activities to that State or to several States including that State, and the contract falls within the scope of such activities.

2.   Where a consumer enters into a contract with a party who is not domiciled in the State bound by this Convention but has a branch, agency or other establishment in one of the States bound by this Convention, that party shall, in disputes arising out of the operations of the branch, agency or establishment, be deemed to be domiciled in that State.

3.   This section shall not apply to a contract of transport other than a contract which, for an inclusive price, provides for a combination of travel and accommodation.

Article 16
1.   A consumer may bring proceedings against the other party to a contract

either in the courts of the State bound by this Convention in which that party is domiciled or in the courts for the place where the consumer is domiciled.

2.   Proceedings may be brought against a consumer by the other party to the contract only in the courts of the State bound by this Convention in which the consumer is domiciled.

3.   This Article shall not affect the right to bring a counter-claim in the court in which, in accordance with this Section, the original claim is pending.

Article 17
The provisions of this Section may be departed from only by an agreement:
   1.   which is entered into after the dispute has arisen, or
   2.   which allows the consumer to bring proceedings in courts other than those indicated in this Section, or
   3.   which is entered into by the consumer and the other party to the contract, both of whom are at the time of conclusion of the contract domiciled or habitually resident in the same State bound by this Convention, and which confers jurisdiction on the courts of that State, provided that such an agreement is not contrary to the law of that State.

Section 5
Jurisdiction over individual contracts of employment

Article 18
   1.   In matters relating to individual contracts of employment, jurisdiction shall be determined by this Section, without prejudice to Articles 4 and 5(5).
   2.   Where an employee enters into an individual contract of employment with an employer who is not domiciled in a State bound by this Convention but has a branch, agency or other establishment in one of the States bound by this Convention, the employer shall, in disputes arising out of the operations of the branch, agency or establishment, be deemed to be domiciled in that State.

Article 19
An employer domiciled in a State bound by this Convention may be sued:
   1.   in the courts of the State where he is domiciled, or
   2.   in another State bound by this Convention:
   (a)   in the courts for the place where the employee habitually carries out his work or in the courts for the last place where he did so, or
   (b)   if the employee does not or did not habitually carry out his work in any one country, in the courts for the place where the business which engaged the employee is or was situated.

Article 20
   1.   An employer may bring proceedings only in the courts of the State bound by this Convention in which the employee is domiciled.
   2.   The provisions of this Section shall not affect the right to bring a counter-claim in the court in which, in accordance with this Section, the original claim is pending.

Article 21
The provisions of this Section may be departed from only by an agreement on jurisdiction:
   1.   which is entered into after the dispute has arisen, or
   2.   which allows the employee to bring proceedings in courts other than those indicated in this Section.

Section 6
Exclusive jurisdiction

Article 22

The following courts shall have exclusive jurisdiction, regardless of domicile:

1. in proceedings which have as their object rights *in rem* in immovable property or tenancies of immovable property, the courts of the State bound by this Convention in which the property is situated.

However, in proceedings which have as their object tenancies of immovable property concluded for temporary private use for a maximum period of six consecutive months, the courts of the State bound by this Convention in which the defendant is domiciled shall also have jurisdiction, provided that the tenant is a natural person and that the landlord and the tenant are domiciled in the same State bound by this Convention;

2. in proceedings which have as their object the validity of the constitution, the nullity or the dissolution of companies or other legal persons or associations of natural or legal persons, or of the validity of the decisions of their organs, the courts of the State bound by this Convention in which the company, legal person or association has its seat. In order to determine that seat, the court shall apply its rules of private international law;

3. in proceedings which have as their object the validity of entries in public registers, the courts of the State bound by this Convention in which the register is kept;

4. in proceedings concerned with the registration or validity of patents, trade marks, designs, or other similar rights required to be deposited or registered, irrespective of whether the issue is raised by way of an action or as a defence,1 the courts of the State bound by this Convention in which the deposit or registration has been applied for, has taken place or is under the terms of a Community instrument or an international convention deemed to have taken place.

Without prejudice to the jurisdiction of the European Patent Office under the Convention on the grant of European patents, signed at Munich on 5 October 1973, the courts of each State bound by this Convention shall have exclusive jurisdiction, regardless of domicile, in proceedings concerned with the registration or validity of any European patent granted for that State irrespective of whether the issue is raised by way of an action or as a defence.

5. in proceedings concerned with the enforcement of judgments, the courts of the State bound by this Convention in which the judgment has been or is to be enforced.

Section 7
Prorogation of jurisdiction

Article 23

1. If the parties, one or more of whom is domiciled in a State bound by this Convention, have agreed that a court or the courts of a State bound by this Convention are to have jurisdiction to settle any disputes which have arisen or which may arise in connection with a particular legal relationship, that court or those courts shall have jurisdiction. Such jurisdiction shall be exclusive unless the parties have agreed otherwise. Such an agreement conferring jurisdiction shall be either:

    (a) in writing or evidenced in writing, or

    (b) in a form which accords with practices which the parties have established between themselves, or

    (c) in international trade or commerce, in a form which accords with a usage of which the parties are or ought to have been aware and which in such trade or commerce is widely known to, and regularly observed by, parties to contracts of the type involved in the particular trade or commerce concerned.

2.   Any communication by electronic means which provides a durable record of the agreement shall be equivalent to 'writing'.

3.   Where such an agreement is concluded by parties, none of whom is domiciled in a State bound by this Convention, the courts of other States bound by this Convention shall have no jurisdiction over their disputes unless the court or courts chosen have declined jurisdiction.

4.   The court or courts of a State bound by this Convention on which a trust instrument has conferred jurisdiction shall have exclusive jurisdiction in any proceedings brought against a settlor, trustee or beneficiary, if relations between these persons or their rights or obligations under the trust are involved.

5.   Agreements or provisions of a trust instrument conferring jurisdiction shall have no legal force if they are contrary to the provisions of Articles 13, 17 or 21, or if the courts whose jurisdiction they purport to exclude have exclusive jurisdiction by virtue of Article 22.

Article 24
Apart from jurisdiction derived from other provisions of this Convention, a court of a State bound by this Convention before which a defendant enters an appearance shall have jurisdiction. This rule shall not apply where appearance was entered to contest the jurisdiction, or where another court has exclusive jurisdiction by virtue of Article 22.

Section 8
Examination as to jurisdiction and admissibility

Article 25
Where a court of a State bound by this Convention is seised of a claim which is principally concerned with a matter over which the courts of another State bound by this Convention have exclusive jurisdiction by virtue of Article 22, it shall declare of its own motion that it has no jurisdiction.

Article 26
1.   Where a defendant domiciled in one State bound by this Convention is sued in a court of another State bound by this Convention and does not enter an appearance, the court shall declare of its own motion that it has no jurisdiction unless its jurisdiction is derived from the provisions of this Convention.

2.   The court shall stay the proceedings so long as it is not shown that the defendant has been able to receive the document instituting the proceedings or an equivalent document in sufficient time to enable him to arrange for his defence, or that all necessary steps have been taken to this end.

3.   Instead of the provisions of paragraph 2, Article 15 of the Hague Convention of 15 November 1965 on the Service Abroad of Judicial and Extrajudicial Documents in Civil and Commercial matters shall apply if the document instituting the proceedings or an equivalent document had to be transmitted pursuant to that Convention.

4.   Member States of the European Community bound by Council Regulation (EC) No 1348/2000 of 29 May 2000 or by the Agreement between the European Community and the Kingdom of Denmark on the service of judicial and extra-judicial documents in civil or commercial matters, signed at Brussels on 19 October 2005, shall apply in their mutual relations the provision in Article 19 of that Regulation if the document instituting the proceedings or an equivalent document had to be transmitted pursuant to that Regulation or that Agreement.

Section 9
Lis pendens – related actions

Article 27
1.   Where proceedings involving the same cause of action and between the

same parties are brought in the courts of different States bound by this Convention, any court other than the court first seised shall of its own motion stay its proceedings until such time as the jurisdiction of the court first seised is established.

2.   Where the jurisdiction of the court first seised is established, any court other than the court first seised shall decline jurisdiction in favour of that court.

Article 28

1.   Where related actions are pending in the courts of different States bound by this Convention, any court other than the court first seised may stay its proceedings.

2.   Where these actions are pending at first instance, any court other than the court first seised may also, on the application of one of the parties, decline jurisdiction if the court first seised has jurisdiction over the actions in question and its law permits the consolidation thereof.

3.   For the purposes of this Article, actions are deemed to be related where they are so closely connected that it is expedient to hear and determine them together to avoid the risk of irreconcilable judgments resulting from separate proceedings.

Article 29

Where actions come within the exclusive jurisdiction of several courts, any court other than the court first seised shall decline jurisdiction in favour of that court.

Article 30

For the purposes of this Section, a court shall be deemed to be seised:

1.   at the time when the document instituting the proceedings or an equivalent document is lodged with the court, provided that the plaintiff has not subsequently failed to take the steps he was required to take to have service effected on the defendant, or

2.   if the document has to be served before being lodged with the court at the time when it is received by the authority responsible for service, provided that the plaintiff has not subsequently failed to take the steps he was required to take to have the document lodged with the court.

Section 10
Provisional, including protective, measures

Article 31

Application may be made to the courts of a State bound by this Convention for such provisional, including protective, measures as may be available under the law of that State, even if, under this Convention, the courts of another State bound by this Convention have jurisdiction as to the substance of the matter.

TITLE III
RECOGNITION AND ENFORCEMENT

Article 32

For the purposes of this Convention, 'judgment' means any judgment given by a court or tribunal of a State bound by this Convention, whatever the judgment may be called, including a decree, order, decision or writ of execution, as well as the determination of costs or expenses by an officer of the court.

Section 1
Recognition

Article 33

1.   A judgment given in a State bound by this Convention shall be recognised in the other States bound by this Convention without any special procedure being required.

2.   Any interested party who raises the recognition of a judgment as the principal issue in a dispute may, in accordance with the procedures provided for in Sections 2 and 3 of this Title, apply for a decision that the judgment be recognised.

3.   If the outcome of proceedings in a court of a State bound by this Convention depends on the determination of an incidental question of recognition that court shall have jurisdiction over that question.

Article 34

A judgment shall not be recognised:

1.   if such recognition is manifestly contrary to public policy in the State in which recognition is sought;

2.   where it was given in default of appearance, if the defendant was not served with the document which instituted the proceedings or with an equivalent document in sufficient time and in such a way as to enable him to arrange for his defence, unless the defendant failed to commence proceedings to challenge the judgment when it was possible for him to do so;

3.   if it is irreconcilable with a judgment given in a dispute between the same parties in the State in which recognition is sought;

4.   if it is irreconcilable with an earlier judgment given in another State bound by this Convention or in a third State involving the same cause of action and between the same parties, provided that the earlier judgment fulfils the conditions necessary for its recognition in the State addressed.

Article 35

1.   Moreover, a judgment shall not be recognised if it conflicts with Sections 3, 4 or 6 of Title II, or in a case provided for in Article 68. A judgment may furthermore be refused recognition in any case provided for in Article 64(3) or 67(4).

2.   In its examination of the grounds of jurisdiction referred to in the foregoing paragraph, the court or authority applied to shall be bound by the findings of fact on which the court of the State of origin based its jurisdiction.

3.   Subject to the provisions of paragraphs 1 and 2, the jurisdiction of the court of the State of origin may not be reviewed. The test of public policy referred to in Article 34(1) may not be applied to the rules relating to jurisdiction.

Article 36

Under no circumstances may a foreign judgment be reviewed as to its substance.

Article 37

1.   A court of a State bound by this Convention in which recognition is sought of a judgment given in another State bound by this Convention may stay the proceedings if an ordinary appeal against the judgment has been lodged.

2.   A court of a State bound by this Convention in which recognition is sought of a judgment given in Ireland or the United Kingdom may stay the proceedings if enforcement is suspended in the State of origin, by reason of an appeal.

Section 2

Enforcement

Article 38

1.   A judgment given in a State bound by this Convention and enforceable in that State shall be enforced in another State bound by this Convention when, on the application of any interested party, it has been declared enforceable there.

2.   However, in the United Kingdom, such a judgment shall be enforced in England and Wales, in Scotland, or in Northern Ireland when, on the application of any interested party, it has been registered for enforcement in that part of the United Kingdom.

Article 39

1.   The application shall be submitted to the court or competent authority indicated in the list in Annex II.

2.   The local jurisdiction shall be determined by reference to the place of domicile of the party against whom enforcement is sought, or to the place of enforcement.

Article 40

1.   The procedure for making the application shall be governed by the law of the State in which enforcement is sought.

2.   The applicant must give an address for service of process within the area of jurisdiction of the court applied to. However, if the law of the State in which enforcement is sought does not provide for the furnishing of such an address, the applicant shall appoint a representative *ad litem*.

3.   The documents referred to in Articles 53 shall be attached to the application.

Article 41

The judgment shall be declared enforceable immediately on completion of the formalities in Article 53 without any review under Articles 34 and 35. The party against whom enforcement is sought shall not at this stage of the proceedings be entitled to make any submissions on the application.

Article 42

1.   The decision on the application for a declaration of enforceability shall forthwith be brought to the notice of the applicant in accordance with the procedure laid down by the law of the State in which enforcement is sought.

2.   The declaration of enforceability shall be served on the party against whom enforcement is sought, accompanied by the judgment, if not already served on that party.

Article 43

1.   The decision on the application for a declaration of enforceability may be appealed against by either party.

2.   The appeal is to be lodged with the court indicated in the list in Annex III.

3.   The appeal shall be dealt with in accordance with the rules governing procedure in contradictory matters.

4.   If the party against whom enforcement is sought fails to appear before the appellate court in proceedings concerning an appeal brought by the applicant, Article 26(2) to (4) shall apply even where the party against whom enforcement is sought is not domiciled in any of the States bound by this Convention.

5.   An appeal against the declaration of enforceability is to be lodged within one month of service thereof. If the party against whom enforcement is sought is domiciled in a State bound by this Convention other than that in which the declaration of enforceability was given, the time for appealing shall be two months and shall run from the date of service, either on him in person or at his residence. No extension of time may be granted on account of distance.

Article 44

The judgment given on the appeal may be contested only by the appeal referred to in Annex IV.

Article 45

1.   The court with which an appeal is lodged under Article 43 or 44 shall refuse or revoke a declaration of enforceability only on one of the grounds specified in Articles 34 and 35. It shall give its decision without delay.

2.   Under no circumstances may the foreign judgment be reviewed as to its substance.

Article 46

1. The court with which an appeal is lodged under Article 43 or 44 may, on the application of the party against whom enforcement is sought, stay the proceedings if an ordinary appeal has been lodged against the judgment in the State of origin or if the time for such an appeal has not yet expired; in the latter case, the court may specify the time within which such an appeal is to be lodged.

2. Where the judgment was given in Ireland or the United Kingdom, any form of appeal available in the State of origin shall be treated as an ordinary appeal for the purposes of paragraph 1.

3. The court may also make enforcement conditional on the provision of such security as it shall determine.

Article 47

1. When a judgment must be recognised in accordance with this Convention, nothing shall prevent the applicant from availing himself of provisional, including protective, measures in accordance with the law of the State requested without a declaration of enforceability under Article 41 being required.

2. The declaration of enforceability shall carry with it the power to proceed to any protective measures.

3. During the time specified for an appeal pursuant to Article 43(5) against the declaration of enforceability and until any such appeal has been determined, no measures of enforcement may be taken other than protective measures against the property of the party against whom enforcement is sought.

Article 48

1. Where a foreign judgment has been given in respect of several matters and the declaration of enforceability cannot be given for all of them, the court or competent authority shall give it for one or more of them.

2. An applicant may request a declaration of enforceability limited to parts of a judgment.

Article 49

A foreign judgment which orders a periodic payment by way of a penalty shall be enforceable in the State in which enforcement is sought only if the amount of the payment has been finally determined by the courts of the State of origin.

Article 50

1. An applicant who in the State of origin has benefited from complete or partial legal aid or exemption from costs or expenses shall be entitled, in the procedure provided for in this Section, to benefit from the most favourable legal aid or the most extensive exemption from costs or expenses provided for by the law of the State addressed.

2. However, an applicant who requests the enforcement of a decision given by an administrative authority in Denmark, in Iceland or in Norway in respect of maintenance may, in the State addressed, claim the benefits referred to in paragraph 1 if he presents a statement from the Danish, Icelandic, or Norwegian Ministry of Justice to the effect that he fulfils the economic requirements to qualify for the grant of complete or partial legal aid or exemption from costs or expenses.

Article 51

No security, bond or deposit, however described, shall be required of a party who in one State bound by this Convention, applies for enforcement of a judgment given in another State bound by this Convention on the ground that he is a foreign national or that he is not domiciled or resident in the State in which enforcement is sought.

Article 52

In proceedings for the issue of a declaration of enforceability, no charge, duty or fee calculated by reference to the value of the matter at issue may be levied in the State in which enforcement is sought.

Section 3
Common provisions

Article 53

1.   A party seeking recognition or applying for a declaration of enforceability shall produce a copy of the judgment which satisfies the conditions necessary to establish its authenticity.

2.   A party applying for a declaration of enforceability shall also produce the certificate referred to in Article 54, without prejudice to Article 55.

Article 54

The court or competent authority of a State bound by this Convention where a judgment was given shall issue, at the request of any interested party, a certificate using the standard form in Annex V to this Convention.

Article 55

1.   If the certificate referred to in Article 54 is not produced, the court or competent authority may specify a time for its production or accept an equivalent document or, if it considers that it has sufficient information before it, dispense with its production.

2.   If the court or competent authority so requires, a translation of the documents shall be produced. The translation shall be certified by a person qualified to do so in one of the States bound by this Convention.

Article 56

No legalisation or other similar formality shall be required in respect of the documents referred to in Article 53 or Article 55(2), or in respect of a document appointing a representative *ad litem*.

TITLE IV
AUTHENTIC INSTRUMENTS AND COURT SETTLEMENTS

Article 57

1.   A document which has been formally drawn up or registered as an authentic instrument and is enforceable in one State bound by this Convention shall, in another State bound by this Convention, be declared enforceable there, on application made in accordance with the procedures provided for in Article 38, et seq. The court with which an appeal is lodged under Article 43 or Article 44 shall refuse or revoke a declaration of enforceability only if enforcement of the instrument is manifestly contrary to public policy in the State addressed.

2.   Arrangements relating to maintenance obligations concluded with administrative authorities or authenticated by them shall also be regarded as authentic instruments within the meaning of paragraph 1.

3.   The instrument produced must satisfy the conditions necessary to establish its authenticity in the State of origin.

4.   Section 3 of Title III shall apply as appropriate. The competent authority of a State bound by this Convention where an authentic instrument was drawn up or registered shall issue, at the request of any interested party, a certificate using the standard form in Annex VI to this Convention.

Article 58

A settlement which has been approved by a court in the course of proceedings and is enforceable in the State bound by this Convention in which it was concluded shall be enforceable in the State addressed under the same conditions as authentic instruments. The court or competent authority of a State bound by this Convention where a court settlement was approved shall issue, at the request of any interested party, a certificate using the standard form in Annex V to this Convention.

TITLE V
GENERAL PROVISIONS

Article 59

1. In order to determine whether a party is domiciled in the State bound by this Convention whose courts are seised of a matter, the court shall apply its internal law.

2. If a party is not domiciled in the State whose courts are seised of the matter, then, in order to determine whether the party is domiciled in another State bound by this Convention, the course shall apply the law of that State.

Article 60

1. For the purposes of this Convention, a company or other legal person or association of natural or legal persons is domiciled at the place where it has its:
    (a)   statutory seat, or
    (b)   central administration, or
    (c)   principal place of business.

2. For the purposes of the United Kingdom and Ireland 'statutory seat' means the registered office or, where there is no such office anywhere, the place of incorporation or, where there is no such place anywhere, the place under the law of which the formation took place.

3. In order to determine whether a trust is domiciled in the State bound by this Convention whose courts are seised of the matter, the court shall apply its rules of private international law.

Article 61

Without prejudice to any more favourable provisions of national laws, persons domiciled in a State bound by this Convention who are being prosecuted in the criminal courts of another State bound by this Convention of which they are not nationals for an offence which was not intentionally committed may be defended by persons qualified to do so, even if they do not appear in person. However, the court seised of the matter may order appearance in person; in the case of failure to appear, a judgment given in the civil action without the person concerned having had the opportunity to arrange for his defence need not be recognised or enforced in the other States bound by this Convention.

Article 62

For the purposes of this Convention, the expression 'court' shall include any authorities designated by a State bound by this Convention as having jurisdiction in the matters falling within the scope of this Convention.

TITLE VI
TRANSITIONAL PROVISIONS

Article 63

1. This Convention shall apply only to legal proceedings instituted and to documents formally drawn up or registered as authentic instruments after its entry into force in the State of origin and, where recognition or enforcement of a judgment or authentic instruments is sought, in the State addressed.

2. However, if the proceedings in the State of origin were instituted before the entry into force of this Convention, judgments given after that date shall be recognised and enforced in accordance with Title III:
    (a)   if the proceedings in the State of origin were instituted after the entry into force of the Lugano Convention of 16 September 1988 both in the State of origin and in the State addressed;

(b)   in all other cases, if jurisdiction was founded upon rules which accorded with those provided for either in Title II or in a convention concluded between the State of origin and the State addressed which was in force when the proceedings were instituted.

TITLE VII
RELATIONSHIP TO COUNCIL REGULATION (EC) NO 44/2001 AND OTHER INSTRUMENTS

Article 64
1.   This Convention shall not prejudice the application by the Member States of the European Community of the Council Regulation (EC) No 44/2001 on jurisdiction and the recognition and enforcement of judgments in civil and commercial matters, as well as any amendments thereof, of the Convention on Jurisdiction and the Enforcement of Judgments in Civil and Commercial Matters, signed at Brussels on 27 September 1968, and of the Protocol on interpretation of that Convention by the Court of Justice of the European Communities, signed at Luxembourg on 3 June 1971, as amended by the Conventions of Accession to the said Convention and the said Protocol by the States acceding to the European Communities, as well as of the Agreement between the European Community and the Kingdom of Denmark on jurisdiction and the recognition and enforcement of judgments in civil and commercial matters, signed at Brussels on 19 October 2005.
2.   However, this Convention shall in any event be applied:
(a)   in matters of jurisdiction, where the defendant is domiciled in the territory of a State where this Convention but not an instrument referred to in paragraph 1 of this Article applies, or where Articles 22 or 23 of this Convention confer jurisdiction on the courts of such a State;
(b)   in relation to *lis pendens* or to related actions as provided for in Articles 27 and 28, when proceedings are instituted in a State where the Convention but not an instrument referred to in paragraph 1 of this Article applies and in a State where this Convention as well as an instrument referred to in paragraph 1 of this Article apply;
(c)   in matters of recognition and enforcement, where either the State of origin or the State addressed is not applying an instrument referred to in paragraph 1 of this Article.
3.   In addition to the grounds provided for in Title III, recognition or enforcement may be refused if the ground of jurisdiction on which the judgment has been based differs from that resulting from this Convention and recognition or enforcement is sought against a party who is domiciled in a State where this Convention but not an instrument referred to in paragraph 1 of this Article applies, unless the judgment may otherwise be recognised or enforced under any rule of law in the State addressed.

Article 65
Subject to the provisions of Articles 63(2), 66 and 67, this Convention shall, as between the States bound by this Convention, supersede the conventions concluded between two or more of them that cover the same matters as those to which this Convention applies. In particular, the conventions mentioned in Annex VII are superseded.

Article 66
1.   The conventions referred to in Article 65 shall continue to have effect in relation to matters to which this Convention does not apply.
2.   They shall continue to have effect in respect of judgments given and documents formally drawn up or registered as authentic instruments before the entry into force of this Convention.

Article 67

1.   This Convention shall not affect any conventions by which the Contracting Parties and/or the States bound by this Convention are bound and which in relation to particular matters, govern jurisdiction or the recognition or enforcement of judgments. Without prejudice to obligations resulting from other agreements between certain Contracting Parties, this Convention shall not prevent Contracting Parties from entering into such conventions.

2.   This Convention shall not prevent a court of a State bound by this Convention and by a convention on a particular matter from assuming jurisdiction in accordance with that convention, even where the defendant is domiciled in another State bound by this Convention which is not a party to that convention. The court hearing the action shall, in any event, apply Article 26 of this Convention.

3.   Judgments given in a State bound by this Convention by a court in the exercise of jurisdiction provided for in a convention on a particular matter shall be recognised and enforced in the other States bound by this Convention in accordance with Title III of this Convention.

4.   In addition to the grounds provided for in Title III, recognition or enforcement may be refused if the State addressed is not bound by the convention on a particular matter and the person against whom recognition or enforcement is sought is domiciled in that State, or, if the State addressed is a Member State of the European Community and in respect of conventions which would have to be concluded by the European Community, in any of its Member States, unless the judgment may otherwise be recognised or enforced under any rule of law in the State addressed.

5.   Where a convention on a particular matter to which both the State of origin and the State addressed are parties lays down conditions for the recognition or enforcement of judgments, those conditions shall apply. In any event, the provisions of this Convention which concern the procedures for recognition and enforcement of judgments may be applied.

Article 68

1.   This Convention shall not affect agreements by which States bound by this Convention undertook, prior to the entry into force of this Convention, not to recognise judgments given in other States bound by this Convention against defendants domiciled or habitually resident in a third State where, in cases provided for in Article 4, the judgment could only be founded on a ground of jurisdiction as specified in Article 3(2). Without prejudice to obligations resulting from other agreements between certain Contracting Parties, this Convention shall not prevent Contracting Parties from entering into such conventions.

2.   However, a Contracting Party may not assume an obligation towards a third State not to recognise a judgment given in another State bound by this Convention by a court basing its jurisdiction on the presence within that State of property belonging to the defendant, or the seizure by the plaintiff of property situated there:

  (a)   if the action is brought to assert or declare proprietary or possessory rights in that property, seeks to obtain authority to dispose of it, or arises from another issue relating to such property, or

  (b)   if the property constitutes the security for a debt which is the subject-matter of the action.

TITLE VIII
FINAL PROVISIONS

Article 69

1.   This Convention shall be open for signature by the European Community,

Denmark, and States which, at the time of the opening for signature, are Members of the European Free Trade Association.

2. The Convention shall be subject to ratification by the Signatories. The instruments of ratification shall be deposited with the Swiss Federal Council, which shall act as Depositary of this Convention.

3. At the time of the ratification, the Contracting Parties may submit declarations in accordance with Articles I, II and III of Protocol 1.

4. The Convention shall enter into force on the first day of the sixth month following the date on which the European Community and a Member of the European Free Trade Association deposit their instruments of ratification.

5. The Convention shall enter into force in relation to any other Party on the first day of the third month following the deposit of its instrument of ratification.

6. Without prejudice to Article 3(3) of Protocol 2, this Convention shall replace the Convention on jurisdiction and the enforcement of judgments in civil and commercial matters done at Lugano on 16 September 1988 as of the date of its entry into force in accordance with paragraphs 4 and 5 above. Any reference to the 1988 Lugano Convention in other instruments shall be understood as a reference to this Convention.

7. Insofar as the relations between the Member States of the European Community and the non-European territories referred to in Article 70(1)(b) are concerned, the Convention shall replace the Convention on Jurisdiction and the Enforcement of Judgments in Civil and Commercial Matters, signed at Brussels on 27 September 1968, and of the Protocol on interpretation of that Convention by the Court of Justice of the European Communities, signed at Luxembourg on 3 June 1971, as amended by the Conventions of Accession to the said Convention and the said Protocol by the States acceding to the European Communities, as of the date of the entry into force of this Convention with respect to these territories in accordance with Article 73(2).

Article 70

1. After entering into force this Convention shall be open for accession by:

(a) the States which, after the opening of this Convention for signature, become Members of the European Free Trade Association, under the conditions laid down in Article 71;

(b) Member States of the European Community acting on behalf of certain non-European territories that are part of the territory of that Member State or for whose external relations that Member State is responsible, under the conditions laid down in Article 71;

(c) any other State, under the conditions laid down in Article 72.

2. States referred to in paragraph 1, which wish to become a Contracting Party to this Convention, shall address their application to the Depositary. The application, including the information referred to in Articles 71 and 72 shall be accompanied by a translation into English and French.

Article 71

1. Any State referred to in Article 70(1)(a) and (b) wishing to become a Contracting Party to this Convention

(a) shall communicate the information required for the application of this Convention;

(b) may submit declarations in accordance with Articles I and III of Protocol 1.

2. The Depositary shall transmit any information received pursuant to paragraph 1 to the other Contracting Parties prior to the deposit of the instrument of accession by the State concerned.

Article 72

1. Any State referred to in Article 70(1)(c) wishing to become a Contracting Party to this Convention:

(a) shall communicate the information required for the application of this Convention;

(b) may submit declarations in accordance with Articles I and III of Protocol 1; and

(c) shall provide the Depositary with information on, in particular:

(1) their judicial system, including information on the appointment and independence of judges;

(2) their internal law concerning civil procedure and enforcement of judgments; and

(3) their private international law relating to civil procedure.

2. The Depositary shall transmit any information received pursuant to paragraph 1 to the other Contracting Parties prior to inviting the State concerned to accede in accordance with paragraph 3 of this Article.

3. Without prejudice to paragraph 4, the Depositary shall invite the State concerned to accede only if it has obtained the unanimous agreement of the Contracting Parties. The Contracting Parties shall endeavour to give their consent at the latest within one year after the invitation by the Depositary.

4. The Convention shall enter into force only in relations between the acceding State and the Contracting Parties which have not made any objections to the accession before the first day of the third month following the deposit of the instrument of accession.

Article 73

1. The instruments of accession shall be deposited with the Depositary.

2. In respect of an acceding State referred to in Article 70, the Convention shall enter into force on the first day of the third month following the deposit of its instrument of accession. As of that moment, the acceding State shall be considered a Contracting Party to the Convention.

3. Any Contracting Party may submit to the Depositary a text of this Convention in the language or languages of the Contracting Party concerned, which shall be authentic if so agreed by the Contracting Parties in accordance with Article 4 of Protocol 2.

Article 74

1. This Convention is concluded for an unlimited period.

2. Any Contracting Party may, at any time, denounce the Convention by sending a notification to the Depositary.

3. The denunciation shall take effect at the end of the calendar year following the expiry of a period of six months from the date of receipt by the Depositary of the notification of denunciation.

Article 75

The following are annexed to this Convention:

– a Protocol 1, on certain questions of jurisdiction, procedure and enforcement;

– a Protocol 2, on the uniform interpretation of this Convention and on the Standing Committee;

– a Protocol 3, on the application of Article 67 of this Convention;

– Annexes I through IV and Annex VII, with information related to the application of this Convention;

– Annexes V and VI, containing the certificates referred to in Articles 54, 58 and 57 of this Convention;

– Annex VIII, containing the authentic languages referred to in Article 79 of this Convention; and

– Annex IX, concerning the application of Article II of Protocol 1.

These Protocols and Annexes shall form an integral part of this Convention.

Article 76
Without prejudice to Article 77, any Contracting Party may request the revision of this Convention. To that end, the Depositary shall convene the Standing Committee as laid down in Article 4 of Protocol 2.

Article 77
1. The Contracting Parties shall communicate to the Depositary the text of any provisions of the laws which amend the lists set out in Annexes I through IV as well as any deletions in or additions to the list set out in Annex VII and the date of their entry into force. Such communication shall be made within reasonable time before the entry into force and be accompanied by a translation into English and French. The Depositary shall adapt the Annexes concerned accordingly, after having consulted the Standing Committee in accordance with Article 4 of Protocol 2. For that purpose, the Contracting Parties shall provide a translation of the adaptations into their languages.
2. Any amendment of the Annexes V through VI and VIII through IX to this Convention shall be adopted by the Standing Committee in accordance with Article 4 of Protocol 2.

Article 78
1. The Depositary shall notify the Contracting Parties of:
   (a) the deposit of each instrument of ratification or accession;
   (b) the dates of entry into force of this Convention in respect of the Contracting Parties;
   (c) any declaration received pursuant to Articles I to IV of Protocol 1;
   (d) any communication made pursuant to Article 74(2), Article 77(1) and paragraph 4 of Protocol 3.
2. The notifications will be accompanied by translations into English and French.

Article 79
This Convention, drawn up in a single original in the languages listed in Annex VIII, all texts being equally authentic, shall be deposited in the Swiss Federal Archives. The Swiss Federal Council shall transmit a certified copy to each Contracting Party.

...

ANNEX I

The rules of jurisdiction referred to in Article 3(2) and 4(2) of the Convention are the following:
...
– in the United Kingdom: the rules which enable jurisdiction to be founded on:
   (a) the document instituting the proceedings having been served on the defendant during his temporary presence in the United Kingdom, or
   (b) the presence within the United Kingdom of property belonging to the defendant, or
   (c) the seizure by the plaintiff of property situated in the United Kingdom.

ANNEX II

The courts or competent authorities to which the application referred to in Article 39 of the Convention may be submitted are the following:
– in the United Kingdom:

...
(b)   in Scotland, the Court of Session, or in the case of a maintenance judgment to the Sheriff Court on transmission by the Secretary of State.
...

ANNEX III

The courts with which appeals referred to in Article 43(2) of the Convention may
be lodged are the following:
– in the United Kingdom:

...
(b)   in Scotland, the Court of Session, or in the case of a maintenance judgment the Sheriff Court.
...

ANNEX IV

The appeals which may be lodged pursuant to Article 44 of the Convention are the
following:

...
– in the United Kingdom: a single further appeal on a point of law.

INDEX OF LEGISLATION